Getting the Most from Utilities on the IBM PC

"The book is an excellent single source on the overall subject of utility programs, and it describes the use of many programs more clearly than their own user manuals. . . . a good guide for finding your way through the utilities jungle."

—Charles Rubin
San Jose Mercury News

Other Brady Books by Robert Krumm

Understanding and Using *dBASE II* and *III*
Understanding and Using Multiplan

Getting the Most from Utilities on the IBM PC

Perfecting the System Environment

Robert Krumm

BRADY
New York

Getting the Most from Utilities on the IBM PC

 BRADY

Simon & Schuster, Inc.
Gulf+Western Building
One Gulf+Western Plaza
New York, NY 10023

DISTRIBUTED BY PRENTICE HALL TRADE

Manufactured in the United States of America

   4   5   6   7   8   9   10

Library of Congress Cataloging-in-Publication Data

Krumm, Robert, 1951-
   Getting the most from utilities on the IBM PC.

   "A Brady book."
   Includes index.
   1. IBM Personal Computer—Programming. 2. Utilities
(Computer programs) I. Title.
QA76.8.12594K78   1986   005.265   86-17010
ISBN 0-89303-926-8

For Carolyn, without whom none of this would have been possible—
so if anything is wrong don't call me—call her.

Limits of Liability and Disclaimer of Warranty

The author and publisher of this book have used their best efforts in preparing this book and the programs contained in it. These efforts include the development, research, and testing of the theories and programs to determine their effectiveness. The author and publisher make no warranty of any kind, expressed or implied, with regard to these programs or to the documentation contained in this book. The author and publisher shall not be liable in any event for incidental or consequential damages in connection with, or arising out of, the furnishing, performance, or use of these programs.

Trademarks

Contents

Part 1. Basics of DOS

1. What You Need to Know / 3
1.1.   Memory / 4
1.2.   Why Two Types of Memory / 5
1.3.   How Memory Is Measured / 6
1.4.   How Memory Is Used / 7
1.5.   The Role of DOS / 7
1.6.   The Structure of DOS Commands / 8
1.7.   How DOS Communicates to You / 9
1.8.   Other Communications from DOS / 9
1.9.   How You Communicate with DOS / 11
1.10.   The Basic Grammar / 12
1.11.   DOS Commands / 12
1.12.   Internal Commands / 14
1.13.   External Commands / 15
1.14.   Parameters and Delimiters / 16
1.15.   Reading and Typing Filenames / 19
1.16.   Wildcards / 19
1.17.   The ? Character / 20
1.18.   The * Character / 20
1.19.   Options / 21
1.20.   Defaults / 22
1.21.   Disk Organization / 22
1.22.   Paths / 24
1.23.   Types of Files / 25
1.24.   Text Files and ASCII / 25
1.25.   How Computers Represent Information / 26
1.26.   The ASCII Code / 27
1.27.   How Programs Create Files / 27
1.28.   What Programs Produce ASCII Files / 29
1.29.   DOS Commands / 29
1.30.   Word Processing Programs / 29
1.30.1.   *WordStar* / 30
1.30.2.   *WordStar 2000* / 30
1.30.3.   *Microsoft Word* / 30

1.30.4.   *MultiMate* / 30
1.30.5.   *DisplayWrite II* / 31
1.30.6.   *DisplayWrite III* / 31
1.30.7.   *WordPerfect* / 31
1.31.   Other Programs / 31
1.31.1.   *Lotus 1-2-3 and Symphony* / 31
1.31.2.   *Framework* / 32
1.31.3.   *dBASE II and III* / 32
1.32.   Extended ASCII Code / 32
1.33.   Print the Full IBM Character Set / 33
1.34.   The Issue of Copy Protection / 35
1.35.   What Is Copy Protection / 36
1.36.   A Brief History / 37
1.37.   When Can You Make Copies / 38
1.38.   Problems with Protected Software / 39
1.39.   Types of Copy Protection / 39
1.40.   Problems with Protection Schemes / 40
1.41.   Making Copies of Copy-Protected Software / 41
1.42.   Copy II PC / 41
1.43.   The Copy Option Board / 41
1.44.   Conclusion / 42

2. Working with DOS Commands / 43
2.1.   Setup / 43
2.2.   Making a Copy / 43
2.3.   Beginning with DOS / 44
2.4.   The Systems Level / 45
2.5.   The Disk Directory / 46
2.6.   Other Drives / 50
2.7.   Limited Searches / 51
2.8.   Editing in DOS / 53
2.9.   Checking the Disk / 54
2.10.   Clearing the Screen / 57
2.11.   The Copy Command / 57
2.12.   Copying to Devices / 58
2.13.   Erasing Files / 59
2.14.   The Type Command / 59
2.15.   Printing / 59
2.16.   The System Prompt / 60
2.17.   Filters / 60

2.18.   Subdirectories / 61
2.19.   Changing the Default Directory / 64
2.20.   Sub-subdirectories / 66
2.21.   Paths / 68
2.22.   Batch Files / 70
2.23.   A Simple Batch File / 71
2.24.   Creating a Batch File / 72
2.25.   The Echo Command / 74
2.26.   Editing Batch Files / 74
2.27.   Autoexec / 76
2.28.   The ANSI System / 77
2.29.   The CONFIG.SYS File / 77
2.30.   Changing Buffers and Files / 78
2.31.   Device Drivers / 79
2.32.   Answer Key / 79

Part 2.   Systems Utilities

3.   Norton Utilities / 83
3.1.   Versions / 83
3.2.   Exploring with Norton Utilities / 84
3.3.   Setup / 85
3.4.   Starting the Program / 86
3.5.   The Directory / 94
3.6.   Display Modes / 95
3.7.   Directory Details / 96
3.8.   Saving the Changes / 98
3.9.   Other Features of the Norton Utilities Main Program / 99
3.10.   Disk Map / 99
3.11.   Searching the Disk / 101
3.12.   Note on Hard Disks / 105

4.   Other Norton Utilities Programs / 109
4.1.   File Programs / 110
4.2.   Directory Sorting / 111
4.3.   Sorting a Floppy Disk / 112
4.4.   Sorting Directories on a Hard Disk / 113
4.5.   File Size / 114
4.6.   File Find / 117
4.7.   File Attributes / 119
4.8.   Listing Files / 120

4.9.   Protecting Files / 121
4.10.   Archive Status / 123
4.11.   List Directories / 125
4.12.   Text Search / 125
4.13.   Looking for Text / 126
4.14.   Finding Text / 128
4.15.   Systems Utilities / 137
4.16.   Testing the Disk / 138
4.17.   Line Print / 139
4.18.   Screen Attributes / 141
4.19.   Screen Attributes in Batch Files / 143
4.20.   System Information / 144
4.21.   Time Mark / 145
4.22.   Options with Time Mark / 146
4.23.   Volume Label / 147
4.24.   Security / 148
4.25.   Wiping a Disk Clear / 149
4.26.   Wiping Out Individual Files / 151

5.   Recovering Erased or Damaged Files / 155
5.1.   What Erasing a File Really Means / 155
5.2.   Setup / 156
5.3.   Erasing a File / 157
5.4.   The Hex View / 158
5.5.   Unerasing the File / 158
5.6.   File Status / 161
5.7.   Selecting Data / 162
5.8.   Recovering Files with Text Search / 166
5.9.   Searching Erased Text / 167
5.10.   Selecting a Sector Number / 174
5.11.   Saving a Damaged File. / 175

6.   Other DOS Enhancements / 179
6.1.   SmartPath / 179
6.2.   What Path Does / 179
6.3.   Making an Auto Execute File / 182
6.4.   SmartPath: Summary / 182
6.5.   Xtree / 183
6.6.   Program Files / 183
6.7.   Basic Organization / 184
6.8.   Display Modes / 187

6.9. Selecting Files / 188
6.10. The Global View—Show All / 188
6.11. Xtree Commands / 190
6.12. Function Keys / 190
6.13. Directory Commands / 190
6.14. File Commands / 191
6.15. Working with Groups of Files / 192
6.16. Xtree: Summary / 192
6.17. EASY DOS IT / 193
6.18. The Files / 193
6.19. DOS Functions in EASY DOS IT / 194
6.20. DOS Commands in EASY DOS IT / 195
6.21. Customizing the Program / 197
6.22. Creating Commands / 200
6.23. Menu Items That Perform Special Tasks / 202
6.24. Custom Tutor Screens / 202
6.25. Other Menu Items / 203
6.26. EASY DOS IT: Summary / 204

Part 3. Keyboard Enhancements

7. Keyboard Enhancing Programs / 207
7.1. What Are Macros? / 207
7.2. Keyboard Macros / 208
7.3. How Many Keys? / 208
7.4. How Part 3 is Organized / 209
7.5. The Basic Concept / 209
7.6. Key Reassignment with DOS / 210

8. ProKey / 213
8.1. The ProKey Disk / 213
8.2. ProKey's Approach / 214
8.3. Special Features / 215
8.4. Using ProKey / 215
8.5. The Interactive Mode / 216
8.6. Recording without Executing / 217
8.7. Saving and Recalling Macros / 218
8.8. Clearing the Memory / 220
8.9. Restoring Macros / 221
8.10. Annotating Macros / 221
8.11. Updating a File / 222

8.12.   Guarding a Macro / 222
8.13.   Delays in Macros / 223
8.14.   Macros with Pauses / 225
8.15.   A Fixed-Length Field / 226
8.16.   Variable-Length Fields / 227
8.17.   Multiple Fields / 228
8.18.   Macros with Names / 229
8.19.   Swapping Keys / 231
8.20.   Text Files / 232
8.21.   Batch Commands / 232
8.22.   Creating the Batch Program / 234
8.23.   More about Batch Commands / 235
8.24.   Text Files / 237
8.25.   Other Features and Modes / 239
8.26.   ProKey's Working Speed / 240
8.27.   Suspending the Program / 241
8.28.   Changing Prokey / 241
8.29.   Changing Prokey Commands / 243
8.30.   Layout / 244
8.31.   Removing and Activating a Keyboard / 248
8.32.   Conclusion / 248

9. SuperKey / 249
9.1.   The Program / 249
9.2.   Memory Space / 250
9.3.   Creating Macros with SuperKey / 250
9.4.   What Keys? / 251
9.5.   Setup for Hands-On / 252
9.6.   The Interactive Mode / 252
9.7.   Using the Menu / 253
9.8.   Editing Keystrokes / 258
9.9.   Special Symbols / 258
9.10.   Saving a Macro in Edit Mode / 259
9.11.   More Macro Editing / 259
9.12.   Cancelling a Macro / 260
9.13.   Clearing a Key / 261
9.14.   Revising Macros / 262
9.15.   Showing Macros / 263
9.16.   Saving and Recalling Macros / 267
9.17.   Clearing the Memory / 270

9.18.   Loading Macros from a File / 270
9.19.   Merging Files / 271
9.20.   Using Commands in Macros / 272
9.21.   Delays and Pauses / 273
9.22.   Delays in Macros / 274
9.23.   Nesting Macros / 275
9.24.   Entering a Function / 275
9.25.   Functions in the Edit Mode / 277
9.26.   Macros with Entry Fields / 278
9.27.   A Fixed-Length Field / 279
9.28.   How Fixed Fields Are Recorded / 280
9.29.   Variable-Length Fields / 280
9.30.   Multiple Fields / 282
9.31.   Data Entry Control / 282
9.32.   Data Control in Fixed Fields / 285
9.33.   Advanced Formats and Functions / 286
9.34.   Alignment within Fields / 287
9.35.   Changing the Fill Character / 289
9.36.   Numeric Formats / 290
9.37.   Advanced Editing Techniques / 292
9.38.   Cut and Paste / 294
9.39.   Functions in Macros / 295
9.40.   A Cut and Paste Macro / 300
9.41.   Playback Delays / 302
9.42.   Options in Macros / 303
9.43.   Keyboard Locking / 303
9.44.   Display Macros / 304
9.45.   Adding Text to Frames / 305
9.46.   Auto Display / 306
9.47.   Pages / 306
9.48.   Video Attributes / 307
9.49.   Display Macros as Menus / 308
9.50.   Submenus / 310
9.51.   Batch Commands / 311
9.52.   The Spreadsheet File / 312
9.53.   Creating the Batch Program / 313
9.54.   Batch Execution / 314
9.55.   The Command Stack / 316
9.56.   Sidekick / 317
9.57.   Other Features and Modes / 320

9.58.   Changing SuperKey Defaults / 322
9.59.   Encryption / 323
9.60.   Layout / 326
9.61.   Removing and Activating a Keyboard / 329
9.62.   Conclusion / 329

10.   Recall / 331
10.1   Vital Statistics / 331
10.2.   Macro Creation / 331
10.3.   Fields / 333
10.4.   Debugging Macros / 334
10.5.   Menus / 334
10.6.   Conclusion / 336

11.   SmartKey / 339
11.1.   Vital Statistics 339
11.2.   Macro Creation / 340
11.3.   Buffer Recording / 341
11.4.   Lists / 342
11.5.   Editing Features / 342
11.6.   Captured Fields / 343
11.7.   DOS Functions / 343
11.8.   Special Functions / 343
11.9   Keyboard Lock / 344
11.10.   Windows and Menus / 344
11.11.   Making Windows Menus / 346
11.12.   Submenus / 348
11.13.   Menus in Macros / 348
11.14.   Batch Commands / 348
11.15.   PCKEY / 349
11.16.   File Encryption / 349
11.17.   Conclusion / 350

12.   Keystroke Enhancement Programs: A Comparison / 351
12.1.   Overall Programs / 351
12.2.   Ratings / 355

Part 4.   Background Utilities

13.   Background Utilities / 359
13.1.   Ramdisks and Spoolers / 359
13.2.   Vdisk / 361

14. Sidekick / 363

14.1.   The Sidekick Program / 363
14.2.   Using Sidekick / 365
14.3.   Activating Sidekick / 367
14.4.   Help / 368
14.5.   The Calculator / 369
14.5.1.   *Using the Memory with the Calculator* / 371
14.5.2.   *Mode Changes in Calculator* / 371
14.5.3.   *Programming Keys* / 372
14.6.   Leaving a Sidekick Application / 373
14.6.1.   *Clearing Programmed Keys* / 374
14.7.   The Calendar / 374
14.8.   Entering an Appointment / 375
14.9.   Entering Appointments / 376
14.10.   Multiple Calendars / 378
14.11.   Printing Calendars / 380
14.12.   Deleting Entries / 381
14.13.   Printing More Than One Day on a Page / 381
14.14.   Program to Change Form Length / 384
14.15.   The Dialer / 386
14.16.   Creating a Phone List with dBASE III / 390
14.17.   The Notepad / 393
14.18.   Notepad as Word Processor / 394
14.19.   Basic Editing / 398
14.20.   Inserting and Deleting / 400
14.21.   Saving the Text / 401
14.22.   Reforming Text / 401
14.23.   Other Editing Commands / 401
14.24.   Changing the Right Margin / 402
14.25.   Indents / 403
14.26.   Opening a New Notepad File / 403
14.27.   Recalling a File / 404
14.28.   Selecting Filenames / 405
14.29.   Combining Files / 405
14.30.   Import and Export of Text / 406
14.31.   Importing Data / 407
14.32.   Time Stamping / 409
14.33.   About Imports / 409
14.34.   Exporting Data / 410
14.35.   Pasting a Key for Export / 411

14.36.   Pasting a Column of Numbers / 412
14.37.   Conclusion / 414

15.   Spotlight / 417
15.1.   Copy Protection / 417
15.2.   Notepad / 418
15.3.   Window Position / 419
15.4.   Using the Menu / 419
15.5.   How the Data Is Saved / 420
15.6.   Help / 421
15.7.   Help Window / 421
15.8.   Calculator / 421
15.9.   Calculator Menu / 422
15.10.   The Appointment Calendar / 422
15.11.   Appointment Calendar Commands / 423
15.12.   Phone Book / 429
15.13.   Phone Book Features and Commands / 430
15.14.   The Filer / 432
15.15.   Index Card File / 434
15.16.   Windows / 434
15.17.   Conclusion / 435

16.   DeskSet / 437
16.1.   What DeskSet Offers / 437
16.2.   Notepad / 438
16.3.   Calculators / 440
16.4.   The DeskSet Pocket Calculator / 440
16.5.   The Financial Calculator / 441
16.6.   Special Modes / 442
16.6.1.   *Statistical Mode* / 444
16.7.   Date Calendar / 444
16.8.   Alarms / 448
16.9.   Batch Processing / 450
16.10.   DOS Access / 451
16.11.   Clipboard / 456
16.12.   Pasting Data from the Clipboard / 457
16.13.   Voice and Modem / 458
16.14.   PopAny / 458
16.15.   Conclusion / 460

17.   Turbo Lightning / 461
17.1.   Vital Statistics / 461
17.2.   Automatic Proofreading / 463
17.3.   The Main Menu / 464
17.4.   Word Check / 464
17.5.   Using Commands / 465
17.6.   Full Screen Checks / 468
17.7.   Sound Alike Words / 469
17.8.   Capitalization / 472
17.9.   The Thesaurus / 474
17.10.   Words Not in the Thesaurus / 476
17.11.   Expanding the Dictionary / 478
17.12.   Making Turbo Lightning Work with Your Software / 479
17.13.   Key Commands / 480
17.14.   Environments / 480
17.15.   New Environments / 482
17.16.   Framework II and Turbo Lightning / 482
17.17.   Arrow Keys / 484
17.18.   WordStar 2000 / 486
17.19.   Saving the Changes / 487
17.20.   Conclusion / 487

18.   Comparing the Background Utility Programs / 489
18.1.   Basic System Design / 489
18.2.   Notepads / 490
18.3.   Calculators / 491
18.4.   Calendars / 492
18.5.   DOS Access / 493
18.6.   Telecommunications / 493
18.7.   Other Features / 494
18.8.   Conclusion / 494

19.   Printing Utilities / 495
19.1.   C-Printer / 496
19.2.   C-Printer Commands / 496
19.3.   Conclusions: C-Printer / 498
19.4.   Printworks / 498
19.5.   The Main Program / 500
19.6.   Advanced Options / 502
19.7.   Font Editor / 503
19.8.   Downloading Fonts / 503

19.9.   Conclusions: Printworks / 504
19.10.   Sideways / 504
19.11.   Indirect Processing / 505
19.12.   Direct Spreadsheet Printing / 506
19.13.   Special Effects / 508
19.14.   Conclusions: Sideways / 509

Appendix: Product List / 511

Index / 513

Foreword

This book is organized in four parts. Part 1 concerns the concepts and use of DOS. Contrary to popular belief, no computer can be run properly without a good understanding of the Disk Operating System. Thus the opening chapters provide the reader with a clear understanding of what DOS is and how it is used by itself as well as in conjunction with other programs. This information will help readers to use their software programs more productively, and to understand the utility programs discussed in later chapters.

Part 2 covers programs that expand and extend the functions of the operating system. It includes programs that recover files and organize hard disks.

Part 3 presents keyboard enhancement programs. There is a surprising variety of useful features provided by these programs, even though at first glance they may seem only peripherally related to the keyboard.

Part 4 is concerned with background utility programs. These are programs that "pop up" in the middle of an application and enable the user to perform all sorts of tasks without having to exit the program being used. Printing utilities also are included in this part.

If the reader has never used a utility program, or doesn't know what a utility program is, this book will explain the incredible array of features and functions. For those who have used utility programs, e.g., Sidekick, this book will expand and broaden their knowledge about how such programs can enhance the capabilities of a computer system. For the experienced user of utility programs, the book provides detailed information about products that allow one to compare and decide which utilities best fit one's needs.

The most popular programs are documented in a "hands-on" style. Not only are the programs discussed, but the chapters contain examples of how their features can be used. These uses can be reproduced in a follow-along style on one's own computer.

Which are the best programs in the book? The answer to that is personal. However, no program was included in the book that was not considered an excellent value and a key productivity tool. However, I cannot say that the opposite is true. Some fine programs could not be included in the book because of lack of space. GEM Desktop and Microsoft Windows are two excellent programs that function as a user interface in place of DOS.

A glossary has not been included because I find that the dictionary-type definitions usually found in book glossaries don't really explain anything. Instead, I have placed extensive technical notes throughout the book, and have used these notes to cross-reference related topics.

It is not often that one finds programs that combine fun and productivity. Utility programs seem to. They have been designed by people who have noticed that their computer doesn't do something that they think it should. Like these designers, it is my desire that this book be a guide to useful tools that increase the productivity of a computer system.

Robert Krumm
Walnut Creek, CA

Part 1.
Basics of DOS

1.

What You Need to Know

When people get involved with computers, one question that comes up frequently is, "How much, if anything, do I have to know about the technical side of the computer?"

Often an analogy to an automobile is used. Many people insist that they don't need to know how a car works; all they want to do is drive it. But the analogy misses a very important point. The main use of computers is for business productivity. People are going to be using the computer as part of their jobs. If your job were to drive, you would expect to know more about driving and the vehicle you drive than a person who drives merely for pleasure.

Experience has shown that in order to use a computer effectively in a job situation you need to know a bit about how the system operates. Owning or simply using a personal computer can be a very rewarding experience. But it can also be complicated, demanding, and often frustrating. For reasons that are obvious, computer manufacturers have always downplayed this aspect of microcomputers.

Most people who use small computers do so as a means to some other end, not as an end in itself. Most users feel that they want to spend as little time as possible learning the ins and outs of computers. While this attitude is understandable, the problem comes in when you begin to be specific about exactly what that minimum amount of knowledge actually is. People will often reason that since microcomputers are small, personal devices, they should be proportionally less complicated than the type of computers used by professional programmers. However, the truth is that this is not the case.

For example, a professional programmer, i.e., a person who writes programming code eight hours a day for a living, working on a large mainframe computer system, usually knows very little about the hardware setup of the computer he or she is programming. This is because, in a professional setup, the jobs more closely related to hardware are performed by operations specialists. By the same token, repairs and installation of equipment are usually the job of other specialists who know little about programming applications. Still other people, systems analysts, for instance, concentrate on the overall picture of hardware and software in a system. The analysts, however, do not get bogged down with the small details of programming or operations.

But when it comes to a personal computer, the user is placed in the position of having at one time or another to wear all those hats. Granted, microcomputers are simpler than large computer systems, but on the other hand the users are not computer professionals.

As you begin to use and subsequently depend upon your personal computer more, you will find a need to know more about it. This is especially true for people who use more than one application. Many people begin working with their computer because they need the function of a single piece of software. It could be word processing or a program that handles bookkeeping. As long as you use just the one program things remain fairly simple. The learning curve gets much steeper when you begin to use several programs to do different tasks. This book is designed to show you how to get more out of your computer by the use of *utility* programs. Utilities do not replace, but enhance, the functions of the major applications with which you work.

To understand how these programs work you should be clear about some basic concepts of microcomputer operations.

1.1. Memory

One of the most confusing terms used in the computer industry is *memory*. The reason is simple: the term is used to describe very different types of computer memory.

For example, suppose that you were asked to recall a specific piece of information, such as the year that the Mexican-American War began. If you knew the answer, you would simply answer the question. On the other hand, if you did not recall this information, you might attempt to look up the answer in a book of some kind.

Notice that for a human who knows how to read there are two sources of information. The first is what is already present in your mind. This can be referred to as your *internal* memory. It is information that is immediately available to you. The other source of information is not part of your mind but external to it. When you read information from a book you are transferring data from an *external* memory to your *internal* memory.

Computers make the same distinction between two types of memory, internal and external. The internal memory of the computer is composed of microchips. The chips are of two types, RAM (random access memory) and ROM (read-only memory). The ROM is permanent and unchangeable. The IBM PC has a minimum amount of ROM information. Since ROMs cannot be altered, a computer with a lot of ROM memory isn't very flexible. When internal memory is discussed in this book it is the flexible RAM memory that is being discussed.

External memory comes in several forms. The most popular form is disk storage. Disks come in several types; the two most popular are 5 1/4 inch floppy disks and 5 1/4 inch hard disk drives.

1.2. Why Two Types of Memory

Why do computers need two types of memory? How do they differ? The answer to the former question can be understood if you look at the latter first.

Internal and external memory differ in some very important characteristics. The positive side of internal memory is its great speed and flexibility. The internal memory of the computer is composed of silicon chips. Movement of data within chips from one place to another is measured in *nanoseconds*. A nanosecond is one billionth of a second.

Internal memory can be used to perform all sorts of tasks. Internal memory can be viewed as a matrix of cells. While this may not mean much to the average user, it enables programmers to perform all sorts of complicated logical and mathematical operations in a very short period of time.

The primary drawback of internal memory (RAM) is that it is volatile. When you turn your computer off all the information that has been so carefully entered and manipulated is wiped clean in a fraction of a second.

It is to overcome this problem that external memory is used. The disks, both hard and floppy, are really recording media. Information entered into the internal memory can be stored on a disk and then recalled at a later time.

Another consideration is the relative cost of the two types of storage. While prices vary greatly from year to year, it is fair to say that internal memory costs about ten times as much as external memory. In addition, the basic design of the computer often limits the maximum size of the internal memory.

Without both internal and external memory you cannot have a usable computer.

1.3.   How Memory Is Measured

Memory is measured in units called *bytes*. A byte is the amount of memory space used to store a character, the letter *a*, for instance. The word *byte*, for example, would take up at least four bytes of memory storage.

The phrase *at least four* is used to indicate that in the real world of computer storage the number of bytes used to store even a simple word like *byte* may include characters that are not visible on the screen. There are almost always *overhead* characters that the computer needs, which are stored along with the characters that you recognize.

The most common unit of computer memory is the *kilobyte* or *K*. One kilobyte is equal to 1,024 bytes.

[A kilobyte is not 1,000 bytes but 1,024. This may seem odd, because the term *kilo* is borrowed from the metric system, where it stands for 10 to the third power, 1,000. However, most computer mathematics is based not on a ten-number system (decimal) but a two-number system (binary). Therefore, *kilobyte* refers to 2 raised to the tenth power, which equals 1,024.]

When computers are sold they are generally rated by the number of kilobytes in the internal memory. If a computer is advertised as a 256K IBM PC, its internal memory is being referred to.

The external memory size can be determined by looking at the rating of the drives, hard or floppy. Many computers have several drives that may vary in the amount of data each can store.

1.4. How Memory Is Used

How much memory do you need? How much internal and how much external? The answer to that question is quite complicated because it depends upon what type of work you intend to do with the computer. It is important to remember that different types of software work with memory, both internal and external, in different ways. Word processing and data management programs usually require more external memory than internal. Spreadsheet programs and integrated programs are more dependent on internal memory. You must carefully consider the requirements of the software you want to use before you decide on the amount of internal and external memory you require.

Keep in mind that you cannot substitute one type of memory for another. For example, if you are working in 1-2-3 and run out of memory, adding a hard disk to your computer system will not have any effect on the problem. On the other hand, if your data base requires more disk memory, adding an internal memory board will not have any effect either.

1.5. The Role of DOS

Understanding that the computer contains two very different types of memory, you might wonder how the complicated and crucial job of moving information back and forth between the two is accomplished. The answer is that every computer is supplied with a master program. Among its several responsibilities is the control of the movement of data to and from the internal and external memories. The program is called DOS, and stands for Disk Operating System.

[DOS has two official names. When you buy the program from IBM it is called PC DOS, Personal Computer Disk Operating System. This system was designed by the Microsoft Corporation, which also sells a version of the program called MS DOS, Microsoft Disk Operating System. Most people use the terms DOS, PC DOS, and MS DOS interchangeably.

DOS also comes in several different versions, because as computers change and grow the operating system is revised. The versions are numbered successively, and the complete name of an operating system includes the version number. Probably the most common version is PC DOS (MS DOS) Version 2.10.]

One of the most talked about and least understood areas of the computer is the DOS. DOS performs three major tasks:

1. Coordinating the hardware. DOS is responsible for making the hardware and software work together. Since the basic setup of DOS stays the same as long as you don't change your hardware, most users don't get involved with this area of DOS.
2. Loading and executing programs. DOS makes it possible to load a program from disk storage and then run that program. This process seems automatic to most users and is of interest chiefly to programmers.
3. File Management. DOS controls the storage of data on the disks. This is the area in which most users come in contact with the operating system.

1.6.   The Structure of DOS Commands

The purpose of this section is to provide you with some background on the way DOS communicates with you and the way in which you can communicate with DOS. The previous section explained why DOS exists. Here you will see how the functions provided by DOS can be used to maintain the data stored on your disks. This is really quite important. Years of teaching about computers have shown me that the more one understands about the operating system, the more in control one feels.

When the topic is utilities the need to understand DOS is even greater. The key to understanding DOS and many of the programs in this book is to understand how DOS commands are structured. Since many of the utilities explained in this book are closely tied to the basic functions conducted by the operating system, you will find that many of the structures and conventions of the operating system apply to these programs.

Many of the basic functions DOS provides are transparent to the user. That is, they take place more or less automatically. Programs that store and retrieve data utilize the operating system. However, the interaction of the program and the operating system takes place so smoothly most users are never aware that DOS and their application are both working. For instance, when a word processing program reads a file on a disk and sends it to a printer, DOS is called upon to handle many of the functions that make that action possible.

As a user of, not a programmer of, a microcomputer, you seldom need to understand these aspects of the operating system. However, there is another area of operation where the average user does need to understand and utilize the operating system. While DOS and your applications perform many functions automatically, decisions about the actual details of what is stored and where it is stored require you, the user, to command the computer. The more you understand about how to use such commands, the better you will be able to utilize the full power of the computer.

1.7. How DOS Communicates to You

Even though DOS is always present when you are working with your computer, DOS indicates its presence by using only a minimal display. This display consists of two characters. The first character is a letter, usually *A* in a floppy drive system or *C* if the system contains a hard disk. The second character is >.

This two-character display is referred to as the *system's prompt*. The system's prompt tells you two important things. First it tells you that DOS has been loaded into the memory of the computer and that it is ready to accept a command from you. The second piece of information comes from the letter used in the prompt. The letter indicates the *default drive*. When DOS is loaded the program assumes that you want to work with the drive from which the DOS program was loaded; the letter indicates which drive that is. When you give DOS a command that requires some reference to a disk drive, DOS automatically uses the drive indicated by the prompt unless you tell it otherwise.

1.8. Other Communications from DOS

The system's prompt is the most basic sign that DOS displays. As you enter various commands DOS will respond by displaying different types of information. The information takes three forms:

1. PROMPTS. Prompts are questions or instructions that DOS prints in response to a command that you enter. For example, if you entered a command to make a copy of a disk, DOS would display the following:

```
Insert new diskette for drive B:
and strike any key when ready
```

[When a prompt says *Press any key to continue* or any variation of this, there are two ways to stop the command from proceeding. The BREAK command is issued by holding down the [Ctrl] key and pressing the [Scroll Lock] key. Or you may prefer to hold down the [Ctrl] key and press the C.

Any other key or combination will result in the command actually taking place. Remember the Escape key, <Esc>, will not break a command. Only [Ctrl Scroll Lock] or [Ctrl C] will do so.]

The display tells you where to place the disk that will become the copy. It also tells you that you need to press a key for the program to continue.

The display is called a prompt because it requires you to take some action. Prompts are used to delay the execution of a command to give you an opportunity to change disks, for instance. Prompts are also used to warn you about the effect of the command you've entered and to make sure you really meant to enter that command. For example, if you entered a command to delete all the files on a disk, DOS would display:

```
Are you sure (Y/N)?
```

Since deleting all the files is a serious step, this prompt gives you a chance to reconsider your command before you proceed.

[This type of prompt is an attempt by the programmers of DOS to anticipate problems or mistakes that you might make. The prompts are a reflection of what the programmers thought you would need to know and be warned about.

You may find that DOS displays too little information for your needs. The art of creating programs, messages, and prompts is what utilities are all about. The programs presented in this book are extensions, additions, and improvements to the basic DOS functions.

Some of the utilities are so useful that newer versions of DOS often include them. DOS 3.0 and 3.1 include commands such as Label and Attrib, previously available only with Norton Utilities.]

2. CONFIRMATIONS. A confirmation is a message that DOS displays after a command has been completed. For example, if you copied three files from drive A to drive B DOS would display:

```
3 File(s) copied
```

The confirmation is used to show that the command was actually carried out.

3. ERROR MESSAGES. An error message is displayed by DOS when it cannot carry out the command entered. They occur on two occasions. The first occurs

immediately after you enter a command. DOS reads the command and checks to see if the instruction is correct and complete. If DOS cannot understand the command or finds it incomplete, a message is displayed. For example, if you entered a command to delete, but forgot to tell DOS what you wanted deleted, the following message would be displayed:

```
Invalid number of parameters
```

DOS messages are supposed to help you understand what was incorrectly entered. Another system's prompt is immediately displayed to indicate that DOS is ready for you to enter a new command.

The second type of error message is displayed while a command is executing. Usually this type of message indicates a hardware problem of some sort. For example, if you told DOS to print a copy of the directory of files on your disk but didn't turn the printer on, you would get this message:

```
Not ready error writing device PRN
Abort, Retry, Ignore?
```

The message tells you that the computer thinks the printer is not ready. You have three options. You can enter an a for Abort, an r for Retry, or an i for Ignore.

[When you see this prompt you can only enter a, r, or i. This is true even if you see the message while you are working with an application, for example, a word processing program. The error handling mechanism of DOS takes over the keyboard until you respond with one of the three letters. None of the commands of the program you are using will be recognized until you respond to the error message with one of the three valid characters.]

Remember that simply entering r, for example, will not solve the problem. In this case you would first turn on the printer, and then enter the r. The idea is that you should correct the problem that caused the error, and then respond to the message.

1.9. How You Communicate with DOS

A much more complex subject is how you communicate with the operating system. The only way to do this is to type in commands that DOS understands. DOS, like your computer in general, does not have any insight into what you want to do. It can only respond to commands that fit exactly into the structure of the command interpreter programmed into it.

[The command interpreter is stored in a file called COMMAND.COM on your DOS systems disk.]

In order to get DOS to do what you want it to do, you have to learn to speak DOS correctly.

1.10.   The Basic Grammar

Computer languages and command environments, like human languages, have a fundamental structure from which all the commands can be constructed.

DOS works with six basic elements:

1. Commands
2. Delimiters
3. Parameters
4. Options
5. Wildcards
6. Input/Output Devices

The most important rule is that all DOS entries must begin with a command. While every DOS command begins with a command word, it is usually followed by one or several of the basic elements above.

Rule #1: All entries in DOS begin with a command.

1.11.   DOS Commands

DOS commands are really the verbs of the DOS language. They represent the basic actions that DOS can perform and are divided into two major classifications:

1. *Internal Commands*. These commands are contained in the memory of the computer at all times when the DOS prompt is displayed. Because these commands are internal, no special disks or files need to be present in the computer to execute an internal command.

2. *External Commands.* These commands are really small computer programs that are stored in disk files until they are needed. External commands are loaded each time they are requested and are erased from memory when the command is finished.

Both types of commands have their advantages and disadvantages. Internal commands are always available because they reside in the memory whenever DOS is active. However, internal memory is limited in a computer. If you increase the number of DOS commands that are resident in the memory of the computer, you decrease the amount of room that can be used for programs and their data.

External commands occupy internal memory only when they are being executed. Otherwise they reside in the external storage medium like other programs and data files. External commands make efficient use of the internal memory, but they are slower to execute than internal commands because they must be loaded into the internal memory each time they are used. In addition, the external commands must be stored on disk space that is immediately available to the computer or these commands cannot be executed. On floppy disk systems, where storage is limited, this can be a problem.

The relevant questions are: What are the DOS commands? How do you know what they do? There is absolutely nothing within DOS that explains what DOS commands are or what they do. There is also nothing that tells you why you need them. When you turn on the computer DOS displays the prompt and waits for you to enter the commands. There is no attempt to indicate what you could or should do. The only way to learn about DOS is to refer to some source of information outside the computer, for example the DOS manual, books like this, or people who know about DOS.

It is very important to understand that not knowing what to tell DOS to do is quite natural. The people who designed DOS assumed that the user would come to DOS with a basic understanding of operating systems. The DOS manual is organized as a reference guide, not as an educational guide. This lack of "friendliness" on the part of DOS has led to the idea that computers that use DOS are hard to use. While this may or may not be true, it is more precise to say that DOS is not easy to learn. The distinction is important and revealing.

If DOS were to present a screen display that was more indicative of what you can and should do, it would be simpler to learn to use the program. However, these abilities would cause the DOS program to become larger and slower. A larger operating system would take memory space away from other applications. Also, once you became well acquainted with the system, you might find that the helpful displays become tedious, and slow down your work.

The tradeoffs are quite clear and point out the general theme of computer software. What is easy to use may eventually become cumbersome. What is not easy to use may take you some time to learn. DOS is designed to maximize the performance of the computer by taking up as little room as possible and executing commands with the least amount of user input necessary. Computers like the Macintosh place the emphasis on assisting the user in getting started. Which is better is decided by the user.

1.12. Internal Commands

Internal commands are the ones that are always available when the system's prompt is displayed. Naturally, they are the commands that you will need to use most frequently. The internal commands in DOS 2.1 are given below:

BREAK	activate/disable [Ctrl] BREAK combination
CLS	clear screen
COPY	transfer data from one device to another
CHDIR or CD	change active directory
CTTY	change standard input/output device
DATE	set system's date
DIR	list filenames
ERASE or DEL	delete files
MKDIR or MD	create directory
PATH	set search path
RENAME or REN	rename a file
RMDIR or RD	remove empty directory
SET	insert text strings into DOS
TIME	enter time
TYPE	display file contents
VER	display DOS version number
VERIFY	verify data when copying
VOL	display volume label

These commands have one thing in common. They can be executed at any time that you see the DOS system's prompt. There is no need for any special disk to be present.

1.13.   External Commands

External commands are not kept resident in the memory of the computer but are loaded from files stored on the disk when you request them. Thus if you ask for an external command and DOS cannot find the corresponding program file on the disk, the command will not operate. In order to access external commands you must make sure that they are available by copying the files from the DOS systems disk onto the disks you are using.

If you are using a hard disk you would normally copy all the DOS files onto the hard disk. However, users of floppy disks need to be more selective because their disk space is quite limited.

Put another way, the DOS external commands are *optional*. Experience and need will indicate which external commands you will need to copy onto which disks. Hard disk users often copy all the external command files onto the hard disk.

Below are the external commands for DOS 2.

Command	File	Size in Bytes
COMMAND	COM	17792
ANSI	SYS	1664
FORMAT	COM	6912
CHKDSK	COM	6400
SYS	COM	1680
DISKCOPY	COM	2576
DISKCOMP	COM	2188
COMP	COM	2534
EDLIN	COM	4608
MODE	COM	3139
FDISK	COM	6369
BACKUP	COM	3687
RESTORE	COM	4003
PRINT	COM	4608
RECOVER	COM	2304
ASSIGN	COM	896
TREE	COM	1513

Command	File	Size in Bytes
GRAPHICS	COM	789
SORT	EXE	1408
FIND	EXE	5888
MORE	COM	384
BASIC	COM	16256
BASICA	COM	26112
EXE2BIN	EXE	1664
LINK	EXE	39936
DEBUG	COM	11904

[Also supplied on the DOS disk are basic programs that are demonstrations of some of the features of the IBM PC. They are not part of the external commands of DOS and do not have to be included when you want to copy the DOS external command files.

The files are:

SAMPLES	BAS
ART	BAS
MUSIC	BAS
MUSICA	BAS
MORTGAGE	BAS
COLORBAR	BAS
DONKEY	BAS
CIRCLE	BAS
PIECHART	BAS
SPACE	BAS
BALL	BAS
COMM	BAS]

1.14.   Parameters and Delimiters

Parameters are additional pieces of information added to commands, and fill the same role in DOS commands that the object does in human languages. Parameters indicate what will be affected by the command.

For example, the command DEL deletes a file from the disk. However, simply entering DEL as a command to DOS is incomplete. DOS needs to know what you want to delete before it can carry out the command. To create a valid command you would have to supply a filename. Example:

DEL FORMAT.COM

The command has two parts: DEL is the command; FORMAT.COM is the parameter.

Notice that there is a space between the command and the parameter. The space is an important part of the grammar of DOS. Commands must be separated from their parameters by such *delimiters*. The space, in this instance, serves to delimit or punctuate the command. Without the delimiter the command would not be interpreted properly.

However, not all commands require parameters. For example, the DATE and TIME commands require no parameters. On the other hand, some commands can accept or even require more than one parameter.

The case of the characters, upper or lower, is irrelevant when entering DOS commands and parameters. When you have typed the command, pressing the <return> key activates the entry.

Rule # 2: Commands that use or require parameters need to be delimited.

Rule # 3: Commands and parameters can be entered in upper or lower case.

[In almost all publications, including most DOS manuals, the space is shown as the delimiter between commands and parameters. However, DOS will accept a variety of characters as delimiters. The equal sign, comma, semicolon, or tab can be used in place of the space. Tab is produced by pressing the <tab> key.

Look at the following commands:

DEL=FORMAT.COM
DEL;FORMAT.COM
DEL,FORMAT.COM
DEL   FORMAT.COM   (the space was created by pressing the <tab> key)

(Some versions of MS DOS will not recognize all delimiters. In the above case, the reference is to PC DOS Version 2.10.)

DOS would recognize all of these as the same as DEL FORMAT.COM. In commands that have several parameters you can mix the delimiters.]

Parameters are used to denote the following:

1. *Disk Drives.* If you want to specify a disk drive as a parameter for a command, you enter a letter corresponding to the drive and a colon. Drive specifications are always exactly two characters. Examples:

   A:
   B:
   C:

2. *Directories.* Directories are subdivisions that can be created on disks. Normally they are used only on hard disk drives, though it is possible to use them on

floppy drives. Directories are indicated by a backslash followed by the name of the directory. Examples:

\DATA
\LOTUS\BUDGET

3. *Filenames.* Filenames are strictly limited. Names consist of two parts, a filename, which is between one and eight characters, and an extension, which is between one and three characters. The extension is optional.

Filenames and extensions are separated by a period. Example:

FORMAT.COM

In this file FORMAT is the filename and COM the extension. The period indicates the separation between the two parts. Extensions are optional for most files; however, program files that are directly executable by DOS are an exception. These files must have an EXE or COM extension.

[In common usage, *filename* usually refers to the filename and extension as a single unit. For all practical purposes the "name" of a file is its filename and extension, if there is one.

In this book most references to the name of a file or filename will refer to the entire name of the file, including the extension.]

Filenames (including extensions) *must* follow these rules. The following characters are permitted in DOS filenames:

A B C D E F G H I J K L M N O P Q R S T U V W X Y Z
0 1 2 3 4 5 6 7 8 9 ! @ # $ % ^ & ( ) { } ' ` ~ _ /

All other characters are forbidden. Keep in mind that a < space > is one of the characters *not* allowed in a filename or extension.

[DOS also uses some special terms that cannot be used as filenames. These names are *reserved* because DOS uses them as the names of devices. For example, the name PRN is the DOS word for the printer. No file can be named PRN. However, PRN1 or PRN% are acceptable. Other reserved words are: CON, AUX, LPT1, LPT2, LPT3, COM1, COM2, and NUL.]

DOS does not recognize the difference in case between letters. Commands and filenames can be typed in upper or lower case letters.

[There is one exception to the rule about the case of letters. A few commands in DOS accept what are called text strings as part of the command sequence. In those instances case will count. Keep in mind that the FIND command is one that uses strings.]

1.15. Reading and Typing Filenames

One cause for confusion to a new user is the discrepancy between the way DOS displays a filename in a directory and the way you should type the name when you want to refer to it. For example:

```
          Volume in drive A has no label
          Directory of  A:\

          ASSIGN   COM     1073    1-01-80    1:46a
          ASTCLOCK COM      813    9-18-82
                  2 File(s)      78848 bytes free
```

This is a typical directory display on a disk. The first file listed is shown as ASSIGN   COM. If you wanted to delete that file from the disk you would refer to it by typing in ASSIGN.COM

Note that your entry is different from the DOS display of the filename. The DOS directory showed spaces (three to be exact) between the name and the extension. When typing in a filename, these spaces must not be included. Instead, a period is entered to indicate the separation of a filename from its extension.

1.16. Wildcards

There are times when you will find it advantageous to refer to files in a more general way. When you issue a command you may want to refer to more than one file at a time, so that the command entered can act upon more than one file.

For example, suppose there were 50 files on a disk that needed erasing. You might enter 50 commands, one to erase each file. However, the most convenient way would be to use a *wildcard*.

The purpose of DOS wildcards is to refer to a group of files with a single command.

DOS recognizes two special characters as wildcards: ? and *.

1.17.   The ? Character

The ? is used as a substitute for a particular character. Suppose that you stored the payroll information for your company in a series of files. The files were named by using the first name of the worker and the extension PAY to indicate payroll files. Here are the filenames:

MARY.PAY
MORRIS.PAY
JOE.PAY
SUE.PAY
WALTER.PAY
SAM.PAY

If you entered a command and specified ???.PAY, DOS would select files with any three characters as a filename, and the PAY extension.

JOE.PAY
SUE.PAY
SAM.PAY

If you wanted to be more specific you might use S??.PAY. Then only the three-letter names that began with an S would appear.

SUE.PAY
SAM.PAY

1.18.   The * Character

The * is even more general than the ?. An * used in a filename indicates that any characters beginning at that position and continuing to the end of the filename or extension are acceptable. For example, entering *.PAY would refer to all files with a PAY extension.

MARY.PAY
MORRIS.PAY
JOE.PAY
SUE.PAY

WALTER.PAY
SAM.PAY

If you entered M*.PAY you would get

MARY.PAY
MORRIS.PAY

When * is used DOS does not care how many characters follow the specified characters. One of the most common wildcards is *.*. When *.* is used it tells DOS to use all the files contained in a directory.

Most DOS commands and many programs allow you to enter file specifications with wildcard characters.

1.19.   Options

Options affect how a command is carried out. They function as adverbs do in human languages, modifying the action of the command verb. Not all commands have options, but those that do have may have several.

Options can be inclusive or exclusive of each other depending upon the command. If options are inclusive, they will function at the same time and produce a combined effect.

The usual form for an option is a slash followed by a letter. For example, the DIR command lists on the screen the names of the files stored in a disk directory. A typical directory display looks like this:

```
Volume in drive A has no label
Directory of  A:\

ASSIGN   COM     1073   1-01-80   1:46a
ASTCLOCK COM      813   9-18-82
         2 File(s)    78848 bytes free
```

DIR has an option, /W, that changes the format of the display to a wide format. Entering the command DIR/W will display the information like this:

```
Volume in drive A has no label
Directory of  A:\

ASSIGN   COM    ASTCLOCK COM
         2 File(s)     77824 bytes free
```

DIR also has a /P option that pauses the listing when the screen is filled. This makes it easier to read the directory display. The command below shows how two options can be used at once.

DIR/W/P

The number of options varies with each command. Also, some commands have no options at all.

1.20. Defaults

In many cases DOS makes assumptions about the parameters of a command if none are entered. These assumptions are called *defaults*. Their purpose is to allow you to simplify the entry of DOS commands. Unless your command contains a specific parameter, default values will always be used by DOS.

One of the most common examples of a default is the drive specification. For example, suppose you entered the DIR (List Directory) command into DOS. DOS would list the files in the *default* drive. Remember that the default drive is always indicated by the letter displayed by the DOS system's prompt. For example, if the prompt shows A>, then A is the default drive; if C>, then C is the default drive.

DOS does not display all its defaults in such a visual manner. Each command has its own set of defaults. When the term *default* is used in this book it refers to the options assumed by a command unless specifically stated otherwise.

1.21. Disk Organization

Although DOS carries out many types of tasks, most computer users only come into contact with the operating system in connection with the use of disks, both hard and floppy.

Disks have one very important characteristic—disk storage is reusable. If you record information on a disk you can later erase that information and use the space it occupied to record new information. The process of erasing old information and storing new information is constantly going on in a computer system.

For example, suppose that you were using a word processing program to type a document, such as a chapter of this book. If you decided to change the first word of the chapter, the computer would have to erase the old word and replace it with a new one.

DOS is charged with controlling and organizing the complex process of moving data to and from disks. In addition, most computer systems use more than one disk type, and often combine them.

The basic units of disk organization are as follows:

1. *Disk* or *Drive*. In computer systems the terms *disk* and *drive* are often used interchangeably, though not correctly so. A disk is placed inside a disk drive; that is, you have a recording medium within a recording device. In a floppy disk drive the medium is a removable plastic disk. In a hard disk drive the disk is aluminum and cannot be removed. Because the hard disk unit is sealed, many people do not realize there is a disk inside that performs about the same function as the plastic disk inserted into a floppy drive. Drives are given letter names, A, B, C, etc.

2. *Volume*. A volume is the same as a disk. The volume name has no function except to confirm to the user what disk is in what drive. Most people rely on the labels placed on their floppy disks instead of the volume labels. Each disk can have one and only one volume name, although that name can be changed.

3. *Directories* and *Subdirectories*. Both of these terms refer to the same thing. Directories are often compared to file cabinets, in that their purpose is to keep track of data and files stored on the disk. Every disk has at least one directory, the basic directory created when the disk is formatted. Prior to formatting, no information can be stored on the disk.

   The basic directory of every disk is called the *root* directory and is indicated by the \ (backslash) character.

   A disk can have more than one directory. As the number of files on a disk increases, it may be easier to divide the file into related groups so that similar groups can be stored together.

   Directories have a hierarchical organization. This means that directories spread out from the root like the branches of a tree. For example, you might decide to divide all your files into three groups: word processing, accounting, and graphics. You would then create three directories for the three types of files.

Later you might decide that the accounting directory should be further divided into payroll and general accounting. This means you would create two subdirectories for the accounting directory. The term *subdirectory* is used to indicate that the directory you are talking about is a division of a broader category, e.g., payroll is a subcategory of accounting. Because every directory is a division of the *root*, each can be viewed as a subdirectory. In normal usage the terms are interchangeable.

Most floppy disks have only one directory, the *root*. Hard disks, because they have more storage capacity, have more than one directory. However, these are not hard and fast rules. Floppy disks may have several directories, and it is possible (though perhaps not desirable) to operate a hard disk with a single directory.

4. *Files*. These are the smallest units of disk storage. To store even one character or number on a disk you must create a file and that file must be given a name. Every file is also assigned to a directory when it is created, even if there is only a *root* directory on the disk.

1.22.   Paths

If a disk has more than one directory, the *path* or *pathname* refers to the name of the file and the names of the directory and/or subdirectories that contain the file.

Pathnames are needed to locate files that may be stored in various directories. It's like calling Information for someone's telephone number. The first question you are asked, even before you give the person's name, is what city they live in. If you can't tell the operator what city the person lives in, the operator won't know what directory to use to find the person's number.

In the same way, when you instruct the computer to use a file on the disk the computer has to know what directory to look in. If you don't correctly identify the file and its pathname, the computer won't find the file.

The term *full pathname* refers to the complete name of a file and the directories in which it is contained. For example:

\ACCOUNT\PAYROLL\WORKERS.85

This means that there is a file WORKERS.85 stored in the PAYROLL subdirectory of the ACCOUNT directory. Note that the pathname lists the items in descending order of generality, with the filename coming last.

The drive can be added to the pathname. Below is an example of the full drive and pathname of a file:

C:\ACCOUNT\PAYROLL\WORKERS.85

1.23.   Types of Files

There are two basic types of files stored on computer disks.

1. *Binary Files.* Binary files are long sequences of numbers that contain coded information to be read directly by the computer. The microprocessor in your computer contains enough information to break the number sequence codes and interpret them as commands and or/data.

   Most programs are provided in the binary form. By convention, files that are program files carry either a COM or EXE extension.

   Binary program files are microprocessor-specific. This means that a program written for an IBM PC will run only on a computer that has the same decoder set as the IBM.

   If data is stored in a binary file it is likely that only the program and computer it was designed to operate with can understand the data.
2. *ASCII Files.* ASCII stands for the American Standard Code for Information Interchange. The purpose of this code is to create files that are stored in a format that is common to many different programs and computers.

   Storage in ASCII format is usually less compact than binary storage. However, the advantage is that ASCII provides a common basis for the interchange of information.

   As a computer user you will want to be aware of which programs work with ASCII files. Programs that can read and write ASCII files can exchange information with other programs that do the same. Programs that use only their own specially coded binary files are much more limited in terms of sharing information.

1.24.   Text Files and ASCII

If you have been working with microcomputers, you may already be acquainted with the terms *ASCII files*, *DOS files*, and *text files*. The three terms generally refer to the same thing: files in which data is stored in a standard format. To understand how the programs explained in this book can be used, it is important to have a clear understanding of what is meant by these terms.

1.25.   How Computers Represent Information

The first step in understanding the ASCII system is to understand the general technique used by computers to store information.

When you press a key on the keyboard of the computer, you do so in response to the letter or the symbol printed on the key that corresponds to something that you recognize. When you want to type an A you press the key with the A symbol on it.

But what really happens when you press that key? The answer may surprise you. When you press a key you generate a series of signals. The signals are a bit like Morse code in that they consist of only two types of information. Morse code represents the letters of the alphabet by using DOTS and DASHES. Computers represent keystrokes by using ON and OFF signals. The ON signal is usually represented as the number 1, the OFF signal as the number 0. For example, when you press the key representing lower case *a*, the following signal is sent:

01100001

If you press the lower case *b* key you send a slightly different series:

01100010

You may have noticed that both keys produce exactly eight signals. Most microcomputers receive signals of that size for each keystroke.

Each signal is called a *bit*. A *bit* is the smallest unit of information a computer deals with. The group of eight signals is called a *byte*. It is common to define a byte as the amount of information generated by a single keystroke.

[It is more accurate to say that at least one byte is created by each keystroke. When you are working with a computer program, each keystroke may set off a chain of events that results in the creation of many bytes. For example, when you are word processing, the computer may store more bytes than the number of keystrokes you typed in. The additional bytes are used to store information about the format of the text. There is usually a certain amount of overhead involved in storing data.]

Computer storage is usually expressed in terms of the number of bytes that can be stored. The standard unit of measurement is the *kilobyte*, which is 1,024 bytes. If a computer is said to have a "64K" memory capacity, this means that it has 64 kilobytes of memory. To find out the exact number of bytes, you would perform the following calculation:

$$64 \times 1,024 = 65,536 \text{ bytes}$$

1.26. The ASCII Code

ASCII, the American Standard Code for Information Interchange, provides 128 standard representations. These 128 ASCII characters include all of the characters shown on the normal keyboard, plus characters that represent special keys, such as <Esc>, <return>, and <Tab>.

A file that is standard ASCII format means that any program that reads standard files can read and understand the information contained in that file. Therefore, the terms *ASCII file*, *DOS text file*, *text file*, and *ASCII standard file* all refer to the same thing.

Thus, files can be divided into two distinct groups:

1. Standard Text Files. These are files that contain data readable by many different programs.
2. Non-Standard Files. These files contain special codes that do not conform to the ASCII conventions. Generally, these files can be understood only by programs that are specifically designed to read them.

1.27. How Programs Create Files

Not all programs can read and write information in ASCII standard form. Many programs add special numeric codes to the information they store. The codes have meaning only to those particular programs. Any other program that attempts to read such a file will be confused by the codes it does not understand.

For example, here is a simple worksheet created with Lotus 1-2-3:

Rate	Hours	Gross
25.00	40.00	1,000.00

The data seems perfectly straightforward. But when the data is saved in a 1-2-3 worksheet file it looks something like this:

```
71710100  0F000B00  FF000000  00275261  7465000F  000C00FF
01000000  27486F75  7273000F  000C00FF  02000000  2747726F
7373000D  000700FF  00000100  1900000D  0700FF01  00010028
0010001B  00FF0200  01000000  00000040  8F400C00  01FEBF00
8001FFBF  00800B03  01000000  1A000000  00000000  00000000
```

Lotus Format In Hex Notation

```
*************'Rate******
****'Hours**********'Gro
ss.***....*.*.*.*..*.*.*
.*.*..*.*......@*@****.
*..*******...........
```

Lotus Format Text Equivalent

Figure 1-1.

The format that Lotus uses to save its data is nothing like the way it appears on the screen. Lotus 1-2-3 does not save worksheets in ASCII format. One reason is that Lotus needs to save more information than just the text that appears on the screen. It needs to save cell locations, formulas, and other data that are used internally by the program. This additional information is often coded into numeric sequences that mean nothing to most users but can be translated by the program being used.

The advantage to storing information in a standard format is that many other programs can use the data. Lotus 1-2-3 can produce an ASCII standard file by using the Print File commands. When Print File is used, Lotus 1-2-3 creates a file that consists of the ASCII codes for the data as it appears on the screen. This file can be read into other programs, such as word processing or data base programs that read ASCII standard files.

Remember that in using the ASCII version of the file, Lotus cannot represent the formulas and cell locations as it could in the Lotus format file. The ASCII file contains the end result but not the calculations that produced it.

ASCII files tend to take up more room than files that compress data into binary sequences.

1.28. What Programs Produce ASCII Files

Many of the utility programs presented in this book make use of standard ASCII files. ASCII text files can be created with a variety of programs. The following sections explain the types of files that various popular applications create. This guide is meant to help you decide if your word processor or even your spreadsheet program can be used to create or revise ASCII standard text files.

1.29. DOS Commands

While not everyone owns WordStar or 1-2-3, it is certain that everyone with a MS DOS system has two simple ways to create DOS ASCII text files:

1. COPY CON: <filename> This method allows you to create a simple text file. Its advantage is that it will work anywhere and anytime that you have a system's prompt. The copy command sends any text that you enter into the specified file. When you are finished typing, you would enter

   [F6] <return>

   This method can be used to create files only. You cannot revise files with this method.
2. EDLIN: The EDLIN program is supplied as part of the MS DOS system. The name stands for LINE EDITOR. It will create and revise standard text files.

1.30. Word Processing Programs

The following is a brief list of popular word processing programs and their use, if any, of ASCII files.

1.30.1.   WordStar

The most popular word processing program for creating and editing text files is probably WordStar. Be aware that WordStar has two modes: the Document mode and the Non-document mode. The Document mode is entered with the D command and does not produce ASCII standard files. Be careful not to use the D command for the non-document mode or you could damage your file.

To create or edit a standard text file use the N command for the Non-document mode. Note that WordStar will not allow entry of the extended character set from the keyboard. However, should you read in a document with extended characters, WordStar will display them as characters after subtracting 128 from the value.

1.30.2.   WordStar 2000

This program will create and revise standard text files. The key is to use UNFORM format when you create the document. WordStar 2000 will display the entire IBM character set. You can type in extended ASCII characters with the [Alt] and keypad numbers.

1.30.3.   Microsoft Word

Any Word document can be saved as an ASCII standard file. Word has two modes for saving files: formatted or unformatted. Make sure to choose the UNFORMATTED option when saving the file. If you accidentally save the file as formatted you can correct this by loading it again and saving it as unformatted. This will strip out the Word formatting codes.

1.30.4.   MultiMate

MultiMate will not directly read or write ASCII files. However, if you want to take the trouble, MultiMate provides a CONVERT program that will change ASCII files to MultiMate files and MulitMate files to ASCII files. Note that MultiMate, unlike WordStar or Word, treats documents as a series of pages, not one long continuous file. This often creates logical problems when constructing ASCII files, which seldom require pages.

MultiMate is problematic when creating ASCII files. If you need them, you might consider using a program that is more ASCII-compatible.

1.30.5. DisplayWrite II

This program does not support ASCII files.

1.30.6. DisplayWrite III

DisplayWrite III does allow you to save text in an ASCII format. The command is accessed on the BLOCK menu (F4). Use the ASCII SAVE command on that menu to mark a block of text to be saved as an ASCII standard file.

Note that only files saved with this command are in ASCII format. All normal DisplayWrite files are non-ASCII. DisplayWrite, like MultiMate, treats documents as pages. This makes this program difficult to use for ASCII file creation.

1.30.7. WordPerfect

WordPerfect can read and write ASCII-compatible files.

1.31 Other Programs

Other programs that can also create ASCII standard files are described below.

1.31.1. Lotus 1-2-3 and Symphony

Both of these programs are able to read and write ASCII files. The output of ASCII files can be accomplished by using the Print File command. This command creates an ASCII output file with a PRN extension. The data in the file is the same type of data that is sent to the printer.

In Symphony, the same thing can be accomplished by setting the Print Destination on the Print Settings Menu for a file.

Both programs can also accept an ASCII text file as data. Version 2 of 1-2-3 and Symphony 1.0 and 1.1 have a parse command that breaks up ASCII text into a series of cell entries.

1.31.2. Framework

Framework can also read and write ASCII standard files. Framework assigns a TXT extension to files that are saved in the ASCII format. The Disk menu contains the Import and Export commands that accept ASCII specifications.

1.31.3. dBASE II and III

Both programs will read and write ASCII files. The dBASE word processor, accessed by the Modify Command command, will write ASCII standard files. dBASE can also copy its data files to ASCII standard or import data from an ASCII text file.

1.32. Extended ASCII Code

As we have said, the ASCII code has 128 standard characters. However, the IBM PC and compatible computers have a built-in character set that consists of 256 characters. The additional characters are often displayed on the screen by programs. They are the ones that form the lines and boxes seen so often in screen displays. Other additional characters include accented *e* and the Greek letters used in mathematics.

The entire set of 256 characters, the 128 ASCII characters and the 128 other characters displayed by the IBM PC, is referred to as the *extended* ASCII system.

The differences between the standard ASCII codes and the extended codes lie in what is called the *high-order bit*. (Remember that each character is composed of a series of eight signals, called *bits*. For example, the letter A (upper case) is represented by 01000001.)

All of the 128 standard ASCII characters can be represented with only seven bits. You can confirm this by calculating the number of permutations possible with seven bits. Each bit can have only two options, ON or

OFF. A seven-bit number can be arranged in 2 to the seventh power, or 128, different ways.

But the eight-bit structure used by the IBM PC allows you to represent data with eight bits. That means there are 2 to the eighth power, or 256, possible arrangements.

In the standard ASCII codes, the leftmost bit is ALWAYS OFF and is called the *high-order* bit.

00000000
↑
Always zero in ASCII code

The extended codes make use of the high-order bit. Extending the ASCII seven-bit code to a full eight-bit code makes use of the full potential of the computer.

On the IBM PC the additional 128 characters in extended ASCII code are shown in Figure 1-2.

The advantage of this extended set is that you can display all types of special characters on the screen that enhance the video display.

There is a little trick that enables you to type the full IBM character set. The trick is to hold down the [Alt] key and type the number which represents the character that you want to appear. For example, you could enter

[Alt/160]

and the screen displays an *a* with an accent.

[Not all applications will accept this extended character set as input. For example, Word-Star will automatically subtract 128 from the value of the extended character and display the character indicated by the first seven bits. Character 160 will appear as character 32, i.e., a blank space.

WordStar uses the high-order bit to control word processing features, such as print justification.]

1.33. Print the Full IBM Character Set

While it is rather simple to display the IBM extended character set, it is not quite so simple to print it. With the exception of high-resolution

	☺	☻	♥	♦	♣	♠	•	◘	○	◙	♂	♀	♪	♫	☼
0	1	2	3	4	5	6	7	8	9	10	11	12	13	14	15
►	◄	↕	‼	¶	§	▬	↨	↑	↓	→	←	∟	↔	▲	▼
16	17	18	19	20	21	22	23	24	25	26	27	28	29	30	31
	!	"	#	$	%	&	'	(	)	*	+	,	-	.	/
32	33	34	35	36	37	38	39	40	41	42	43	44	45	46	47
0	1	2	3	4	5	6	7	8	9	:	;	<	=	>	?
48	49	50	51	52	53	54	55	56	57	58	59	60	61	62	63
@	A	B	C	D	E	F	G	H	I	J	K	L	M	N	O
64	65	66	67	68	69	70	71	72	73	74	75	76	77	78	79
P	Q	R	S	T	U	V	W	X	Y	Z	[	\	]	^	_
80	81	82	83	84	85	86	87	88	89	90	91	92	93	94	95
`	a	b	c	d	e	f	g	h	i	j	k	l	m	n	o
96	97	98	99	100	101	102	103	104	105	106	107	108	109	110	111
p	q	r	s	t	u	v	w	x	y	z	{	|	}	~	⌂
112	113	114	115	116	117	118	119	120	121	122	123	124	125	126	127
Ç	ü	é	â	ä	à	å	ç	ê	ë				ì	î	ì	Ä	Å
128	129	130	131	132	133	134	135	136	137	138	139	140	141	142	143
É	æ	Æ	ô	ö	ò	û	ù	ÿ	Ö	Ü	¢	£	¥	₧	ƒ
144	145	146	147	148	149	150	151	152	153	154	155	156	157	158	159
á	í	ó	ú	ñ	Ñ	ª	º	¿	⌐	¬	½	¼	¡	«	»
160	161	162	163	164	165	166	167	168	169	170	171	172	173	174	175
░	▒	▓	│	┤	╡	╢	╖	╕	╣	║	╗	╝	╜	╛	┐
176	177	178	179	180	181	182	183	184	185	186	187	188	189	190	191
└	┴	┬	├	─	┼	╞	╟	╚	╔	╩	╦	╠	═	╬	╧
192	193	194	195	196	197	198	199	200	201	202	203	204	205	206	207
╨	╤	╥	╙	╘	╒	╓	╫	╪	┘	┌	█	▄	▌	▐	▀
208	209	210	211	212	213	214	215	216	217	218	219	220	221	222	223
α	β	Γ	π	Σ	σ	µ	τ	Φ	Θ	Ω	δ	∞	ø	ε	∩
224	225	226	227	228	229	230	231	232	233	234	235	236	237	238	239
≡	±	≥	≤	⌠	⌡	÷	≈	°	∙	·	√	ⁿ	²	■	
240	241	242	243	244	245	246	247	248	249	250	251	252	253	254	255

**Fig. 1-2. Extended Character Set. IBM character above,
ASCII number below.**

graphics, all printing is done by sending the ASCII codes to the printer.
The printer then translates the codes into the corresponding characters.

If the printer is a dot-matrix printer, the ASCII code is translated into a
pattern of dots. If the printer is a daisy-wheel printer the ASCII code will
be translated by turning to a particular spoke on a print wheel.

The advantage of having printers ASCII-compatible is that they can accept data from a wide variety of sources, such as computers or other de-

vices that send out ASCII codes. As a computer owner you have a wide variety of printers to choose from because the ASCII establishes a standard method of coding information sent from the computer to the printer.

However, when you look at a daisy-wheel printer you quickly realize that there is a problem. The average wheel on a daisy-wheel printer contains 96 spokes. No matter what codes you send to that printer, it can only print the 96 characters on that wheel. The computer has more than double that number of characters when you include the extended IBM graphics set.

[The extended ASCII code comprises 256 characters. However, not all of the characters have a printable character by which they can be represented. For example, character 13 in the ASCII code is the CR (carriage return) character. When it is sent to a printer the printer returns the carriage instead of printing a letter.

Of the total of 256 characters, the full IBM set contains 223 printable characters. It is this set of 223 printable characters that printers are concerned with.]

Dot-matrix printers do not have the same physical limitation as daisy-wheel printers. Most printers will respond to the full extended character set. However, not all printers do so in the same way. The EPSON MX, RX, and FX series prints italic characters when the IBM PC shows lines and boxes on the screen. If you have the IBM labeled version of the EPSON printer you can get the full character set to print.

[If you have a printer like an EPSON MX or FX series you can still produce the full IBM character set. However, you will need a utility program to do so. Part 4 contains information about these programs.

If you have a printer with the full PC character set built in, you still must make some adjustments if you want your printout to look exactly like the IBM screen. The line height used in standard print mode places space between the lines. This is fine for text, but box drawings or vertical lines that look continuous on the screen will appear chopped into pieces on the printer.]

If you have an HP Laser Printer you will also find problems printing the full IBM character set since many of the fonts designed for that printer do not include the full IBM character set, at the time of this writing.

1.34. The Issue of Copy Protection

The concepts of DOS techniques are complex and require some time to understand and utilize. The issue of copy protection adds additional complexities to the way in which programs operate.

DOS has the ability to transfer data from one disk to another. For example, if you have the DOS file FORMAT.COM on a disk, you can use the copy command to copy FORMAT.COM to any other DOS disk that has room for that file. The copy contains exactly the same information as the original, and therefore will operate exactly like the original when the program is run.

This makes it possible for you to make as many copies of the Format program as you need. Traditional computer wisdom says that you should always make at least one copy of every valuable disk you have, especially programs. When you work, you work with the copies, not the originals.

But there is a disadvantage to this system, according to the software companies. If you can make copies of software programs, what is to stop you from making copies of a program that you bought and giving or even selling them to other people? This type of action is a violation of the copyright laws, but unfortunately that does not stop people from doing it.

There is no general agreement about the extent to which programs are copied and used in violation of copyrights. Since the activity is illegal, it is unlikely that people who do such things will be entirely truthful about it.

This book is not meant to judicate the legal issues surrounding copying programs. However, the schemes employed by some software companies to protect their programs from being copied illegally add a layer of complexity to operating a computer system.

1.35.   What Is Copy Protection

Copy protection is used to prevent computer users from making illegal copies of programs. In order to create a disk that cannot be copied, the common practice is to store the information on the disk in such a manner that the DOS COPY or DISKCOPY commands will fail to recognize and/or copy some part of the program onto the new disk. When a user tries to use the copy, the program will be incomplete, and will therefore fail to run.

In order to hide information from DOS, programmers must violate the normal rules for storage of data in DOS. Copy protection schemes come in many varieties. How the program you buy is copy protected will determine how it can be used. Some programs offer you limited ability to make copies; others cannot be copied, even once to a hard disk; still others cannot be backed up onto a tape; and so on.

One question often asked is: "How does one know if a program is copy protected when it is bought?" The answer is that one doesn't know. Although companies put a lot of effort into creating copy protection schemes, they do not advertise the fact to potential customers. I know of no program packaging that indicates that the program contained within is copy protected.

[In recent months some companies have begun to advertise that their software is not copy protected. Borland, makers of Sidekick, Superkey, and Turbo Lightning (discussed in this book) consider their lack of copy protection as a benefit for the user and promote their software as unprotected.]

Even in the documentation, the idea of copy protection is rarely stated. Often, the only way to find out if a program is protected is to read the installation procedure. If the program uses DOS commands like COPY *.* or DISKCOPY to make copies of the original, that indicates that the program probably isn't protected. If the program has a special INSTALL or SETUP program, this might indicate that there is a special protection scheme used.

For the average user, it is a very hard thing to judge. One doesn't usually read the installation guide until the program is bought. Though copy protection schemes are necessary, copy-protected programs present problems for legitimate owners.

1.36.   A Brief History

Anyone who sells ideas is always nervous about people stealing them. This is true of inventors, writers, or programmers. Where copyrights are concerned, the law takes the view that you cannot copyright an idea but only the implementation of the idea. For example, if a computer is designed to be compatible with an IBM computer, the maker can duplicate the functions of the IBM model, but the functions must be implemented in a different way.

The problem with software is not just that it can be copied but that it is so inexpensive and easy to copy. Like the book you are reading, most books are protected by copyright. If you wanted to make a copy of this book and sell it you would need to have a copying machine and paper, and perhaps a binder for the pages. In making the copy, chances are that the cost in time, paper, use of the machine and the binder would exceed the cost of the book itself. Therefore not only is the publisher's copyright protected by law, it is also protected by the practical economics of printing.

With computer programs just the opposite is true. While many programs cost hundreds, even thousands of dollars to buy, to duplicate a disk costs a fraction of the original fee. This unfortunate circumstance tends to wreak havoc on the finances of the industry.

[Of course, many programs are accompanied by large and complex manuals that explain their use and functions. Anyone copying a program would do well to consider if the program will be of use without its manual. This creates a much-needed drawback to illegal copying.]

Before the IBM PC, the computer world was divided into protected and unprotected operating systems. By tradition, Apple II programs were generally protected. CP/M programs generally were not. When the PC arrived, software companies began to convert their programs to run on the IBM. It was here that the two worlds met.

Programs like WordStar and dBASE II were not protected as CP/M programs and remained unprotected as MS DOS programs. The big change came with Lotus 1-2-3. Unlike the other major programs transported over from CP/M to MS DOS, 1-2-3 was copy protected. Since then new programs like dBASE III and WordStar 2000 have been released with copy protection.

[WordStar 2000 was originally released as a copy-protected program. The reaction by users familiar with WordStar (unprotected) was so vehement that within a few months a new version of WordStar 2000 was released without copy protection.]

1.37.   When Can You Make Copies

Whether or not your software is copy protected does not affect your rights as a consumer to make copies for your own personal use or the rights of the manufacturer to be protected by copyright laws. When you buy a software program you are purchasing the right to work with a copy of the program. The program is still the property of the company that sold it to you. You are required by law to respect their rights and not produce copies for illegal purposes.

However, some legitimate users feel a need to make backup copies to protect their investment. These backup copies are intended to be used only if the original program becomes damaged. In some cases, however, backup copies are provided with the purchase and you needn't spend the effort to make further copies. The backup copies can be used in place of, but not along with, the originals. This means that only you can use your copies or the original.

Remember, even if the software isn't copy protected, your rights are extended only to making backup copies for your own use. Giving or selling the copies to other people to use is a violation of the copyright laws.

1.38. Problems with Protected Software

Copy-protected software can create a number of compatibility problems for users.

1. Some copy-protected programs will fail to operate in some IBM-compatible computers. For example, I have found that the Lotus 1-2-3 version 2 will not run on my Eagle PC. The original copy-protected version of WordStar 2000 failed to run on a Panasonic portable.
2. In the case of hard disks, many programs require that the master disk be placed in the A drive before you can run your program.

1.39. Types of Copy Protection

The methods used to create copy protection schemes are quite varied. From the user's point of view they fall into the following types:

TYPE A. This type of program is created to be run only from the master disk or backup disk which is supplied with the program. It does allow you to copy the program to a hard disk and use the master as a key disk. The program disk must be in the A drive at all times. This type of protection is common in game software but less common with business software. Further, the disk's directory is often hidden and you can only load the software by booting the disk. *Example*: Flight Simulator

TYPE B. Type B software is a little more flexible than type A. This type of protection allows the user to copy the files from the floppy disk to a hard disk. However, the program will not run unless the master disk is in drive A when the program is loaded. The program will automatically seek the master disk in drive A when it is run. Failure to find the disk will result in a failure to run the program. *Example*: Lotus 1-2-3 Version 1A

TYPE C. This type of program allows you to make a limited number of copies, usually one, to a hard disk. The copy made to the hard disk will operate with a key disk in drive A. You cannot make copies of the floppy disks to other floppy disks at all. *Examples*: Microsoft Word, dBASE III Version 1.0

TYPE D. This type of protection has one change from type C. Once you have installed a copy onto the hard disk you can uninstall it at a later time. This means that you can move the software from one hard disk to another by uninstalling it on one and reinstalling it on a different computer. *Examples*: Lotus 1-2-3 Version 2, dBASE III Version 1.1

1.40. Problems with Protection Schemes

The various schemes present different types of problems. The simplest is type B. You can make as many copies to your hard disk as you like. Should your hard disk fail, you can simply copy the files back onto the disk when it is repaired.

With type C there is no way to restore the program if your hard disk fails. Type D would in theory allow you to uninstall the program. But disk problems may make this impossible. In that case type D is no different than type C.

Type B also has the virtue of not creating problems with backups. For example, with programs that use types C and D, if you backed up your data onto floppy disks and then restored the data from the floppies to the hard disk, the program would treat the restored files as unauthorized copies.

The reason is that types C and D of copy protection transfer special hidden files to your hard disk. DOS cannot correctly copy these files. The normal procedure of backup and restore looks like illegal copying to the program.

You can avoid this problem by not backing up the root directory where the programs store their special files. Of course, this makes backups a bit more complicated.

1.41. Making Copies of Copy-Protected Software

There is help for users in this area. Because the law recognizes the right of individuals to make backup copies of software, some companies market products that will create these copies. One of the most popular is Copy II PC.

The program is an intelligent copying program. It examines the disk as it copies and attempts to create a full working duplicate of the original. Of course, not all software can be copied with this program. The makers of software know that these programs exist, and they try to make their software more difficult to copy. Thus, the honest consumer is caught in the middle.

1.42. Copy II PC

The Copy II PC program provides a number of aids to users:

1. COPY. This function makes a copy of the diskette that will operate the way the master does.
2. NOKEY. An additional program furnished by Copy II PC. This program makes it possible to run copy-protected type B software from a hard disk. The NOKEY program is loaded into the computer first. When the copy-protected files are run, they do not search for the master disk but load directly into memory.
3. NOGUARD. This additional program can in some cases remove the copy protection from a disk. This creates a non-copy protected version of the program that can be copied to other disks or a hard disk using the normal DOS copy command. This type of protection works with type C and D software.

1.43. The Copy Option Board

For those pieces of software that cannot be copied by the Copy II PC software program, one can purchase a board that will extend the functions of the floppy disk controller. The board is a hardware solution to the problem of copy protection.

The board is installed directly into one of the slots of the computer. The cables between the floppy drives and the floppy drive controller card are reconnected so that the Copy Option board sits between them.

In normal use the board has no effect. However, when a special program is run the board can duplicate the data from almost any disk. The board does not eliminate the copy protection like NOGUARD, but simply makes an exact duplicate of the disk. Unlike software copying programs, the Copy Option Board can copy data stored in unusual places on the disk. Both the Copy II PC program and the Copy Option Board take more time to make copies than does a normal DOS copy command.

Note that if you use a IBM-compatible computer you may find the cables supplied with the copy-option board do not fit connectors in your computer. Carefully check these connections before trying to install this board.

1.44. Conclusion

This chapter contains some basic concepts that apply generally to software and hardware in the IBM PC and compatible market. You will find that the DOS concepts introduced here will help you understand how utilities work within the context of the entire computer system.

For readers who would like a better understanding of DOS, the next chapter contains hands-on examples of DOS commands.

This chapter also contains information on copy protection, problems connected with copy protection, and options available to users to produce copies for legitimate use of the protected programs. The topic was meant as a matter-of-fact discussion of the technical issues involved. It is in no way intended to promote the duplication of copyrighted programs or the use of illegally duplicated programs.

2.

Working with DOS Commands

The purpose of this chapter is to give you a workable understanding of how DOS commands are used. The principles and techniques illustrated here will be used again and again in working with the utilities discussed in this book.

   The hands-on presentation assumes that you are working with DOS 2.0 or higher. Users with the DOS 1.0 level can follow most of the commands with the exception of the sections on redirection, filters, and subdirectories.

2.1.   Setup

The setup is quite simple. Place a copy of the MS DOS or PC DOS systems disk in drive A. (If you are not sure how to make a copy, refer to the next section. If you have a copy, you can proceed. Note, however, that you should use a copy of the systems disk, since some of the instructions will change the way that disk is currently set up.)

2.2.   Making a Copy

Floppy Disk Systems:
Place a DOS systems disk in drive A.
Place a blank or new disk in drive B.

Enter **diskcopy,a: = b: <return>**

The program will pause. Press any key to begin the copying. When the copying is complete the program will ask you if you want to make another. Enter **n**, for no more copies. Place your newly made copy in drive A and you are ready to begin.

Hard Disk Systems:
Place the DOS systems disk in drive A. This disk will be referred to as the *source disk*. Enter **diskcopy,a: = a: <return>**

Press any key to begin copying. When the program asks for the *target* disk, place a blank disk into drive A and remember to close the door of the disk drive. Enter **<return>**

The program will continue to ask for *source* and *target* disks until a complete duplicate of the first disk is created. Then it will ask you if you want to make more copies. Enter **n** for no more copies. After placing your *target* disk in drive A, you are ready to begin.

2.3. Beginning with DOS

Modern computer memory has one basic drawback. It cannot store information after the electricity has been turned off, even for a fraction of a second. In order to store information you need some way of recording the information handled by the computer. The most common devices used for this task are disk drives, both hard and floppy.

When information is stored on a disk, it is stored as a group. A given group of related information is called a FILE. A disk can have many files that contain either instructions for the computer or data stored by the user. Each file must be given a unique name so that the computer can later refer to that group of information and load it from the disk into the computer again.

A file that contains instructions for the computer is a PROGRAM file. A file that contains data entered by a user is called a DATA file. Both program files and data files may be stored on disks. Every computer that uses disks (hard or floppy) must have a master program that coordinates the flow of information from computer to disk, and from disk to computer. The Disk Operating System is assigned the task of integrating the various devices that make up a computer system. The three major tasks the operating system must carry out are:

1. Coordination of the parts of the system, such as monitors, printers, disk drives, and modems, for input and output.
2. Allowing the user to load and execute programs.
3. Maintaining an orderly system of files on the disk.

Note that all programs that operate on an IBM or compatible depend on MS DOS to handle the movement of data between input and output devices. A computer system is really not one machine but a group of related devices; thus the term *system* is used. Devices can be attached to the computer internally, inside the same metal box, or externally, in separate boxes attached by cables. Look at the list below:

DEVICE	*FUNCTION*
Keyboard	INPUT ONLY
Screen	OUTPUT ONLY
Printer	OUTPUT ONLY
Disks	INPUT and OUTPUT

Note that the disk drives can be both input and output devices. Most of the commands in MS DOS refer to the complex process of input and output from and to the disk drives. When you first turn the computer on, it goes through a process called *booting* or *bootstrapping*. The process is necessary before the computer can actually be usable for real work. The bootstrap process is used to load the MS DOS into the memory of the computer. Once MS DOS is in the memory, you can begin to work.

The first display you see will ask for today's date. You do not have to enter a date. You can simply press return. If you do want to set the date to the current date, notice that you should enter the date in this format: MM-DD-YY. After the date prompt, you are prompted to enter the time. Once again this is optional. If you do want to enter the time, enter it in the form HH:MM. Press return to skip the time if you wish.

2.4. The Systems Level

The Disk Operating System is automatically loaded from the disk when you turn on the computer. Therefore, there must always be a disk present in drive A before turning on the computer. If you have a hard disk, then that disk is always ready and takes the place of the floppy disk in drive A.

To see how MS DOS shares the computer memory with the program and your data, look at the figure below.

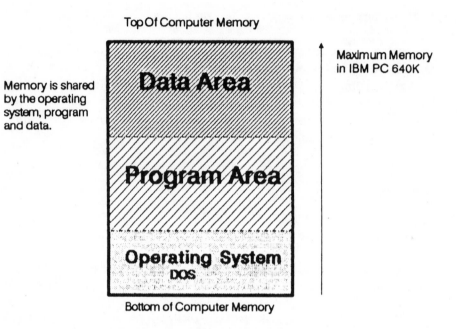

Fig. 2-1. Memory Map.

The A prompt, A>, shows that MS DOS is active. Whenever you see the A>, it means MS DOS is ready to accept a command from you, and you are not working within an application program yet. Unless specified otherwise, all commands will affect data on the active drive only. Later you will learn how to change that A to B or C. You are now ready to work with MS DOS.

2.5.   The Disk Directory

You can usually tell what files are stored on a disk by reading the disk label. But that label may not have the correct information on it. The only

way to be sure about what is really on a disk is to display a directory of its
files. MS DOS has a command called DIR that will do just that. Enter the
following command: **dir‹return›**

All the disk files on the active drive, A, are displayed. You might also
notice that the red light on that drive turns on, indicating that the device
is activated. Whenever you see the red light you know that the disk drive
is reading from, or writing to, the disk. Never remove a disk from a drive
when the light is on!

The display of the A> prompt means this directory belongs to the disk
in drive A. Below is a sample of how a directory looks:

```
      Volume in drive A has no label
      Directory of  A:\

      COMMAND   COM     17792   10-20-83   12:00p
      ANSI      SYS      1664   10-20-83   12:00p
      FORMAT    COM      6912   10-20-83   12:00p
      CHKDSK    COM      6400   10-20-83   12:00p
      PRINT     COM      4608   10-20-83   12:00p
      RECOVER   COM      2304   10-20-83   12:00p
             39 File(s)      63488 bytes free
```

The list of files is scrolled on the screen. At the bottom of the display the
amount of space left on the disk for new files is shown. The list is too long
to be seen at one time. (There is a way of controlling this which you will
learn later.)

Each line that appears represents a file that is stored on the disk. Look
at the line below:

```
      BACKUP    COM      3687   10-20-83   12:00p
         ↑                ↑        ↑          ↑
      Filename           Size     Date      Time
```

MS DOS displays four pieces of information about each file: the filename, its size, and the date and time of its creation or last update. The
most important aspect of the display is the filename listing. Each filename
potentially has three parts:

1. Drive name (optional)
2. Filename
3. Extension (optional)

The general form of a filename is as follows: d:filename.ext

Note that the first and last parts are optional. When you enter a filename you enter it in a different manner than MS DOS displays it. Below is a typical line from a directory as MS DOS lists it.

BACKUP   COM   3687 10-20-83 12:00p

The name appears as BACKUP   COM but when you enter the name you must enter it as backup.com. Note that MS DOS does not care if the letters are upper or lower case. However, you cannot enter spaces as part of a filename even though that is the way they appear in the directory listing.

The drive name can be any letter from A to Z. However, you must have a device connected to the computer to correspond to the drive designation. For example, two drives allow you to use A or B. Filenames can be between one and eight characters long. You can use any of the following characters:

A B C D E F G H I J K L M N O P Q R S T U V W X Y Z
0 1 2 3 4 5 6 7 8 9 ! @ # % ^ & ( ) { } - _ $

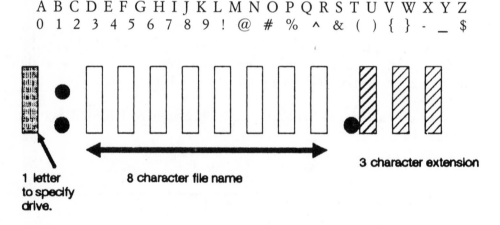

1 letter
to specify
drive.

8 character file name

3 character extension

Fig. 2-2. Filenames.

Remember, you cannot use a blank space as part of a name. The filename below, for instance, would not be acceptable to MS DOS:

MY FILE

However, MY_FILE would be acceptable. The space was replaced with a _ which is a legal character.

The extension is limited to three characters. The extension is separated from the filename by a period and the drive name is separated from the filename by a colon.

Below are examples of filenames. Test yourself to see if you can tell which are valid names and which are not. (An answer key can be found at the end of the chapter.)

		Circle Valid or Not Valid	
1.	A:LETTER.TXT	Valid	Not Valid
2.	SAMPLE DAT	Valid	Not Valid
3.	X	Valid	Not Valid
4.	MY:FILE	Valid	Not Valid
5.	msdos.les	Valid	Not Valid
6.	Sample.File	Valid	Not Valid
7.	C.test.doc	Valid	Not Valid
8.	b:user.fil	Valid	Not Valid

The drive specification and extension are optional. The usual purpose of the extension is to group together files with different names of the same type. By tradition, file extensions such as .BAS (basic program), .COM (machine language file), .DAT (data file) have been used to identify the type of information contained within certain files. You are under no obligation to follow such traditions.

As discussed earlier, the directory of a disk may be too long to be displayed on a single screen at one time. There are two ways to display a directory. Enter **dir/w<return>** and the directory will look like this:

```
Volume in drive A is BASICS
Directory of  A:\

COMMAND  COM    ANSI     SYS    FORMAT   COM    CHKDSK   COM    SYS      COM
DISKCOPY COM    DISKCOMP COM    COMP     COM    EDLIN    COM    MODE     COM
FDISK    COM    BACKUP   COM    RESTORE  COM    PRINT    COM    RECOVER  COM
ASSIGN   COM    TREE     COM    GRAPHICS COM    SORT     EXE    FIND     EXE
MORE     COM    BASIC    COM    BASICA   COM    DEBUG    COM    SETUP
SETUP_C  COM    SETUP_A  COM    MESS     TXT    X        BAS    MONO
AUTOECEC BAT    CHNGPROM BAT    SAMPLE          AUTOEXEC BAT
        39 File(s)      64512 bytes free
```

This is called the wide directory because the files are listed across instead of vertically. This means that more names can fit on a single screen. Note that MS DOS no longer displays the size, date, and time of each file in order to save space on the display. Now try this. Enter **dir/p<return>**

Note that the screen fills and the list pauses until you press another key. Enter **<return>** and the next screen of filenames is displayed.

In summary, there are three styles of directory listings:

DIR   full listing of all files, including size, date, and time.
DIR/W   wide directory, file size, date, and time are not shown
DIR/P   pause directory listing when one screen is filled. Size, date, and time
            are shown.

2.6.   Other Drives

You can specify another drive's directory by following the DIR command with the letter that indicates the drive. Try the following (only if you are using a two-drive system with a disk in the second drive):

dir b:<return>   (floppy drive systems)
dir c:<return>   (hard drive systems)

The computer will display the list of disk files on drive B or C. You can also get a wide display of drive B. Enter

dir b:/w<return>   (floppy drive systems)
dir c:/w<return>   (hard drive systems)

As mentioned earlier, the A> indicates that MS DOS will assume you want to work with drive A unless you specify otherwise. Thus A is considered the default drive for all commands. You can change the default drive by simply typing in the new drive that you want to become the default. Again, drive names are always followed by a colon. Enter

b:<return>   (floppy drive systems)
c:<return>   (hard drive systems)

and the prompt has changed to B> or C>. You can get a listing of drive A by entering **dir a:<return>**

Now change the default back to drive A on your own. The correct command is listed at the end of the chapter.

2.7. Limited Searches

While the DIR command is useful in displaying the names of the files, there are some practical problems that require other techniques. For example, you might want to know if the disk in the drive contains a file called ASSIGN.COM. Enter **dir<return>**

Did you see the file you were looking for? It might be better to narrow down the display to just the files that begin with the letter A. That would make it much simpler to find out whether or not the file you wanted was on this disk. MS DOS allows the user a certain degree of ambiguity in asking for files. This means that there are ways to ask for a directory of files that meet certain criteria. As seen in Chapter 1, the * is used as a wildcard symbol. If you wanted a list of all files that begin with the letter A you would enter **dir a*<return>**

MS DOS will display a listing that looks like this:

```
        Volume in drive A has no label
        Directory of  A:\

        ASSIGN   COM     896   10-20-83   12:00p
        AUTOEXEC BAT      34    3-01-85    6:27p
              2 File(s)     124928 bytes free
```

It is now a much simpler matter to determine if ASSIGN.COM is on that disk because DOS has displayed only a couple of specific files. Suppose you want to see if the disk in drive A contained a file called WS.COM. Enter **dir w*<return>**

MS DOS will display a listing that looks like this:

```
         Volume in drive A has no label
         Directory of  A:\

         File not found
```

The above display indicates that there are no files that begin with the letter W on the disk in drive A; therefore the file WS.COM is not on that disk. Wildcards can be used to select listings of files by their extensions as well as their filenames. Suppose that you wanted to list all the files on disk A that ended with a DAT extension. Since you don't care what the filename is, an * can be used. Enter

dir *.dat < return >

MS DOS lists all the files, in this case only one, that have that extension.

You have already been introduced to the concept of the ? as a wildcard. The ? will search for one character as opposed to the * which can stand for a number of characters. Try this example:

dir ????.com < return >

MS DOS will display a listing that looks like this:

```
        Volume in drive A has no label
        Directory of  A:\

        COMP    COM    2534  10-20-83  12:00p
        MODE    COM    3139  10-20-83  12:00p
        MORE    COM     384  10-20-83  12:00p
        SYS     COM    1680  10-20-83  12:00p
        TREE    COM    1513  10-20-83  12:00p
             5 File(s)    122880 bytes free
```

The common theme is that the ????.COM told MS DOS to include in the list files that have filenames of four characters or less and also have a COM extension.

Look at the following command. What type of files will it list? Try the command and see if your prediction is correct: **dir s???.com** < return >

The next two commands combine the * and the ? wildcards. Try to predict what effect they will have, then enter the commands.

dir ??s?????.* < return >
dir ??s*.* < return >

Both of the above commands will have the same effect. The reason is that both commands told MS DOS to list only those files that contain the letter S as the third character in the filename. That is the only thing that the files were required to have in common.

You can direct a DOS search to the disk in drive B by adding b: to the wildcard. To list all the files on B that begin with F, enter **dir b:f*** **<return>**

Now that you know how it works, try to figure out how to command the computer to get the following lists of files. (The answers can be found at the end of this chapter.)

1. All files on drive A that begin with M.
2. All files on drive A that end in .COM.
3. All files on drive B that begin with S.

2.8.   Editing in DOS

What happens if you make a mistake? Well, there are a few editing controls in MS DOS that you may find handy. Type in the following but do not press <return>: **dir b:*.com**

Your cursor should be on the space just beyond the last character you typed. To erase a character, enter **<back space>**

The M will disappear and the cursor has moved one space to the left. To erase the next character, the O, enter **<back space>**

Continue pressing the **<back space>** until the entire command is removed.

Suppose that you entered a command and decided before you pressed the <return> key that you wanted to cancel it. One way would be to use the <back space> to remove all the characters. MS DOS has a special command that will cancel the entire line with a single keystroke: the escape key, <Esc>. Enter the following (DO NOT press <return>): **dir b:*.exe**

To cancel the command with a single keystroke enter **<Esc>**

A \ mark appears on the line you typed and the cursor moves to the next line. This indicates that the command will be ignored. Note that the command is not erased from the screen. You are now free to enter another DOS command of your choice. Enter the following: **dir<return>**

The DIR command will execute. MS DOS holds the last command you issued in a special place in its memory. If you press the special function key located on the left side of the board you can bring the last command back. Enter the following command: **dir c*.* < return >**

Now press **[F3]**. The command is reentered on the line. Press **< return >**

Enter the following command: **dor b:*.com < return >**

DOS responds with *Bad command or filename*. This makes sense because the command should have been entered as **dir**. You might think that the only way to correct this mistake is to retype the entire command. DOS has a way to edit the previous command. The [F1] key will recall one letter at a time from the previous command. Enter **[F1]**

The letter *d* appears. Now type the correct letter. Enter **i**

To recall the rest of the line, which was entered correctly, enter **[F3]**

The corrected command is ready to be executed. Enter **< return >**

The [F1] and [F3] keys are handy DOS tools to use.

2.9.   Checking the Disk

A program provided with the MS DOS system is one called CHKDSK.COM. If you call the directory for drive A, DIR < return >, you should see this file listed.

You will use this command quite often to check the amount of disk space, used and unused. One of MS DOS's drawbacks is that is does not pack information as densely on the disk as is possible. Files that contain large amounts of information, for example, the file that contains this chapter, will take up a significant amount of disk space. The CHKDSK command will give more detailed information than DIR about the files on the disk. Try the following command: **chkdsk < return >**

Below you will see a summary of the amount of space available on each disk that this command will give you.

```
Volume BASICS        created Apr 17, 1984 7:50a

   362496 bytes total disk space
    22528 bytes in 3 hidden files
   274432 bytes in 39 user files
    65536 bytes available on disk

   262144 bytes total memory
   237568 bytes free
```

CHKDSK will give you information about the following kinds of files on the disk:

TOTAL SPACE: Tells you the total amount of bytes of storage available on that disk before any files were added.

HIDDEN FILES: These are files that are used by MS DOS and are usually hidden from the user's view when a directory is listed. There are two files that may be hidden on a disk: IBMBIO.COM and IBMDOS.COM.

USER FILES: These are the files created by the users of the system, and that appear on the directory.

BAD SECTORS: These are sectors that have been blocked off from use due to some defect detected by the computer system. If all sectors are good then no Bad Sector display will appear.

FREE SPACE: This tells you the amount of space left for adding a new file to a disk.

The last two numbers on the CHKDSK display *do not* deal with the disk drive. They tell you about the internal memory of the computer.

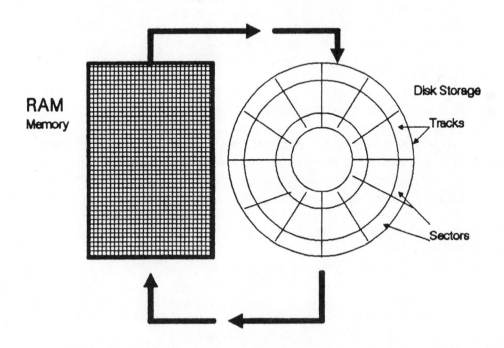

Fig. 2-3. Memory Management.

There are some special uses of CHKDSK in relation to the File Allocation Table. From the computer's point of view the disk is divided into a series of circles called *tracks*. Each track is further divided into blocks called *sectors*, as shown in Fig. 2-3.

Each sector contains 512 characters. In DOS 1.1 there are eight sectors per track. In DOS 2.0 and 2.1 there are nine sectors on each track.

It is possible for programs to create problems in the File Allocation Table. This is often the result of programs that begin to create files but stop because of an error. A special form of CHKDSK command will list all FAT errors and also tell you if the files are stored in contiguous sectors. Note that there is nothing wrong with files in noncontiguous sectors except that large files in noncontiguous sectors process slower than files in contiguous sectors. Enter **chkdsk *.* <return>**

The results might look like this:

```
Volume BASICS        created Apr 17, 1984 7:50a

  362496 bytes total disk space
   22528 bytes in 3 hidden files
  274432 bytes in 39 user files
   65536 bytes available on disk

  262144 bytes total memory
  237568 bytes free

A:\BASIC.COM
    Contains 2 non-contiguous blocks.
```

Note that if a CHKDSK command lists file allocation errors, you need to enter a special command to fix the errors. CHKDSK/F will collect lost or misallocated sectors into a series of files named FILE0000.CHK, FILE0001.CHK, and so on.

Another variation on the CHKDSK command is the /V option. This displays a list of the files on the disk as they are being checked. Enter **chkdsk/v <return>**

2.10.   Clearing the Screen

As you proceed with various DOS commands you may want to clear off all of the current screen display and begin again with a clear screen. MS DOS contains a command to do this. Enter **cls<return>**

The screen is cleared. The A> prompt appears at the top of the screen with the cursor next to it. Note that clearing the screen erases nothing in the computer's internal or external memory. It simply clears the display of text left over from previous commands.

2.11.   The Copy Command

Making copies of files is a very important ability to have in a computer system, especially a floppy disk system. This is because although a single-sided, double-density diskette holds about 180,000 bytes, the space is limited. It is often necessary to transfer files from one disk to another for organization or backup purposes.

Among other uses, the COPY program will move files from one device to another. First you will learn how COPY can make copies of files.

On drive A you have a file called FORMAT.COM. You will make a copy of that information and call the copy FORMAT1.COM.

COPY FORMAT.COM   FORMAT1.COM   <return>
          ↑   ↑
        source   destination

Here the first name is the name of the file to copy. The second name is the name of the new file to be created. Both files will contain the same information. Enter **copy format.com format1.com<return>**

Use DIR to check the results of the command: **dir f*.*<return>**

You should see two files listed in the directory: FORMAT.COM and FORMAT1.COM

To copy all the files from disk A to disk B or C you would enter a command like the one below. (Do not enter the command. If you do, you will copy all the files.)

copy *.* b: < return >
copy *.* c: < return >

Note that if disk B already contains files, you may find that there is not space to hold all the files from A as well as the the files on B. If this is the case DOS will display a message that says *Insufficient Space.*

2.12.   Copying to Devices

COPY can exchange information between the disk and other devices such as the screen and keyboard (CON:) or the printer (LPT1:).

COPY can also allow the user to enter text into a file. If you use CON: as the source device you can use the keyboard to transfer information from the keyboard through the computer to a disk file. Enter the following command: **copy con: text.dat < return >**

Nothing seems to happen except that the A> does not appear. This is an indication that you are not at the systems level. DOS will now allow you to enter text directly from the keyboard. Anything that you type will eventually be stored in the file TEXT.DAT. Enter the following lines of text:

This is an example of keyboard entry< return >
into a text file. < return >

To end the file you need to enter the character that MS DOS uses to mark the end of a file, CTRL Z (Control Z). Enter the following control character by holding down the CTRL and pressing the letter z.

< hold down CTRL> < Press z>

A ^Z appears on the screen. To complete the file enter **< return >**

The disk drive spins. Now the data is saved as a file. To see the data you can simply reverse the objects in the COPY command. Enter the following: **copy text.dat con: < return >**

The text is displayed just as it was typed in.

2.13. Erasing Files

The DEL command will work in place of ERASE. It is two characters shorter and therefore a bit faster to use. Enter the following:
del text.dat<return>

Enter the following to check your results: **dir *.dat<return>**

The ? and * also work with ERASE or DEL, so that you can erase groups of related files with a single command. Be careful with ERASE or DEL, since they will erase files without asking for confirmation. Enter the command below, then check the directory to see that it has been removed.

del *.dat<return>

Since there were no more DAT files none were erased.

[Files that have been erased can sometimes be recovered by using the Norton Utilities program described in Chapter 3.]

2.14. The Type Command

The TYPE command is similar to the COPY CON: command. TYPE can show the contents of an ASCII file. (Note: For future reference TYPE is a good way to view the contents of BATCH files. Although you may not yet have encountered BATCH files, you will later, so make a note of the TYPE command).

2.15. Printing

There are several ways to get information to be printed on the printer in addition to, or instead of, the screen. One simple method is to use the redirection ability of the computer.

The > can be used to redirect the output of a command to another device. The letters PRN can be used to indicate the printer. Make sure that you have a printer cabled to your computer before entering the following command: **dir>prn<return>**

This command will send the directory listing to the printer instead of the screen. The >prn can be used to send to the printer the output of any MS DOS commands. Try the following: **chkdsk>prn<return>**

2.16   The System Prompt

The A> prompt is the standard prompt for MS DOS. You can, however, change that prompt.

MS DOS has a number of special characters that can be included as part of the prompt display. A $ is used to indicate a special character. For example, $t displays the current system's time. The $d displays the current system's date. A $_ (underscore) creates a multiline prompt. Enter **prompt t_$d<return>**

Note the time and date are now displayed as part of the prompt.

To return to the normal prompt, enter **prompt<return>**

2.17   Filters

Another interesting feature of DOS 2.00 and higher is its use of filters to process data output directly from the operating system. The SORT filter is one of the most useful filters and is stored on the disk as a file SORT.EXE.

SORT is used to filter the output of programs or DOS commands. With the DIR command, the SORT filter can be used to create a directory listing that is sorted. This is very helpful because normal directory display does not arrange files by name.

Filters work by using the | (vertical bar) mark. This is the character located next to the letter Z on the IBM keyboard. Enter the following command: **DIR | SORT<return>**

This command sends the output of the DIR command to the SORT filter before it is sent to the screen. The result is a sorted directory display. The SORT filter allows the user to choose some options for sorting. For example, the /R parameter tells the program to sort in reverse (ascending order). Enter **DIR | SORT/R<return>**

The result is a directory listed in reverse alphabetical order.

DOS 2.00 and higher have two other filter programs: FIND and MORE. FIND will select lines from the output of a command or program that contain a certain character or group of characters. For example, the following command would list only those files that contain the letters CO. Enter (note that the letters CO inside the quotation marks must be in upper case): **DIR | FIND "CO"** < **return** >

Note that such a command would include files COMP and FOR-MAT.COM since both contain CO, although not in exactly the same position. FIND will include the line if the search criteria are found anywhere in that line.

FIND can also be used to count the number of line matches by invoking the /C parameter. How many COM files are on the disk? Enter: **DIR | FIND/C "COM"** < **return** >

You can use both the sort and find filters together. Enter **DIR | SORT | FIND "EXE"** < **return** >

Now you get a sorted listing of the EXE files.

The MORE filter is used to pause the screen display in the same way that the /P is used with the DIR command. Why not just use the /P with the sort filter? Try it and see what happens. Enter **DIR/P | SORT** < **return** >

The cursor is blinking but nothing is happening because of the way in which the filter works. When data is filtered it is stored in a temporary file; then the output is filtered. Since the output is filtered, you do not see any output. However, the pause required for the /P occurs anyway. Thus the computer is paused but the pause does not have the desired effect. Enter < **return** >

Now the listing is displayed but no pause. The proper way to handle pauses with filters is to use the MORE filter. Enter **DIR | SORT | MORE** < **return** >

The MORE filter works because it pauses the output of the SORT filter, not the input from the DIR command. Enter < **return** >

2.18   Subdirectories

When IBM created the XT hard disk system it also created a new operating system for it. This operating system is known as DOS 2.0. One of the features of this new version, and all subsequent versions of DOS, is its ability to create subdirectories, making it easier to organize files on a hard disk drive.

The only difference inherent in a hard drive is that it can hold more information than a floppy disk. Look at the chart below:

Type of disk	Total storage in bytes	Number of 20K files
FLOPPY	360K	18
HARD	10mb	500

The hard disk will store the same amount of data as 27.7 floppy disks. More significantly, if the average size of your files is 20,000 bytes, then a hard disk would hold 500 files with 500 different filenames.

If the average file is smaller, say 10,000 bytes, then you could have 1,000 different files on the disk. This raises the problem of keeping order among a huge list of files.

DOS 2.0 and higher allows you to create units of organization that divide the hard disk into sections called *subdirectories* or simply *directories*.

Directories are like separate drawers in the same file cabinet. Files can be stored in the subdirectories and isolated from other files. This system makes disks more manageable.

[While subdirectories are usually associated with hard disk drives, DOS can create subdirectories on floppy disks. Subdirectories function exactly the same on floppy disks as they do on hard disks. They differ only in the volume of data they are capable of holding.]

The term *subdirectory* refers to any directory on a disk other than the root directory. To create a subdirectory you can use either MKDIR or MD. Both commands have the same effect; the MD is shorter to type. At this point a subdirectory called UTIL will be created. Its purpose will be to hold the DOS utility programs now currently in the root directory of the disk in drive A. Without subdirectories, you would have to store all the files in the *root* directory.

Enter the following (note that the \ is the backslash character located next to the Z key, not the slash character located next to the period key):
MD\UTIL <return>

Now enter: **DIR <return>**

The directory display will look like this:

```
Volume in drive A has no label
Directory of  A:\
COMMAND   COM     17792   10-20-83   12:00p
BASIC     COM     56816    1-01-80   12:25a
M         1         107    1-01-80    1:02a
MESS      TXT       640    1-01-80   12:16a
ASSIGN    COM       896   10-20-83   12:00p
BACKUP    COM      3687   10-20-83   12:00p
BASICA    COM     26112   10-20-83   12:00p
CHKDSK    COM      6400   10-20-83   12:00p
COMP      COM      2534   10-20-83   12:00p
UTIL            <DIR>      1-01-80   12:06a
SYS       COM      1680   10-20-83   12:00p
SORT      EXE      1408   10-20-83   12:00p
AUTOEXEC BAT         3    1-01-80   12:01a
       29 File(s)       91136 bytes free
```

The directory has a new type of entry marked with the <DIR> symbol. This symbol tells you that UTIL is not a file but the name of a subdirectory. The difference is that directories contain files and files contain data. You can indicate that a command should work with a subdirectory by using the name of the directory preceded by the \. Enter
DIR\UTIL <return>

The screen will show:

```
Volume in drive A has no label
Directory of  A:\util
.              <DIR>      1-01-80   12:06a
..             <DIR>      1-01-80   12:06a
        2 File(s)       91136 bytes free
```

This is the directory of the files stored in this new subdirectory UTIL. Naturally there are no files listed, because you have not created or copied any files into this directory. The files that you had before are still there, but they are in the main or *root* directory. To see them, enter
DIR\ <return>

Just as DOS allows you to select a default drive, you can select a default directory for the selected disk. Now that you have created a new directory you can tell the operating system that you want it to be the default directory rather than the root. The purpose of changing the default is to allow you to work with only that directory unless you specifically refer to some other subdirectory. This saves you the trouble of entering the subdirectory name before each command.

2.19   Changing the Default Directory

The command used to change directories is the CHDIR or CD command. Enter **CD\UTIL** **< return >**

Now enter **DIR** **< return >**

The screen shows:

```
Volume in drive A has no label
Directory of  A:\util
.              <DIR>      1-01-80  12:06a
..             <DIR>      1-01-80  12:06a
        2 File(s)     91136 bytes free
```

This is the directory for the UTIL subdirectory. The CD command set the default directory as UTIL. Thus the DIR command lists only the directory for UTIL. Now that you have created a subdirectory you can use it to store files. The basic DOS commands, COPY, DEL, RENAME, etc., will work with subdirectories. Copy the FORMAT.COM from drive A into this subdirectory. Enter **COPY \FORMAT.COM** **< return >**

Now enter **DIR** **< return >**

The directory appears:

```
Volume in drive A has no label
Directory of  A:\util
.              <DIR>      1-01-80  12:06a
..             <DIR>      1-01-80  12:06a
FORMAT   COM    6912  10-20-83  12:00p
        3 File(s)     83968 bytes free
```

This confirms that the file has been copied into the subdirectory. Transfer another file. Enter **COPY \CHKDSK.COM** **< return >**

Now enter **DIR** **<return>**
You have added another file to this subdirectory.

```
Volume in drive A has no label
Directory of  A:\util
.               <DIR>      1-01-80  12:06a
..              <DIR>      1-01-80  12:06a
FORMAT   COM     6912  10-20-83  12:00p
CHKDSK   COM     6400  10-20-83  12:00p
        4 File(s)     76800 bytes free
```

You can return to the main or root directory by entering the CD command and using the \ without a name. Enter **CD** **<return> dir <return>**

This is the root directory. Note that the files copied into \UTIL appear in this directory also. Subdirectories allow you to have two copies of the same file on the same disk as long as they are in different directories.

[There can be only one active directory at a time. If you use the CD command to make a directory active, it is implicit that all the other directories are inactive.]

The purpose of subdirectories is to separate files into related groups. How is this accomplished with subdirectories? The answer is that DOS attaches a *prefix* to every file that is stored in the subdirectory. Normally you cannot see the prefix displayed when you use the DIR command. However, there is a special form of the CHKDSK command that reveals the prefixes attached to files. Enter **A:CHKDSK/V** **<return>**

The screen will display a directory similar to this:

```
Directory A:
        A:\IBMBIO.COM
        A:\IBMDOS.COM
        A:\COMMAND.COM
        A:\RESTORE.COM
Directory A:\UTIL
        A:\UTIL\FORMAT.COM
        A:\UTIL\CHKDSK.COM
        A:\TREE.COM
        A:\AUTOEXEC.BAT

    362496 bytes total disk space
     22528 bytes in 2 hidden files
      1024 bytes in 1 directories
```

```
262144 bytes in 30 user files
 76800 bytes available on disk

524288 bytes total memory
499712 bytes free
```

The /V parameter stands for VERBOSE. To return to the root directory, enter **cd\ <return>**

2.20   Sub–subdirectories

You can create subdirectories of subdirectories. For example, you might create a subdirectory of \UTIL. Enter **MD\UTIL\SPECIAL<return>**
   Enter **DIR<return>**
   The new subdirectory does not appear on the root directory because SPECIAL is a subdirectory of UTIL. In order to see this listing you must first log into \UTIL. Enter **CD\UTIL<return>DIR<return>**
   The screen shows:

```
Volume in drive A has no label
Directory of  A:\util

    .            <DIR>       1-01-80   12:06a
    ..           <DIR>       1-01-80   12:06a
FORMAT   COM      6912    10-20-83   12:00p
CHKDSK   COM      6400    10-20-83   12:00p
SPECIAL          <DIR>       1-01-80    1:35a
        5 File(s)       75776 bytes free
```

And the entry for SPECIAL is displayed. Return to the root directory. Enter **CD\ <return>**
   Many DOS commands allow you to specify the subdirectory in which the files are to be found or placed. The COPY command can accept this type of parameter. For example, suppose that you wanted to copy the EDLIN.COM file into the subdirectory \UTIL\SPECIAL. Enter the following: **COPY,EDLIN.COM = \UTIL\SPECIAL<return>**
   The files that were just copied do not appear on the root directory. How would you get a listing of those files?

Below are four commands. One of them would correctly list the files you just copied. Decide which one. (The correct answer is at the end of the chapter.)

1. DIR B:
2. DIR\UTIL M*.*
3. DIR\UTIL\SPECIAL
4. DIR\SPECIAL

Interestingly, command 4 will not work. In order to get through to \SPE-CIAL you must first go through \UTIL.

These directories are arranged like a tree with branches:

ROOT→ \UTIL→ \UTIL\SPECIAL

The series of subdirectories that are linked together is called a *path*. You can see by the way the tree is structured that each subdirectory has a unique path from the root directory.

While subdirectories are an important tool, they can become quite confusing very quickly. DOS has some commands that make it easier to navigate through the complex tangle of directories. The TREE command enables you to get a summary of the directories and subdirectories on a disk. TREE is stored in a command file called TREE.COM. which must be present on one of the disks in order to execute the TREE command. Suppose TREE.COM is located on the A drive. Enter

TREE < **return** >

The program will list all the subdirectories and any sub-subdirectories that they are related to.

```
DIRECTORY PATH LISTING FOR VOLUME ??????????
Path: \UTIL
Subdirectories:  SPECIAL
Path: \UTIL\SPECIAL
Subdirectories:  None
```

You can get a tree display that also lists the specific files in each subdirectory. Enter

TREE/F < return >

The listings looks like this:

```
DIRECTORY PATH LISTING FOR VOLUME ??????????
Path: \UTIL
Subdirectories:    SPECIAL
Files:             FORMAT   .COM
                   CHKDSK   .COM
Path: \UTIL\SPECIAL
Subdirectories:    None
Files:             EDLIN    .COM
```

It is hard to use a TREE listing displayed on the screen because it generally is too long. If you have a printer you can get a printed copy of the screen display by entering

TREE/F > PRN < return >

2.21   Paths

The main purpose of the subdirectory system is to separate groups of files. However, there may be instances when you will want or need to reach a file in another directory to find a program.

Delete the files from the root directory that have been copied into the subdirectories. Enter

DEL FORMAT.COM < return >
DEL CHKDSK.COM < return >
DEL EDLIN.COM < return >

For example, there are utility programs located in different subdirectories. CHKDSK is located in \UTIL and EDLIN is stored in \UTIL\SPECIAL\FINAL.

To execute the CHKDSK command, enter

CHKDSK < return >

The computer tells you that you have entered a bad command or file-name. This is because you are currently logged into the root directory and the CHKDSK file is located in \UTIL. DOS tells you that it has searched the active directory and could not find the CHKDSK program.

DOS allows you to enter a command that will open a path for searching. When a path is opened, the computer will search the subdirectories to find the command file you are looking for. To create a path from the root directory to the \UTIL directory, enter

PATH\UTIL<return>

This command opens a path between the root directory and the subdirectory in which the file can be found. Now enter

CHKDSK<return>

The program executes because it is along the defined path.

The PATH command does not change the active directory. It simply tells DOS to search another directory if the program requested is not listed in the active directory.

The PATH command can be used to search a directory for files with the following extensions:

.COM
.EXE
.BAT

DOS will not search the path directories for files with other extensions. Nor will DOS search those drives for data files not found in the active drive.

Some programs, such as WordStar, dBASE II, and Lotus 1-2-3, require special overlay or driver files to load properly. These files have extensions like OVR and DRV. The path command can load the WS.COM or 123.EXE file, but will fail to locate the required OVR and DRV files.

Programs with these supporting files cannot be run as was CHKDSK by simply opening a path to the directory in which they are stored.

[SmartPath is a special utility that can be purchased and used with DOS to overcome this problem. SmartPath will allow WordStar to function properly with directories. However, you still cannot reference data files in other directories with PATH or SmartPath.]

If you have forgotten or become confused, you can get DOS to show you the current search PATH. To see what the current defined path is, enter

PATH <**return**>

To close the path, enter the PATH command with a semicolon (;) alone. This indicates that all paths are closed. Only the active directory will be searched for programs. Enter

PATH; <**return**>

You can open paths to several directories at once by entering a series of pathnames separated by semicolons. Enter

PATH\UTIL;\UTIL\SPECIAL;\UTIL\SPECIAL\FINAL <**return**>

You have now opened three paths at the same time.

The purpose of multiple paths is to open paths to several directories so that you can access programs in those directories. When a request to run a program is entered, DOS will search the active directory first. If the program is not found it will search each of the paths in the order in which they were entered for the program.

Certain features of DOS are difficult to understand. However, these features can be very important because they allow you to make your own computer system easier to use, as well as more powerful. A batch file is an example of such a feature.

2.22   Batch Files

What is a batch file? What is its purpose? Up to this point you have learned about DOS commands. When you want to execute a DOS command you type in the command at the prompt. When the command is complete, DOS displays the prompt again; then you can enter another command. (Notice that when you work with DOS you must enter the commands one at a time.)

Batch files are used to allow you to enter a preset series of DOS commands automatically. A batch file is really a series of ordinary DOS commands that the computer can execute as a group instead of one at a time. The term refers to a group or *batch* of DOS commands that are meant to execute automatically.

This simple idea has some unexpected benefits. For instance, the ability of DOS to understand batch files allows you to create DOS programs. Programs, like batch files, contain a series of commands that can contain special elements, such as variables, conditional statements, and subroutines. Version 2.0 and higher of DOS allows the user or programmer to create simple or complex batch files to aid in using the system.

In the following sections you will learn some of the basic techniques used in working with batch files.

2.23   A Simple Batch File

Batch files can be as simple or complex as you want them to be. Begin with a simple task. Suppose that you want to display the directory of all the program files on your DOS disk. Program files always end with either a .COM or .EXE file extension. To get the listing you might begin by clearing the screen. Enter the DOS clear screen command.

cls < return >

Now enter a command to list the COM files.

dir *.com/w < return >

Now a command to list the EXE files. Enter

dir *.exe/w < return >

You have issued three commands to complete the task. If this were a task that you performed often, a batch file containing those commands would automate the task. Below you will create a batch file that will accomplish the same thing as the three previous commands.

2.24   Creating a Batch File

For a file to be a *batch* file there are only three rules:

1. The file must be a DOS ASCII standard text file. Standard files contain normal ASCII characters and each line ends with a carriage return. This definition may not mean much to novice computer users, but it is important to know which programs can produce files like these. Many word processing programs create ASCII standard files, while others can convert their files to ASCII standard. (See Chapter 1.28.)
2. ASCII files designed to be used as batch files must have a BAT file extension. For example: *files.bat, start.bat*.

   Note that you should never create a batch file that has the same name as a DOS command. Examples: *dir.bat, format.bat*.

   The reason is that DOS executes batch files the same way programs are executed, by entering the name of the batch or program file without the extension. Thus DIR.BAT can be created but never used because DOS will always assume that when you type in DIR you want a directory command, not the DIR.BAT file.
3. The batch file contains only DOS commands, i.e., commands that work at the DOS prompt.

How, then, can a batch file be created? The simplest way is to use the COPY CON: command to create a DOS file from the console (keyboard). Enter

copy con: files.bat < return >

The command you have just entered will create a DOS file, FILES.BAT. Remember that when you enter a COPY CON: command you are entering text into a file as you type. This means that nothing actually happens when you type in a command. You are simply "writing" a list of commands into a file. Only after the file has been written can you tell DOS to execute the instructions contained within.

Now you are ready to enter the instructions into the list. The first instruction is to clear the screen. Enter

cls < return >

Note that the screen does not clear. You are only writing the list, not executing the commands. Enter another command into the list.

dir *.com/w < return >

Now add another. Enter (DO NOT PRESS RETURN)

dir *.exe/w

Because this command is the last one in the batch file, you do not enter return. Instead you must enter a special character that DOS recognizes as the indicator for the *end of a file*. That character is [Ctrl Z]. DOS automatically programs the [F6] function key to type a [Ctrl Z]. Therefore, press

[F6]

DOS prints ^Z on the line. To complete the entry enter

< return >

The prompt returns. Now you are ready to execute the batch file by typing in the name of the batch file without the .BAT extension.

Batch File Name	*Execute by Entering*
files.bat	files < return >
install.bat	install < return >
demo.bat	demo < return >

Enter

file < return >

DOS executes all three commands in a row without further assistance from you. The screen will look like this when the batch has concluded:

```
A>DIR *.COM/W

 Volume in drive A has no label  Directory of  A:\

COMMAND COM BASIC   COM  ASSIGN COM BACKUP COM BASICA   COM  CHKDSK   COM
COMP   COM  DEBUG   COM  DISKCOMP COM DISKCOPY COM EDLIN   COM  FDISK
COM  FORMAT   COM  GRAPHICS COM MODE  COM  MORE    COM  PRINT COM
RECOVER  COM RESTORE COM SYS   COM TREE   COM  COR   COM  22 File(s)
124928 bytes free

A>DIR *.EXE/W

 Volume in drive A has no label  Directory of  A:\

FIND   EXE   SORT   EXE
2 File(s)   124928 bytes free

A>
```

2.25   The Echo Command

You might have noticed that the batch file displays the command lines contained within the batch file as they execute. The ECHO command controls this display. Normally in DOS the ECHO is ON. This means that DOS commands executed from a batch file are displayed as they are executed.

The display of the command might be improved if the commands were not displayed. To see how this will work you can add the ECHO command to a batch file.

2.26   Editing Batch Files

The COPY CON: command is O.K. when all you want to do is create a batch file. However in this case you want to add commands to a batch file that already exists. DOS provides a special program called EDLIN (line editor) that helps you make changes in your batch files.

Note that word processors can be used to edit batch files if they can create ASCII standard DOS text files.

To use the EDLIN program enter EDLIN followed by the name of the file you want to edit. Note that EDLIN requires the FULL filename including the extension. Enter

edlin files.bat < return >

DOS displays a *, the EDLIN prompt. This means that you are working in the EDLIN program. EDLIN has some simple commands to help you change the contents of text files like batch files.

The L command lists the lines in the file. Enter

L < return >

EDLIN displays:

```
        *l
              1:*cls
              2: dir *.com/w
              3: dir *.exe/w *
```

The i (insert) command is used to add lines. To add a line at the beginning of the file, enter **1i < return >**

The 1:* appears. You can now type a new line 1. Enter **echo off < return >**

EDLIN displays another blank line, number 2. You could enter another command if you wanted. To stop adding lines press **[Ctrl/c]**

To see the file as it is now, enter **L < return >**

The file now has four lines beginning with the echo command. Now add a line at the end of the file. Enter **5i < return > echo on < return >**

Exit the insert mode by entering **[Ctrl/c]**

To save the file and return to DOS enter the e (end) command. Enter **e < return >**

Now execute the batch file. Enter **files < return >**

DOS displays the following. (Note that only the results of the commands, not the commands themselves, are displayed.)

```
  Volume in drive A has no label
Directory of  A:\
COMMAND COM BASIC    COM ASSIGN COM BACKUP    COM BASICA COM CHKDSK  COM COMP
COM   DEBUG    COM    DISKCOMP COM DISKCOPY COM EDLIN    COM   FDISK     COM
```

```
FORMAT    COM GRAPHICS COM MODE    COM  MORE     COM PRINT    COM    RECOVER
COM RESTORE COM SYS     COM  TREE    COM COR     COM 22 File(s)      123904
bytes free
 Volume in drive A has no label
Directory of  A:\
FIND    EXE    SORT    EXE
2 File(s)    123904 bytes free
```

The second A> is caused by EDLIN inserting a carriage return before the End of File marker in FILES.BAT. Do not be concerned; this extra return will not cause any harm.

2.27.   Autoexec

DOS allows you to create a special DOS file called AUTOEXEC.BAT. When the computer is turned on and DOS is loaded, it scans the directory of the disk for a file called AUTOEXEC.BAT. If it finds that file it automatically executes the batch file.

AUTOEXEC is a valuable tool. In floppy disk systems you can make your program disks automatically load the program when the computer is turned on. In hard disk systems (with several programs stored on a disk) the AUTOEXEC can be used to execute DOS commands (e.g., setting the time when the system is booted, if you have a battery powered clock in your computer).

Creating an AUTOEXEC.BAT is the same as creating any other batch file. Make sure that the name is exactly AUTOEXEC.BAT. Enter

edlin autoexec.bat < return > i < return >

In this example, you can create an autoexec that will automatically run BASIC when the system is booted. The simplest way to do this is to enter the command BASIC as the AUTOEXEC.BAT. However, you can use some of the other batch commands you have learned. Enter

echo off < return > cls < return >
echo System set to load BASIC < return >
pause < return > basic < return >

Save the file. Enter **[Ctrl/c]e < return >**

You can execute an autoexec like any other batch file, by entering the name AUTOEXEC. Enter **autoexec < return >**

Press any key. BASIC appears with the characteristic OK prompt. To return to DOS, enter **system < return >**

The special attribute of the AUTOEXEC batch is that it will automatically execute when the system boots. To see how this works issue a warm boot command. Hold down the [Ctrl] and the [Alt] keys and press [Del] while they are being held down. You will note that after the computer boots, the batch file begins automatically. Press any key and BASIC loads. Return to DOS by entering **system < return >**

2.28   The ANSI System

While looking at a DOS 2.00, 2.10, or 3.00 program disk you may have noticed a file called ANSI.SYS. The ANSI.SYS file is a *device driver*. The purpose of a device driver is to install additional hardware options into the DOS system. Device drivers can be stored on the disk and automatically loaded when the system is booted. The concept of using files to change the setup of DOS is called configuring the system. It is very similar to using the batch file AUTOEXEC.BAT to automatically run programs when the system is booted. Below is a general discussion of how device drivers are used.

2.29   The CONFIG.SYS File

When an IBM system is turned on, it runs though a built-in program called the *bootstrap*. The first part of the IBM bootstrap is a memory test. The more memory the system contains, the longer the test will take. If you have recently expanded the memory of your system, you have probably noticed the difference.

Following the memory test, attempts are made to find DOS on one of the drives in the system. IBM computers always begin with drive A. That is why, even if you have a hard disk, the light on the A drive comes on before the hard drive is accessed.

When the drive that has a copy of the DOS files on it is found, the computer reads the information into its memory. The last thing DOS does is to scan the root directory of the drive from which it has read the DOS files for a special file called CONFIG.SYS. If the file does not exist DOS displays an A> prompt and sets up the system according to the built-in default values.

However, if CONFIG.SYS is present, it will contain a list of special device drivers to be added to the memory of the computer. While CONFIG.SYS seems a lot like AUTOEXEC.BAT there are several differences:

1. AUTOEXEC.BAT can execute only normal DOS commands. CONFIG.SYS is used to alter the setup of DOS itself.
2. AUTOEXEC.BAT can be activated at any time DOS is active by typing in AUTOEXEC. CONFIG.SYS can only be activated by booting or rebooting the computer.
3. CONFIG.SYS files can contain only FILES, BUFFERS, and the DEVICE command. AUTOEXEC can use all the DOS commands, including the special batch commands, such as ECHO, GOTO, and IF.

2.30   Changing Buffers and Files

What types of changes would the average user want to make to DOS with a CONFIG.SYS file? Probably none. But users of some of today's sophisticated programs may find that to run programs like WordStar 2000, dBASE III, or Framework, the installation instructions require the creation of a special CONFIG.SYS file. These programs work with a number of files open at the same time. This requires you to change the normal DOS defaults for FILES.

BUFFERS refer to the way DOS manages the input and output of data to and from the disk. When a command is issued by a program to read information from a file, DOS loads the information into a buffer area. When another such command is given, DOS checks the information in the buffer before it tries to read the disk. This can sometimes eliminate the need to actually read the disk. The result is that some programs will perform certain operations faster. A BUFFER holds about 512 bytes. If you increase the number of buffers, DOS loads more data each time a disk read is performed. Note that you should have more memory than the application calls for if you intend to increase the size of the buffers.

2.31   Device Drivers

Another use of the CONFIG.SYS file is to load additional software drivers into DOS. Device drivers extend the command range of DOS. They also take up more memory, which is why they are optional. DOS 2.0 furnishes a special driver called ANSI.SYS. It extends the functions of DOS to include reprogramming of keys and screen colors in DOS.

DOS 3.0 has a driver called VDISK.SYS which is used to create a RAMDRIVE. A RAMDRIVE is an area of the memory that functions as an additional disk drive. (Note that memory used for a RAMDRIVE cannot be used by programs.)

To create a typical CONFIG.SYS file, enter

edlin config.sys < return > i < return >

dBASE III, for example, requires the files specification to be set at 20 (the upper limit on files). Enter **files = 20 < return >**

Now set the buffers. Enter **buffers = 25 < return >**

Finally add the DEVICE command. This command is used to load files that alter the way DOS performs. All device drives end with .SYS. Enter the command to enter ANSI driver. Enter **device = ansi.sys < return >**

Save the CONFIG.SYS file. Enter **[Ctrl/c] e < return >**

There is only one way to activate a CONFIG.SYS file; you must reboot the computer. Hold down the [Ctrl] and the [Alt] keys and press [Del] while they are being held down. You will note that after the computer boots, the batch file begins automatically. CONFIG.SYS does not interfere with the AUTOEXEC. Press any key and BASIC loads. Return to DOS by entering **system < return >**

2.32.   Answer Key

Filenames (p. 49):

1.	A:LETTER.TXT	Valid
2.	SAMPLE DAT	Not Valid—contains a space.
3.	X	Valid
4.	MY:FILE	Not Valid—two characters precede the colon. Drive specifications can be only a single letter. Colon cannot be used in a filename

5.	msdos.les	Valid
6.	Sample.File	Not Valid—file extension can be only three characters.
7.	C.test.doc	Not Valid—drive specifications must be followed with a colon. Only one period can be used in a filename.
8.	b:user.fil	Valid

Wildcard Commands (p. 53):
1. dir m*
2. dir *.com
3. dir b:s*

Listing Files (p. 67):
dir b:<return>

Part 2.
Systems Utilities

3.

Norton Utilities

The Norton Utilities program was one of the first and by far the most popular utility program for enhancing and extending operations that the user could perform from DOS. The Norton Utilities program is not a single program but a collection of small programs that perform interesting and useful functions. The functions provided by these programs fall into two types:

1. *Enhancements*. An enhanced function is one that is already provided in DOS but is implemented in the Norton Utilities program in a different way. The Norton Utilities version of the function is designed to allow you to perform the task more simply and with some additional options.
2. *New Functions*. The Norton Utilities program also provides a number of functions that are possible in DOS but not implemented by the standard DOS programs provided with your computer.

Of these, the Norton Utilities ability to UNERASE files is the most well known. Chapter 5 is devoted to the UNERASE functions.

The Norton Utilities programs provide a broad variety of features and functions that open up the computer and allow the average user to explore the intricate world of operating systems and disk storage.

3.1. Versions

Like DOS itself, the Norton Utilities have changed since they were first developed. The version of the program used in this book is version 3.0.

[At the time of this writing version 3.1 of the Norton Utilities programs has been announced.]

The Norton Utilities programs are provided on one single-sided, eight-sector diskette.

The files contained on the disk are:

READ.ME	DEMO.BAT	BEEP.COM	DS.COM	DT.COM
FA.COM	FF.COM	FS.COM	LD.COM	LP.COM
NU.COM	SA.COM	SI.COM	TM.COM	TS.COM
VL.COM	WIPEDISK.COM	WIPEFILE.COM	NU.PIF	README.BAT
LONG.BAT	SHORT.BAT			

There are 22 files that occupy 130,048 bytes of disk space. The 16 files that end with COM are programs. The remaining files are not required for Norton Utilities functions. READ.ME and README.BAT contain additional information about the programs not included in the documentation. DEMO.BAT is a batch file that demonstrates some of the programs included in the Norton Utilities collection.

The batch files LONG.BAT and SHORT.BAT are used to change the names of the Norton Utilities program files. The files are supplied with "short" names (NU.COM, FS.COM). The LONG.BAT batch file is used to change the Norton Utilities program files to files with longer, more descriptive names.

The SHORT.BAT file will change the names back to their short names. The advantage of short names is that they are easy to enter. Long names are more cumbersome to type, but are more descriptive. The files WIPEFILE.COM and WIPEDISK.COM do not have short names. This is because these programs are destructive and should be used with care.

The file NU.PIF is provided to allow the Norton Utilities program to operate under IBM's Topview operating environment. If you do not use Topview this file is irrelevant.

3.2. Exploring with Norton Utilities

The Norton Utilities programs are designed to allow the average user to gain access to all sorts of interesting information about the computer, and especially about the way data is stored on the disk.

As an introduction to the Norton Utilities program, the following sections explore the computer and the disks by using the main Norton Utilities program. The main program contains a variety of special functions, including the UNERASE program. Since UNERASE is so important, it will be considered in a separate chapter.

In what follows, the Norton Utilities program will be used to explore a typical floppy disk. Following that will be a discussion of how hard disks are organized.

3.3.   Setup

Norton Utilities will allow you to explore any disk, floppy or hard. In this hands-on section, you will want to create a floppy disk that is formatted as a systems disk.

Floppy Disk Systems:
Drive A: DOS systems disk
Drive B: Blank Disk

Enter

format b:/s < return >
< return >

This creates a blank systems disk. When the formatting is complete, enter **n** when asked to format another. Then place the disk you just formatted in drive A. Place a copy of the Norton Utilities program in drive B. You are ready to start.

Hard Disk Systems:
Drive A: Blank Disk
Drive C: Change to the directory that contains the DOS files, usually called DOS. Enter **cd\dos < return >**

Format the disk in drive A by entering

format a:/s < return > < return >

When asked if you want to format another, enter **n**.

Now change the directory to the directory that contains copies of the Norton Utilities program. Example: **cd\nu<return>**

Finally, change the active drive to A. Enter **a:<return>**

Now you are ready to explore the disk.

3.4.　Starting the Program

Most PC users are quite familiar with floppy disks. Even people with a hard drive system must use floppy disks at some time, either to load programs or make backup copies of their hard disk data. In addition, the organization of a floppy disk is quite similar in design to that of a hard disk. The major difference is that the hard disk will hold more data. DOS treats both disks in the same manner.

Exploring the design of a floppy disk tells you a lot about how your computer works. The Norton Utilities program makes it simple to peer into the actual structure of the disk. For this exploration, any version of DOS will do, but keep in mind that the display may be a bit different from the ones shown in the illustrations.

The basic concept of disk organization remains the same in all versions of DOS. This is one of the secrets of the success of the IBM PC and its compatibles. New improved versions of the operating system have not caused major incompatibility problems for users.

To start the program enter

b:nu<return>　　(floppy disk systems)
c:nu<return>　　(hard disk systems)

[The Norton Utilities main program is designed to operate in color when it finds that a color graphics board has been installed in the computer. If you are using a single color composite video monitor (e.g., an Amdek 300a) with a color graphics adapter, you will find that the program's display is difficult to read.

If this is the case, exit the program by entering <Esc>. Then restart the program adding the /nocolor option. Example:

b:nu/nocolor<return>　　(floppy disk systems)
c:nu/nocolor<return>　　(hard disk systems)]

When the program has read the information from the disk the main menu appears:

```
                   Top Level Menu
     Choices:
       f1   Change Selection
              (of drive, directory, file, or disk sector)
       f2   Explore Disk Information
              (discover or change data)
       f3   Recover Erased File
              (UnErase a deleted or erased file)
      Esc   End This Program
     Press 1, 2, 3, or Esc:
```

There are three major sections to the program. You will find that the boundaries are not very strict. As you learn more about the program you will see how the various features are interrelated.

Look at the bottom of the screen.

```
     Currently selected:  No file or disk sector selected
              Drive A:  Directory: root directory
```

This indicates currently selected data. Since you have just loaded the program, no special selection values appear except the drive specification, A, and the directory which defaults to the root directory.

In this case you will begin with option #2. Enter **2**

The program displays:

```
Menu 2
                        Explore Disk Information
             Choices:

                f1   Change Selection
                f2   Display Disk Technical Information
                f3   Map Space Usage of Entire Disk
                f4   Display Information about Selected Item
                f5   Display or Change Contents of Selected Item
                f6   Display Directory Information, Entry by Entry
                f7   Search Disk for Data

               Esc   Return to Top Level Menu

             Press 1, 2, 3, 4, 5, 6, 7, or Esc:
```

In the upper left-hand corner of the screen the program indicates that you are in Menu 2. The program will number each menu, giving you reference points throughout the program. To begin, choose option #2. This will provide some fundamental information about the disk. Enter **2**

This displays the next menu.

```
                Display Disk Technical Information
Drive A:
Type of disk:
   Double-sided, double-density, 9-sector
Basic storage capacity:
   360 thousand characters (kilobytes)
   89% of disk space is free
Logical dimensions:
   Sectors are made up of 512 bytes
   Tracks are made up of 9 sectors per disk side
   There are 2 disk sides
   The disk is made up of 40 tracks
   Space for files is allocated in clusters of 2 sectors
   There are 354 clusters
   Each cluster is 1,024 bytes
Press any key to continue...
```

To most people this display has very little meaning. But a simple explanation of terms will reveal a lot about how DOS goes about the very complicated job of organizing a disk for rapid and efficient storage and retrieval of data.

The fundamental unit of disk storage is the *sector*. All information stored on a disk is stored in some sector. Each sector has a number and represents a unique area of the disk. The sector number is used by DOS to identify each physical location on the disk.

The display tells you that each sector can store 512 bytes. A byte is the basic unit of information stored by the computer. The next unit described is the *track*. Each circular *track* is divided into smaller units called *sectors*. DOS 1.0 places eight sectors on each track; DOS 2.0 and 3.0 place nine sectors on a track.

On a double-sided disk, sectors appear on each side. Adding together the nine sectors on the top and the nine sectors on the bottom, each track holds 18 sectors.

How many tracks are there on a disk? The display tells you there are

40 tracks. Some quick arithmetic will enable you to calculate the amount of space available on a disk. 512 bytes per sector times 18 sectors per track times 40 tracks equals a grand total of 368,640 bytes per disk. If you divide 368,640 by 1,024 (1,024 bytes equal a kilobyte) you will get 360. The double-sided, double-density disk is referred to as a 360K disk.

The next line of the display tells you that file space is allocated in *clusters* of two *sectors*. What does this mean?

A cluster is equal to 512 times 2 or 1,024 bytes. Further, a cluster represents the "minimum" allocation unit for a file. For example, suppose that you created a file with your word processor that contained only a single letter "A". How much disk space would be taken up?

The answer is that to store a single character you would use up 1,024 bytes of disk storage space. That is because DOS assigns disk space to files 1,024 bytes at a time. The idea of a minimum allocation unit makes a lot of sense. After all, you don't walk into a drug store and buy one aspirin. You have to buy a minimum amount to get the one that you need. It is too costly to package each aspirin individually.

The issues in a computer system are similar. DOS must choose an allocation unit that strikes a balance between wasted disk space and the speed with which it can retrieve information.

The smaller the allocation unit, the more units DOS needs to keep track of on each disk. The more units, the more time it takes to search for a particular unit. However, the larger the allocation unit the more potential wasted space when files fail to fill up an entire unit.

[The relationship between sectors and clusters varies with the type of disk used. On a single-sided disk each cluster is exactly one sector. There is no difference between them. However, when a disk is double-sided, each cluster contains two sectors. A 10-megabyte hard disk will typically assign eight sectors to each cluster.]

The next line in the display tells you that there are 354 clusters on the disk. Wait a minute! Some of you may have noticed what appears to be an inconsistency. If each cluster contains 1,024 bytes, then 354 clusters contain 362,496. This is 6,144 bytes less than the calculation for total disk space made previously.

[Double-sided DOS disks have 720 sectors. However, it is possible to create disks with more or fewer sectors. This is one of the techniques employed in certain copy protection schemes. If you have a copy-protected disk, such as Lotus 1-2-3 version 1A, you can use the Norton Utilities disk to display the technical information about that disk. You will notice that the disk has more than the usual 720 sectors.]

Why the difference? The answer involves the technique used by DOS to keep track of all the information on the disk. 6,144 divided by 1,024 tells you that there are six clusters that are not used to store file data. What are they used for?

Let the program help answer this question. Enter **<Esc> 1 5**

Menu 2.1.5 appears

```
                    Select Disk Sector

     You may select a sector numbered from 0 through 719

   Enter sector number:
   Press Esc or Enter to return to Explore Disk Information
   Outline of Sector Usage on This Disk

              0           Boot Area (used by DOS)
            1 - 4         FAT Area (used by DOS)
            5 - 11        Directory Area (used by DOS)
           12 - 719       Data Area (where files are stored)
```

This menu is used to select and view the contents of any of the 360 sectors on the disk. Note that at the bottom of the screen there is an outline of disk usage.

[The relationship between sector numbers and cluster numbers can be understood in terms of the display. Because sectors 0 through 11 are used for non-data items, the first cluster on the disk begins at sector 12. Because double-sided disks use two sectors for each cluster, cluster 1 consists of sectors 12 and 13. Cluster #2 consists of sectors 14 and 15. This number process continues until the final cluster #354, containing sectors 718 and 719.]

The first sector on the disk is called the *boot area*. (The term *boot* is used quite a lot around computers.) The boot area of the disk is the sector that the computer tries to read when it is turned on. To see what the boot area contains, enter

0<return>5

The screen looks like this. (Note that * has been substituted for IBM graphics characters. Your screen will show assorted graphics characters in those positions.)

```
Sector 0 in boot area in hex format        Cursor at offset 0, hex 0
EB2990A9 424D2020 332E3100 02020100 027000D0 02FD0200 ***IBM  3.1*************
09000200 00000000 00000000 0F000000 000100FA 33C08ED0 *.*.........*....*.*]***
BC007C16 07BB7800 36C5371E 5616S3BF 207CB90B 00FCAC26 ********6*7*************
803D0074 03268A05 AA8AC4E2 F1061F89 4702C707 207CFBCD ***********************
137267A0 107C98F7 26167C03 061C7C03 060E7CA3 347CA32C ***********************
7CB82000 F726117C 8B1E0B7C 03C348F7 F301062C 7CBB0005 ***********************
A1347CE8 9600B801 02E8AA00 72198BFB B90B00BE BE7DF3A6 ***********************
750D8D7F 20BEC97D B90B00F3 A67418BE 5F7DE861 0032E4CD ***********************
165E1F8F 048F4402 CD19BEA8 7DEBEBA1 1C0533D2 F7360B7C ***********************
FEC0A231 7CA12C7C A3327CBB 0007A12C 7CE84000 A1187C2A ***********************
06307C40 50E84E00 5872CF28 06317C76 0C01062C 7CF7260B ***********************
7C03D8EB D98A2E15 7C8A161E 7C8B1E32 7CEA0000 7000AC0A ***********************
C07422B4 0EBB0700 CD10EBF2 33D2F736 187CFEC2 8816307C ***********************
33D2F736 1A7C8816 1F7CA32E 7CC3B402 8B162E7C B106D2E6 ***********************
0A36307C 8BCA86E9 8B161E7C CD13C30D 0A4E6F6E 2D537973 ****************Non-Sys
74656D20 6469736B 206F7220 6469736B 20657272 6F720D0A tem disk or disk error**
5265706C 61636520 616E6420 73747269 6B652061 6E79206B Replace and strike any k
65792077 68656E20 72656164 790D0A0D 0D0A4469 736B2042 ey when ready*****Disk B
6F6F7420 6661696C 7572650D 0A004942 4D42494F 2020434F oot failure***IBMBIO  CO
4D49424D 444F5320 20434F4D 00000000 00000000 00000000 MIBMDOS  COM............
00000000 00000000 00000000 00000000 00000000 00000000 .......................
00000000 000055AA                                     ......U*
```

What in the world does this display mean? The display shows, byte by byte, the contents of the first sector on the disk, the *boot* sector.

The display shows two ways to picture the same information. The left side of the screen displays a hexadecimal representation of the actual information stored in the 512 bytes of sector zero. The right side of the screen shows the corresponding ASCII code characters for the hex numbers on the left.

What are hexadecimal numbers and why are they used? The answer is a bit involved. Almost all of the arithmetic done in daily life involves the decimal system. The decimal system uses ten numbers, 0123456789, to represent all possible numbers. However, even though most people never encounter them, there are many other number systems. In the computer field, binary (two numbers, 01), octal (eight numbers, 01234567), and hexadecimal (sixteen numbers, 0123456789ABCDEF) number systems are used as well as the decimal system.

Why different number systems? There are many reasons why people in the computer field choose to represent data with different number systems. Binary (01) is the most detailed way to show computer data. Binary numbers are made up of only two numbers, zero or one. In a binary number each one or zero represents an actual switching element in the computer system. For example, if the number stored was 175 it would look like this in binary:

10101111

Why? The answer has to do with place value. In any number system the value of each place is a multiple of the total number of characters in the number system. In a binary system there are two numbers, zero and one. Thus the place value of the numbers are multiples of two.

128	64	32	16	8	4	2	1
1	0	1	0	1	1	1	1

The value of a binary number can be found by adding together all the place values of the places that have ones in them.

$128 + 32 + 8 + 4 + 2 + 1 = 175$

While a binary display most closely resembles the actual structure of the byte as it is stored in the computer, it is a bit unwieldy. Programmers often want to use a more concise way of displaying the bytes. Hexadecimal notation allows you to display half a byte with a single character. Any byte can be shown as a two-character symbol.

Binary	Decimal	Hexadecimal
0000	0	0
0001	1	1
0010	2	2
0011	3	3
0100	4	4
0101	5	5
0110	6	6
0111	7	7
1000	8	8
1001	9	9
1010	10	A
1011	11	B
1100	12	C
1101	13	D
1110	14	E
1111	15	F

The decimal and hexadecimal systems are the same for zero through nine. The hexadecimal number system uses ABCDEF to represent the two-digit numbers 10 though 15. The number 175 can be shown:

Binary	Decimal	Hexadecimal
10101111	175	AF

You can see that hexadecimal is the most concise way to represent a byte.

What about the right portion of the screen? It shows the ASCII characters represented by the numeric value of the bytes. The A(merican) S(tandard) C(ode) for I(nformation) I(interchange) is a system used to translate the numeric value of bytes into characters and symbols for display.

The characters displayed on the right side will not always make sense. This is because much of the information stored on a disk is meant for only the computer to understand.

If you look at the right side of the screen you can probably make out some characters that you will recognize.

Look at the first line. You can see IBM 3.1. This tells you the version of DOS that was used to format the disk. The table below shows how the number codes match up with their character representations.

49	42	4D	20	20	33	2E	31
I	B	M			3	.	1

The figure shows how the IBM DOS is coded numerically. Look at the bottom of the display. There you can see some familiar text. If you have ever tried to boot your computer with a NON-SYSTEM disk you will recognize the text of the message.

```
*****************Non-Sys
tem disk or disk error**
Replace and strike any k
ey when ready*****Disk B
oot failure***IBMBIO  CO
MIBMDOS  COM...........
```

This text is used to create the message:

```
Non-System disk or disk error
Replace and strike any key when ready
```

Following that is another message: *Disk Boot Failure*. You can see that the messages that DOS displays are stored in the boot sector of the disk. You could use the Norton Utilities to change the text of the message.

Following the two messages there is another interesting item. In the section on DOS concepts the hidden files used to "boot" the computer were mentioned. You can now see clearly the names IBMBIO COM and IBMDOS COM at the bottom of the boot sector. DOS writes these names into the boot sector of the disk when the disk is formatted. When the boot sector is read, during booting, the names IBMBIO COM and IBMDOS COM are loaded into the computer. The computer then checks to see if those files are the first and second entries in the directory. If they are, the files are loaded and executed.

Many non-IBM systems use MS DOS. Their boot sectors look slightly different. Below is a portion of the boot track from an Eagle computer.

```
n-System disk or disk er
ror..Replace and strike
any key when ready.....D
isk Boot failure...io
   sysmsdos   sysibmbio
 comibmdos   com.........
.........................
......U*
```

Notice that IO SYS and DOS SYS are used in addition to IBMBIO COM and IBMDOS COM.

3.5.   The Directory

One of the most important parts of any disk is the directory. The directory is really a block of sectors that are used to hold information about the files stored on the disk. To see how the directory is constructed, enter **[Pg Dn]**

The next screen is displayed. This is the contents of sector 2. Sector 2 is part of the FAT (File Allocation Table). This table is used by the directory to record the allocation of sectors to files as they grow or shrink. To move past the FAT and see the directory, enter **[Pg Dn]** (4 times)

The screen displayed is quite different from what you have seen before.

Sector 5 in root directory shown in directory format

```
Filename Ext    Size      Date         Time  Cluster Attributes
========.=== ======== ============= ======== ====== ==========================
IBMBIO   COM   4,736 Thu Oct 20 83 12:00 pm       2 Read-Only Hidden System Ar
IBMDOS   COM  17,024 Thu Oct 20 83 12:00 pm       7 Read-Only Hidden System Ar
COMMAND  COM  17,792 Thu Oct 20 83 12:00 pm      24 Archive
   unused directory entry
    unused directory entry
     unused directory entry
      unused directory entry
       unused directory entry
        unused directory entry
         unused directory entry
         unused directory entry
          unused directory entry
           unused directory entry
            unused directory entry
             unused directory entry
             unused directory entry
```

Each entry in a disk's directory contains the following information.

1. Filename
2. Extension
3. Size in bytes
4. Date of creation or update
5. Time of creation or update
6. Number of the starting cluster
7. File attributes

3.6. Display Modes

Norton Utilities has three modes by which the contents of a sector can be viewed. The program selects the mode it thinks most appropriate. Because this sector is a directory, the directory mode has been selected. You can change modes by pressing <return> twice. Enter **<return>** (2 times)

The display has now been changed to the HEX format. This is the format that displays each byte as a hexadecimal number and as an ASCII character. Enter **<return>** (2 times)

The mode is changed once again. This time the mode is the TEXT mode. In the TEXT mode only normal text characters are displayed. AS-CII codes that are used for graphics (128 and higher) are not displayed in this mode. Also the display endeavors to show the information in a line of horizontal text.

Which mode should you use? That depends on the type of information you are looking at and also upon what you want to find out about the information. The directory mode is useful for directory sectors. The text mode is clearer for sectors that contain text information such as that produced by word processors. (Note that not all word processing programs store information in ASCII format.) Enter **<return>** (2 times)

The display format returns to the directory display.

3.7.   Directory Details

When a file is created an entry is made into the directory sectors of the disk. The entry consists of a fixed number of bytes. The numeric value of the bytes determines the characteristics of the directory entry. The first 11 characters of the entry are the filename and extension. The twelfth character plays a special role. It controls the attributes of the files.

For example, the first file in the directory is the IBMBIO COM file.

```
Filename Ext   Size  Date          Time     Cluster Attributes
======== === ======== ============= ======== ======= ===========================
IBMBIO   COM   9,564 Thu Mar  7 85 1:43 pm        2 Read-Only Hidden System Ar
```

Note that this file is currently a Read-Only, Hidden, System, Archive file. You might have noticed that the file IBMBIO.COM does not appear in the directory listing. Files are hidden so that you cannot erase them accidentally. IBM hides these files to protect them. However, your DOS disk will function quite correctly even if these files have the same attribute (archive) as the remainder of the files.

You can change the attribute of the file by changing the twelfth byte in the directory entry. This sounds complicated but the Norton Utilities makes it quite simple.

Of the three display modes, Directory, Text, and Hex, you can make changes *only* from the Hex mode. Enter **<return>** (2 times)

Data can be changed in two ways:

1. Entering the Hex number that you want on the hex number display.
2. Use the <Tab> key to change the cursor position to the ASCII display. Then you type in the text character you want to use.

You can try both methods. To enter a Hex number, move the cursor to the number that you want to change. Move the cursor under the 2 in the number 27, the twelfth character in the sector. Enter **<right arrow>** (22 times)

[At the top of the screen on the right-hand side there is a display that shows the position of the cursor in the display. The display shows the number of bytes from the beginning of the display. If you move your cursor to the twelfth byte, then the display will show: Cursor at offset 11, hex B. The display shows one byte less than the cursor position.]

Enter **20**

The entry is highlighted. The value of 20 Hex tells DOS that is is an Archive file. This shows that you have made a change in the data in this sector. Later you will have to decide whether or not you want the change to actually be written onto the disk. To see the effect, return to the directory display mode. Enter **<return>** (4 times)

The IBMBIO.COM file is no longer hidden but archive like the majority of the files. Return to the Hex display. Enter **<return>** (2 times)

[The cursor is still in the same position that you left it in. Changing display modes will not alter the position of the cursor.]

You will now change the attribute of the IBMDOS.COM file. This time you will use the ASCII method. To change the cursor position to the ASCII display area, enter **<tab>**

Position the cursor to the 44th byte. Enter

<down arrow>
<right arrow> (7 times)

The top of the screen will show:

```
Sector 5 in root directory in hex format    Cursor at offset 43, hex 2B
```

The value of Hex 20 is produced when you press the <space bar>. To enter the ASCII character all you need to do is press the <space bar>. Enter **<space bar>**

Check the directory format. Enter **<return>** (4 times)

Now all the files have the same attributes.

3.8. Saving the Changes

The changes you have made have been recorded in the memory of the computer. They have not been written to the disk itself. Remember, CHANGING DISK DATA IN THIS WAY PERMANENTLY ALTERS THE DISK. Only make changes when you are sure about their effect or you have made a backup copy of the disk to protect yourself from disaster. Enter <**Esc**>

The screen displays:

```
          Save or Discard Changes Made to Data

     You have made changes to the disk data in memory

        (Changes are made and shown highlighted when
        data is displayed in the hexadecimal format)

     You may now:

        Write the changed data, saving it on the disk
        Ignore the changes, leaving the disk data unchanged
        Return to review the changed data

     Press W, I, or R ...
```

You have three choices.

W—This command writes the changes made in the memory of the computer to the disk. This disk is permanently changed.

I—This command ignores the changes. The display screen for that sector is returned to the original values as loaded from the disk. This option can be used to start your sector modifications over again.

R—This command returns you to the sector you were working with. Your alterations are preserved on screen but not saved to the disk.

You must choose one of these three. In this case enter **w**

The two bytes you have changed are written to the disk. To see the effect of the changes exit the program. Enter <**Esc**> (2 times)

Enter **dir**<**return**>

Note that the two files, IBMBIO.COM and IBMDOS.COM, appear on the directory.

```
        Volume in drive A has no label
        Directory of  A:\

        IBMBIO    COM      4736   10-20-83   12:00p
        IBMDOS    COM     17024   10-20-83   12:00p
        COMMAND   COM     17792   10-20-83   12:00p
                3 File(s)      321536 bytes free
```

3.9.   Other Features of the Norton Utilities Main Program

To continue exploring the disk with the Norton Utilities program, enter

b:nu < return >   (floppy disk systems)
c:nu < return >   (hard disk systems)

Once again the main menu appears. Enter **2**

3.10.   Disk Map

One of the interesting displays offered by the Norton Utilities program is the map of disk usage. Enter **3**

The program displays a map that shows the clusters that are occupied and those that are unused.

```
              Map of Space Usage for the Entire Disk

                   89% of disk space is free

                   Proportional Map of Disk Space
          ~ ~~~~~~~~~~~~~~~~~~~~~~~~~~~~~~~~~~~~~~~~~~DDDDDDDDDD
represents DDDDDDDDDDDDDDDDDDDDDDDDDDDDDDDDDDDDDDDDDDDDDDDDDDDDD
    space  DDDDDDDDDDDDDDDDDDDDDDDDDDDDDDDDDDDDDDDDDDDDDDDDDDDDD
    in use DDDDDDDDDDDDDDDDDDDDDDDDDDDDDDDDDDDDDDDDDDDDDDDDDDDDD
```

```
0000000000000000000000000000000000000000000000000000000000
0000000000000000000000000000000000000000000000000000000000
0000000000000000000000000000000000000000000000000000000000
0000
```
Each position represents 1/354th of the total disk space

Press any key to continue...

The display shows that 89% of the disk is unused. You can also see clearly where on the disk the used and unused clusters are located. Enter **<return>**

You can also display the files one at a time. Enter **6**

```
Menu 2.6            1st of 112 entries in this directory
                       Display Information about a File

                              Name: IBMBIO.COM
                        Attributes: Archive
                    Date and time: Thursday, October 20, 1983, 12:00 pm
           Starting cluster number: 2 (sector number 12)
                              Size: 4,736 bytes, occupying 5 clusters
                                    in 1 area of the disk

                       Proportional Map of Disk Space
              F  FFFFF0000000000000000000000000000000000000000000000000
     represents 0000000000000000000000000000000000000000000000000000
          space 0000000000000000000000000000000000000000000000000000
         in use 0000000000000000000000000000000000000000000000000000
        by this 0000000000000000000000000000000000000000000000000000
           file 0000000000000000000000000000000000000000000000000000
                0000000000000000000000000000000000000000000000000000
                0000
          Each position represents 1/354th of the total disk space
```

This map shows information about one particular file, IBMBIO.COM. This is the first entry in the directory. The top portion of the screen supplies details about the file. You may recognize this data as the same data that is stored in the file directory. Norton Utilities has simply changed the way the information is displayed. The visual impact of this display is much greater than the directory display. Enter **<right arrow>**

The screen display now reflects the data stored about the file
IBMDOS.COM. You may notice that this file is much larger than the
IBMBIO.COM file. Enter **<right arrow>**

This displays the data for the final file on this disk, COMMAND.COM.
To return to the main menu, enter **<Esc>**

3.11. Searching the Disk

The Norton Utilities program provides a means of searching the disk
space to locate a particular character or group of characters. Enter **7**

The Norton Utilities program displays:

```
             Search Disk for Data
      Choices:
        f1   Specify Where to Search
        f2   Specify What to Search For
        f3   Begin Searching
        f4   Continue Searching
       Esc   Return to Explore Disk Information
      Press 1, 2, 3, 4, or Esc:
```

The search menu has four commands:

1. *Specify Where to Search.* This command selects the area of the disk to search.
   The Norton Utilities allows you to distinguish between the file space and the
   space not used by files.
2. *Specify What to Search For.* This command allows you to enter a string of 1 to
   48 characters that will be searched for. The character can be entered as text
   characters directly from the keyboard or entered as hexadecimal numbers.
   This allows you to search for non-keyboard characters such as graphics characters and control codes.
3. *Begin Searching.* This command tells Norton Utilities to initiate the search.
   Note that commands 1 and 2 must be entered before this command can be
   used. The Begin Search command always starts at the first data cluster on the
   disk.

   [If *files only* or *unused only* is specified in step 1, then the program skips the sectors
   that do not qualify.]

4. *Continue Searching.* This command continues the search from the point where
   it was last stopped. It does not restart the search at the first cluster.

Enter **1**
Norton Utilities displays:

```
You may search:
  All of the disk
  File data space (in use by files or not)
  Erased file space (data space not in use)
Press A, F, or E ...
```

You now must specify what area of the disk you want to search:

A—All: This option tells the Norton Utilities program to search the entire data
area of the disk.
F—Files: This option searches only those clusters currently in use by files. Unused clusters are skipped.
E—Erased: This option selects only those clusters not in use by a file to search.

Why would you want to search clusters that are not in use? What could
be in them? The answer reveals something very significant about the operation of DOS. What is in the unused clusters may be data that was stored
in files that have been erased. When a file is erased, DOS does not actually destroy the data. Why not?

It would simply waste too much time. If DOS had to wipe out the
actual data every time a file was erased, it would have to fill in all the
clusters with some character like zero. The larger the file, the longer this
would take. More to the point, it would serve no purpose.

When a file is erased with the DEL or ERASE commands, DOS simply
changes the disk directory and the file allocation table to show that the
clusters used for that file are now available for new data. As new data is
added to the disk the new data overwrites the existing data. However, you
can see that if a file is erased and no new data is written to the disk, the
clusters still contain the data.

If you search these clusters you can find the data that is stored there.
You may already have figured out that all you need to do to recover this
erased data is to change the file directory and file allocation table back to
show that this cluster belongs to a file. In a nutshell, that is how Norton
Utilities unerases a file. You will learn about that in detail in Chapter 5.

For now, enter **a**
Now enter **2**
The program displays the *Enter the data to search for* menu:

```
Enter the data to search for
 in character or in hexadecimal format

Press Esc or Enter to return to Search Disk for Data

Use the Tab key to switch between character and hex

Search data, in character format:

   1...5...10...15...20...25...30...35...40...45.48

Search data, in hexadecimal format:
```

This menu allows you to enter up to 48 characters to search for. The characters can be entered as text characters typed from the keyboard or as hexadecimal codes. The <Tab> key switches entry modes. The default mode is text entry.

[Search strings must be exact matches. The case of the letters, upper or lower, is significant. If you are not sure in which case the data is stored, you may have to make several searches using different combinations of upper and lower case letters.

Also note that the data may be stored in a way that you do not realize. Many programs use special formats to store data. For example, when a 1-2-3 worksheet is stored the data is organized in a format that looks very different from the way that it appears on the screen.

This is also the case with many word processing programs. For example, document files created with WordStar contain a number of non-keyboard characters. These are not visible in the WordStar document mode but they are stored on the disk.

Norton Utilities has no way of knowing what program created the file or the format that was used. Keep this in mind when you are looking for information stored in disk files.

One technique is to look for very simple sequences of characters. They may appear in the file exactly as they appear on the screen.]

In this example you will search the disk to find the text AUTOEXEC. You may be familiar with the fact that file called AUTOEXEC.BAT can automatically execute DOS commands when the system is loaded. (See Chapter 2.27.)

Note that the following entry should be made in UPPER case. Enter **AUTOEXEC<return>**

Now begin the search. Enter **3**

The search will display the sectors as they are searched. When the text is located the screen will show:

```
                    Searching for Data
        Press any key to interrupt the search...
        Searching sector 63 Found!
        Go to menu 2.5 to see the data found
        Press any key to continue...
```

To view the contents of the disk sectors that contains the AUTOEXEC, enter **<return> <Esc>5**

The program displays the sector on the screen. If you look at the bottom of the right side of the display you see the sector contains the text \AUTOEXEC.BAT. To find out what file contains this text, enter **<Esc>6**

The screen displays:

```
  Menu 2.6            3rd of 112 entries in this directory
                       Display Information about a File


                        Name: COMMAND.COM
                  Attributes: Archive
               Date and time: Thursday, October 20, 1983, 12:00 pm
      Starting cluster number: 24 (sector number 56)
                        Size: 17,792 bytes, occupying 18 clusters
                              in 1 area of the disk


                    Proportional Map of Disk Space
            F  000000000000000000000000FFFFFFFFFFFFFFFFFFF0000000000
    represents 0000000000000000000000000000000000000000000000000000
         space 0000000000000000000000000000000000000000000000000000
        in use 0000000000000000000000000000000000000000000000000000
       by this 0000000000000000000000000000000000000000000000000000
          file 0000000000000000000000000000000000000000000000000000
               0000000000000000000000000000000000000000000000000000
               0000
         Each position represents 1/354th of the total disk space
```

The screen shows that the text that was searched for is stored in the file COMMAND.COM. Why does DOS look for a file called AUTOEXEC.BAT when it loads?

The reason is now clear. The file COMMAND.COM contains the names of the files that will be automatically executed when the system is booted.

If you wanted, you could use the Norton Utilities program to change the name of the file automatically executed by typing in a new filename into the COMMAND.COM file. To exit the program, enter **<Esc>** (3 times)

3.12.   Note on Hard Disks

The techniques illustrated in this chapter will operate approximately the same on a hard disk as they do on a floppy disk. The main difference is that the hard disk contains a much larger volume of information. Below are the disk statistics of a ten-megabyte hard disk as displayed by Norton Utilities.

```
              Display Disk Technical Information
    Drive C:
    Basic storage capacity:
      10 million characters (megabytes)
      25% of disk space is free
    Logical dimensions:
      Sectors are made up of 512 bytes
      Tracks are made up of 17 sectors per disk side
      There are 4 disk sides
      The disk space is made up of 305 cylinders
      Space for files is allocated in clusters of 8 sectors
      There are 2,586 clusters
      Each cluster is 4,096 bytes
      The disk's root directory can hold 512 files
    Press any key to continue...
```

Scrutinizing the logical dimensions of the disk you will notice that the sectors remains exactly the same size, 512 characters. This is part of the secret of how DOS can operate so many different types of disks. No matter what the capacity of the disk, the basic unit is always the same.

The next few lines reveal that there are 17 sectors on each track and that there are four sides.

[Hard disk drives often contain more than one disk plate. A drive with four sides indicates that there are two plates being read on the top and the bottom of each plate.

This is a clever design. Suppose that you wanted to make a 20-megabyte drive. If you made the disk larger, all the other hardware would have to be redesigned. It is much simpler to stack more plates of the same size on top of each other. All the parts, armatures, etc., remain the same.]

The next line introduces the term *cylinder*. This term is similar to *track*. It refers to all the tracks that are the same distance from the center of the disk. In this example there are four tracks on each cylinder because there are four disk sides.

The significance of the cylinder is that data can be written to all the tracks and subsequent sectors in the same cylinder without having to be repositioned. When data is written without moving to another cylinder it takes place faster than when other cylinders must be accessed. The disk has 305 cylinders. (This also means that each disk plate has 305 tracks.)

Finally, note that the hard disk uses clusters that are four times the size of clusters on a double-sided disk. This means that every file, no matter how few characters it contains, takes up a minimum of 4,096 characters.

The sector usage outline for the same hard disk would reveal:

```
Outline of Sector Usage on This Disk
    0          Boot Area (used by DOS)
  1 - 16       FAT Area (used by DOS)
 17 - 48       Directory Area (used by DOS)
 49 - 20,736   Data Area (where files are stored)
```

The first 49 sectors are used by DOS. The remainder of the sectors are used for data storage.

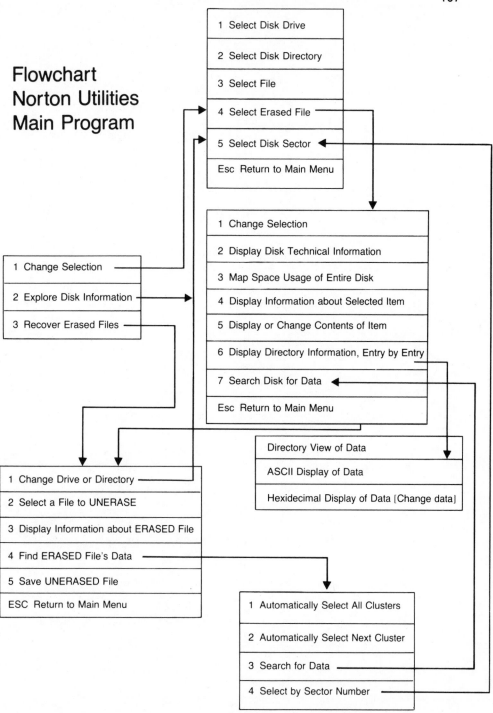

**Flowchart
Norton Utilities
Main Program**

1 Select Disk Drive

2 Select Disk Directory

3 Select File

4 Select Erased File

5 Select Disk Sector

Esc Return to Main Menu

1 Change Selection

2 Display Disk Technical Information

3 Map Space Usage of Entire Disk

4 Display Information about Selected Item

5 Display or Change Contents of Item

6 Display Directory Information, Entry by Entry

7 Search Disk for Data

Esc Return to Main Menu

1 Change Selection

2 Explore Disk Information

3 Recover Erased Files

Directory View of Data

ASCII Display of Data

Hexidecimal Display of Data [Change data]

1 Change Drive or Directory

2 Select a File to UNERASE

3 Display Information about ERASED File

4 Find ERASED File's Data

5 Save UNERASED File

ESC Return to Main Menu

1 Automatically Select All Clusters

2 Automatically Select Next Cluster

3 Search for Data

4 Select by Sector Number

4.

Other Norton Utilities Programs

In addition to the main Norton Utilities program, the Norton Utilities is supplied with a number of smaller programs that perform single functions. These programs provide a number of special functions that help in maintaining a computer system. The programs are designed to supplement and extend MS DOS functions.

The other programs are divided into three categories:

1. *Programs that help manage files.* These programs are designed to extend or modify the facilities provided in DOS that manage files stored on disk, both hard and floppy. Some programs present commands not provided in DOS. Others present facilities already provided in DOS but implement them in a different way, making them easier to use. The programs included in this section are:

Program	Filename
Directory Sort	DS.COM
File Attribute	FA.COM
File Find	FF.COM
File Size	FS.COM
List Directories	LD.COM
Text Search	TS.COM*

2. *Programs that affect the entire operating system.* These programs modify and extend DOS functions that have a broader scope than just a file or group of files. The programs explained in this section are:

Program	Filename
Beep	BEEP.COM
Disk Test	DT.COM
Line Print	LP.COM
Screen Attributes	SA.COM*
System Information	SI.COM
Time Mark	TM.COM
Volume Label	VL.COM

3. *Programs that provide data security.* These programs are provided as a means of removing data from disks. Note that the DOS commands ERASE and DEL do not actually remove data from the disk. The programs in this section are:

Program	Filename
Wipeout Disk	WIPEDISK.COM
Wipeout File	WIPEFILE.COM

There are two files marked with an *. This indicates that these programs use or require the ANSI.SYS device driver to be installed in the operating system. Text Search does not require the ANSI driver but it is recommended. Screen Attributes *requires* the driver. For details about the ANSI driver and how to install it see Chapter 2.28.

4.1.   File Programs

The programs in this section help you manage the files stored on your disks, both hard and floppy. The hands-on sections that follow require the following setup:

Drive A—A copy of the DOS system disk. The version used in the examples is PC DOS version 2.1.

Drive B—A copy of the Norton Utilities program diskette.

or

Drive C—Change the directory to one that contains copies of all the files from the Norton Utilities program diskette.

4.2.   Directory Sorting

In what order are files stored in the directory of the disk? The answer is that MS DOS stores files in the order that they are created. Of course, the situation becomes more complex when you begin to erase and add files. When you examine exactly how directories function (see Chapter 3), you can see that the situation begins to get quite complex. If you are working on a hard drive on which you are constantly adding and removing files, the pattern of directory entries can seem quite random.

No matter what the reason, the directory of a disk is almost never presented in a logical order. Sorting the directory listing makes the list much simpler to read and understand.

The DS.COM program, Directory Sort, is used to rewrite the contents of a directory into some logical order. The directory sort program has no effect on the contents of the files and will not affect the way any program functions.

The Directory Sort program recognizes five qualities for each entry:

1. n, Name = the first eight characters of the filename
2. e, Extension = the three-character extension, if used
3. d, Date = the date assigned to the file by DOS
4. t, Time = the time assigned to the file by DOS
5. s, Size = the size of the file as stored in the directory

[Attribute names and extensions are user created. The qualities of date, time, and size are created by DOS when a file is created or updated. The time and date are drawn from the MS DOS system's clock. If you do not use a battery-powered clock/calendar the system's date in your computer will be set by the creation date of the version of DOS you are using. For example, PC DOS 2.1 will always set the system's date at 1/1/81 and 12:00 A.M.

If you intend to use dates and times in a meaningful way you must take care to properly enter the date and time in your computer each time it is turned on. Further note that if you perform a warm boot, the date and time must be reentered.

Even if you have a clock/calendar in the computer, you still must make sure that you run a program that transfers the date in the clock to the operating system. For example, the AST Six-Pak card is supplied with a clock calendar. In addition, there is a program called ASTCLOCK supplied on a disk. Each time the computer is booted, warm or cold, the ASTCLOCK program must be run in order to place the correct date and time into the operating system.

The usual way to handle this is to place an AUTOEXEC.BAT file on the boot disk. In this batch file you can automatically execute the clock command. (See DOS batch file for more information.)]

The program sorts the directory for any one of these qualities. In addition, these qualities can be strung together to create a multilayered sort. For example, sorting on dt would sort first by date. Then if any two files had the same date, the time would be used to break the tie and rank them according to time within the same date.

[Sorting of time is based on a 24-hour clock.]

You must specify at least one of the qualities to sort by. The Directory Sort program does not have a default value.

4.3.   Sorting a Floppy Disk

SETUP:
Floppy Drive System:
Drive A: Any disk that you want to sort
Drive B: Norton Utilities program disk

Hard Drive System:
Drive A: Any disk that you want to sort
Drive C: Directory that contains Norton Utilities programs

Suppose that you wanted the floppy disk to be sorted by name. Enter

ds n a:<return>

The command has three parts. The first, Directory Sort, is the name of the program. Next, *n* tells the program how to sort the directory. Finally, *a:* tells the program what disk to sort. The disk specification is optional. Without a disk specified, the program will use the active drive as the default and sort its directory. To see the results, enter **dir a:<return>**

You can see that the directory is now ordered by name.

Probably the most useful way to sort a directory is by extension followed by name. This type of sort uses the extension to group together similar types of files, COM, EXE, BAT. The name is then used as a secondary criterion to alphabetize the files within their type grouping. Enter **ds en a:<return>**

Check the results. Enter **dir a:<return>**

Try a sort by date and time. Enter

ds dt a:<return>
dir a:<return>

Sort the directory by size. Enter

ds s a:<return>
dir a:<return>

Finally, sort by all five qualities. Enter

ds ensdt a:<return>
dir a:<return>

It is interesting to note the difference between the DS.COM program and the DOS filter SORT.EXE. The directory sort program actually rewrites the directory sectors of the disk. This means that the order in which the files appear is permanently changed.

The SORT filter used by DOS is used to sort the "output" of a program before it is sent to the designated output device, the screen, printer, disk, or modem. The SORT filter has no permanent effect on the directory as it is written on the disk. The files remain in the order they were in before the SORT filter was used.

The sorting of the directory will be correct only as long as you don't alter the disk. If you add or rename files the directory may appear out of order. If you have sorted the files by date or time, updating the files will cause the order to appear incorrect.

In order to get the files correctly listed you must issue another Directory Sort command.

4.4. Sorting Directories on a Hard Disk

When you work with the Directory Sort program on a hard drive, you need to take into account some additional considerations. These involve the presence of more than a single directory on the hard drive.

The Directory Sort program will operate on only one directory at a time. Therefore it is not possible to organize the entire hard disk with a single command. Each directory will need to be sorted on its own.

Just as the Directory Sort command can accept the drive specification, you can also specify a directory. The assumption is made that you are currently in the directory of your disk that contains the Norton Utilities programs. Suppose that you have a directory on your hard drive called \123. To sort that directory, enter **ds en \123 <return>**

Check the results. Enter **dir \123 <return>**

You can sort any directory on the hard disk by using the pathname of the directory in the Directory Sort command.

Another approach to the same problem is to use the PATH and CD commands. Suppose that your Norton Utilities programs are stored in a directory called \DOS and your word processing program and documents are stored in a directory called \WP. You can first change the active directory to WP. Enter **cd\wp**

Enter **ds en <return>**

If DOS displays "Bad command or filename" that is because the DS.COM program is in the DOS directory. To solve this problem, enter

path\dos <return>
ds en <return>

When a path is open to the directory in which the Norton Utilities programs are stored they can be used in any directory on the disk in which you happen to be working.

4.5.   File Size

SETUP:
Floppy Drive System:
Drive A: Copy of MS DOS diskette
Drive B: Norton Utilities program disk

Hard Drive System:
Drive A: Copy of MS DOS diskette
Drive C: Directory that contains Norton Utilities programs

DOS provides some information about files' sizes. For example, the DIR (directory) command tells you the size of each file based on the number of records in the directory and the number of bytes free on the disk. While this information is helpful, it is far from complete.

One useful piece of information that DOS does not provide directly is the amount of space occupied by a file or group of files. This information is important when you think about copying files. The File Size, FS, program displays and adds up the amount of space occupied by a selected file or group of files. This information allows you to know how much room those files take up, and therefore how much room is needed if you are going to copy those files to another disk.

If you are a hard disk user and you want to copy files to a floppy, you need to know if all the files to be copied will fit on the disk.

The File Size program is needed because the DOS directory display gives a misleading display when it comes to the size of files. Suppose that you wanted to know how much space the Norton Utilities program takes up. Enter **dir ??.com<return>**

The display will look like this:

```
Volume in drive B has no label
Directory of  B:\
DS       COM      6292    1-21-85     3:00p
DT       COM      6236    1-21-85     3:00p
FA       COM      3584    1-21-85     3:00p
FF       COM      4618    1-21-85     3:00p
FS       COM      5108    1-21-85     3:00p
LD       COM      2980    1-21-85     3:00p
LP       COM      6406    1-21-85     3:00p
NU       COM     48054    1-21-85     3:00p
SA       COM      2976    1-21-85     3:00p
SI       COM      6762    1-21-85     3:00p
TM       COM      3814    1-21-85     3:00p
TS       COM      9400    1-21-85     3:00p
VL       COM      3934    1-21-85     3:00p
        13 File(s)     202752 bytes free
```

If you were to use a calculator and add up the sizes as shown in the directory listing, you would get a total of 110,164 bytes of space occupied by those files. You might conclude that if a disk had 110,592 bytes free, the 13 files listed could be copied to that disk.

The fact is that if you attempted to actually make the transfer, DOS would report that there was "insufficient" disk space to copy all 13 files. Why?

The answer lies in the way DOS actually stores files (see Chapter 3). DOS has a minimum allocation unit. When a file is stored, DOS records the actual number of bytes in the file. But, for practical reasons, most files take up more space than that number indicates. For example, in a disk formatted to 360K, the minimum space allocation is 1,024 bytes. If a file is only 100 bytes in size, it is still allocated 1,024 bytes of disk space. That is because the minimum block of space assigned to a file is 1,024 bytes.

Files grow in increments of 1,024 bytes. Thus, if the a file contained 1,025 bytes it would still use up 2,048 (1,024 + 1,024) bytes of disk space. What this means is that, unless a file's size is evenly divisible by 1,024, there will be some slack space. This slack represents space allocated to but not used by the file.

This slack space is *not* represented on the file directory display. The File Size program does provide the true file space figure. Enter **fs ??.com <return>**

The program displays an output like this:

```
FS-File Size, Version 3.00, (C) Copyright 1984, Peter Norton

        6,292 DS.COM
        6,236 DT.COM
        3,584 FA.COM
        4,618 FF.COM
        5,108 FS.COM
        2,980 LD.COM
        6,406 LP.COM
       48,054 NU.COM
        2,976 SA.COM
        6,762 SI.COM
        3,814 TM.COM
        9,400 TS.COM
        3,934 VL.COM

      110,164 total bytes in 13 files
      115,712 bytes disk space occupied, 5% slack
```

The second figure, 115,712 (1,024 × 113) represents the true amount of space used by the 13 files. You can see that the minimum amount of space required to copy the files is 5% larger than you would have been led to believe by the directory display.

The File Size program can be used to obtain the sizes of groups of files or entire directories. For example, if you have a directory on a hard disk called \DOS, the following command would list the size of the files in that directory. Enter **fs \dos<return>**

[File Size cannot add up the amount of space used by all the files on a hard drive because it will work with only one directory at a time. The XTREE program, explained in Chapter 6, will perform that function.]

4.6.   File Find

The FF (File Find) program is an alternative to the DOS directory command. It differs from the DOS directory command, DIR, in two respects:

1. The program displays directories in a different format than does DIR.
2. The program will list files on the disk regardless of what directories they are stored in. This is of benefit mainly to users of hard disk systems. The DOS DIR command will list only the files in a given directory.

Let's examine these features; first, the alternate display format. Enter **dir ??.com<return>**

DOS displays something like this:

```
        Volume in drive B has no label
        Directory of  B:\

        DS        COM       6292    1-21-85    3:00p
        DT        COM       6236    1-21-85    3:00p
        FA        COM       3584    1-21-85    3:00p
        FF        COM       4618    1-21-85    3:00p
        FS        COM       5108    1-21-85    3:00p
        LD        COM       2980    1-21-85    3:00p
        LP        COM       6406    1-21-85    3:00p
        NU        COM      48054    1-21-85    3:00p
        SA        COM       2976    1-21-85    3:00p
        SI        COM       6762    1-21-85    3:00p
```

```
        TM        COM      3814    1-21-85    3:00p
        TS        COM      9400    1-21-85    3:00p
        VL        COM      3934    1-21-85    3:00p
        13 File(s)      202752 bytes free
```

Now enter **ff ??.COM < return >**
The FF program displays something like this:

```
FF-File Find, Version 3.00, (C) Copyright 1984, Peter Norton

B:
  DS.COM         6,292 bytes    3:00 pm  Mon Jan 21 85
  DT.COM         6,236 bytes    3:00 pm  Mon Jan 21 85
  FA.COM         3,584 bytes    3:00 pm  Mon Jan 21 85
  FF.COM         4,618 bytes    3:00 pm  Mon Jan 21 85
  FS.COM         5,108 bytes    3:00 pm  Mon Jan 21 85
  LD.COM         2,980 bytes    3:00 pm  Mon Jan 21 85
  LP.COM         6,406 bytes    3:00 pm  Mon Jan 21 85
  NU.COM        48,054 bytes    3:00 pm  Mon Jan 21 85
  SA.COM         2,976 bytes    3:00 pm  Mon Jan 21 85
  SI.COM         6,762 bytes    3:00 pm  Mon Jan 21 85
  TM.COM         3,814 bytes    3:00 pm  Mon Jan 21 85
  TS.COM         9,400 bytes    3:00 pm  Mon Jan 21 85
  VL.COM         3,934 bytes    3:00 pm  Mon Jan 21 85

13 files found
```

The second and most important feature of the FF program is that it will search all the directories on a given disk for the specified files. This is primarily of use to users who are working with hard disks.

For example, many programs create .BAK or backup files when working. These backup files usually do not serve any purpose after you have finished the session of work with that program. However, most programs do not automatically erase those files. The result is that over a period of time the .BAK files begin to occupy disk space that could be used for other files.

In order to find the .BAK files, you would need to take a directory listing for each directory on the hard disk. The FF program makes this task much simpler. Enter **ff *.bak < return >**

The FF program will produce a display that will look something like this:

```
FF-File Find, Version 3.00, (C) Copyright 1984, Peter Norton

C:
   NU2.BAK         14,720 bytes    4:00 pm  Sun Nov 10 85

C:\WS
   KEYS.BAK        50,816 bytes    7:02 pm  Thu Oct 31 85
   SK.BAK          24,832 bytes   11:56 am  Sat Nov  9 85

C:\DBASE
   NU2.BAK         14,720 bytes    4:00 pm  Sun Nov 10 85

4 files found
```

The FF program can locate files of a certain type no matter what directory they are stored in.

4.7.   File Attributes

One of the less obvious characteristics of DOS is the fact that not all files are treated equally. In the section on DOS you learned that DOS stores special "hidden" files on disks when they are formatted as "systems" disks.

Most operating systems allow for distinctions to be made among the types of files stored in the system. The reasons for different types of files usually relate to issues of security. On large computer systems files are assigned various types so that only users with the proper clearance can gain access to those files.

On a personal computer the issue is generally less important, because the computer is designed to be operated by a single person. DOS does maintain file types. Some file types are employed as a means of implementing copy protection schemes. The "File Attributes" program is not concerned with those "hidden" files.

[Hidden files can be manipulated with the main Norton Utilities program by directly changing the data stored in the disk directory.]

The FA program is chiefly concerned with two qualities of a file.

1. READ-ONLY DOS allows you to designate where or not a file can be changed or erased. Files that can be erased or edited are said to be

"READ/WRITE" files since they can be read into the memory, altered, and then rewritten. Such files can also be erased entirely.

Files designated as "READ-ONLY" can be loaded into the memory, but DOS will refuse to rewrite or erase the file on the disk. This attribute allows you to designate files that can and cannot be erased. This action can protect you from accidental erasures of valuable material.

The attribute can be of particular use when you are copying files from one drive to another. Normally DOS will overwrite files with the same names, thereby destroying the old files on the receiving disk by replacing them with the files being copied from the source disk. The READ-ONLY attribute can protect you from destruction of files by accidental copying.

2. ARCHIVE-DOS 2.0 and higher keeps track of which files have been backed up by using the backup command. The purpose of this attribute is to help users with hard disks avoid backing up files that have not been altered since the last backup.

Since backing up files onto a floppy disk is quite time-consuming, the use of the ARCHIVE attribute can save a good deal of time.

Normally the ARCHIVE attribute is changed on a file by the BACKUP command as it backs up the files. The FA program gives you another means by which you can change the designation of a file's ARCHIVE attribute.

The FA program can be used for three actions:

1. List the files and their current attributes.
2. Turn on READ-ONLY or ARCHIVE attributes of specified files.
3. Turn off READ-ONLY or ARCHIVE attributes of specified files.

Note that the ARCHIVE and READ-ONLY attributes are separate attributes and can be changed independently of each other.

4.8.   Listing Files

The simplest use of the FA program is to list the attributes of a file or group of files. Since DOS does not list this information when it lists a directory, this is a handy program. Enter

fa < return >

The program will produce a list like this:

```
FA-File Attributes, Version 3.00, (C) Copyright 1984, Peter Norton

          Archive   BEEP.COM
          Archive   DS.COM
          Archive   DT.COM
          Archive   FA.COM
          Archive   FF.COM
          Archive   FS.COM
          Archive   SI.COM
          Archive   TM.COM
          Archive   TS.COM
          Archive   VL.COM
          Archive   WIPEDISK.COM
          Archive   WIPEFILE.COM
23 files shown
no files changed
```

The files are listed and their attributes shown.

4.9.   Protecting Files

The FA program can be used to protect files that you do not want to erase or change by altering the READ-ONLY attribute of a file or group of files. For example, suppose that you want to protect the NU.COM files from erasure. The characters /R tell the program to affect the READ-ONLY status of the file. Following the /R with a + will tell the program to turn the attribute on. Following the /R with a − will turn the attribute off. Enter

fa nu.com/r+ <return>

The screen will display:

```
FA-File Attributes, Version 3.00, (C) Copyright 1984, Peter Norton

Read-only  Archive   NU.COM

1 file changed
```

To confirm the results, list the file attributes again. This time the /p option is used to pause the listing when the screen has been filled. Enter

fa /p < return >

You will see that the NU.COM file now shows Read-only Archive NU.COM. Press any key to complete the listing.

Next, test the effect of that change. Enter

del nu.com < return >

DOS displays the message *File is Not Found*. Normally this would mean that you had used a filename not found on the directory of the disk. But in this case it indicates that you have protected the file from erasure by the DEL command.

What would DOS do if you tried to copy a file with the name NU.COM onto this disk? Enter

copy vl.com nu.com < return >

DOS displays this message: *File creation error*. The message is not very specific about the problem. In this instance the error was caused by the fact that NU.COM was a READ-ONLY file and therefore could not be copied over.

The FA command will accept a wildcard argument. You could change the attributes of an entire group of files at one time. For example, you might want to change all the Norton Utilities programs to READ-ONLY files. Enter

fa ??.com/R + < return >

The program tells you that there have been 12 files changed and 13 files listed. Why were only 12 changed? Remember that NU.COM had already been changed. The files can be returned to the READ-WRITE status by reversing the pattern. Enter

fa ??.com/r − < return >

Now all 13 files have been changed back to READ-WRITE status.

The /T option tells the program to display only the total count of the files changed. Enter

fa ??.com/r + /t < return >

Thirteen files are changed but only the total is displayed by the FA program. Once more change the file back to READ-WRITE status. Enter

fa ??.com/r − /t < return >

4.10.   Archive Status

The other use of the FA program is to control the way the backup command performs its work. This section is of use only to those users with hard disk drives. Before you work with FA in this regard, let's take a moment and discuss BACKUP.

BACKUP.COM is a program provided with DOS versions 2.0 and higher. Its purpose is to provide users of hard disks a way to backup their disks using floppy disks. The major question to ask about BACKUP is how is it different from the DOS COPY command.

The COPY command is not adequate for hard disks because it does not cope with the problems created when the file being copied from the hard disk cannot fit onto a single floppy disk.

The BACKUP command is designed to provide a means by which a series of floppy disks can be used to backup a large amount of data from a hard disk.

However, BACKUP differs from COPY in many technical aspects that are not obvious at first.

1. Files placed on floppies with BACKUP are not written the same way as they are when the COPY command is used. BACKUP files are compressed. This means that the disk can hold more data, about 11% more than could the same disk if COPY were used. The down side is that files created by BACKUP cannot be loaded and used by programs directly. The file must be recopied onto the hard disk using another specialized program provided by DOS called RESTORE.COM.
2. The BACKUP command changes one of the file's attributes when it is copied. In that way, should you request BACKUP to do so, it can tell those files that have already been backed up and those that are new or have been changed

since the last backup. The COPY command does not mark files as having been copied. The purpose of marking files as backed up is to save time and disks by backing up only those files that actually represent new information.

Normally the only way to change the archive attribute is to actually BACKUP the file.

[If you want to change a file so that DOS will think that it needs to be backed up you must make some change in that file. For example, if the file is a word processing document, you would load the file into the word processor and then save it again. Even though you didn't actually change the text, the act of saving the file again will fool DOS into thinking that the file has been altered.

In dBASE II and III placing a file in USE, e.g., USE NAMES, will cause its attribute to be changed even though you don't actually change any of the data.]

The previous listing told you that all of the Norton Utilities files showed "Archive" as their attribute. When the word "Archive" appears, it indicates that DOS needs to backup these files. As an example, backup the files to the A drive. In order to perform this task you must place a BLANK FORMATTED disk in drive A.

Enter **backup ??.com a:<return>**

BACKUP warns you that you will erase any files on drive A. Enter **<return>**

The files are backed up onto the disk in drive A. Now check the attributes of those files. Enter **fa ??.com <return>**

Instead of "Archive" the attribute shows "Normal File." This indicates that the files have been backed up. The /M option (modified) of the BACKUP command tells DOS to ignore the "normal files" and back up only the "archive" files. Enter

backup ??.com a:/m<return> <return>

What happens? DOS displays the message: Warning! No files were found to backup. Another way to look at it is that all the files specified already had a "normal" attribute.

As you can see, the BACKUP command changes the attribute of the files. FA can perform the same change but without actually having to backup the file. For example, suppose that you wanted to make DS.COM "Archive" again. The /A option is used to change this attribute. Enter **fa ds.com/a+ <return>**

Now enter the backup command again. Enter

backup ??.com a:/m < return > < return >

This time DOS finds one file, DS.COM, to backup. Return all the files to their original status as archive files. Enter

fa ??.com/a + < return >

4.11.   List Directories

The LD.COM program is used to display a list of directories. This command is generally of interest to users who have hard disks and therefore have created a sequence of directories on that disk. Enter **ld < return >**
  The screen will display something like this:

```
LD-List Directories, Version 3.00, (C) Copyright 1984, Peter Norton

   C: (root)
   C:\WS
   C:\WS\SPELL
   C:\DOS
   C:\BOOK
   C:\TERRY
   C:\CORY
   C:\123
8 directories
```

4.12.   Text Search

This program is one of the most valuable programs provided in the Norton Utilities collection. The function that it performs is quite simple. It searches the data on a disk to determine if and where certain groups of characters are stored.
  Word processing programs provide a similar function when they SEARCH a document for a word or group of characters. However, search features provided by word processors are usually limited to files that are

created with that word processor. Also, they usually search the contents of one file at a time.

Text Search will examine all the data stored on a disk, including space that is occupied by erased files. The Text Search program has been one of the most popular parts of the Norton Utilities system. Normally the only clue as to the contents of a file is the filename. The Text Search program gives users another way to locate information. This may account for its importance and popularity.

[As of the writing of this book, Peter Norton has announced version 3.1 of the Norton Utilities programs. Included are a revised and improved version of the Text Search program. The version described in this book is version 3.0 of the Norton Utilities programs.]

4.13.   Looking for Text

The term *text* is used to describe a portion of the type of information your computer is capable of understanding. The Text Search program is designed to search only for data that is stored in the ASCII text format. Generally speaking, non-text characters like <Esc> or [Ctrl] combinations cannot be searched for. The search is usually limited to the characters that you see on your keyboard.

[As you will see, there is a way to search for some [Ctrl] characters with Text Search. You can also search for graphics characters that the IBM PC displays but does not supply specific keys for on the keyboard. The search program provided within the main Norton Utilities program can search for data based on the hexadecimal value of the data. This allows you to search for all 255 possible characters.]

The Text Search program allows you to choose the scope of the search. The scope is used to limit the search to a particular portion of the data on the disk. You can choose to search:

1. *F—Files*. This type of search is limited to the portions of the disk that are indicated by the disk directory as belonging to active files. The search will not include areas of the disk used by DOS, e.g., directories or file allocation tables, or portions of the disk not used by files, e.g., erased areas.

   This option also indicates the sequence in which the disk is searched. The search proceeds in the order in which the files are entered in the disk directory.

[The Directory Sort command will rewrite the disk directory into a specific order based on filename, extension, time, date, size, or some combination of these characteristics. For example, if you wanted to search your files in chronological order for some data, you could use Directory Sort to order the files in date order and then use Text Search to search the files. Of course the assumption is made that you have been entering the correct date into the system or are using a battery-powered clock to do so.]

When you search by files, Text Search displays the name of the file that is being searched. If the search finds a match then the text is displayed on the screen. The program also displays surrounding text, if any, to help you see the context of the selected text.

Text Search also provides the offset number of the first byte in the file that is part of the matching text. For example, if you searched for the word FOOD in a group of files created by the Lotus 1-2-3 program, you might see a display like this:

```
Enter specific text to search for
Or press enter for any text
   Text: FOOD


Searching BUDGET.WKS


Found at byte offset 1,342


.'FOOD...
```

This display tells you several things. First, *Searching BUDGET.WKS* tells you the name of the file being searched.

Next, *Found at byte offset 1,342* tells you the place within the file that the word *FOOD* was found. This tells you that the *F* in *FOOD* is the 1,343rd character in that file—1,342 characters precede the *F*. You will see how this number can be used with the main Norton Utilities program to locate the exact spot in the file where the text is stored.

The *.'FOOD...* displays the context in which the word was found. Lotus users will recognize the ' which is used to indicate a left-justified label in 1-2-3. The periods stand for non-text characters.

2. *D—Disk*: This search looks at all the data stored on the disk starting with sector 0. This means that the entire disk is searched, including the boot sector, file allocation table, and directories. The search is conducted consecutively by sector or cluster number, not in order of files. When an entire disk is searched, the matches are recorded differently than when the search is performed by files. For example, if you were to search the disk for the word *FOOD*, you would get a display that looks like this:

```
Searching A: cluster number 3, sectors 14 - 15

Found at byte offset 318

.'FOOD...
```

The location on the disk is given in terms of cluster number, 3, and sector numbers, 14–15. The offset shows how many bytes into cluster #3 the text was found. You are also shown the context of the match.

3. *E—Erased*: This search uses only those portions of the disk that are not allocated for use by files. The display for erased searches is the same as that used for disk searches. This makes sense because the data is not assigned to any files, so that there are no filenames to report.

Erased searches are also conducted sequentially beginning with the first unused cluster on the disk.

The ability to specify the areas to search is quite important. If you know in advance if the data is in an active or erased area, you can cut down on the search time quite a bit.

4.14. Finding Text

As an example of how to work with the Text Search program, you can perform searches on the files found on the DOS systems disk. It is interesting to note that the files on the DOS systems disk are not text files at all. They are all programs. However, even programs often contain sections of text. The reason is quite simple. The menus, prompts, and messages that programs display must be stored in those programs in the first place. They may not be stored in exactly the form you see them in on the screen, but they are stored in the file in some form.

For example, the CHKDSK program (Check Disk) displays the words *bytes free* as part of its functions. You should be able to search the DOS disk and locate the exact position of those characters on the disk. To begin, enter the Text Search command:

ts < return >

The program displays:

```
TS-Text Search, Version 3.00, (C) Copyright 1984, Peter Norton

Select search within FILES, all of DISK, or ERASED file space of disk
Press F, D, or E ...
```

You must enter the a letter to choose what type of search you want to perform. Enter **f**

Next Text Search displays:

```
Enter the file specification for the files to search
   File:
```

You can now enter the wildcard specification you desire. If you enter <return> then Text Search will assume you want to search all the files (*.*) in the active drive and directory. You can enter any valid DOS wildcard specification. In this case enter

a: <return>

This selects all the files from the disk in drive A. Next you need to enter the specific text to search for.

```
          Enter specific text to search for
          Or press enter for any text
             Text:
```

Enter **bytes free <return>**

[Text Search does not recognize differences in case between the search text and the disk data. This means that text will be considered a match if the same letters appear in either upper or lower case.]

Text Search begins to examine the files on the disk. While searching COMMAND.COM, it will display:

```
          Searching IBMBIO.COM
          Searching IBMDOS.COM
          Searching COMMAND.COM

          Found at byte offset 13,941
```

This tells you that the text has been found in the COMMAND.COM files beginning at byte 13,942 of the file. The text found is the text used to display the number of free bytes at the bottom of each directory listing. Text Search asks you if you want to continue seaching the disk.

Before you continue the search, consider a question. How will you remember the information currently on the screen for later reference? Although the Text Search program gives you the location of the data you seek, it does not record the locations. As the program progresses the information will gradually scroll off the screen. If you want to refer to the locations later on you must record the information. A fast way to do this is to use the [Shift PrtSc] combination to dump the data on the screen to your printer.

[If you have a background program like Sidekick or Deskset you could copy the information directly off the screen. See Sidekick, notepad import function, or Deskset, POPCLIP program, for details.]

Enter **y**

The search continues. Text Search lists the files as they are searched. The next time the program stops the screen will look like this:

```
        Searching COMMAND.COM
        Searching ANSI.SYS
        Searching FORMAT.COM
        Searching CHKDSK.COM

        Found at byte offset 5,741
```

This time the text has been found with the CHKDSK.COM file at byte 5,742. You can terminate the search by entering **n**

[You can stop a search while the files are being examined by entering [Ctrl Scroll Lock] or [Ctrl/c].]

Now try the same search but search the entire disk instead of just files. Enter **ts<return>d**

This time Text Search displays the prompt *Press a letter to select the drive to search...* Enter **a**

The next prompt reads:

```
  To copy text into a file, enter file specification,
  Or press enter to not copy
    File:
```

What does this mean? When Text Search is used in the D, entire disk, mode you have the option to copy the clusters selected into a new file. This gives you the ability to extract the data you are searching for from the disk you are searching and place it into a new file. This feature provides a way to recover data in a similar fashion as the UNERASE section of the main Norton Utilities program.

The advantage of this method is that the data is copied into a new file on another disk. The UNERASE function always tries to recover data on the disk it was erased from. Text Search allows you to transfer data to a new disk. Since the disk level search includes both active and erased files, you can assemble data from both into a new file.

[While it is possible to use Text Search to copy data onto the same disk that it is searching, you would probably want to avoid doing so. If the data you were copying came from an erased file, it is possible that when Text Search went to write the recovered text it might write over other data on the same disk. To avoid this problem always copy data to a different disk than the one you are searching. This is simple to do on a floppy system. If you are working on a hard disk you will have to copy the data onto a floppy in drive A to be safe.]

When data is copied into the specified file, an entire cluster is copied. If you are copying text on a floppy disk, 1,024 characters will be copied. If you are copying on a hard disk, 4,096 characters will be copied each time. You will probably be coping a great deal more text than you might ideally like.

Enter **search.dat < return >**

This tells the program to store that information in a file called SEARCH.DAT. Now enter the search text:

bytes free < return >

The first match displays the following information:

```
Searching A: cluster number 73, sector 80

Found at byte offset 117


Copy this cluster into output file (Y/N) ?
```

This time you can see that the location is given in terms of clusters and bytes. You do not know what file, if any, the text is stored in. Text Search wants you to decide if the data should be copied to the SEARCH.DAT file. Enter

y

The search continues. The next match is displayed. Enter

y (2 times)

Next another match. Enter

y (2 times)

Continue the search. Enter

y (2 times)

The search will continue until the entire disk has been searched. At the end of the search the file SEARCH.DAT is completed. It now contains the data stored in the clusters that you selected. To display the copied text, enter

type search.dat < return >

The results may not mean much to you. The first part displays a cluster that contains many of the error messages displayed by DOS. The other sectors are just a bunch of symbols. This tells you that the cluster selected was probably written in machine code and not really text at all.

Although copying these sectors didn't accomplish much in this example, it serves as an illustration of the degree of control you can gain over the information stored in your computer system when you use programs like Norton Utilities.

The last type of search is the search of the erased areas of the disk. To illustrate how this works you will first erase some files from the disk in drive A. Remember that the disk should be a copy of your system's disk, *not* the original. Enter

del a:chkdsk.com < return >

Text Search working on the erased or unused areas of the disk functions exactly like Text Search when it searches the entire disk. The only execption is that the program will skip the portions of the disk that are already in use and begin with the first unused area. Now start a Text Search. Enter **ts <return>**

Select drive A. Enter **a**

This time, don't bother with an output file. Enter **<return>**

Specify the text to search for by entering **bytes free <return>**

The program will now find the data in the erased area of the disk. To stop the program enter **[Ctrl Scroll Lock]**

The Text Search program is closely related to the main Norton Utilities program. The Text Search is very helpful in locating text on the disk. This makes it a valuable tool in figuring out where data to be unerased is located, if it exists.

The combination of Text Search and the main Norton Utilities program allows you to have some fun with the programs that display text messages. You can use the programs to modify the text of various prompts and messages. This ability can be beneficial in making prompts more understandable to people using your system.

[What follows shows how programs can be modified by using the Norton Utilities program. CHANGING PARTS OF PROGRAMS CAN POSSIBLY DAMAGE OR DESTROY THE PROGRAM. Always work with a copy of the original program. Keep in mind that a program modified in any way may fail to function properly.]

To get the idea of how this might be done, you can take one of the standard DOS programs. For example, the DISKCOPY program is used to make duplicates of diskettes. The program refers to two disks, the *source* and *target* disks. It might be simpler to understand if, instead of *source*, the prompt read *original*.

First, take a look at the current display of the program. Enter

a:diskcopy a: a: <return>

The screen shows:

```
Insert source diskette in drive A:
Strike any key when ready
```

Your task is to change *source* to *original* in the DISKCOPY program. First, cancel the command you have just entered. Enter **[Ctrl Scroll Lock]**

Next use the Text Search program to locate the places in the DISK-COPY.COM where the word *source* is stored. Enter

ts < return > f a:diskcopy.com < return > source < return >

The screen will display:

```
Searching DISKCOPY.COM
Found at byte offset 1,622
```

That is the place in the text you want to change. Note the exact location, byte offset 1,622. Continue the search to find any other instances of the same word. Enter **y**
The screen displays:

```
Found at byte offset 1,769
```

This is another location to alter, 1,769. Enter **y**
The program completes its search of the file. You now know that there are two places to change to make the word *source* become *original*.
The next step is to use the Norton Utilities main program to change the text in the DISKCOPY file. Enter **nu a: < return >**
Select the file to work with. Enter **1 3**
Use the arrow keys to highlight DISKCOPY.COM. Press **< return >**
Look at the bottom of the screen. The program displays the name of the currently selected file:

```
Currently selected:  File: DISKCOPY.COM
Drive A:  Directory: root directory
```

Now use the Display Contents option to display the contents of the file. Enter **2 5**
The Norton Utilities program displays the contents of the first sector of the DISKCOPY.COM file. A sector consists of 512 bytes. The top line on the screen tells you the filename, the sector number and the cursor position relative to the beginning of the sector.

```
DISKCOPY.COM sector 123 in hex format        Cursor at offset 0, hex 0
```

In this example, the first sector of the file begins at sector 123 of the disk.

The Text Search program told you that the word *source* appears following the 1,622nd byte in this file. Your task is to find that position in the file.

How will you do it? Although Norton Utilities makes many complicated computer functions quite simple, there are times when you still need to put a little brain power to work on a problem.

In the current mode, the cursor position indicated at the top of the screen begins at 0 and continues to 511. Each sector viewed resets the counter back to 0. You need to locate the 1,622nd byte from the beginning of the file. This can be done by figuring out how many sectors you have to skip in order to bring up the right one on the screen.

Because each sector has 512 bytes, you can divide 1,622 by 512 (1,622/512 = 3.168).

This means that you must skip the next three sectors to locate the one that contains the word *source*. The [PgDn] key will advance the display to the next sector in the file. Enter **[PgDn]**

The display now shows the next sector, in this example sector 124. Enter **[PgDn]** (2 times)

The cursor is now positioned at the first byte in the third sector of the disk. If you multiply 512 by 3 you will calculate that the cursor is located at offset 1,536. How will you get to 1,622?

First subtract 1,536 from 1,622. This tells you that you need to move the cursor to offset 86 of this sector.

Use the arrow keys to move the cursor to offset 86.

Now switch the cursor to the text display side of the screen. Enter <tab>

The cursor should land exactly on the *s* in the word *source*. Of course you probably could have found the word *source* by simply looking for it on the display. Working exactly by the numbers illustrates how precisely you can locate specific data if you need to do so.

[In some instances, your modfiications will not be to text information. For example, many of WordStar's defaults and setups can be changed by directly modifying the WS.COM file. MicroSoft Word provides instructions about the bytes that control printer functions in their PRD printer control files.

The Norton Utilities program is a great help if you need to perform these types of operations. These files will not be text at all. You will have to go strictly by the numbers in these files.]

Now you can enter your substitute text. Enter

ORIGINAL DISK <space> <space>

As you typed, Norton Utiltiies entered the text on the right side of the screen and the equivalent hex numbers on the left side of the screen.

[Modifications of text strings done in this manner require that any new text fit into the space in the file occupied by the old text. This means that you can change the text but not add or delete. The text displayed will almost always be the same length. All you can do is change the specific characters that are displayed. You cannot, by this method, increase or decrease the amount of the display or its position on the screen.]

The next occurrence of the word *source* in the file is at 1,769. If you subtract 1,536 (512×3) from 1,769 you find out that the word *source* should appear at offset 233 of this sector. You may have already spotted it.

Use the arrow keys to position the cursor at offset 233.

In this case you can only change six characters. Enter **ORIGIN**

The changes you have made have been made in the internal memory of the computer only. You now must decide if you want the data written on the disk to be changed. Enter <**Esc**>

The program displays the following screen. This screen appears *only* if the sector is modified.

```
        Save or Discard Changes Made to Data
  You have made changes to the disk data in memory
    (Changes are made and shown highlighted when
     data is displayed in the hexadecimal format)
  You may now:
     Write the changed data, saving it on the disk
     Ignore the changes, leaving the disk data unchanged
     Return to review the changed data
  Press W, I, or R ...
```

In this example you want to write the changes to the sector on the disk. Enter **w**

You can now leave the Norton Utilities program. Enter

<**Esc**> (twice)

The test of this procedure will be the prompt displayed when the DISK-COPY program is run. Enter **a:diskcopy a: a:** <**return**>

The screen displays:

```
Insert ORIGINAL DISK    in drive A:
Strike any key when ready
```

The prompt now displays the text you inserted into the file.

4.15.   Systems Utilities

The next group of programs described provide functions that are not directly related to files. The simplest program is BEEP.COM.

The BEEP program has one very simple function. Whenever it is executed the computer sounds a tone on its speaker. Enter

beep < return >

The purpose of BEEP is to provide a means to create an audio feedback during batch files. The feedback can be used as a warning or to signal you by sound when a task has been completed. This allows you to be out of sight of the monitor display and still keep track of the computer. Create a simple example. Enter

copy con: sound.bat < return > dir < return > beep < return >
beep < return > beep[F6] < return >

The batch file will list the directory and BEEP three times. Enter
sound < return >
The directory is listed and the beeps are sounded.

[The beeping of the computer is an interesting example of how technology evolves. The computer keyboard and ASCII system were originally designed for use with teletype machines. You will often see references to "teletype-like" printers in word processing programs. Many have a printer choice called TTY (Teletype).

One curious leftover from the teletype devices is the BELL. Some keyboards still label the G key with the word BELL, even though the IBM PC does not. The BELL served the same function on a teletype machine that the BEEP does on a computer. It was an audio signal that something important was happening on the teletype machine. When important news stories were sent over the teletype, the BELL characters were sent first to alert the people in the newsroom that there was a special story being sent. The more important the story, the more bells. For example, the death of a president was considered a seven-bell story.

As a vestige of this, the combination of [Ctrl g] will still sound a tone on the IBM PC. To prove this, create another batch file called sound1. Enter
copy con: = sound1.bat < return >

Enter **dir** <**return**>
Next enter the control-g combination [**Ctrl g**]
The characters ^G appear on the screen. Enter [**Ctrl g**][**Ctrl g**]
Close the file. Enter [**F6**] <**return**>
Now execute the program. Enter **sound1** <**return**>
The same beep is sounded as is produced by the BEEP program.]

4.16.   Testing the Disk

This program is designed to test the data storage areas of a disk to determine if they can be read successfully. The purpose of this program is to locate sectors that potentially can create a problem and mark those areas as unusable for data storage.

Disks can fail for a number of reasons. The purpose of testing the disk is to find the sectors, if any, that cannot be used and prevent them from being used by programs.

There are three conditions that Disk Test can reveal.

1. A sector of a disk is unreadable. However, the sector has already been marked as a *bad sector*. The marking is done by DOS when the disk is formatted or at a later time by the Disk Test program. In this instance there is nothing to worry about. Since DOS knows that the sector is "bad," it will simply ignore the sector when writing data. The only disadvantage is that you have less space available to you on the disk.
2. A sector is found that is unreadable. The sector is not part of a file but has not been marked as a bad sector. Once again, there is nothing to worry about. The bad sector is unused and therefore does not affect any of the the files on the disk. The Disk Test program can be used to mark this sector so that DOS will know to avoid using it.
3. A sector is unreadable and is part of an existing file. This is a problem. The Disk Test program will indicate which files have this problem. You then must attempt to recover the data as best you can.

The Disk Test program does not fix disk problems but warns you of their existence. The major function of this program is preventive. You should run the Disk Test on important disks at regular intervals. If you are using hard disks, you should test the entire disk regularly to avoid data problems.

[The purpose of Disk Test and the DOS program CHKDSK are the same. However, they go about their work in different ways. The Norton Utilities Disk Test program is designed to read all of the sectors on a disk and determine if they can be read properly. The DOS

CHKDSK command focuses on the relationship between files and the allocations of space made to them in the file allocation table. It is a good idea to use *both* programs to determine the status of a given disk. You can never be too careful with your data.]

Since the Disk Test program reads all the sectors on a given disk, it takes some time to work. The larger the disk space, the longer it will take. In order to give you more control over the program three options are provided:

1. /D—Disk Test—This test checks all the sectors of the disk, beginning with sector 2, until the entire disk has been examined. If errors are found they are reported by the sector number. Example: DT A:/D
2. /F—File Only—This test looks at only those sectors that are in use by files. The purpose of this test is to determine if any of the files contain sectors that are unreadable. This test reveals problem with existing files. Example: DT A:/F
3. /B—Both—This option performs the disk test first and then the file test. Example: DT A:/B

If you do not specify any of the options when you enter the command, Disk Test will display the following prompt:

```
Select DISK test, FILE test, or BOTH
Press D, F, or B...
```

To see how a Disk Test is performed, enter **dt a:/b <return>**
In most cases no errors will be reported.

```
..Errors message for disk testing
```

4.17. Line Print

The Line Print program is used to transfer data from a disk file to the printer. The assumption is made by the Line Print program that the data stored in the selected file is ASCII standard. The program cannot be used to print non-text files. The Line Print program is not a word processing program. Its main feature is that the program can automatically number each line as it prints.

Line Print has the following parameters:

1. *What to Print?* You must specify the files that are to be printed. You can enter any valid DOS filename including drive specification and path. Examples:

```
lp read.me
lp c:\dos\screen.bat
```

You can also enter a DOS wildcard and all files that qualify will be printed. Example: lp r*.*

2. *Output Device.* The second parameter is the destination of the output of the Line Print command. The default is to send the output to the printer. However, the file can be redirected to a disk file or another output device, such as a modem, if desired.

As an example of how Line Print functions, print out the READ.ME file that comes with the Norton Utilities program. Enter

lp read.me < return >

Note that the Line Print program adds a line at the top of the file that prints the filename, systems date, and page number.

The Line Print program also contains options that control the format of the output.

1. /N—This option numbers the lines as they are printed. Example:
   lp read.me/n (prints file with line numbers)
2. /Tn—This option sets the top margin of each page at the specified number of lines. The default value is 6 lines (one inch) that includes the page heading line. Examples:
   lp read.me/t3 (prints file with top margin of 3 lines)
   lp read.me/n/t10 (prints file with a top margin of 10 lines and numbers the lines)
3. /Bn—Changes the number of lines printed as a bottom margin. The default is 6. Example:
   lp read.me/t0/b0 (prints the file with no top or bottom margin. This places the maximum amount of text on a page.)
4. /Ln—Changes the left margin setting. The left margin is the number of spaces added to the left side of each line when the file is printed. The default is 6 spaces. Example:
   lp read.me/l10 (prints file with a left margin of 10 characters)
5. /Rn—Changes the right margin. The default is 4. Example:
   lp read.me/l0/r0 (prints file with no margins. The lines are 85 columns wide based on the width setting.)
6. /Pn—Sets the starting page number at a specific page. Example:
   lp read.me/p10 (prints first page as page 10)
   lp read.me/p5/n (prints first page as 5 and numbers lines)

7. /Hn—Determines the page length in lines. Normal spacing on computer printers is 6 lines per vertical inch. The default value for page length is 66 lines, i.e., 11 inches. Example:
lp read.me/h42 (prints file on pages 7 inches long)

8. /Wn—Determines the page width in columns. The default value is 85 columns. If the printer is printing at 10 pitch, this corresponds to 8.5 inches. Example:
lp read.me/h49/w140 (prints file on legal-sized paper turned lengthwise, 8.5 by 14)

9. /80 or /132—This setting is used to place the printer into compressed or normal print modes. It is important to remember that when the printer is placed into compressed print mode it will remain compressed until you enter the /80 code to return the print to its normal pitch. After the first /132 command all printing will be compressed even if you don't use the /132 option. The default is 80 column mode. Example:
lp read.me/132/n (prints the file in compressed mode and numbers the lines)

[The compression is based on common printer codes such as those used by the Epson family of printers. Of course not all printers will conform to this standard.]

10. /Sn—This option sets the line spacing. The default is single-spaced type. Example:
lp read.me/s2/n (prints the file double-spaced and numbered)

[In the above example, only the text lines are numbered. The extra lines used for spacing are not numbered.]

4.18.   Screen Attributes

The Screen Attributes program is used to change the attributes of the screen display. If you have a color monitor, this means that you can select color combinations. If you have a monochrome screen display, then you will be able to select an attribute that can be displayed on a monochrome screen, such as reverse video and blinking.

The Screen Attributes program will function *only* if the ANSI device drive has been installed. If you need more information about the ANSI system and how it is installed, see Chapter 2.31.

The Screen Attributes program sets three types of characteristics for the screen:

1. *Main Setting.* The main settings are NORMAL, REVERSE, and UNDER-LINE. These settings are mutually exclusive. While it is possible for the IBM

PC monochrome displays to show REVERSE UNDERLINED text, Norton Utilities will show one or the other but not both. Generally speaking this is not much of a shortcoming.

2. *Prefix*. A prefix can be used with any of the main settings. The are two prefixes, BRIGHT (or BOLD) and BLINKING.

3. *Colors*. Colors apply *only* to computers with color/graphics adapters and color monitors. If you attach a single-color, composite video monitor (e.g., Amdek 300G) to a color/graphics card, the colors will appear as patterns. Many of the patterns will make the text very difficult or impossible to read.

The standard IBM PC color graphics boards generate eight distinct colors: BLACK, BLUE, GREEN, CYAN, RED, MAGENTA, YELLOW, WHITE. The colors can be displayed as BRIGHT colors, making a total of 16 colors.

[The actual colors displayed may not match your expectations based on their names. For example, YELLOW appears closer to what most people call brown. Real yellow is produced by using BRIGHT YELLOW. If you display WHITE vs. BRIGHT WHITE you would probably call WHITE gray because it is much less intense than the BRIGHT WHITE.]

To see how the Screen Attributes program affects the screen display, enter **sa reverse < return >**

The screen is changed to dark letters on a white background. Enter **sa normal < return >**

The display is set back to the original. If you have a color monitor you can try some of the following settings. Enter **sa bright yellow on blue < return >**

That is the setting I use on my computer. Enter **sa blue on red < return >**

To return to the usual setting, enter **sa normal < return >**

NORMAL on a color monitor is white on black. While it is possible to create a background on the IBM PC that uses a bright color as the background, the BRIGHT setting affects only the foreground color. You cannot enter **sa blue on bright yellow < return >**

The Screen Attributes program will display an error message like the one below if you do.

```
            Invalid parameters
            Examples: SA NORMAL
                      SA REVERSE
                      SA YELLOW ON BLUE
                      SA BRIGHT GREEN
```

[Color monitors have some odd reactions to commands. For example, enter the following command to set the display into UNDERLINE mode: **sa underline < return >**

This command creates a screen full of lines on a monochrome monitor, but on a color monitor the UNDERLINE mode is displayed as blue letters on a black background.

You may have noticed that same effect if you use word processing programs like Multi-Mate that underline on screen. On color monitors the underlined text appears simply as blue, with no underline.

The reason for this has to do with the fact that monochrome and color displays use a different size matrix to display the characters. On a monochrome screen each character is created with a grid 9 dots wide by 14 dots long. A color card creates characters in an 8 by 8 grid.

The monochrome grid allows room below the character to display an underline. The color grid is too small to display the underline without overwriting part of the character. This also explains why monochrome displays are easier to read than color screens. Another computer oddity is the idea of BRIGHT BLACK. In normal terms black is the absence of light. However, due to the nature of video displays you will find that the two commands below display the text in a slightly different manner:

sa bright black on white < return >
sa black on white < return >

On most screens, the BRIGHT BLACK will not be as dark as simply using BLACK.]

4.19.   Screen Attributes in Batch Files

The Screen Attributes program can add a bit of zest to batch files by using color and/or screen attributes to communicate messages to the user. To see this program work, create a batch file that uses the Screen Attributes program. Enter

copy con: screen.bat < return >
echo off < return >
sa reverse blinking < return >
echo ***** WARNING ******** < return >
echo Computers can be Dangerous to Your Health
[F6] < return >

Run the batch, enter **screen < return >**

The message will be displayed in an emphatic manner. To return the screen to normal, enter **sa normal < return >**

The Screen Attributes program has one option, /N. The /N is used to exclude the screen border from the color change. The screen border is the area of the screen in which text display does not take place. Enter **sa reverse/n < return >**

The screen reverses video only in the text area. The screen border remains unaffected. Return to normal. Enter **sa normal < return >**

[The Screen Attributes program requires longer command lines than do most of the other programs in the Norton Utilities collection. You can cut down on the length of the entry by using only the first three letters of the parameters. For example, the command SA REVERSE BLINKING could be entered as: **sa rev bli < return >**
If you wanted to enter a color command you might have to type:
sa bright magenta on yellow < return >
This could be shortened to: **sa bri mag on yel < return >**]

4.20.   System Information

The System Information program, SI.COM, does not change files or systems attributes. Its only purpose is to display information about the computer system. This information tells you some interesting and useful facts about your system that would be very hard to find out without this program.

The System Information program is the simplest of the Norton Utilities collection in that it has no parameters or options. To get the information, enter **si < return >**

The screen will display something like this:

```
SI-System Information, Version 3.00, (C) Copyright 1984, Peter Norton
IBM/PC
Built-in BIOS programs dated Wednesday, October 27, 1982
Operating under DOS 2.10
3 logical disk drives, A: through C:
The operating system reports 640K of memory
A test of random access memory (RAM) finds:
  640K from hex paragraph 0000 to A000
   32K from hex paragraph B800 to C000
(some may be phantom memory)
BIOS signature found at hex paragraph C800
Programs are loaded at hex paragraph 1C97
following 117,104 bytes of system memory

Computing performance index relative to IBM/PC: 1.0
```

The information breaks down into the following:

1. *Name of the computer.* In the example, IBM/PC was displayed.
2. *Built-in BIOS programs.* This is a very important piece of information. It tells you when the built-in, hard-wired ROM programs that are part of your computer were created. As your computer gets older, you will find that new products designed for later model computers are incompatible. Knowing the date of the BIOS programs can tell a manufacturer whether or not their product will run on your computer.

   [BIOS upgrades are available for some computers. These upgrades allow newer products like boards and hard disks to operate in older computers. While not expensive, these upgrades are often hard to find, since they are considered spare parts and not stocked by most dealers.]

3. *Operating under.* This tells you the version of DOS running in the computer at the moment.
4. *Logical disk drives.* This tells you the number of drives DOS is working with. The term *logical* refers to the fact that DOS need not actually have a physical disk drive in the computer for each logical drive it reports. If you created a RAMDRIVE by allocating part of the internal memory to function like a disk drive, DOS would consider that a logical drive.
5. *System reports memory.* The total amount of internal memory available in the computer. If this figure shows a different number than you expect, there may be something wrong with your computer.
6. The remainder of the information is quite technical. It explains details about how the memory is organized. This information is mainly for programmers, and a full explanation is beyond the scope of this book.
7. *Computing performance index relative to IBM/PC.* The final item on the display is the result of a test performed by the System Information program. The test compares the processing speed of your computer to a typical IBM PC. A value of 1.0 indicates that the computer is equal to the PC. A lower value indicates that the computer is slower, while a higher value shows an improvement over the PC.

4.21. Time Mark

The Time Mark program, TM.COM, is used to time the actions of programs or commands. Time Mark can be used in three ways:

1. Used by itself, Time Mark displays the current time and date as calculated by the system's clock.

   [The system's clock depends upon you to enter the "real" date and time when the computer is first turned on. Otherwise the system's clock begins at zero. If you have a battery-powered clock in the computer, you must use the AUTOEXEC.BAT batch file to set the time when the computer boots.]

2. START. The Time Mark program can act as a stop watch. The START parameter starts a timer that begins to run when the command is issued. The Time Mark program can operate up to four timers simultaneously.
3. STOP. This parameter displays the current time in one of the four timers. Despite the name of the parameter, the timer will continue to run. If you enter another STOP, the accumulated time will be displayed. When another START command is issued for the timer, it will be recycled back to zero.

Enter **tm ‹return›**
The current date and time are displayed as in the example below:

```
8:20 pm, Monday, December 2, 1985
```

To start a timer, enter **tm start ‹return›**
The time and date are displayed. Wait a few moments and enter **tm stop ‹return›**
The time and date are displayed and the elapsed time is shown as well:

```
8:20 pm, Monday, December 2, 1985
            1 minute, 10 seconds
```

Next, enter **tm stop ‹return›**
Notice that the time elapsed has increased. This indicates that the STOP command does not turn off the timer but merely displays the elapsed time.

4.22. Options with Time Mark

Time Mark has the following options:

1. /Cn—This option is used to select a timer. The *n* is a number from 1 to 4. The option can be used with both the START and STOP commands. Enter **tm start/c2 ‹return›**
   Now display the time. Enter **tm stop ‹return› tm stop/c2 ‹return›**
   Note that the times are different. If you do not specify a timer with the /Cn option, Time Mark uses C1.

2. /N—This option suppresses the display of the date and time and shows only the elapsed time display. Enter **tm stop/c2/n<return>**

3. /L—This option places the Time Mark display on the left side of the screen as opposed to its usual position on the right side of the screen. Enter

tm stop/c2/l<return>
tm stop/l/n<return>

4.23.   Volume Label

What is a volume label and what purpose does it serve? A volume label is simply a name that you give to a disk. The purpose of volume labels goes back to larger computer systems in which a variety of disk or tape drives were used. The volume label identified the name of the disk or tape to the user.

On small computers volume labels are of very little practical importance. However, they can help you recognize a disk without having to read the entire directory.

The volume label of a disk is displayed when a directory listing is displayed. Example:

```
Volume in drive B is UTILITIES
Directory of  B:\
```

In DOS, version 2, volume labels can be created when a disk is formatted by using the /V parameter with the FORMAT command. However, after a disk is formatted, DOS provides no way to add or revise the label. That is the purpose of the Volume Label command.

Volume labels perform no logical function. They affect no commands or files.

[DOS, version 3, provides a command LABEL which performs the same function as VL.COM with the exception that all labels entered with LABEL are converted to upper case.]

To change or create a volume label enter **vl a:<return>**

The Norton Utilities displays:

```
VL-Volume Label, Version 3.00, (C) Copyright 1984, Peter Norton
No old label.
Enter volume label, up to 11 characters,
or nothing for no label: "            "
```

Enter **sample disk** **< return >**

Note that your letters were automatically capitalized. To enter lower case letters you need to use the /L option. Example: vl a:/L

The program displays the message:

```
        Putting new label into place.
```

To see the label enter **dir a:/w**

```
        Volume in drive A is SAMPLE DISK
        Directory of  A:\
```

4.24.   Security

Norton Utilities' ability to *unerase* files indicates that erasing a file or a group of files does not prevent the recovery of all or some of the data. In some instances you will want to make sure that all the data has been cleared from a file or a disk for purposes of security and confidentiality.

Norton Utilities provides two programs that make secure erasure of data stored on disks. They are WIPEFILE.COM and WIPEDISK.COM.

Both of these programs go farther than the DOS commands DEL and ERASE. DEL and ERASE affect only the directory and file allocation table. The data stored on the disk is left intact until new information is written into the sectors formerly occupied by the erased files. This means that it is possible to view the data even after it has been erased.

WIPEFILE and WIPEDISK actually rewrite the sectors on the disk. They type over all the characters by entering zeros. This means that when a disk or file is wiped, the information is gone forever.

[Data encryption allows you to make copies of files that are coded to prevent unauthorized users from reading those files. Both SuperKey and SmartKey provide this feature. Note that to complete the data security process, you can use WIPEFILE or WIPEDISK to eradicate the original file.]

WIPEDISK and WIPEFILE are very dangerous programs in that their effect cannot be reversed. Take caution when you consider using these commands that you have correctly chosen the files or disk that will be affected.

4.25.   Wiping a Disk Clear

The DISKWIPE command is used to eradicate the contents of an entire disk. Unlike ERASE (DEL) or even FORMAT, DISKWIPE destroys data stored in every portion of the disk. Naturally, exteme caution should be used when working with this program. There are some built-in safeguards that help you prevent mistakes.

1. You must specify a drive to wipe. The DOS FORMAT command will function without a drive specification. For example, if you were working on a hard disk, drive C, and entered FORMAT < return >, DOS would proceed to format the hard disk, thereby wiping out all the files stored on the hard disk.

   If you fail to specify a disk with the WIPEDISK program, it will fail to operate. For example, if you were working on a hard disk, drive C, and entered WIPEDISK < return >, the program would display:

   ```
   WD-Wipe Disk, Version 3.00, (C) Copyright 1984, Peter Norton

   Invalid drive specification
   ```

2. The WIPEDISK program works in the opposite direction of the FORMAT command. The DOS FORMAT command begins by changing the most frequently used sectors of the disk first. This means that if you begin a format command and use the [Ctrl Scroll Lock] (BREAK) command to stop the formatting, it is certain that some data has been lost. This data usually includes the file directory, which makes data recovery quite difficult.

   WIPEDISK begins with the least used portions of the disk and works backwards towards the directory. Thus if you use [Ctrl Scroll Lock] to stop the program, you can still use any data that has not actually been wiped out. The program scans the keyboard for the entry of the [Ctrl Scroll Lock] command after each sector is wiped.

If you want to try out this command, place a disk in drive A that contains data that you do not want or need any longer. Warning: make sure that the disk you have chosen is *really* unneeded.

Enter **wipedisk a: \<return\>**
The program displays:

```
WD-Wipe Disk, Version 3.00, (C) Copyright 1984, Peter Norton
Wiping the disk in drive A:
DANGER! This will wipe-out the entire disk.
Proceed (Y/N) ?
```

Enter **y**
The program displays the sector number as each sector is wiped out. When the program is complete you can use the Norton Utilities main program to see what was done to the disk. Enter **nu a: \<return\>**

Pick a sector to examine. Enter **1 5 30 \<return\>**

Display the contents of that sector. Enter **2 5**

The sector looks like this:

```
Sector 30 in data cluster 25 in hex format  Cursor at offset 0, hex 0
00000000    00000000    00000000    00000000    00000000    00000000
00000000    00000000    00000000    00000000    00000000    00000000
00000000    00000000    00000000    00000000    00000000    00000000
00000000    00000000    00000000    00000000    00000000    00000000
00000000    00000000    00000000    00000000    00000000    00000000
00000000    00000000    00000000    00000000    00000000    00000000
00000000    00000000    00000000    00000000    00000000    00000000
00000000    00000000    00000000    00000000    00000000    00000000
00000000    00000000    00000000    00000000    00000000    00000000
00000000    00000000    00000000    00000000    00000000    00000000
00000000    00000000    00000000    00000000    00000000    00000000
00000000    00000000    00000000    00000000    00000000    00000000
00000000    00000000    00000000    00000000    00000000    00000000
00000000    00000000    00000000    00000000    00000000    00000000
00000000    00000000    00000000    00000000    00000000    00000000
00000000    00000000    00000000    00000000    00000000    00000000
00000000    00000000    00000000    00000000    00000000    00000000
00000000    00000000    00000000    00000000    00000000    00000000
00000000    00000000    00000000    00000000    00000000    00000000
00000000    00000000    00000000    00000000    00000000    00000000
00000000    00000000    00000000    00000000    00000000    00000000
00000000    00000000    Press Enter for help    ........
```

Exit the Norton Utilities program. Enter **\<Esc\>** (3 times)

4.26.   Wiping Out Individual Files

The WIPEFILE program functions in the same way as the WIPEDISK program except that it blanks the contents of individual files one at a time or in groups. WIPEFILE can also be used to perform a deleting function such as that of the DOS commands ERASE and DEL. WIPEFILE allows you to select which functions—data wipe out, deleteing, or both—are to be performed.

[Unlike WIPEDISK, WIPEFILE does not delete files as they are wiped clear. When WIPEFILE is used to wipe out the contents of a file, the file remains part of the directory just as it was when it contained data. The only difference is that instead of containing data, the file contains all zeros. Therefore, when you wipe out files, the directory of the disk will appear unchanged. You will only be able to tell that the file has been wiped out if you try to access the data.]

The WIPEFILE program has three options:

/D—This option tells WIPEFILE to delete the files from the disk directory as they are wiped clean of data. Example: WIPEFILE *.*/D

/N—This option places WIPEFILE into a DELETE ONLY mode. This means that selected files will be deleted from the disk but not wiped clean. The effect is exactly the same as the DOS ERASE or DEL commands. Example: WIPEFILE *.*/N

    The advantage of this option over the ERASE or DEL commands is that the WIPEFILE program will display the names of each file and allow you to select the ones you want to delete.

/P—The PAUSE option tells WIPEFILE to pause as each filename is displayed and ask for confirmation for each file. Example: WIPEFILE *.*/P

[Even if you don't use the /P option, the WIPEFILE program will always ask you if you want confirmation when it starts.]

The WIPEFILE command *requires* a file specfication. The file specification can be any valid DOS wildcard or any valid DOS filename. Examples are:

wipefile *.*—On a floppy disk this would select all the files on the disk. On a hard disk this would select all the files in the current directory.

wipefile a:—This specification would select all the files on the disk in drive A.

wipefile *.com—This selects all the files that end in a COM extension.

wipefile \dos—This specification selects all the files in the DOS directory on the active drive. This type of specification is used with hard disks that have multiple directories.

In order to work with WIPEFILE you should place a disk in drive A that contains files that you no longer want or need. The disk used in the examples is a copy of the PC DOS systems disk provided with an IBM PC (Version 2.1).

Enter **wipefile a:*.com < return >**

The program displays the following:

```
WF-Wipe Files, Version 3.00, (C) Copyright 1984, Peter Norton
Over-writing Files
Proceed without pausing (Y/N) ?
```

The display tells you that you have selected to overwrite the data in the files. You are now asked to decide if you want to be prompted for each file. Entering **n** tells WIPEFILE to stop and ask you about each of the slected files before it is wiped clean. Entering **y** tells WIPEFILE to automatically wipe out all the selected files without pausing. Enter **n**

The first file encountered is a hidden READ-ONLY file, the IBMBIO.DOS. As discussed previously (see Chapter 4.7), DOS can assign attributes to files. One of these attributes tells DOS whether or not a file is a READ-WRITE file (normal) or a READ-ONLY file (protected). The purpose of READ-ONLY files is to prevent accidental erasure. In this example, you see that the WIPEFILE program displays a special message when it encounters a READ-ONLY file.

```
IBMBIO.COM  Read-only file; remove read-only restriction (Y/N) ?
```

You are given the choice to remove the READ-ONLY status and therefore wipe out the contents of the file or not. In this case you will leave this file as it is. Enter **n**

The program displays the message *IBMBIO.COM Skipped*. The next file is also a READ-ONLY file. Skip this one by entering **n**

The next file is a normal file. The program simply asks you if you want to wipe out this file. Enter **y**

The program wipes out the contents of the file and displays the next file selected. To stop the program at this point, enter **[Ctrl Scroll Lock]**

The system's prompt appears. This indicates that the program has been terminated. List the directory of the disk in drive A. Enter **dir a:*.com < return >**

Note that the file COMMAND.COM, which you had selected to be wiped out, is still listed on the directory along with the other COM files.

The size of the file, 17,792 bytes remains unchanged. The only difference is that the file contains all zeros now.

[The file size shown for the COMMAND.COM is for DOS 2.10. Other versions of DOS have different size COMMAND.COM files. For example, DOS 1.1 has a COM-MAND.COM file of 4,949 bytes while DOS 3.1 has a COMMAND.COM file of 23,210. New versions of DOS have been designed to add new features, and larger command files are required.]

As explained earlier, the reason that the wiped-out file still appears in the directory is that WIPEFILE only changes the information inside the file. It does not automatically delete the filename from the directory. If you wanted to wipe out and delete at the same time you would use the /D option as in the command: **wipefile a:*.com/d<return>**

To delete only, i.e., to perform the same action as the DOS ERASE and DEL commands, use the /N option as shown: **wipefile a:*.com/n<return>**

5.

Recovering Erased or Damaged Files

One of the main reasons for learning about programs like Norton Utilities is to learn how to recover, as much as possible, erased or damaged files.

Recovering files is part science and part art. Many factors determine the success of the recovery process. The Norton Utilities program provides some of the basic tools by which you can attempt to successfully locate and recover whole or partial files.

5.1. What Erasing a File Really Means

The idea of unerasing a file many seem like a contradiction in terms. It also implies that the ERASE or DEL commands do not completely eradicate the information in a file. This is true. You may have noticed that it takes a very much shorter amount of time to erase files than it does to save them. To understand how this can be so, you should start by understanding what erasing and unerasing means in the first place. When a file is erased with the DEL or ERASE commands, the data that was stored in the file is not actually destroyed. The only change that takes place is that the entries in the disk directory and file allocation table for that file are altered to indicate that the operating system can reuse the space that was formerly occupied by that file for storage of data from other files.

When you erase a file, all of the data is still intact. However, if you add new files or add data to old files on the disk, you may overwrite some or all of the data that once belonged to the erased file. Whether or not a file can be recovered depends upon how much the disk has been altered since the file was erased.

[Formatting a disk is destructive to the majority of the information on that disk. If you format a disk that previously contained information, the information is unrecoverable. Erasing all the files, DEL *.*, is not nearly as destructive as formatting a disk.]

If you begin recovery before new data has been written to the disk, your chances of recovering the file are very good. However, this is not always the case. Recovery of files from a disk that has been written to after erasure is a hit or miss operation.

If the file contained text information that you would recognize, you can use the text search facility of Norton Utilities to find the text and recover all or part of the file.

5.2.   Setup

In this example, you can use a copy of your DOS systems disk and a copy of the Norton Utilities program.

Floppy Systems: Place the DOS disk in drive A and the Norton Utilities disk in drive B.
Hard Drive Systems: Load the Norton Utilities programs into an appropriate directory on your hard disk . For example, you might create a directory called Norton Utilities by entering **md\nu <return>**

Then copy the file from the original Norton Utilities disk into that directory. Enter **copy a:*.* c:\nu <return>**

Make the Norton Utilities directory the active directory. Enter **cd\nu <return>**

Then place a copy of the MS DOS disk in drive A. Make drive A the active drive. Enter **a: <return>**

[You can make a copy of the DOS diskette even if you have only a single floppy drive. Use the DOS DISKCOPY command. Enter **diskcopy a: a:**
    The program will prompt you to place the source and target disks into the drive.]

Make sure that you have changed the default drive to A, (the A> prompt will appear on the screen). If you are working on drive C or B, entering A: <return> will change the default drive to A.

5.3. Erasing a File

In order to learn how to recover a file, you will need to erase a file first. Then you can use the Norton Utilities program to recover the file that was erased. In this example, you will erase the CHKDSK.COM program from the disk in drive A and then recover it.

The first task is to erase the file. Enter **del chkdsk.com < return >**

You have now erased the format command. To test this fact, enter **chkdsk < return >**

The computer displays the message *Bad command or filename*. This tells you that DOS cannot find the CHKDSK program. This makes sense because you have just erased it.

The Norton Utilities program enables you to see quite clearly exactly what happened when you erased the file. Start the Norton Utilities program. Enter

b:nu < return >   (floppy disk systems)
c:nu < return >   (hard disk systems)

When the program comes up move to menu 2.1.5 by entering **2 1 5**

This menu allows you to select a specific sector of the disk space to look at. The sector you are interested in is the sector that contains the directory information. On a 360K floppy disk that sector is number 5. Enter **5 < return >**

The display should look like this:

```
Sector 5 in root directory shown in directory format

Filename Ext     Size      Date       Time  Cluster Attributes
         .
IBMBIO   COM    4,736 Thu Oct 20 83 12:00 pm      2 Read-Only Hidden System Ar
IBMDOS   COM   17,024 Thu Oct 20 83 12:00 pm      7 Read-Only Hidden System Ar
COMMAND  COM   17,792 Thu Oct 20 83 12:00 pm     24 Archive
ANSI     SYS    1,664 Thu Oct 20 83 12:00 pm     42 Archive
FORMAT   COM    6,912 Thu Oct 20 83 12:00 pm     44 Archive
?HKDSK   COM    6,400 Thu Oct 20 83 12:00 pm     51 Archive
SYS      COM    1,680 Thu Oct 20 83 12:00 pm     58 Archive
DISKCOPY COM    2,576 Thu Oct 20 83 12:00 pm     60 Archive
DISKCOMP COM    2,188 Thu Oct 20 83 12:00 pm     63 Archive
COMP     COM    2,534 Thu Oct 20 83 12:00 pm     66 Archive
EDLIN    COM    4,608 Thu Oct 20 83 12:00 pm     69 Archive
MODE     COM    3,139 Thu Oct 20 83 12:00 pm     74 Archive
FDISK    COM    6,369 Thu Oct 20 83 12:00 pm     78 Archive
BACKUP   COM    3,687 Thu Oct 20 83 12:00 pm     85 Archive
RESTORE  COM    4,003 Thu Oct 20 83 12:00 pm     89 Archive
PRINT    COM    4,608 Thu Oct 20 83 12:00 pm     93 Archive
         .
       Filenames beginning with '?' indicate erased entries
```

In the middle of the display there is an entry that begins with a ?.

```
?HKDSK   COM    6,400 Thu Oct 20 83 12:00 pm    51 Archive
```

This indicates that the file is erased. Note that all the information about the file is still intact. Only the first character of the filename has been altered. That is what happens when a file is erased.

This raises one very crucial point about recovery of erased files that must be stressed again. A file can usually be recovered completely immediately after it has been erased. However, if new information has been written to the disk, part or all of the space formerly occupied by the erased file may have been overwritten by new data. Any data that has been written over cannot be recovered.

[If you do not see the ?HKDSK entry on your screen you need to move to the next sector. Enter **[Pg Dn]**

The next section of the directory will appear. Continue this until you locate the erased file.]

5.4.   The Hex View

You can gain an even clearer view of what happens when a file is erased by changing the Norton Utilities view to the Hex mode. Enter **< return >** (2 times)

The screen displays:

```
Sector 5 in root directory in hex format    Cursor at
49424D42 494F2020 434F4D27 0000000 0000000 0000060
54070200 80120000 49424D44 4F532020 434F4D27 0000000
0000000 00000060 54070C00 80420000 434F4D4D 414E4420
434F4D20 0000000 0000000 00000060 54072E00 80450000
414E5349 20202020 53595320 0000000 0000000 00000060
54075100 80060000 464F524D 41542020 434F4D20 0000000
0000000 00000060 54075500 001B0000 E5484B44 534B2020
434F4D20 0000000 0000000 00000060 54076300 00190000
53595320 20202020 434F4D20 0000000 0000000 00000060
54077000 90060000 4449534B 434F5059 434F4D20 0000000
0000000 00000060 54077400 100A0000 4449534B 434F4D50
434F4D20 0000000 0000000 00000060 54077A00 8C080000
434F4D50 20202020 434F4D20 0000000 0000000 00000060
54077F00 E6090000 45444C49 4E202020 434F4D20 0000000
0000000 00000060 54078400 00120000 4D4F4445 20202020
434F4D20 0000000 0000000 00000060 54078D00 430C0000
46444953 4B202020 434F4D20 0000000 0000000 00000060
54079400 E1180000 4241434B 55502020 434F4D20 0000000
0000000 00000060 5407A100 670E0000 52455354 4F524520
434F4D20 0000000 0000000 00000060 5407A900 A30F0000
5052494E 54202020 434F4D20 0000000 0000000 00000060
5407B100 00120000            Press Enter for help
```

Use the arrow keys to move the cursor to offset byte 160. This is the place in the directory that was occupied by the first character in the file-name CHKDSK.COM. The Hex code for C is 43. Instead of 43 the byte contains the value E5. When you erase a file DOS changes the first character of the file name to E5. This tells DOS that the file is no longer active and the space that it occupies can be used by other files.

5.5.   Unerasing the File

Now that you have an idea of what DOS actually does when an ERASE or DEL command is issued, you can use the Norton Utilities program to change the status of the file from erased to active. To begin the unerase process, move to menu 3. Enter **<Esc> <Esc>3**

The Unerase menu appears.

```
Menu 3
                        Recover Erased File
                Choices:

                  f1   Change Selected Drive and Directory

                  f2   Select an Erased File to UnErase

                  f3   Display Information about Erased File

                  f4   Find Erased File's Data

                  f5   Save UnErased File

                 Esc   Return to Top Level Menu

              Press 1, 2, 3, 4, 5, or Esc:

     See the Norton Utilities manual for an outline of the steps to follow

                  Currently selected:  Disk Sector: 5
```

The first step in unerasing a file is to use option #2. Enter **2**

The program now lists all the files on the disk or directory which have been erased.

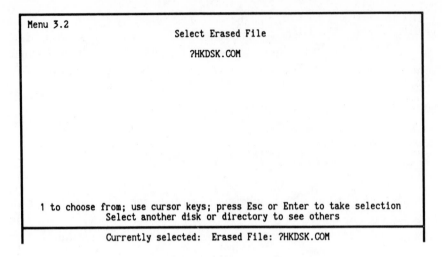

```
Menu 3.2
                              Select Erased File
                                ?HKDSK.COM








           1 to choose from; use cursor keys; press Esc or Enter to take selection
                    Select another disk or directory to see others

                  Currently selected:  Erased File: ?HKDSK.COM
```

[If you have erased other files from the disk you should see additional files listed.]

The next step is to choose the file that you want to recover. In this example there is only one file to choose. In a real situation you might see quite a few files. You can use the arrow keys to move the highlight to the file you want to recover.

Note that all the files are missing their first letter. This is a result of the way MS DOS marks the files when they are erased. When the proper file is highlighted, enter **<return>**

This selects the file for recovery and displays the next menu.

In order to proceed with the unerasing, you need to supply a legitimate character for the beginning of the filename. It really does not matter to the program what letter you choose. From a practical point of view you would usually want to use the character that was originally there. However, should you not remember what that character was you can actually use any letter that you like. In this case enter **c**

You return to menu 3. The bottom section of the screen displays:

```
        Currently selected:  Erased File: CHKDSK.COM
               Drive A:  Directory: root directory
```

This tells you that the program is ready to begin the process of recovering data from that file.

5.6.   File Status

The next step to take in recovering a file is to display the information about the file. Enter **3**

The program displays:

```
Menu 3.3

                Display Information about an Erased File

                        Name: CHKDSK.COM
                  Attributes: Archive
                Date and time: Thursday, October 20, 1983, 12:00 pm
      Starting cluster number: 99 (sector number 106)
                        Size: 6,400 bytes, occupying 13 clusters


      The beginning of the space formerly used by this file
      is not in use by the data of another file.

      Successful UnErasure of this erased file is possible.


         Press any key to continue...
```

The screen tells you some important facts about the file and its current status on the disk. The top section displays the basic information stored in the directory section of the disk. This is the same information that you saw when you displayed sector 5 of the directory.

The second section is an evaluation of the file allocation table (FAT). The file allocation table tells DOS which disk sectors are related to which files. If the sectors formerly occupied by the CHKDSK.COM file have not been used by another file, you can usually recover the entire file without a problem.

The display indicates that this is the case with the file you want to recover. This is the best of all possible cases for successful recovery.

The illustration below shows an example of a file which has been wholly or partially used by other files:

```
Menu 3.3

                  Display Information about an Erased File


                        Name: PROGRAMS.COM
                  Attributes: Archive
                Date and time: Thursday, January 10, 1985, 12:00 pm
        Starting cluster number: 1,844 (sector number 14,785)
                        Size: 11,520 bytes, occupying 3 clusters


        The beginning of the space formerly used by this file
        is in use by the data of another file.

        Successful UnErasure of this erased file is unlikely.
        Only attempt UnErasing if partial data can be used.

          Press any key to continue...
```

When you see this type of display, you have a much more difficult job of recovering the file. As the display suggests, at least part of the erased file's space has been used by another file. You would only attempt to recover a file in this condition if partial recovery would be useful to you. If the file were a program, partial recovery would probably not be useful to you.

However, if the file were a data file, in particular a text file produced by a word processor or data base program, partial recovery would allow you to get back some of the text or data. Techniques for partial recovery are explained later in this chapter. Fortunately, the CHKDSK file has not been overwritten. To continue on to the next step, enter **<return>**

5.7.   Selecting Data

The next step in unerasing a file is to select data to be included in that recovered file. Enter **4**

This displays menu 3.4, used to select disk sectors for the file that you want to recover.

```
┌─────────────────────────────────────────────────────────────────┐
│ Menu 3.4                                                          │
│                       Find Erased File's Data                     │
│                                                                   │
│        File data is stored in units of disk space called clusters│
│                                                                   │
│           The erased file CHKDSK.COM occupied 13 clusters         │
│                                                                   │
│           You may now ...                                         │
│              f1  Automatically Select All Data Clusters (Best Guess)│
│              f2  Automatically Select One Cluster (Best Guess)     │
│              f3  Search for Specific Data                          │
│              f4  Select One Cluster by Sector Number               │
│                                                                   │
│           Press 1, 2, 3, 4, or Esc:                               │
│                                                                   │
│                                                                   │
└─────────────────────────────────────────────────────────────────┘
```

At the top of the screen, the Norton Utilities program tells you the number of clusters that the file formerly occupied. This information is important in the recovery process.

The number of clusters indicates the size of the file you want to recover. The cluster is the basic unit of data storage. This means that you can recover a file by selecting one or more clusters of data. In this example, Norton Utilities indicates that 13 clusters should be selected to recover the entire file. Since the file CHKDSK.COM is a program, a useful recovery must contain all 13 clusters.

The key to file recovery is the selection of clusters. Norton Utilities has four ways of accomplishing this:

1. *Automatically Select All Data Clusters (Best Guess)*—This method is the simplest way to recover a file. The Norton Utilities program looks at the file allocation table (FAT) and attempts to figure out where the clusters formerly assigned to that file were located.

   This option works best on files that have not been written to since the erasure was made. The more the disk has been written to, the less likely this operation will be to correctly recover the file.

   If the file you are attempting to recover is a program this option is probably the only one that will be of use to you. If this option does not work, the file is probably not completely recoverable. Since programs are stored in computer language, it is unlikely that you would recognize parts of the program even if they were displayed.

   If the file you want to recover is a text file of some kind, i.e., information which you would recognize when it was displayed on screen, options 2, 3, and 4 can be used to recover some or all of the file.

2. *Automatically Select One Cluster (Best Guess)*—This option also uses the information found on the file allocation table, but selects only a single cluster at a

time. The purpose of this option is to allow you to inspect each cluster to see if it really belongs to the file.

This option is useful mainly for files that contain ASCII information. Programs stored in binary computer language would make very little sense to you when displayed. ASCII text files, such as those produced by many word processing and data base programs, would be recognizable.

By inspecting the contents of various clusters you can determine which ones belongs to the file you are trying to recover and which ones have been used for other purposes.

3. *Search for Specific Data*—The first two options use the file allocation table to locate the clusters. This option is used when you really don't know where to begin looking for your data.

With option 3, you select a string of characters or hex numbers that you want to find. For example, if the file was a word processing document that contained the name "Joe Flynn", you would use the search option to find sectors on the disk that contained those characters.

You would then use the display sectors information option of Norton Utilities to look at the information and decide if it is part of the file you want to recover. The assumption is that you know what information was stored in the file you are trying to recover.

4. *Select One Cluster by Sector Number*—This option is usually used after you have used the search option to locate a potentially useful sector. For example, if your search for "Joe Flynn" indicated that those characters could be found in sector 55 of the disk, you would use this option to select, inspect, and, if necessary, add the cluster that the sector is part of to the file you are recovering.

In this case the first option will probably be the correct one to use. Enter **1**

Norton Utilities displays:

```
Menu 3
                        Find Erased File's Data

          File data is stored in units of disk space called clusters

             The erased file CHKDSK.COM occupied 13 clusters
             You have selected 13 clusters

             To finish UnErasing the file, go to menu 3.5
             You may review the selected data at menu 3.3
             To undo the selection so far, go to menu 3.2

             You may now ...
                 f1  Automatically Select All Data Clusters (Best Guess)
                 f2  Automatically Select One Cluster (Best Guess)
                 f3  Search for Specific Data
                 f4  Select One Cluster by Sector Number

                 Press 1, 2, 3, 4, or Esc:
```

At this point you have a decision to make. You have three alternatives:

1. To finish unerasing the file—This means that you are ready to save the clusters that have been selected as the recovered file.
2. To review the selected data—This option displays the contents of the selected clusters, one sector at a time, so that you can inspect their contents. This selection makes sense if the file contains ASCII or text data. If it contains program information it is unlikely that the review will have any value for you.
3. To undo the selection—This option takes you back to the beginning of the selection process and allows you to gather the data again. You would use this option if you felt that the clusters selected were not the correct ones for the file.

In this example, choice 1 is appropriate. To reach those choices you must backup to the Unerase menu, menu 3. Enter **<Esc>**

To save the selected clusters, enter **5**

The program displays:

```
Menu 3.5


                        Save UnErased File


             Saving record of file's data ... done
             Saving file's directory entry ... done

             UnErasing CHKDSK.COM is complete
             Press any key to continue...




           Currently selected:  File: CHKDSK.COM
                 Drive C:  Directory: DOS
```

The display indicates that the file has been saved. To confirm this you must leave the Norton Utilities program. Enter **<return> <Esc>** (2 times)
   Enter **chkdsk <return>**

The command executes normally. The file that had been erased is once again a usable file. This file was recovered by using the simplest possible method. Unfortunately, not all file recovery situations will be as clear cut as this example. In the next section you will learn some of the other tools provided by Norton Utilities to recover files.

5.8.   Recovering Files with Text Search

When an erased file is a program file, e.g., COM or EXE file, you are usually limited in the ways that you can attempt to recover it. Because the file is a program, its contents are coded to be understood directly by the computer.

However, if the file is a text file, i.e., if it contains information that can be understood directly by someone reading it, you have several alternatives when you are trying to recover lost information.

To illustrate these techniques you will need a text file. Luckily, Norton Utilities comes supplied with several text files in the form of batch files.

To set up this type of recovery, copy the BAT files from the Norton Utilities disk or directory onto the disk in drive A. Enter

copy b:*.bat<return>   (floppy disk systems)
copy c:*.bat<return>   (hard disk systems)

The screen will show that four files have been copied: DEMO.BAT, README.BAT, LONG.BAT, and SHORT.BAT. To see the contents of the files, you can use the TYPE command. To make it easier to read, the MORE filter can be used. Enter **type readme.bat | more<return>**
The screen will show:

```
ECHO OFF
CLS
ECHO      Norton Utilities, Version 3.00
ECHO
ECHO      dated Monday January 21, 1985
ECHO
ECHO      This "READ ME" file provides additional information
ECHO      to supplement the Norton Utilities manual.
ECHO
ECHO      You'll find the following information here:
ECHO
ECHO       * The computers supported by the Norton Utilities, Version 3
ECHO       * TopView and the Norton Utilities
ECHO       * Special notes about the TI Professional,
ECHO          Wang PC, and NEC APC-III computers
ECHO
```

To see more of the file, enter **<return>**
The purpose of displaying this file on the screen is to make sure that you know some of the data contained within this file. Otherwise you wouldn't know what to search for when you tried to recover the file. It is hard to recover a file when you don't know what is stored in that file. Usually, people know all too well what data was accidentally erased. To stop the listing, enter **[Ctrl Scroll Lock]**
The next step is to erase the files. Enter **del *.bat<return>**
The files are erased. You can test this by entering the TYPE command again. Enter **dir *.bat<return>**
This time DOS tells you that the file is not found. This makes sense because the all the BAT files has been erased. Start the Norton Utilities program. Enter

b:nu <return>   (floppy disk systems)
c:nu <return>   (hard disk systems)

5.9.   Searching Erased Text

The first step is to proceed to the UNERASE section. Enter **3**
   Next you need to select the file to UNERASE. Enter **2**
The screen shows the files that have been erased.

```
        Select Erased File
          ?EMO.BAT
          ?EADME.BAT
          ?ONG.BAT
          ?HORT.BAT
          ?PIPE1.$$$
          ?PIPE2.$$$
```

[You may notice that there are two files, ?PIPE1.$$$ and ?PIPE2.$$$, listed as erased files. Where did they come from? The answer is that they were created by the MORE filter used in the TYPE command. Filters are special programs that control the output of other programs. In DOS 2 and higher you have such programs available. In order to perform these functions the DOS filters create temporary files.]

The next step is to choose one of the files to recover. Use the <down arrow> to highlight ?EADME.BAT. Then enter **<return>**
   You now need to fill in the first letter of the filename of the file that you want to recover.

[The first letter of the filename is missing because of the method employed by DOS to indicate deleted files. When a file is deleted, DOS replaces the first letter of the filename with ASCII character 229 (E5 in hexadecimal notation). That is why you must always add the first character to the filenames when you attempt to recover them.]

Enter **r**
   You are now looking at menu 3. The next task is to select data to be included in the file that is to be recovered. Enter **4**
   Menu 3.4 appears:

```
              Find Erased File's Data
     File data is stored in units of disk space called clusters
        The erased file README.BAT occupied 8 clusters
        You may now ...
          f1  Automatically Select All Data Clusters (Best Guess)
```

```
f2  Automatically Select One Cluster (Best Guess)
f3  Search for Specific Data
f4  Select One Cluster by Sector Number
Press 1, 2, 3, 4, or Esc:
```

In the previous section you used the program's ability to automatically select the necessary clusters. While that method will work in this instance, there will be times when it will not correctly recover the data. The purpose of this section is to point out other methods by which data can be recovered.

One very important piece of information to take note of is the line on the display that reads:

```
The erased file README.BAT occupied 8 clusters
```

The Norton Utilities program has read the directory entry for the erased file and found that before it was erased the file contained eight clusters of information. The number is important when you are using data selection techniques other than #1, Automatically Select All Data Clusters (Best Guess). It tells you that to fully recover the file you must find eight clusters.

Because the information in the erased file was text, you can use option #3 to search the disk for specific text characters. If you know a word or phrase that was part of the file that was erased, you can find out where on the disk that data is stored and recover at least that part of the erased file. Notice that you cannot use Option #3 unless you have some idea what you are looking for.

Enter **3**

The text search menu appears:

```
              Search Disk for Data
      Choices:
         f1    Specify What to Search For
         f2    Search from Beginning
         f3    Continue Searching
        Esc    Return to Find Erased File's Data
      Press 1, 2, 3, or Esc:
```

This menu displays three commands:

1. *Specify What to Search For.* This command allows you to specify the characters that should be searched for. The idea is to enter a group of characters that will as closely as possible identify the data as belonging to the erased file. This means that you should try to avoid, whenever possible, searching for very common words that can occur in any file such as "the".
2. *Search from Beginning.* This command begins the search for the specified data at the first sector on the disk that is not occupied by data from an existing file.
3. *Continue Searching.* The continue command is used to restart the search after it has been stopped. Typically, the search will be halted if the program finds a match for the data that you specified in step 1. Using this command allows you to continue the search without having to start at the first sector again.

Begin by choosing step 1. Enter **1**
The Specify What to Search For screen appears:

```
              Specify What to Search For
      Enter the data to search for
         in character or in hexadecimal format
      Press Esc or Enter to return to Search Disk for Data
      Use the Tab key to switch between character and hex
      Search data, in character format:

         1...5...10...15...20...25...30...35...40...45.48

      Search data, in hexadecimal format:
```

You can enter up to 48 characters to search for. The characters can be entered in two ways:

1. Text Format. You can simply type the characters that you want to search for.
2. Hexadecimal Format. You can enter the hexadecimal value that corresponds to the characters you want to search for.

Normally the text format is the one you would use. However, the hexadecimal format allows you to search for special characters, such as graphics or control codes that normally cannot be typed in directly from the keyboard.

What should you search for? This is an important question and can often be a hard one to answer. You should try to remember a word or phrase that typifies the information in the file. If the file was a data base you might look for a name or city that you know was part of the file. In this case you might have remembered that the date January 21, 1985, was listed at the beginning of the file. Enter **January**

Why did I only enter January and not the entire date January 21, 1985? The reason is a practical one. I can be reasonably sure that the word in the file was January. However, the remainder of the date contained spaces. While it might be correct to assume that the text was typed with a single space between each of the parts of the date, it is always possible that the date had extra spaces.

[Some programs add or alter the characters in a file without displaying them on the screen. For example, WordStar in the document mode alters the ASCII value of the characters that begin and end words. This means that you might think you entered "January" but WordStar would have stored something else. In that case you might restrict the search key to "anuar".]

By using only the word "January" you avoid making a mistake about the actual number of spaces. If the search text is different from the actual stored text by even so much as an additional space, the Norton Utilities program will not consider it a match. Therefore, to be on the safe side you will search only for the characters you are absolutely sure of.

[Remember that the case of the letters used in the text is significant. For example, "january" would not match "January". If you are unsure of the case of the text you might search simply for "anuary".]

Enter **<return>**

You return to the Search for Data menu. You are now ready to search the disk space. Enter **2**

The search begins. When a match is found the following screen is displayed:

```
            Searching for Data
     Press any key to interrupt the search...
     Searching cluster 301 Found!
     The next step is to Review the Data Found
     to see if it is the data you wish to UnErase

     Press any key to continue...
```

The screen indicates that text that matches the specified characters was found in sector 301 of the disk. The next step is to look at the contents of that sector to see if they are really the text that you want to recover. Enter **<return>**

The next screen is displayed:

```
     Review the Data Found
A data cluster has been found
that is a candidate for inclusion
in the file being UnErased
You may now ...
   Review the contents of the data cluster
   Add the data to the file being UnErased
   Skip this data, look for other data

Press R, A, or S ...
```

This menu allows you to review that data selected by the search. You can perform three actions:

R—Review: This allows you to look at the contents of the sector to determine visually whether or not the data in that sector belongs to the file that you want to recover.

A—Add: This command adds the cluster that includes the chosen sector.

[The relationship between sectors and clusters is important to keep in mind. The data search program searches sector by sector on the disk. However, when data is added to a file it is added in clusters. The cluster is the minimum allocation unit for files. Clusters vary in size depending upon the type of disk in use.

The simplest relationship occurs on a disk that is formatted as a single-sided disk. For example, the DOS 2-level master disk supplied by IBM (the disk copied for this exercise) is formatted as a single-sided disk. On this type of disk a cluster is one sector.

On disks that are formatted as double-sided there are two sectors in each data cluster(1,024 bytes). On a typical hard disk each cluster contains eight sectors (4,096 bytes).

This means that if you decide to add the data to the file you are attempting to recover, you will be adding more data than you see displayed on the screen. Since files are created in clusters, recovering the entire cluster is often exactly what you want to do. Finding the sector, you need to also find additional sectors because they belong to the same cluster.

However, if the file has been badly overwritten and is only partially recoverable, the cluster may contain both good and bad data.]

S—Skip: This command tells the program to skip the selected sector. The data is not added to the file and you may resume the search.

The first step is to review the data. Enter **r**
The program displays:

```
README.BAT sector 308 shown in text format
  ECHO OFF
  CLS
  ECHO    Norton Utilities, Version 3.00
```

```
ECHO      dated Monday January 21, 1985
ECHO
ECHO      This "READ ME" file provides additional information
ECHO      to supplement the Norton Utilities manual.
ECHO      You'll find the following information here:
ECHO
ECHO          * The computers supported by the Norton Utilities, Version 3
ECHO          * TopView and the Norton Utilities
...more
                    Press Enter for help
```

You immediately recognize the data as that which was contained in the file README.BAT. Because you can see that this is the correct data for the file, you will want to add the cluster which contains that sector to the file being recovered. To return to the Review Data Menu, enter **<Esc>**

[Pressing <return> at the previous screen will not bring you back to this menu. Rather it will change the display mode from text to hex and then to the directory format.]

To add the data to the file, enter **a**
The program displays the Find Erased Data menu:

```
                Find Erased File's Data
    File data is stored in units of disk space called clusters
        The erased file README.BAT occupied 8 clusters
        You have selected 1 cluster
        7 more clusters are needed
        You may review the selected data at menu 3.3
        To undo the selection so far, go to menu 3.2
        You may now ...
            f1  Automatically Select All Data Clusters (Best Guess)
            f2  Automatically Select One Cluster (Best Guess)
            f3  Search for Specific Data
            f4  Select One Cluster by Sector Number

        Press 1, 2, 3, 4, or Esc:
```

There is, however, a significant change. The top section of the display indicates that one cluster has been selected, and that to fully recover the file seven more must be added. In most instances you would use options 1 or 2 to automatically select the remaining sectors. However, there may be a time when the automatic selection commands cannot find the next sector.

To illustrate how you would handle that situation, assume that functions 1 and 2, the automatic selection, are not applicable to this recovery problem. Since you are now working on your own, you must decide what the next step is to be. One technique is to select the adjacent sector as a feasible choice for containing the data you are searching for. To select data by the sector number, enter **4**

The program displays the Select Disk Sector menu:

```
                    Select Disk Sector
      You may select a sector numbered from 9 through 359
      It must be part of an available data cluster
      Enter sector number:
      Press Esc or Enter to return to Find Erased File's Data
      Outline of Sector Usage on This Disk
           0          Boot Area (used by DOS)
         1 - 4        FAT Area (used by DOS)
         5 - 8        Directory Area (used by DOS)
         9 - 359      Data Area (where files are stored)
```

The display tells you some interesting things about the disk you are working with. The outline of the disk usage explains that there are 360 sectors on the disk numbered from 0 to 359. The first 9 sectors are taken up with special information. The remaining 351 sectors, numbered 9 through 359 are used to store data. A little arithmetic tells you that cluster #1 is the same as sector #9. On this disk, the cluster number is equal to the sector number minus 8. This is not the case with all disks.

5.10.   Selecting a Sector Number

You have just found data that appears to be the beginning of the file. Logically you will want to examine the contents of the next cluster on the disk. However, this is not as straightforward as it might seem. The number of sectors stored in each cluster depends upon the capacity of the disk you are working with.

In this example, the disk is formatted as a single-sided disk. Each cluster contains only one sector. A disk that has been formatted as a double-sided disk would contain two sectors in each data cluster. Its disk usage outline would look like this:

```
Outline of Sector Usage on This Disk
     0          Boot Area (used by DOS)
   1 - 4        FAT Area (used by DOS)
   5 - 11       Directory Area (used by DOS)
  12 - 719      Data Area (where files are stored)
```

There are 708 sectors used for data storage. Divided into clusters that contain two sectors apiece, you get a total of 354 clusters on a double-sided disk. The first data cluster on the disk would contain sectors 12 and 13. The last data cluster, 354, would contain sectors 718 and 719.

Hard disks store even more sectors in each cluster. Below is the outline of disk usage for a typical 10-megabyte hard disk:

```
Outline of Sector Usage on This Disk
     0          Boot Area (used by DOS)
   1 - 16       FAT Area (used by DOS)
  17 - 48       Directory Area (used by DOS)
  49 - 20,736 Data Area (where files are stored)
```

On the hard disk each cluster is composed of eight sectors. The 20,688 sectors are used to store data. Divided into clusters of eight sectors, you find that there are 2,586 clusters.

[For more information about sectors and clusters, see the beginning of Chapter 3.]

All these numbers may seem confusing, but if you think about them for a little while they give you a very concrete map of where the data that you need is stored. Naturally, most people would prefer to avoid the complexities of disk organization. But when you are trying to recover lost data, the numbers may be your key to solving the problem. Necessity supplies the motivation to attack these complicated subjects.

The next sector you choose to add to the file should not belong to the cluster you just selected. If you tried to select that sector or any other sector that was in use by a file already, the program would display this message:

```
Sector is not part of an available cluster; try another
```

In this example, to do so is a simple matter since there is only one sector in each cluster. Since you just selected sector 308, 309 is the next logical choice. Enter **309 < return >**

Now review the contents of that sector. Enter **r**

The data appears to belong to the file. Enter **<Esc>a**
Now you have two out of the eight clusters.

5.11.   Saving a Damaged File

If the file that you are trying to recover is undamaged, you would continue until you had found all eight clusters that belong to it. What would happen if you found that the remainder of the clusters had been used by another file, so that you could only recover two of the eight original clusters?

Because you cannot restore the file to its original size, there is another very important step that you must remember to take in order to correctly salvage the two clusters you have found.

To see what is required of you in this type of situation, pretend that you have searched extensively for the rest of the data and have concluded that it has been lost due to use of the disk for storing data after the file was originally erased.

Your task is to save the clusters that you have found. The first step is to move to the main UNERASE menu. Enter **<Esc>**

Now choose option 5, *Saving the recovered data*. Enter **5**

Because the data recovered is less than the original file, Norton Utilities displays a special menu:

```
            Save UnErased File
   You have selected less data
   than the erased file originally held
   You may now ...
     Save the file's data as already selected
     Adjust file's size to the selected data and Save
     Return to the UnErase menu for other data
   Press S, A, or R ...
```

The chief question is the adjustment of the directory to reflect the new size of the recovered file. As a general rule you will want to adjust the record of the file's size. If you fail to do this you may find that the recovered data will be difficult to access. Enter **a**

The two clusters have been correctly recovered. The data can now be used. To exit the Norton Utilities program, enter **<Esc>** (3 times)

The techniques illustrated in this chapter reflect the ability provided by the Norton Utilities for exploring the data stored on a disk and using that information to recover valuable data. The subject is a tricky one because no two disks present the exact same combinations of erased and unerased data. If you have had trouble recovering files, it will pay to run though the exercises in this section several times until the concepts are clear to you. The knowledge and ability they provide may one day prove invaluable in recovering erased data or damaged files.

UNERASE OPTIONS

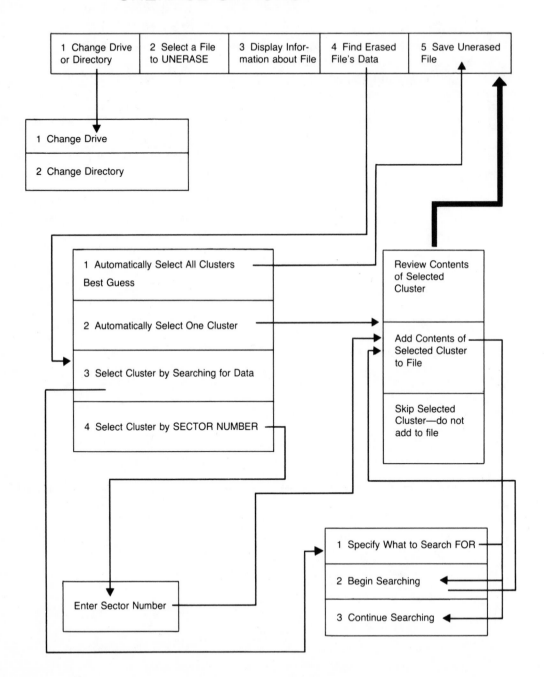

6.

Other DOS Enhancements

This chapter discusses three very interesting programs—SmartPath, Xtree, and EASY DOS IT—that extend the range of commands provided by DOS.

6.1. SmartPath

SmartPath is an excellent example of a very simple utility that can add a tremendous amount of value to your computer system by supplementing a function that already exists in DOS but doing it a little bit better. SmartPath solves a tricky problem that is often encountered by users with hard disks. The principle applies to floppy disk systems in theory but is not usually of practical value, since most floppy disks hold only one program at a time.

To understand the value of SmartPath, you first must understand the shortcoming in DOS that creates the problem that SmartPath solves.

6.2. What Path Does

To understand PATH you must begin with an even more fundamental question: How does DOS run programs?

When you want to format a disk you must run the FORMAT program. To do so you enter a command that looks like this: **format a:**

How does DOS understand what you mean when you type in that command? The answer is that when you enter a command in DOS, the program takes the following steps:

1) First DOS checks to see if the word FORMAT is a special DOS command word like COPY or DIR.
2) If the word is not a special DOS command, DOS scans the directory you are working in for the presence of a file called FORMAT.COM. DOS is designed to add the .COM as part of its search, even though you don't type it in. If it can't find a FORMAT.COM file, it proceeds to the next step.
3) DOS next searches the disk for a file called FORMAT.EXE. If it cannot find that file, it proceeds to the next step.
4) Finally DOS will look for a file called FORMAT.BAT.
5) If DOS cannot find any of these files, it displays BAD COMMAND OR FILENAME.

One of the most interesting and potentially useful commands in DOS is the PATH command. The purpose of PATH is to allow you to access programs stored in directories other than the one in which you are currently working. When a PATH command is used, DOS will repeat the search for a requested file in other directories.

The advantage of this command is that you can create many directories that are devoted strictly to data. The programs can be kept in directories that contain no data files. This simplifies the task of locating data files by allowing the directory to function as a "file folder" and the directory name as the heading for that folder. You also avoid mixing data files with program files. This simplifies backing up and restoring data.

Briefly, the PATH command tells DOS where to look for a program when you request DOS to run a program.

[For more information about the DOS path command see Chapter 1.22.]

Unfortunately, the PATH command fails to live up to its potential. Its main shortcoming is that DOS searches will locate only files with one of three specified extensions, COM, EXE, or BAT. At the time when the IBM PC began to dominate the business market, the major programs running on eight-bit computers were converted to operate on MS DOS systems.

One of the secrets of the IBM strategy was to use the 8088 microprocessor. The 8088 allowed programs written for eight-bit computers with Z80 microprocessors to be quickly converted to run on the IBM. Thus WordStar, dBASE II, SuperCalc, and other major CP/M programs were available for the IBM PC.

The XT brought with it a new operating system, DOS 2. DOS 2 (and DOS 3 as well) allow the user to create multiple directories so that a 10-megabyte hard disk can be sectioned into work areas that are simpler to manage. However, this created some problems for programs like WordStar and dBASE II. Because they were designed before the implementation of DOS 2, they could not take advantage of the multiple directory structure of this operating system.

The problems occur in two areas: execution of the program and reference inside the program to files in another directory. The first problem is caused by the fact that programs are divided into several files. WordStar is actually three files: WS.COM, WSMSGS.OVR, and WSOVLY.OVR. If you have Mailmerge and CorrectStar you will find two additional files, CORRSTAR.OVR and MAILMRGE.OVR.

When WordStar is run, it will load data from the OVR files. WordStar was designed this way to allow it to run in a computer with a small internal memory, e.g., 64K. DOS 2 and 3 allow you to specify a search path. A *path* is the name of a directory or directories that DOS will search in addition to the current directory for programs (.COM and .EXE files) and batch files (.BAT). DOS can find WS.COM if the proper path is open. However, DOS cannot find the overlay files (.OVR), even with a path open.

The problem is not limited to older programs. Version 1A of Lotus 1-2-3 makes use of .DRV files. Normally you must run 1-2-3 from the same directory in which the drivers (DRV file) are stored. DOS cannot search a path for .DRV files. The result is an ERROR LOADING DRIVER message when you try to run the program.

In addition, programs like dBASE III and Framework also use overlay files and are subject to path problems.

SmartPath solves this problem and allows you to take full advantage of the directory structure of DOS 2 and 3. The product is used in conjunction with the DOS PATH command to extend the search to overlay and driver files. The result is that you can run WordStar or 1-2-3 from *any* directory on your hard disk as long as you have opened a path to the directory in which the WordStar files are kept.

For example, suppose that you have the WordStar files stored in a directory called \WS. To be able to run WordStar from any directory you would use the DOS PATH command: **path\ws <return>**

Next you would use the SmartPath program to include the overlay files. SmartPath functions just like PATH. Enter **spath\ws <return>**

The result is that you can run the WordStar program from any directory on the disk. SmartPath makes it simple to store groups of related documents in specific directories without having to make copies of the

WordStar files for each directory. The DOS BACKUP can be used to backup an entire directory without unnecessarily saving the WordStar files each time.

You can open several directories at once by entering a series of path-names separated by semicolons.

path \ ws; \ 123; \ dbase < return >
spath \ ws; \ 123; \ dbase < return >

6.3.   Making an Auto Execute File

The AUTOEXEC.BAT batch file is one that will be mentioned through-out this book. For a full explanation of AUTOEXEC.BAT see Chapter 2.27.

One of the best uses of PATH and SPATH commands is to place them in the AUTOEXEC.BAT file so that they are set automatically when you boot your computer.

Generally speaking, the PATH command should be the first command that is issued by an AUTOEXEC.BAT file. Once the PATH command is given you should then issue the SPATH command.

[SPATH is a program, SPATH.COM, that must be stored on the disk. PATH is part of DOS and is loaded as part of the COMMAND.COM file. This means that in order to set the SPATH, the PATH command must be issued to open a search path to the directory that contains the SPATH.COM file.

That is why PATH should usually precede the SPATH command in a batch file. The only time this rule can be violated is if the SPATH.COM program is stored in the root directory along with the COMMAND.COM file.

Issuing the PATH command first allows you to store the SPATH.COM program in a directory other than the root and still include it in the AUTOEXEC.BAT file.]

You can use EDLIN or any ASCII text editor or word processor to add the SPATH command to your AUTOEXEC.BAT file.

6.4.   SmartPath: Summary

SmartPath is an outstanding value and makes the DOS environment more flexible. If you own a hard disk this program is really a must. The cost-performance ratio of this product is remarkable.

[SmartPath can slow down the performance of some IBM-compatible computers. This problem can be solved by changing the FILES specification in DOS to the maximum, 20 files. This operation is performed by adding the FILES = 20 command to the CON-FIG.SYS file. For details about CONFIG.SYS see Chapter 2.29.]

6.5.   Xtree

The Xtree program is a utility that helps you organize and maintain your hard disk. The program has several practical advantages over the normal DOS commands. The primary advantage of Xtree is that it provides the user with a global view of the disk. DOS tends to limit the user's view of the disk to one directory at a time.

Xtree is primarily of interest to users with hard disk drives. However, most users will find the menu-driven DOS commands a fast and accurate way to clean up and organize floppy disks also.

DOS commands like DIR or DEL affect only the active or specified directory. The Xtree program reads information about the entire disk into the memory of the computer. The program then presents the disk data in a form that allows you to view the information in a more flexible way than DOS does.

In addition, many of the common DOS commands can be implemented through Xtree menus. The Xtree commands contain prompts and messages that try to prevent you from making mistakes, such as accidentally copying over a file while using the COPY command.

Xtree also contains features and abilities that cannot be duplicated in DOS. The main advantage of the program is its ability to present a global view of a hard disk.

A "global view" is one that includes all the files on the hard disk, no matter what directory they are stored in or if they are assigned the DOS attribute "hidden".

6.6.   Program Files

The Xtree program consists of three files:

CRTDRV.DAT	15,488
XTREEINS.EXE	8,912
XTREE.EXE	34,866

The program files will occupy about 64 kilobytes of disk space when copied to a hard disk. Two files are required for operation, CRTDRV.DAT and XTREE.EXE. The file XTREEINS.EXE is used to install the program. If you do not need to change the program's setup or you have finished installing the program, you can remove this file from your hard disk.

[Do not erase this file from your master copy. Only erase the XTREEINS.EXE file from your hard disk, if it is not needed, in order to free the disk space.]

6.7. Basic Organization

To start the program, enter **xtree** **< return >**

[You can operate Xtree from any directory on your hard disk if you open a path to the directory that contains the XTREE.EXE file. For example, if you stored the files in the directory \DOS you would open the path by entering **path\dos< return >**]

When the program first loads, it reads all the information about the drive into the memory of the computer. If you have a large number of files on your disk this may take a few moments.

When the information has been read, Xtree presents its main display screen.

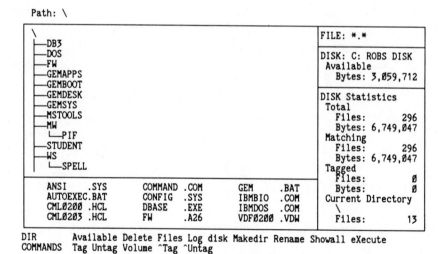

Path: \

```
\                                          FILE: *.*
 ├─DB3
 ├─DOS                                      DISK: C: ROBS DISK
 ├─FW                                        Available
 ├─GEMAPPS                                     Bytes: 3,059,712
 ├─GEMBOOT
 ├─GEMDESK                                  DISK Statistics
 ├─GEMSYS                                    Total
 ├─MSTOOLS                                     Files:        296
 ├─MW                                          Bytes: 6,749,047
 │  └─PIF                                    Matching
 ├─STUDENT                                     Files:        296
 ├─WS                                          Bytes: 6,749,047
 │  └─SPELL                                  Tagged
                                              Files:          0
  ANSI    .SYS   COMMAND .COM   GEM    .BAT   Bytes:          0
  AUTOEXEC.BAT   CONFIG  .SYS   IBMBIO .COM  Current Directory
  CML0200 .HCL   DBASE   .EXE   IBMDOS .COM   \
  CML0203 .HCL   FW      .A26   VDF0200 .VDW  Files:         13
```

DIR   Available Delete Files Log disk Makedir Rename Showall eXecute
COMMANDS   Tag Untag Volume ^Tag ^Untag

Fig. 6-1. Xtree Main Display.

At the very top of the screen Xtree displays the current directory path-name. Below that line is an area divided into five boxes.

The box in the upper left-hand corner of the display is a map of the directories on the disk. The map is displayed in a "tree" fashion.

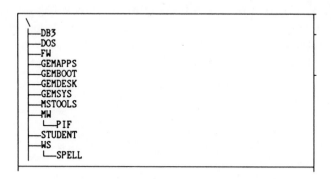

```
\
 ├─DB3
 ├─DOS
 ├─FW
 ├─GEMAPPS
 ├─GEMBOOT
 ├─GEMDESK
 ├─GEMSYS
 ├─MSTOOLS
 ├─MW
 │   └─PIF
 ├─STUDENT
 ├─WS
     └─SPELL
```

Fig. 6-2. Directory Map Section.

The box on the lower left displays some or all of the files that are con-tained in the directory indicated on the top line. Xtree always begins with the root directory of the disk.

```
ANSI      .SYS     COMMAND .COM    GEM     .BAT
AUTOEXEC.BAT       CONFIG  .SYS    IBMBIO  .COM
CML0200 .HCL       DBASE   .EXE    IBMDOS  .COM
CML0203 .HCL       FW      .A26    VDF0200 .VDW
```

Fig. 6-3. File Box.

[For more information about directories see Chapter 2.18.]

On the right side of the display are three other boxes. The top box displays the current file specification. Xtree allows you to select the files that are displayed by entering a DOS wildcard specification. The default value is *.*, meaning all files.

[For a full discussion of wildcards see Chapter 1.16.]

Fig. 6-4. File Specification Box.

The middle box on the right side contains information about the disk as a whole. The volume label (if any), the total number of files on the disk and the total amount of bytes remaining free on the disk are displayed.

```
DISK: C: ROBS DISK
  Available
    Bytes: 2,990,080
```

Fig. 6-5. Disk Facts.

The box at the bottom right of the display contains statistics about the disk and directory. This portion of the display is the most active in that it will change as you change directories, tag files, or select files.

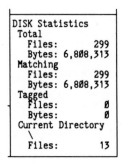

Fig. 6-6. Disk Statistics.

At the bottom of the screen the Xtree commands are displayed:

```
DIR        Available Delete Files Log disk Makedir Rename Showall eXecute
COMMANDS   Tag Untag Volume ^Tag ^Untag
```

6.8.   Display Modes

Xtree has three display modes. The first is the one that is displayed when the program is loaded. In this mode you can move the cursor through the directory map display. As you do, the Disk Statistics box will change the current directory and number of files display.

The modes are changed by pressing the <return> key. The first time you press <return>, Xtree moves the cursor into the lower left box. You are now in the file mode. In this mode you can perform actions on files or groups of files.

Pressing <return> changes the mode once again. This mode displays the files contained in a directory in a full screen mode.

```
┌─────────────────────────┐   ┌─────────────────────────┐
│ ANSI     .SYS           │   │ FILE: *.*               │
│ AUTOEXEC.BAT            │   │                         │
│ CML0200 .HCL            │   │ DISK: C: ROBS DISK      │
│ CML0203 .HCL            │   │  Available              │
│ COMMAND .COM            │   │   Bytes: 2,990,080      │
│ CONFIG  .SYS            │   │                         │
│ DBASE   .EXE            │   │ DIRECTORY Stats         │
│ FW      .A26            │   │  Total                  │
│ GEM     .BAT            │   │   Files:          13    │
│ IBMBIO  .COM            │   │   Bytes:     398,085    │
│ IBMDOS  .COM            │   │  Matching               │
│ VDF0200 .VDW            │   │   Files:          13    │
│ VDF0203 .VDW            │   │   Bytes:     398,085    │
│                         │   │  Tagged                 │
│                         │   │   Files:           0    │
│                         │   │   Bytes:           0    │
│                         │   │  Current File           │
│                         │   │   ANSI     .SYS         │
│                         │   │   Bytes:       1,664    │
└─────────────────────────┘   └─────────────────────────┘
```

Fig. 6-7. Full Screen File Display.

In this mode, the map box is erased and the left side of the screen is filled with the files from that directory.

Pressing <return> once more changes modes back to the default. You can cycle through these modes as much as you like.

6.9.   Selecting Files

One of the principal advantages of Xtree over DOS is its ability to present a coherent visual display of disk data. The ability to select files enhances that capacity.

The file selection command has a global effect. For example, suppose that you wanted to track down all all the backup (.BAK) files that were currently taking up space on your disk.

[The backup files referred to are files that end with the extension .BAK. Many programs produce backup (.BAK) as part of their normal functioning. The purpose of backup files is to protect your work while the files are being edited. Some popular programs that create .BAK files are WordStar, Word, dBASE II and III, and even the EDLIN program.

These files generally serve no purpose after the original file has been successfully saved. Over a period of time these files can accumulate and take up a large amount of disk space. Removing these unnecessary files can free up disk space.]

To select only .BAK files you would enter **f *.bak <return>**

Xtree will now display only files that meet the wildcard specification. If there are no files that meet the specification, Xtree then displays NO FILES!in the file window.

To return to the normal display you would enter **f *.* <return>**

6.10.   The Global View—Show All

The file specification command allows you to filter each directory you select for the desired files. Xtree allows you to expand your search to a global search. The S, Show All, command opens the file window and displays all the files on the entire disk that meet the specification.

This global view is something that is unavailable in DOS. It can save you a lot of time in tracking down files. It is also very helpful in finding duplicate files.

Also pay attention to the Matching area of the Disk Statistics display. The Matching area tells you the number of files that meet the file specification and the total amount of disk space.

For example, to find all the .BAK files on the entire disk, enter **f *.bak <return> s**

Path: \WS2000

```
  CLIENTS  .BAK                          FILE: *.BAK
  ELLIE    .BAK
  FIRST    .BAK                          DISK: C: ROBS DISK
  JGR      .BAK                           Available
  PAGES2   .BAK                             Bytes: 2,990,080
  SPECIAL  .BAK
  TABS     .BAK                          DISK Statistics
                                          Total
                                            Files:        299
                                            Bytes: 6,808,313
                                          Matching
                                            Files:          7
                                            Bytes:      9,926
                                          Tagged
                                            Files:          0
                                            Bytes:          0
                                          Current File
                                            CLIENTS .BAK
                                            Bytes:      3,291
```

Fig. 6-8. Global View of Backup Files.

When the Show All mode is in effect the directory indicator at the top of the screen tells you what directory the files are stored in. The Matching Section of the Disk Statistics display indicates the amount of space occupied by .BAK files.

[A word about the numbers used to indicate the disk space used by each file. The number that appears in Xtree is the same number that is stored in the disk directory indicating the number of bytes in the file.

However, the number of bytes in the file *is not the same* as the amount of space occupied by the file on the disk. Suppose that you have a file that Xtree and DOS indicate contains 2,500 bytes. How much disk space does the file use up?

The answer is 4,096 bytes. Why? Because DOS allocates file space based on the minimum allocation for each file. The minimum unit is called a cluster. On a typical hard disk DOS allocates 4,096 bytes to each cluster. Even if a file only requires 2,500 bytes the smallest unit DOS can allot is 4,096 bytes. This inevitably leads to "slack" space. Slack space pertains to the space that is allocated to a file but is not actually filled with data from that file.

In the example, the Matching area showed that the files totaled 9,926 bytes. You might think that erasing all these files would free only the 9,926 bytes of disk space. In fact the seven files must occupy at least seven times 4,096 bytes, or 28,672 bytes of disk space. You can see that looking only at the figure displayed by Xtree and DOS gives you a misleading impression of the amount of disk space that would be recovered if these files were erased.

The Norton Utilities program FS (File Size) displays the true disk allocation for files and calculates the percentage of slack space. The issue is further complicated by the fact that cluster sizes vary with the type of disk being used. For example, double-sided floppy disks have clusters that hold 1,024 bytes. Thus the minimum allocation for seven files on a floppy disk would be 7,168 bytes.]

6.11.   Xtree Commands

There are three sets of commands in Xtree:

1) Function Keys: active all the time.
2) Directory Commands: active only in the main window mode.
3) File Commands: active when Xtree is in the file window.

6.12.   Function Keys

Xtree has four function keys that operate anywhere in the program:

F1—Quit: Exit Xtree and return to DOS.
F2—Help: Display help screens (not available during commands that are executing)
F3—Cancel the command in progress. (Note that the <Esc> key does not perform this function. To cancel you must use F3.)
F4—Turn the display of the Directory and File Command lines ON or OFF.

6.13.   Directory Commands

A—Available: Displays the amount of free space available on any disk.
D—Delete: Removes the selected directory from the disk. (Note that a directory cannot be removed if it contains files. Only empty directories can be removed.)
F—Files: Allows you to enter a wildcard for file selection.
L—Logged disk: Changes the active disk drive.
M—Make directory: Create a new directory on the disk. (Duplicates the DOS command MD.)
*R—Rename: This command allows you to change the name of a directory.
*S—Show all files: This command presents a global view of the disk and displays all files on the disk that meet the current file specification, if any.
*T—Tag: Tag all the files in a directory. (Tagging is discussed below.)
*U—Untag: Removes the tag mark.
*V—Volume: Changes the disk volume label.
X—eXecute: Executes a program from DOS.

Xtree uses the ∧ symbol to indicate that the following commands should be issued with the [Ctrl] key pressed down:

[Ctrl t]—Tag all the matching files in all directories on the disk.
[Ctrl u]—Untag all the matching files in all directories.

The * indicates that these functions are *not* available in DOS.

6.14. File Commands

The following commands are used when Xtree is in one of its two file display modes:

*A—Attribute: This command performs two functions. It displays and allows you to change the attributes of a file. (For a full discussion of file attributes see Chapter 4.7.) The two most significant attributes for most users are "Hidden" and "Read-Only". A hidden file does not appear on a DOS directory but can be seen in Xtree. A "Read-Only" file is one that DOS will not delete.

   Xtree allows you to change file attributes by entering a two-character command. The first character is either a + or − sign. The plus sign adds an attribute to a file. The minus sign removes an attribute from a file. The second character is a letter indicating the attribute to be added or removed.
A—Archive File
H—Hidden File
R—Read-Only File
S—System File
C—Copy: Copies the current file to a new disk and/or path.
D—Delete: Deletes the current file.
F—Files: Allows you to enter a wildcard for file selection.
L—Logged disk: Changes the active disk drive.
R—Rename: Renames the current file.
T—Tag: Tags the current file.
U—Untag: Removes the tag from the current file.
V—View: This command displays the contents of the file. (Note that not all files make visual sense when viewed. Program files contain data stored in binary code, which seldom makes sense to view, although many programs contain some text data. You cannot edit any of the data displayed.)
X—eXecute: Executes a program from DOS.

The * indicates that these functions are *not* available in DOS.

6.15.   Working with Groups of Files

Another reason why Xtree is helpful is its ability to tag files. Tagging a file allows you to create groups of files. Xtree will allow you to tag individual files or an entire directory of files. When a file is tagged a diamond appears next to the filename. The untag command reverses the process and removes the tag mark. The commands [Ctrl t] and [Ctrl u] will tag or untag an entire directory respectively. Once a group of files has been tagged you can perform the following actions on all the tagged files at once:

[Ctrl a]—Attribute: Modify the attributes of the tagged files.
[Ctrl c]—Copy: Copy the tagged files to a new disk and/or path.
[Ctrl d]—Delete: Delete the tagged files.
[Ctrl r]—Rename: Rename the tagged files.

The Rename command is a bit tricky. DOS does not allow two files with the same name. The purpose of this command is to change the names of a group of files that contain similarities in their filenames. For example, you might have a series of files with the extension .DAT. If you enter *.TXT as the new name, all the files will receive a TXT extension.

6.16.   Xtree: Summary

Xtree is a valuable tool if you are working with hard disks. Its primary advantages are:

1) Global View. Xtree provides commands that are not limited by the directories, as are most DOS command. The directory map provides a clear visual representation of a hard disk's subdirectory organization. While many of Xtree's functions can be performed by DOS, Xtree provides a more supportive environment than does DOS.
2) Xtree provides some functions not supported by some versions of DOS, such as renaming a directory or changing attributes.
3) Tagging files allows you to create groups of files to copy, delete, rename, and change attributes.

6.17. EASY DOS IT

The EASY DOS IT program is designed to create a menu-driven system to replace the interface that DOS presents the user. While this program is primarily of interest to users with hard disks, the program will operate within a floppy disk system.

[With floppy disks the program provides a menu-driven way of implementing DOS commands.]

EASY DOS IT is really a system of menus that interacts with the user to guide him/her through the use of DOS. The DOS command menus are provided with the system. In addition, EASY DOS IT allows you to create menus of your own choice that will run the programs that you have on your hard disk.

These custom-made menus can also perform specialized tasks such as backing up data files and erasing backup files. EASY DOS IT accepts lists of DOS commands and executes them from user-designed menus. In some senses, the program coordinates batch files. However, to the person using the system, all signs of DOS are hidden.

[For more information on batch files see Chapter 2.22.]

The major value of EASY DOS IT is to create a simple, menu-driven interface for the computer. The program greatly accelerates the speed at which one can learn to operate a hard disk and the programs stored on it.

6.18. The Files

The program is supplied on a single diskette. There are 33 files in all, that occupy 135,168 bytes of disk space. The files divide into three types. The EXE files are program files. The DTA files are text files that are used to construct the menus and provide the data for the commands. The BAT files are DOS batch files used to install the program and then run it. When you install the program a directory called EZDOSIT is created on your hard disk. The files are then copied into that directory.

6.19.   DOS Functions in EASY DOS IT

To run the program you must first make sure that you have logged into the correct directory. Enter the command **cd\ezdosit<return>**

[Before you run EASY DOS IT you should make sure that you have a path open to the directory that contains the DOS command files. EASY DOS IT will not operate DOS commands without this path open.

EASY DOS IT requires that DOS system files be on your hard disk and available to the EASY DOS IT program to run.]

To execute the program enter **easy<return>**
The main EASY DOS IT menu appears.

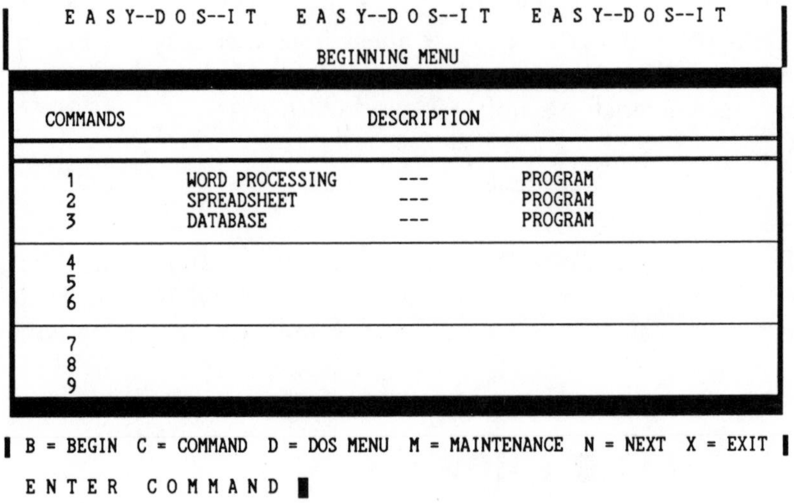

```
EASY--DOS--IT   EASY--DOS--IT   EASY--DOS--IT

                    BEGINNING MENU


COMMANDS                        DESCRIPTION


    1          WORD PROCESSING     ---      PROGRAM
    2          SPREADSHEET         ---      PROGRAM
    3          DATABASE            ---      PROGRAM

    4
    5
    6

    7
    8
    9


 B = BEGIN  C = COMMAND  D = DOS MENU  M = MAINTENANCE  N = NEXT  X = EXIT

 ENTER  COMMAND
```

Fig. 6-9. Main EASY DOS IT Menu.

The display of commands that appears is a false setup. It is meant only as a suggestion of how a user-defined menu might appear. Pressing the command numbers now will not accomplish anything. The commands that do count are the ones at the bottom of the screen. They are:

B—BEGIN: This command displays the main EASY DOS IT menu. Right now you are looking at the Main menu. However, as you use other menus, this command is used to return to this display.

C—COMMAND: This allows you to directly enter a DOS command.

D—DOS MENU: This command brings up the main DOS command menu.

M—MAINTENANCE: This brings up the menu that allows you to customize the EASY DOS IT program to run your applications and DOS commands.

N—NEXT: Displays the next menu screen.

X—EXIT: This exits the EASY DOS IT program and returns you to the DOS systems prompt.

6.20. DOS Commands in EASY DOS IT

One of the purposes of EASY DOS IT is to present DOS functions in a simpler, easy to use manner. To use DOS commands, enter **d**

The program displays the main DOS menu.

COMMANDS			DESCRIPTION
1	CHKDSK	---	CHECK DISK
2	COPY	---	COPY FILES
3	DIR	---	DIRECTORY
4	ERASE	---	ERASE FILES
5	FORMAT	---	FORMAT DISK
6	DOS (A-D)	---	COMMANDS
7	DOS (D-M)	---	COMMANDS
8	DOS (M-S)	---	COMMANDS
9	DOS (S-Z)	---	COMMANDS

Fig. 6-10. DOS Command Menu.

Options 1 through 5 bring up specific menus for each of the specified commands. These five options are considered the most common DOS commands. Options 6 through 9 bring up menus of DOS commands listed alphabetically. To get a feel for how these menus work, bring up the format menu by entering **5**

```
E A S Y--D O S--I T    E A S Y--D O S--I T    E A S Y--D O S--I T

FORMAT: PREPARES A NEW DISKETTE FOR USE BY THE COMPUTER
```

COMMANDS			DESCRIPTION
1	FORMAT	DISKETTE	TUTOR SCREEN
2	FORMAT	DRIVE A	FOR DATA
3	FORMAT	DRIVE A	WITH SYSTEM
4	FORMAT	DRIVE B	FOR DATA
5	FORMAT	DRIVE B	WITH SYSTEM
6	RETURN	TO DOS	SUMMARY MENU
7	RETURN	TO DOS	MENU (D-M)

```
B = BEGIN  C = COMMAND  D = DOS MENU  M = MAINTENANCE  N = NEXT  X = EXIT

E N T E R   C O M M A N D
```

Fig. 6-11. The Format Menu.

Note that none of the choices allow for formatting of drive C. It is a common accident for people to attempt to format a floppy disk and accidentally format their hard disk, thereby losing all the data stored on the hard drive. This menu eliminates that danger because each format option specifies the drive that will be formatted.

Options 2 though 4 format the disks on A or B as data for system disks. Option 1 is a tutor screen. The screen displays a brief explanation of the format command. Enter **1**

The tutor screen appears:

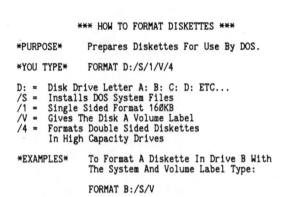

```
            *** HOW TO FORMAT DISKETTES ***

*PURPOSE*     Prepares Diskettes For Use By DOS.

*YOU TYPE*    FORMAT D:/S/1/V/4

D: =  Disk Drive Letter A: B: C: D: ETC...
/S =  Installs DOS System Files
/1 =  Single Sided Format 160KB
/V =  Gives The Disk A Volume Label
/4 =  Formats Double Sided Diskettes
      In High Capacity Drives

*EXAMPLES*    To Format A Diskette In Drive B With
              The System And Volume Label Type:

              FORMAT B:/S/V
```

Fig. 6-12. Format Tutor Screen.

At the bottom of the screen you can enter a DOS command of your own if you desire. To return to the previous menu, enter **<return>**
The screen clears and EASY DOS IT presents this prompt:

```
THIS COMMAND WILL FORMAT THE DISKETTE IN DRIVE A.
ALL EXISTING DATA ON DRIVE A WILL BE DESTROYED.

DO YOU WANT TO CONTINUE (Y/N) ?
```

If you want to format the disk in A enter **Y**; if not, enter **N**.
When complete you will return to the previous menu. To return to the main program screen, enter **b**

6.21. Customizing the Program

The other main feature of this program gives you the ability to create custom menu screens that run the applications you have on your hard disk, as well as special tasks, such as backing up data files. To customize the menu you will use the Maintenance menu. Enter **m**

```
E A S Y--D O S--I T    E A S Y--D O S--I T    E A S Y--D O S--I T

 COMMANDS                          DESCRIPTION

    1        CHANGE        ---      MENU SCREENS
    2        CHANGE        ---      LOADING COMMANDS
    3        RUN           ---      EASYMAKE

    4
    5
    6

    7
    8
    9        CHANGE        ---      SUB-MENUS    (OPTIONAL)

 B = BEGIN  C = COMMAND  D = DOS MENU  M = MAINTENANCE  N = NEXT  X = EXIT
 E N T E R   C O M M A N D ▮
```

Fig. 6-13. Maintenance Menu.

There are three steps to creating custom menus:

1) Edit the Menu Display. This option changes the text that is displayed on the menu. It does not create the commands that run the program.
2) Enter the Command Sequences. In this step you enter the DOS commands that are necessary to carry out the functions described on the menu. For example, if you put Lotus 1-2-3 on the menu, then you must enter the DOS commands that actually tell DOS how to run 1-2-3.
3) Compile the Commands. To make command entry simple, EASY DOS IT allows you to enter the commands as text in a file. EASY DOS IT supplies a program that reads the text commands and creates a file that EASY DOS IT can execute. The process of changing text commands into more specialized computer commands is referred to as *compiling*.

As an example, assume that there are at least three directories on the hard disk:

1) \LOTUS. This directory contains the Lotus 1-2-3 program files.
2) \WS. This directory contains the WordStar program files.
3) \DB3. This directory contains dBASE III program files.

The task is to create a menu that runs these three programs.

Begin with the menu creation program. Enter **1**

EASY DOS IT asks you if you are sure that you want to change the menu. Enter **y**

The screen now shows the file EASY0001.DTA. This file contains the data that is displayed by the program when EASY DOS IT is run.

To understand how menus are created, you need to look at the structure of the file. The file is divided into menu areas. On each menu there are nine lines. Each line can contain a command that can run a program or perform a task.

Menus begin with a special designation: $$.START .MENU101. The .MENU101 gives the menu a name. Menus are ended with $$ END MENU. Each line in the menu is named by USER followed by a four-digit number. Later you will link the menu number with a series of commands that will be executed when that number is chosen from the menu. The file contains four menus, a total of 36 possible commands. To change the text, enter **x**

The cursor is now free to move about the screen. Use the arrow keys to position the cursor to the USER0001 line. Move the cursor to the right until it is positioned on the W in WORD PROCESSING. Enter **WORDSTAR PROGRAM**

```
Again, Buffer, Copy, Delete, Find, -find, Get, Insert, --space--
----- reading file: EASY0001.DTA
-------------------------------------------------------------------------------
            STEP 1 - HIT THE X KEY TO BEGIN EDITING.

            STEP 2 - MOVE CURSOR WITH ARROW KEYS AND CHANGE THE DESCRIPTIONS
                     TO MATCH YOUR PROGRAMS.

            STEP 3 - END EDITING BY HITTING [ESC] Q U E
-------------------------------------------------------------------------------

$$.START .MENU101                               BEGINNING MENU
USER0001        1           WORD PROCESSING     ---         PROGRAM
USER0002        2           SPREADSHEET         ---         PROGRAM
USER0003        3           DATABASE            ---         PROGRAM
USER0004        4
USER0005        5
USER0006        6
USER0007        7
USER0008        8
USER0009        9
$$ END MENU

$$.START .MENU102                               SECOND MENU
```

Fig. 6-14. Changing the Menu Display.

Move the cursor to the next line. Type over SPREADSHEET and change the text to LOTUS 1-2-3. Then change the database line to DBASE III. On line 4 enter the title BACKUP DBASE FILES. The screen should look like this:

```
$$.START .MENU101                               BEGINNING MENU
USER0001        1           WORDSTAR PROGRAM    ---         PROGRAM
USER0002        2           LOTUS 1-2-3         ---         PROGRAM
USER0003        3           DBASE III           ---         PROGRAM
USER0004        4           BACKUP DBASE FILES
USER0005        5
USER0006        6
USER0007        7
USER0008        8
USER0009        9
$$ END MENU

$$.START .MENU102                               SECOND MENU
```

Now that the menu has been revised it can be saved. Enter **<Esc>**
The cursor moves to the command line. The command to enter is Quit Update. Enter **q u**

Now exit the menu section. Enter **e**
The Maintenance Menu appears once again.

6.22.   Creating Commands

The next step is to tell EASY DOS IT what commands to carry out when
you press the numbers on the menu. Enter **2 y**

This time the file that is loaded is the EASYCMND.DTA file. This file
contains the commands that are to be associated with the menu items.
The purpose of this file is to associate the menu items with actual DOS
commands. Each command section begins with $$ START followed by
the name of the menu, e.g., USER0001. The default setup is to assign
three ECHO commands to each menu item. The ECHO command has no
purpose except to hold the place for commands that you want to enter.

The files consist of 17 user items ready to be filled in. If needed, you
can add more command sections to the file.

When you do create a command section you must remember to create
the $$ START and $$ END lines. To begin entry, enter **x**

Move the cursor down to the first ECHO under $$ START USER0001.
It is here that you want to type in the commands that will run the Word-
Star program. The commands follow a basic pattern:

Step #1: Change the directory to the program directory.
Step #2: Execute the program
Step #3: Change the directory back to EZDOSIT so that the menu will
        reappear.

When you follow this pattern the programs will run and the user is
always returned to the EASY DOS IT menu. The effect is that of a closed
system. People can operate the computer without ever having to change a
directory or run a program from DOS.

[Access to DOS is always available through the X, EXIT command.]

To run WordStar, enter **cd\ws <return>**

Notice that the <return> caused the insertion of a new line. This is
permissible because the ECHO commands have no effect. If you wanted,
you could delete the ECHO commands after you have entered the DOS
commands, but it is not necessary. The next command runs WordStar.
Enter **ws <return>**

Finally return to the EASY DOS IT directory. Enter **cd\ezdosit**

You have now set up menu item 1 to actually run the WordStar program. Move the cursor to the ECHO command in the section following the $$ START for USER0002. Enter the following to run Lotus 1-2-3. Enter **cd\lotus <return>**

Instead of immediately entering the command to run LOTUS, there might be something else you can to do help your user or even yourself. Version 1A of Lotus 1-2-3 is a copy-protected program that cannot operate on a hard disk without having a copy of the original system disk in drive A. This is part of the copy protection scheme. It might be useful to display a message that reminds the person using the computer that, unlike WordStar, 1-2-3 requires a disk to be placed in drive A.

You can use the DOS ECHO command to display a message and the PAUSE command to pause the flow of commands. Why pause? The purpose of a pause is to give users an opportunity to react to the message. They might have to go get the master disk. When they return and press a key, the commands continue. Enter

echo 123 requires the master disk to be in drive A<return>
echo place the disk in drive A NOW!<return>
pause <return>

Now complete the command sequence. Enter

lotus <return> cd\ezdosit

[The Nokey program provided with Copy II PC can permit 1-2-3 to operate on a hard disk without placing the master disk in drive A. For more information see Chapter 1.34.]

Next move the cursor to the area for USER0003. This section will execute dBASE III. Enter

cd\db3 <return> dbase <return> cd\ezdosit

6.23. Menu Items That Perform Special Tasks

Although the most common use of the menu items is to run programs, they are also very useful for special operations that are conducted periodically. One good example is backing up files. Backing up is like exercise, something that you really should be disciplined about but often put off.

Placing the backup command as part of the menu makes it simple to do and also serves to remind users that it should be done. As an example, create a menu option that will backup all the data base files to a floppy disk.

All dBASE III data files are assigned the extension of DBF. You can use that extension to select those files for backup. Move the cursor to the section for USER0004. Enter **backup c:\db3*.dbf a:**

[The BACKUP command requires you to place a series of FORMATTED disks in drive A. You might want to add further commands that explain to the user what is required.]

You have now filled out the commands to match the menu items you created. Save this file. Enter **<Esc>q u e**

You return to the Maintenance menu. You are ready to take the final step. This step requires little effort on your part but it is crucial for the EASY DOS IT system. The RUN option compiles the command sequences you just entered so that EASY DOS IT can use them. If you do not take step 3, the menu will function as it did before. Your commands will not be effective. Enter **3 y**

You are now ready to operate your menus. Return to the main menu. Enter **b**

Try some of the options and see how they work. You can continue to update and revise the menu system as your needs change and grow.

6.24.   Custom Tutor Screens

If you want to design your own tutor screen you can do so by typing an * at the beginning of the command line. The * does not print but tells EASY DOS IT to display the text that follows. For example, below is a tutor screen designed for menu item # 9:

```
$$ START USER0009
*                   ABOUT MENUS
*
*   To choose a menu item simply press the number
*   of the program you want to work with
*
$$ END
```

Tutor screens can be up to 17 lines. Each line cannot be longer than 75 characters.

There is one other change that must be made in order to work a tutor screen. You must use Maintenance option #1 to change the user item. If the item—in this example, USER0009—is going to be used, an @ must follow the item. For example:

```
$$.START .MENU101                                    BEGINNING MENU
USER0001        1        WORDSTAR PROGRAM     ---        PROGRAM
USER0002        2        LOTUS 1-2-3          ---        PROGRAM
USER0003        3        DBASE III            ---        PROGRAM
USER0004        4        BACKUP DBASE FILES
USER0005        5
USER0006        6
USER0007        7
USER0008        8
USER0009@       9        ABOUT MENUS
$$ END MENU
```

6.25.   Other Menu Items

The EASY DOS IT system allows for more complex menu relationships. You can create submenus. A submenu is a menu that appears when you choose an item from the displayed menu.

For example, instead of having a menu choice for backing up dBASE files, you might make a menu item that says BACKUPS. When you choose that item, a new menu with a listing of several backup options would appear. A submenu can be called by placing a special command in the menu item position. In the example below, item 8, USER0008, is replaced with a reference not to a command item but another menu. The reference begins with a period:

```
USER0001        1       WORDSTAR PROGRAM    ---     PROGRAM
USER0002        2       LOTUS 1-2-3         ---     PROGRAM
USER0003        3       DBASE III           ---     PROGRAM
USER0004        4       BACKUP DBASE FILES
USER0005        5
USER0006        6
USER0007        7
.USER001        8       BACKUP DATA FILES
USER0009        9
$$ END MENU
```

The .USER001 refers to a submenu. You can add items and commands to the submenu by using option # 9 on the maintenance menu.

Another interesting feature is the ability to reference any of the built-in DOS menus from a user menu. Each DOS menu is given a special name. For example, the COPY menu is *.copy...* (Note that the periods are part of the name, one before and three after.)

If you place *.copy...* in a menu, EASY DOS IT will automatically bring up the copy command. A full list of these special names can be found in the program's documentation.

6.26.   EASY DOS IT: Summary

EASY DOS IT is valuable for two reasons. First, EASY DOS IT creates a straightforward, easy to use interface that simplifies the complexities of hard disk usage for the new user. The program is supplied with a complete set of menu-driven DOS commands.

Second, the system allows for a full range of custom menus, tutors, and submenus. You can run DOS commands, programs, and even preset EASY DOS IT menus from your own system of menus.

Part 3.
Keyboard
Enhancements

7.

Keyboard Enhancing Programs

Most computer users take the keyboard for granted in a literal sense, since it seems logical to assume that the keys will type the letters, numbers, or symbols that are painted on them. The reality, however, is that the face value of the keys is only the beginning of the capacity of the keyboard. The link between the computer and the keyboard is not fixed but programmable. The programs discussed in this chapter allow you to redefine the way the keyboard works. You can use this ability to personalize and simplify a variety of computer tasks. Since most computer users spend a lot of time typing on the keyboard, many people use these utility programs every day. In fact, you may become completely dependent on them.

7.1.   What Are Macros?

The term *macro* is used often today when users talk about computer software. It is a term that is hard to define.

On the most basic level, *macro* refers to a software command that is assembled by stringing together a series of simpler commands. The command that is created in this way is considered a "super" or "macro" command because it carries out a task that would normally require several simpler commands to accomplish.

Macros offer two advantages:

1. Performance. Macros make computers' work simpler. The number of commands that need to be remembered and entered to accomplish a task can be reduced to a few "super" commands, thus making computer work easier and faster.
2. Customization. Every computer user has the potential to create a system of macros that fits his or her own unique requirements. By definition, most software programs are designed to be used by as wide an audience as possible. Macros make it possible for users to shape the software more closely to their particular usage.

The definition of macro is not too far away from the definition of computer programming. In fact, the distinction is getting more and more fuzzy as computer software evolves. From a practical point of view, the creation and use of macros are often the first introduction to programming concepts that users of microcomputers encounter.

The process by which simple commands are combined to make a set of larger macro commands takes many forms. This chapter will be concerned with a specific form of macros called *keyboard macros*.

7.2.   Keyboard Macros

The term *keyboard macro* implies that the creation of these "super" commands is done by using ordinary keystrokes. This means that if you know the sequence of keystrokes that need to be entered in order to accomplish a particular task, you should be able to create an appropriate keyboard macro to accomplish the same task more simply. Keyboard macros have become popular largely as a result of Lotus 1-2-3's ability to create keystroke macros.

The fundamental idea of a keystroke macro is to list the keystrokes you would normally enter, in a form that can be recorded by the program and then played back when that function is needed.

7.3.   How Many Keys?

The idea of keystroke macros is quite simple. What makes them practical are two features of the IBM PC. First, the IBM has an expandable memory. This means that often users have more memory available than is actually required by the application they are using. This leaves memory space available to store the keystroke macros.

Second, the IBM PC keyboard has more keys and key combinations than are needed to run a single application. This means that there are always keys or combinations of keys that have no particular use in an application and are free to be assigned as macro keys.

The IBM keyboard allows you to press most of the keys four ways:

1. The key by itself.
2. Hold down the [Shift] and press the key.
3. Hold down the [Ctrl] and press the key.
4. Hold down the [Alt] and press the key.

For example, Lotus 1-2-3 uses the [F2] to toggle the program in and out of the Edit mode. However, the combinations of [Shift/F2], [Ctrl/F2], and [Alt/F2] are not used by the program at all. They are free to be defined as macro keystrokes.

7.4.   How Part 3 Is Organized

In Part 3 a number of products that perform similar functions are presented. In order to achieve some consistency, the basic functions of the programs are illustrated using MS DOS commands and functions. This allows users with different libraries of software to take advantage of the tutorials to learn how to use the functions.

The use of MS DOS commands as a common base has another advantage. Each product is explained based upon the same task. This allows the reader to make direct comparisons between comparable functions in different products.

There are, of course, some features that cannot be duplicated in every program. A summary at the end of the chapter will recap these functions.

7.5.   The Basic Concept

As with many of the programs and techniques described in this book, the basic concept is embedded in DOS. In fact you can create some simple keyboard macros by using DOS itself.

When DOS loads into the computer, the keyboard is set up automatically. Six of the function keys, [F1] through [F6], are automatically programmed to perform special functions on the systems level.

[The six functions are:

F1 = retype the last DOS command one character at a time.
F2 = retype the last command up to a specified character.
F3 = retype the entire last command.
F4 = sets the F3 key to retype the last command starting at a specified character to the end of the command. F4 does not type the characters. The F3 key must be used after the F4 to actually type the characters.
F5 = stores any text on the current line to the memory, moves the cursor down a line. This allows you to correct typing mistakes entered into a command.
F6 = Enter a [Ctrl z]]

DOS normally does not allocate room in the memory for additional key assignments. However, as part of the ANSI system, DOS does set aside additional memory space for key redefinition.

In order to take advantage of this, you must load the ANSI driver (ANSI.SYS). Then you are capable of creating new key assignments.

7.6.   Key Reassignment with DOS

The first concept to understand is the numbering system that is used to identify keys. While you recognize keys by the symbols painted on them, the computer knows the keys by means of a special numeric code. The ASCII coding system assigns most of the standard keys a number. (For more on ASCII see Chapter 1.26.)

When the ANSI driver is loaded into the computer along with DOS, the numbering system is extended to include special keys that appear on the IBM keyboard but not necessarily on the standard ASCII keyboard.

When you want to redefine a key with DOS you need to know what number is assigned to that key. You can redefine any of the ASCII or ANSI keys. However, from a practical point of view, you usually only redefine keys that don't already serve a purpose.

For example, suppose you wanted to set up your keyboard so that the [Home] key issued a directory command and the [End] key issued a wide directory command.

A command that will redefine a key requires the following elements:

1. An Escape code.
2. A [character.

```
 3          Null character, NUL
15          Shift Tab
16-25       Alt Q, W, E, R, T, Y, U, I, O, P
30-38       Alt A, S, D, F, G, H, J, K, L
44-50       Alt Z, X, C, V, B, N, M
59-68       F1, F2, F3, F4, F5, F6, F7, F8, F9, F10
71          Home
72          <up arrow>
73          [Pg Up]
75          <left arrow>
77          <right arrow>
79          [End]
80          <down arrow>
81          [Pg Dn]
82          [Ins]
83          [Del]
84-93       Shifted F1, F2, F3, F4, F5, F6, F7, F8, F9, F10
94-103      [Ctrl] F1, F2, F3, F4, F5, F6, F7, F8, F9, F10
104-113     [Alt] F1, F2, F3, F4, F5, F6, F7, F8, F9, F10
114         [Ctrl/PrtSc]
115         [Ctrl/<left arrow>]
116         [Ctrl/<right arrow>]
117         [Ctrl/End]
118         [Ctrl/Pg Dn]
119         [Ctrl/Home]
120-131     Alt 1, 2, 3, 4, 5, 6, 7, 8, 9, 0, -, =
132         [Ctrl/Pg up]
```

Fig. 7-1. Extended Keyboard Codes on the IBM PC.

3. A number indicating whether the key to be redefined is being specified with an ASCII number or an ANSI number.
4. The list of characters you want to assign to the selected key. You can enter the characters as literals or as number codes using their ASCII numbers.

"DIR" is an example of a literal. Literals are always enclosed in quotation marks. If you wanted to use the ASCII codes instead of the literal representation you would enter 68;73;82.

The ASCII code number 13 stands for the character entered when the <return> key is pressed. The number 13 is usually entered as the last character in a definition, to make the command automatically execute when the defined key is pressed.
5. The letter p. The p indicates the end of a reassignment command.

The trouble with the above specifications is that entering an <escape> character is not simple. It cannot be done by simply pressing the <Esc> key. DOS assigns the <Esc> key a special function, to cancel a command.

The trick is to use the PROMPT command to enter the necessary characters. To enter the <Escape>, PROMPT can be used with $e. Enter the following command while at your computer:

prompt $e[0;71;"DIR";13p <return>

When you use the PROMPT command in this way the system's prompt, A> or C>, disappears. To bring the prompt back, enter

prompt < return >

If all has gone correctly, you should be able to issue a directory command by pressing the [Home] key. Try this now. Enter

[Home]

Now enter the following to assign a wide directory command to the [End] key. Enter

prompt $e[0;79;"DIR/W";13p < return >

Restore the prompt by entering

prompt < return >

Now you can use the [Home] and [End] keys to issue the directory commands. Enter

[End]

Now enter

[Home]

This simple example illustrates the potential of keyboard macros. The programs discussed in Part 3 expand upon this simple concept.

[The assignments you have given to the keys have been stored in the internal memory of the computer. They are not a permanent part of DOS. If you turn off the computer or reboot it, the assignments will be lost. You will have to enter the commands again to assign keystrokes to the keys.

Further, note that the key assignments made at the system level will not function when a software program is active. These assignments are applicable to DOS only.]

8.

ProKey

ProKey is designed to allow the user to create keystroke macro commands. Unlike the ANSI examples shown, ProKey allows you to use macros with a variety of software programs. ProKey also allows you to customize keys to work with word processors, spreadsheets, data bases, and other applications.

[The program discussed in this section is ProKey version 4.0.]

ProKey is memory-resident. This means that when you load ProKey into the memory of your computer, it will remain there until you turn off the computer or reboot the system. Once installed, ProKey allows you to define keystroke macros for almost any key or combination on the IBM PC keyboard.

When you load a software program such as WordStar or Lotus 1-2-3, ProKey remains active in the background. Thus ProKey macros are global. This means that they are accessible to any program that is running in your computer.

[As always, there are some exceptions. Because of the way in which certain programs use and/or alter the memory setup of the computer, programs like ProKey may not function properly. Specific examples are covered later in this chapter.]

8.1. The ProKey Disk

The ProKey program is supplied on a single disk which contains the following files:

PKLOAD.COM	KEYTRON.LAY	123.DOC	OW.PRO
PROKEY.COM	DSK.LAY	WS.PRO	OW.DOC
LAYOUT.COM	DSKR.LAY	WS.DOC	PEACH.PRO
READ.ME	DSKL.LAY	DB.PRO	DATE.BAS
IBM.LAY	TI.LAY	DB.DOC	TODAY.BAT
AT.LAY	EAGLE.LAY	EDIT.PRO	TODAY.PRO
IBMSEL.LAY	123.PRO	EDIT.DOC	SURVEY.TXT

The 28 files take 136,704 bytes of disk space. However, only the PKLOAD.COM file is required for the majority of functions of the program. PROKEY.COM and LAYOUT.COM are additional programs that work with PKLOAD.COM. The files that end with PRO extensions are macro files that are provided with ProKey as examples of how the program can be used with other programs. For example, WS.PRO contains macros for WordStar.

The files with DOC extensions are text files that contain explanations of the macros provided in the PRO files. For example, WS.DOC contains explanations of the macros stored in WS.PRO. The DOC files can be read by any word processing program that loads standard ASCII files, e.g., WordStar, WordStar 2000, Microsoft Word.

The DOS command TYPE can also be used to view or print the contents of these files. The following command will display the contents of the WS.DOC file on the screen: **type ws.doc‹return›**

[The contents of the file will scroll by too quickly to read. To stop the scrolling enter [Ctrl/s] or [Ctrl/Num Lock]. The display will pause until another key is pressed. Pressing any key will continue the scrolling.]

To obtain a printed copy, enter **type ws.doc›prn**

The files with the LAY extensions are examples of the LAYOUT program. Layout is used to change the overall keyboard layout of your computer and is discussed later in this chapter. The disk is not copy protected. This allows floppy disk users to copy files needed, to any disk. Hard disk users can copy the files to a hard disk and no longer need the original ProKey disk as a key.

8.2. ProKey's Approach

ProKey version 4.0 allows creation and revision of macros for all the keys on the IBM PC keyboard with the following exceptions:

[Alt] [Ctrl] [Shift] [Num Lock] [Caps Lock] [Scroll Lock] [PrtSc] [Ctrl Esc]

There are three methods by which you can create and revise macros with ProKey:

1. Interactive Mode. In the interactive mode ProKey records the keystrokes you type while you are actually performing some task.
2. Record-Only Mode. In this mode you record the keystrokes you want by typing them. However, ProKey does not allow the keystrokes to flow through to the application. When you have recorded the macro, you return to where you were in the application when you began the recording.
3. ASCII Text File entry and editing. Methods 1 and 2 store the macro directly into the memory of the computer. They can be used immediately after they have been created. The ASCII text file method creates text files that contain symbols for keystrokes. These are then loaded into the memory and become macros.

8.3. Special Features

In addition to these basic functions, ProKey has a number of special features:

1. One-finger mode. The [Alt], [Shift], and [Ctrl] keys are normally used in combination with other keys. Individuals who use only one finger at a time can place the keyboard into the one-finger mode. This allows you to enter a [Alt], [Shift], or [Ctrl] combination as two consecutive keystrokes rather than a single combination. Programs like WordStar and MultiMate which rely heavily on keystroke combinations can then be used by pressing one key at a time.
2. Time Delay. ProKey allows you to enter a specific time into a macro so that it will execute at a predetermined time. Thus a command can be automatically executed when you are away from your computer.
3. Revise Keyboard Layout. ProKey comes with an additional program called Layout. This program is used to alter the layout of the keyboard. A touch typist can rearrange the keyboard to conform more closely to the type of layout he/she prefers.

8.4. Using ProKey

ProKey's primary function is to create macros. As you will see, there are three ways to work with, create, and revise keystroke macros in ProKey.

The first two methods, explained above, Interactive and Record-Only, have one thing in common. They directly enter the macros into the memory of the computer. This means that they can be replayed immediately after they have been created.

The first step in using ProKey is to load the PKLOAD program. At the system's prompt, A> or C>, **enter pkload <return>**

ProKey will display:

```
ProKey 4.00 (C) Copyright RoseSoft Incorporated 1983,84,85 All Rights
Reserved.
Installing ProKey
```

[Once ProKey is installed it is not necessary that a disk with the PKLOAD.COM file be present in the computer. The program will remain resident in the memory until the computer is turned off or rebooted. Further, if you intend to use ProKey in the Interactive or Recording modes only, PKLOAD.PRO is the *only* file that you need to copy from the original ProKey disk. If you have a floppy-based system this means that you can add ProKey to any program disk that has 32K (32,768 bytes) of free space left.]

To learn how ProKey works, you can duplicate the two simple macros created in the section on the ANSI system. These macros defined the [Home] and [End] keys as directory commands.

8.5.   The Interactive Mode

One way to create a macro with ProKey is to use the interactive mode. This mode tells ProKey to record each keystroke entered. When you work in the interactive mode, two things happen:

1. Your keystrokes are executed by the application with which you are working.
2. They are also recorded in the memory of the computer as a keystroke macro.

When you complete the entry of the keystrokes you can play back the recording as a macro by pressing the specified key. ProKey uses three special keystrokes with the interactive mode:

[Alt=] Turns on the recording mode
[Alt-] Turns off the recording mode
[Ctrl Esc] Stops recording or playback of macro.

To begin the interactive recording mode, enter [**Alt = **]

At the top of the screen, the program displays: Press Key to Define. This display confirms that you have entered the Interactive mode. The next key that you press will tell ProKey which key to assign the macro to. Enter [**Home**]

The prompt changes to Defining <home>   TEXT

Next enter **dir < return >**

[When you are working in the interactive mode your keystrokes will have the same effect that they normally do when you are working with that application. Often this will mean that the program you are working with will overwrite the ProKey messages on the screen. Remember that even though the ProKey messages have been erased, the interactive recording mode is still active.

It is easy to get confused when the prompt has been wiped off the screen. Make sure that you remember to turn off the interactive mode when you are finished creating the macro.]

When the directory display has completed, turn off the recording mode. Enter [**Alt-**]

The macro has been created. Test the macro by entering [**Home**]

The recorded keystrokes are automatically replayed.

8.6. Recording without Executing

When you recorded the previous macro, you were doing two things at once. You were executing a command and recording the keystrokes simultaneously. The advantage of this method is that you can see how each keystroke is used while you are creating a macro. However, there may be occasions when it is more advantageous to enter the macros without having the keystrokes execute at the same time.

ProKey has another method of recording the keystrokes but *without* executing the command at the same time. This is the *recording* mode. This method also introduces the ProKey pop-up menu. Enter [**Alt/**]

The ProKey menu contains a number of commands that affect the operation of the program. At this point you are interested in the command that will allow you to define a macro. The Edit command will both create new macros and allow you to revise an existing macro. Enter **e**

Next, ProKey needs to know the name of the key that you want to define. Enter [**End**]

ProKey displays Editing <end> at the top of the screen to confirm that you are actually editing the key you intended to edit. Below are some special ProKey keystrokes:

[Alt enter] or [Alt Return] saves the keystrokes and returns you to the ProKey Command menu.

[Alt Esc] clears the keystrokes you have already entered and allows you to start the entry over again.

[Ctrl Esc] cancels the the entry and returns you to the ProKey Command menu.

[Backspace] will erase the character to the left of the cursor position.

[Home] moves the cursor to the left end of a line.

[End] moves the cursor to the right end of a line.

The arrow keys position the cursor.

[Del] erases the character, if any, at the cursor position.

[Ins] toggles the edit mode between inserting and overtype entry modes.

Note that these special keys cannot be used as part of the macro's definition when you are working in the edit mode. When you press these keys, they perform their editing function instead of being recorded as part of the macro.

[If you want to enter the editing keys as part of your macro, you can do so by typing out the ProKey symbol for that key. For example, if you want the Home key included in the macro, you would enter the six-character symbol <home> by typing it out character by character. When the macro is executed, the symbol will be correctly translated as the Home key.]

Enter the keystrokes that will define the key: **dir/w<return>**

ProKey types the characters as you type them. They have no effect on the computer. They are simply being recorded by ProKey for later playback. Special keystrokes like <return> appear as symbols in ProKey. The program has its own symbol for each of the keys and key combinations that can be used with the program. A full listing of the key symbols used by ProKey can be found in Appendix A of the ProKey manual.

To complete the creation of the macro, enter **[Alt Return]**

This returns you to the ProKey menu. To return to DOS and execute the macro, enter **<return>**

Now test the macro you have created. Enter **[Home]**

The command is typed and executed.

8.7.   Saving and Recalling Macros

As mentioned previously, macros can work only if they are stored in the internal memory of the computer. However, turning off the computer will erase any information stored in its internal memory. In order to avoid the need to create the macros over again each time the computer is turned off and on, you need some method of storing the macros.

[In ProKey, the responsibility for saving macros is on the user. If you create macros but forget to save them, ProKey does not warn you about the potential loss of the macros. Always remember to save any macros or changes to old macros before you turn off the computer.]

ProKey stores macros in standard ASCII DOS text files. Macros created with the interactive and recording modes can be saved by using the ProKey Command menu.

To save the two macros you have created, return to the ProKey Command menu by entering **[Alt/]**.

ProKey has four commands which are concerned with saving and restoring macros:

W—WRITE: This command stores all the macros currently in the memory to a specified text file. The macros in the memory are not erased. They remain as they were before the command.

R—READ: This command loads all the macros stored in a specified text file into the memory. Any macros that are currently in the memory will be automatically erased when you read the macros from the disk.

M—MERGE: This command loads the macros from a file but does not erase the macros currently in the memory of the computer. This feature allows you to combine macros from different files.

If the file being loaded contains a macro for the same key as one currently in the memory, the active macro is erased and the macro being loaded takes its place.

[When you merge macro files, be aware that the total amount of space used by all the macros cannot exceed the space allocated for ProKey. The default setting is 4,096 keystrokes. If ProKey displays the message "Macro too long" when you are merging a file, this means that you have run out of room for those macros.]

C—CLEAR: This command erases all of the macros currently in the memory. Macros erased with CLEAR and not previously saved cannot be recovered.

Also of interest is the L command. The L command displays a list of all the active macros. Enter **l**

ProKey displays the macros that have been created. You can see the keystrokes that were used to create them. To return to the ProKey Command menu, enter **<return>**

To save the macros use the WRITE command. Enter **w**

You need to enter a filename for the macros. Enter **dir.pro <return>**

ProKey saves the macros in a text file called dir.pro.

[ProKey does not require you to use a special type of filename, nor does it automatically add a file extension, as do some programs, for example, SuperKey. The macro files supplied with the program all have the .PRO extension. This is only a convention and there is no reason why you must use the .PRO extension with a ProKey file. In fact, the file can be named without an extension. For example, KEYS is a legal filename. In short, any legal DOS filename will suffice for ProKey.

If you are working on a hard disk, note that ProKey will accept filenames with directory specifications. For example, assuming you have a directory called \DOS on your hard disk, you could enter the filename C:\DOS\DIR.PRO

The result would be that the macros would be stored in the DOS directory, no matter what directory you were working in when you entered the command. This allows for storage of all the macro files in the same directory, even if you create macros while you are in other directories. Doing so makes it simpler for you to remember where you stored your macro file.

You can also store the macros on a different disk drive than the one that you are working on. This is accomplished by simply preceding the filename with the drive specification, e.g., B:DIR.PRO.]

Writing macros to a file has no effect on the memory of the computer. This means that the macros remain in the memory exactly as they were before they were saved. Any changes made in the memory will not appear in the file unless the W, WRITE, command is used to save a new version of the file.

8.8. Clearing the Memory

Once you have entered macros into the memory of the computer, you can remove them in one of two ways:

1. Use the E, EDIT, command to remove them one at a time.
2. Use the C, CLEAR, command to remove all the macros.

When a macro is removed it means that the key will function as it normally would. As an example, remove the macro defined for the the Home key. Enter **e**

When ProKey asks for the key, enter **[Home]**

The macro appears on the screen. To clear this one key, enter **[Ctrl Esc]**

ProKey beeps and asks Clear this entry? [y/n] Enter **y**

The keystrokes have been eliminated. You now have three possible actions:

1. Enter a new macro by typing the desired keystrokes.
2. Leave the key *undefined* by entering [Alt Return]
3. Restore the previous macro by entering [Ctrl Esc]

In this example, choose option #2 to leave the key undefined. Enter
[Alt Return]

Enter **l**

You can see that only one macro, [End], is now in the memory. Return
to the menu by entering **<return>**

You can clear all the macros in the memory by using the C, CLEAR,
command. Enter **c**

To clear the memory, enter **<return>**

Enter **1**

ProKey tells you that there are no macros defined. Enter **<return>**

Once again you are at the ProKey Command menu.

8.9.   Restoring Macros

The purpose of saving macros is to have the ability to restore them when
you want them. The R, READ, command will read a macro text file and
create from it the macro definitions. In this example you have saved a
macro file called dir.pro. Now that the memory is clear, you can get the
two macros back by entering **r**

Now you must enter the name of the file that you want to load:
dir.pro<return>

The ProKey Command menu appears. To check to see if the macros
have been restored, enter **l**

The list shows they have been. To test to see if they still function correctly, enter

<return> <return> [Home][End]

The macros function exactly as they did when you first created them.

8.10.   Annotating Macros

The macros we have been discussing are simple enough to understand just
by looking at the keystrokes. However, as your macros get longer and
more complex you may find that it is not as simple to remember what
function the macros were designed to carry out.

ProKey allows you to add a comment or explanation to the macro. This process is referred to as *annotation*. To annotate the macros currently in the memory, return to the ProKey Command menu: **[Alt/]**

You are back to the ProKey Command menu. To annotate a macro, enter **a**

Next select the key to annotate. Enter **[Home]**

Now enter the text which will explain the function of the home key. Enter **displays normal directory listing<return>**

To annotate the [End] key, enter

a [end]display a wide directory<return>

To see the effect of these annotations, list the macros: **l**

The screen shows the macro keys, but instead of the keystrokes you see the explanation of the keys' functions. Return to the main menu: **<return>**

8.11.   Updating a File

Now that you have made changes to the macros, you must use the WRITE command to store the changes to the disk if you intend to maintain them.

[If you make changes and do not update the file, the changes will not appear the next time you load that file. This may be desirable if the changes you have made are for a temporary purpose, or simply mistakes that you do not want to preserve.]

To save the changes, enter **w dir.pro<return>**

[ProKey does not warn you if you are using the WRITE command to save a file that already exists. In this example, saving the macros as DIR.PRO erases the old DIR.PRO file and replaces it with a new file containing the macros as they exist in the memory of the computer. Take care not to accidentally erase a macro file by using a name that already exists.]

8.12.   Guarding a Macro

Another feature of ProKey is its ability to "guard" a macro in memory. The purpose of guarding is to prevent erasure when you use the CLEAR, READ, or MERGE commands.

For example, when you enter the CLEAR command, all the currently defined macros are cleared from the memory. However, if you designate macros as guarded, they will *not* be affected by the clear command.

When you READ or MERGE macro files, guarded macros will also be unaffected by the macros being loaded.

[In the case of the MERGE command, guarding a macro reverses the normal procedure in case of name conflicts. Normally, when two macros have the same name, ProKey erases the existing macro and replaces it with the new macro of the same name. If the old macro is guarded, the new macro is ignored and the old macro remains in memory.]

To see how guarding works, enter **g**

ProKey asks which key do you want to Guard/Unguard. The guard command can be used to mark a macro as guarded, or to unmark it. Enter **[Home]**

ProKey tells you that the Home key is currently unguarded. Entering a + sign will mark the macro as guarded, while entering a − will unmark the macro.

[If you are using an IBM PC keyboard you can use either the gray or the white + or − keys.]

Enter **+l**

You can see that an * appears next to the Home key. This indicates that the macro is guarded. Enter **<return>**

You are back to the ProKey Command menu. To test the effect of guarding a macro use the C, CLEAR, command. Enter **c<return>**

Use the L, LIST, command to display the macros in memory. Enter **l**

You can see that the macro defined for the Home key is still in memory. The other macro was erased by the clear command. Macros saved as guarded will be defined as guarded when they are read back into the memory of the computer.

8.13. Delays in Macros

One interesting feature of ProKey is its ability to insert timed delays into macros. In most simple situations you want a macro to execute as quickly as possible. However, there are situations in which it is advantageous to have a delay inserted between the keystrokes of a macro. ProKey allows you to insert a special command that will halt the execution of a macro for a length of time as short as one-tenth of a second or as long as 256 hours.

Why use a delay? Perhaps to create a screen display pause. This would allow the user to read the information displayed by one part of the macro before the next display appears.

As a simple example, suppose that you wanted to create a macro that displayed the directory of both drive A and drive B. It might be useful to pause between the commands to allow the user to view the results of each command.

Delays can be entered in both the interactive and the recording modes. This example will create a macro by both methods.

Begin with the interactive mode. Enter **[Alt=]**

The prompt at the top of the screen asks you to press the key you want to define. Enter **[F10]**

Now begin to enter the macro. First display a directory of drive A. Enter **dir/w<return>**

If this were the end of the macro you would enter the [Alt-] command to terminate the interactive mode. Instead, you will create a delay. Enter **[Alt/]**

The ProKey Command menu appears. Choose the D, DELAY command. Enter **d**

Next you need to enter the amount of delay time. Time is entered using a hh:mm:ss.t format. There is no need to type leading zeros for the time. For example

15	equals a 15-second delay
.1	equals a delay of one-tenth of a second
10:5	equals 10 minutes and five seconds
1:30:0	equals one hour and thirty minutes

In this example, enter **15<return>**

A 15-second delay has been created in the macro. To complete the macro, enter **cls<return>dir b:/w<return>**

[If you are working on a hard disk, drive C, substitute the floppy drive A for the B drive. Enter **cls<return>dir a:/w<return>**]

Terminate the interactive mode. Enter **[Alt-]**

Now replay the macro by entering **[F10]**

The directory of drive A will be displayed. Instead of playing back the next command, the cursor will blink next to the prompt. After a 15-second delay the screen will clear and the directory for drive B will appear.

To see how a delay is recorded, enter **[Alt/] l**

The macro looks like this:

```
<f10>    dir/w<enter><cmd>D15<enter>cls<enter>dir b:/w<enter>
```

The delay portion was entered as <cmd>D15<enter>. The <cmd>, meaning command, indicates the entry of the keystroke [Alt/]. The D15 represents a 15-second delay. Create a macro with a delay using the E, EDIT command from the ProKey Command menu. Create a macro for the F9 key by entering **[Alt/]e[F9]**

Now enter the keystrokes for the macro **dir<return>**

The next step is to enter the pause. Enter **[Alt/]**

The **<cmd>** appearing on the screen is the ProKey symbol used to depict the [Alt/] combination. Now enter the delay, (The delay is simply entered as the letter d followed by the amount of time for the delay): **d20<return>**

The delay has been entered. Enter **cls<return>**

Just to make this one different, place a second delay command in the macro by entering **[Alt/]d10<return>**

Finish the macro by entering

dir b:<return>[Alt Return]<return>

Now execute the macro. Enter **[F9]**

Notice that the macro executes with two delays, the first for 20 seconds, the second for 10 seconds. You can have as many delays as you like in a macro.

[Some programs, such as dBASE II and III, have a tendency to lose keystrokes when macros execute. The reason is that when dBASE performs certain operations, typically reading or writing information to or from the disk, it ignores any characters entered on the keyboard. Since characters entered by macros appear to be coming from the keyboard, the program will miss some of the keystrokes in the macro. You can solve this problem by inserting a delay of .1 or .2 seconds between each keystroke. This makes the macro a bit clumsy to type, but it will eliminate the lost keystrokes and allow your macro to operate properly. If you find that even with these delays keystrokes are lost, increase the time of the delay.]

8.14. Macros with Pauses

Another variation on the theme of macros is a macro that stops while it is executing and allows the user to enter a piece of information. After the information is entered, the macro will continue to execute until the task is complete.

The advantage of this type of macro is that you can add a crucial piece of information, such as a filename, to the macro as it executes.

Macros with pauses come in two types:

1. Fixed-Length Pauses. A fixed-length pause is used when the response of the user will always be the same number of characters. For example, if you wanted the user to specify a disk drive, you would leave a fixed-length pause of one character, since all drive names are single letters. The advantage of fixed-length pauses is that the macros will automatically continue as soon as the character or characters have been typed. It is not necessary to signal the computer that you have finished by entering a **<return>.**
2. Variable-Length Pauses. The variable-length pause allows the user to enter as many characters as needed while the macro is paused. However, because the computer cannot know for sure when you have finished, the user must type in a **<return>** to signal that the entry is completed.

[The final <return> is not part of the macro and will not be sent to the application. Its only function is to tell ProKey you have completed your variable field entry.]

Pauses can be entered into macros in both the interactive and recording modes.

8.15.   A Fixed-Length Field

Pauses allow you to create more generalized macros. As an example, if you had three disk drives in your system, A, B, and C, you might create three macros, one to list a directory of each drive. On the other hand, you can get a similar result by creating a single macro with a pause that would allow you to enter the drive specification. As an illustration, the next macro will list the directory of any drive.

The first example will use the edit mode. Enter **[Alt/]e[F7]**

Begin the macro by typing the directory command. Enter **dir<space>**

The change comes next. Instead of typing the letter of the drive, enter the ProKey command to create a fixed-length field pause. The command is a combination of holding down the Ctrl key and pressing the right bracket key,]. Enter **Ctrl]**

The ProKey symbol for a fixed-lenght field is <ffld>. It now appears as part of the macro. The next task is to tell ProKey how many keystrokes should be entered. This is done by typing in periods. Each period reserves space to enter a single character. In this case there is only one character needed. Enter **.**

To complete the fixed-length field entry, enter the ProKey command for fixed-length field. Enter **Ctrl]**

The ProKey symbol < ffld > appears once again. Enter the remainder of the macro. Enter **: < return > [Alt Return] < return >**

Test the macro by entering **[F7]**

The directory command appears and pauses. You can enter a single character: **a**

The macro completes its playback and the directory of drive A is displayed. Enter **[F7]**

Once again the macro pauses for your entry. This time enter a different drive letter (B if you have a floppy system, C for a hard disk system). To create the same macro in the interactive mode, first clear the macros in the memory. Enter

[Alt/]c < return > < return >

Turn on the interactive mode by entering **[Alt =]**

Select the F7 key to be defined by entering **[F7]**

Begin by entering the keystrokes for the macro: **dir < space >**

Now, enter the command to set a fixed-length field pause. Enter **Ctrl]**

Note that in the interactive mode, the fixed-length field command does not display anything on the screen. You must remember that you have pressed that key and have paused the recording of keystrokes. Enter a character to create the fixed-length field. (Any character will do.) ProKey will not record which keys you enter, only the number of keys pressed. It is the latter that will determine the length of the fixed-field pause. Enter **a**

Now mark the end of the fixed-length field and restart the interactive mode. Enter **Ctrl]**

Complete the macro by entering **: < return > [Alt-]**

Now replay the macro. Enter **[F7]a**

Run the macro again, this time using the B drive. Enter **[F7]b**

8.16. Variable-Length Fields

Variable-length fields are required when it is not possible to know in advance the number of characters that need to be entered into a macro.

As an example, a macro will be created that will search the disk for files that are of certain specifications. The method employs the use of the CHKDSK and FIND commands. The assumption is made that the CHKDSK.COM and FIND.EXE DOS program files are currently on your default drive (either A or C). Both these programs can be found on the MS DOS system disk, 2.0 or higher.

The macros will execute a special form of the CHKDSK command using the /V option. The FIND command will be used to filter the filenames to select those that contain certain characters. Look at the following command: **chkdsk/v I find"TXT"**

This command would find all the files that had the letters TXT in their filenames or extensions. The I is the vertical line character found on the same key as the backslash character, \.

[Similar results can be obtained with a DIR *.TXT command with two exceptions. First, the *.TXT will select only files with TXT as the extension. The CHKDSK command will select files in which the characters appear in any part of the filename or extension, such as NEWTXT.DOC or TXT.COM. Second, the DIR command will search only one directory at a time. The CHKDSK command will examine all the files on the disk no matter what directory or subdirectory they appear in.]

Since this command is awkward to type, it is a perfect candidate for a macro. In addition, since the characters being searched for will vary with each use of the command, it will require a variable-length pause. Like fixed-length pauses, variable-length pauses can be entered from the interactive and the recording modes. We begin with the interactive mode. Enter **[Alt =][F8]**

Begin to enter the keystrokes for the macro. Enter **chkdsk/v I find"**

Next you need to tell ProKey to pause for the entry of a variable-length field. The command to enter a pause for a field of variable length is Ctrl– (Hold down Ctrl and press the dash key.) Enter **Ctrl-**

As with the fixed-length command, when it is entered in the interactive mode, the variable–length command displays nothing on the screen. In the case of a variable–length field it really doesn't matter what is entered next. The fixed–length field counted the number of keystrokes entered but this is not the case with variable-length fields. There is no need to enter anything at all. You can simply enter another variable-field command: **Ctrl- "<return>**

The CHKDSK command will execute. No filenames will be displayed because no characters were entered between the quotation marks. Complete the macro by entering **[Alt-]**

Now replay the macro. Enter **[F8]**

The macro pauses after the first quotation has been displayed. Now enter the characters to match (remember they *must* be entered as upper case characters): **BAS**

To tell ProKey to continue with the replay of the macro, enter **<return>**

ProKey completes the command. Any files on the disk that contain the letters BAS are listed.

8.17. Multiple Fields

It is possible to create a macro that pauses several times during playback. Suppose that you wanted to select different drives to be checked with the CHKDSK command. The macro would have to pause twice, once for the drive letter and another time for the characters to match.

This time the ProKey Command menu will be used to create the macro. Enter **[Alt/]e[Shift F8]**

Begin by entering the CHDKSK command. Enter **chkdsk/v<space>**

Now insert a fixed-length field for a single character. Enter **Ctrl].Ctrl]**

Now enter the FIND filter. **: | find"**

Now insert the variable-field command. Enter

Ctrl-
Ctrl-

Finally, complete the macro by entering
"<return>[Alt Return]<return>

Playback the macro: **[Shift F8]**

The first pause is for the drive letter. Enter **a**

Note that because the field was fixed-length, no return was necessary. The macro plays back more keystrokes and then pauses again. Enter **EXE<return>**

The command then lists the file, if any, on drive A that contain the letters *EXE*.

8.18. Macros with Names

For the most part it is usually enough to name macros with single keystroke names—[Alt w], [Shift F1], etc. Execution of these macros is quite simple. All you need do is type the keystroke with which the macro is associated.

The disadvantage is that the single keystroke commands may be hard to remember. ProKey has an alternative method of naming macros in which you can use names that are longer than a single keystroke. For example, you might give macros names like *exit*, *close*, or *address*. The advantage to such names is that it is much simpler to remember what a macro does when its name is more descriptive. The disadvantage is that it takes longer to type in a long name than it does a single keystroke.

From a practical point of view, you need to balance the advantages and disadvantages of both naming methods. Usually you would use single key names for macros that type out short amounts of text or commands. Long names make more sense when the macro is long or executes a command that takes some time to complete.

Long names have a second advantage. Suppose that the application for which you wish to design macros uses many of the key combinations typically used as macro keys, e.g., [Alt letter], for its normal program functions. For example, a Lotus 1-2-3 spreadsheet may have been created with [Alt letter] combinations defined as Lotus 1-2-3 macros. Long names can be used to create macros that will not conflict with the already established functions of the [Alt] combinations.

Long-name macros can be created in either the interactive or recording modes. Below, we begin with the interactive mode to create a simple macro that will perform a CHKDSK command on all the drives in your system. Enter **[Alt =]**

The next step is the crucial one. ProKey is waiting for you to press the key that will be associated with the macro. However, if you enter a comma, ProKey will not use the comma as the macro's name. Rather, ProKey will allow you to enter a name up to eight characters long. Enter **[Alt,]**

The cursor moves to the prompt at the top of the screen. You can now type in up to an eight-character name for the macro. Enter **check <return>**

The name of the macro will be *check*. Enter

chkdsk b: <return>   Floppy Disk Systems
chkdsk c: <return>   Hard Disk Systems

Terminate the macro. Enter **[Alt -]**
To play back the macro, enter **[Alt,]check <return>**

The macro is played back. The CHKDSK command is executed and both disks are checked. Next, use the ProKey Command menu to create a macro with a long name. Enter

[Alt/]e[Alt,]chks <return> chkdsk <return>
chkdsk b: <return>   Floppy Disk Systems
chkdsk c: <return>   Hard Disk Systems
[Alt Return] <return>

Execute the macro. Enter **[Alt,]chks <return>**

8.19. Swapping Keys

A very specialized type of macro is used to swap functions between the upper and lower cases of a key. A typical example is the semicolon/colon key. The IBM PC defines the lower case of the key as the semicolon and the upper case as the colon character. In computer usage, the colon character is much more common than the semicolon. It would be advantageous to swap the functions to avoid having to SHIFT every time a colon was needed.

Swapping a key's function is tricky. This operation can be performed *only* in the interactive mode. It cannot be performed with the E, EDIT command on the ProKey Command menu. Attempting to do so will create an endless loop, and prompt ProKey to refuse to allow the macro to be entered.

The accent key is used in the swapping function. On the IBM PC keyboard it is located to the right of the quotation key. When ProKey is in the computer's memory, the function of the accent key is reserved for the special task of swapping upper and lower case characters.

To begin the swap, define the semicolon key as the colon: **[Alt =]**

You have turned on the interactive recording mode. Enter the key you want to define. Enter `

The computer beeps and displays: OK to redefine this key Y/N? ProKey will display this message whenever an attempt is made to redefine a standard key. Enter **y**

You are now ready to redefine the semicolon key. The next step is to enter the accent key. Note that when you enter this key nothing will appear to happen. Enter `

Now type the colon character. Enter :

To complete the macro, enter [Alt-]

The semicolon key will now type a colon. To test this enter ;

A colon prints on the screen. You have completed the first part of the swap. Now define the colon key as a semicolon by entering [Alt =]:y`;[Alt-]

The advantage of the accent key is clearer in this example. The accent key gave you access to the original value of the semicolon key so that you could assign its value to the colon key. The functions of the semicolon and the colon keys are now swapped. Test the swap by typing :::;;;

You can see that the keys have been swapped. To return the keys to their original functions, enter [Alt/]c<return>

8.20.   Text Files

When a macro file is stored on the disk it is stored in the form of an ASCII standard file. This implies that programs that edit ASCII standard files can be used to create and edit macro files. To see the relationship between a macro and its text storage format, some simple macros will be created. First, make sure that the memory is clear of existing macro commands: [Alt/]c

8.21.   Batch Commands

The advantages of programs like ProKey that alter and expand the function of the keyboard lead logically to the design of "turnkey" applications. This refers to the use of generalized programs like 1-2-3 or dBASE as specific applications.

The purpose of turnkey applications is to allow someone to use a complex program to accomplish a task by using macro functions prepared in advance. With macro functions, tasks that might take considerable time and knowledge can be executed by anyone who knows what macro keys to press.

For example, you might create a macro for the F1 key that loads a Lotus 1-2-3 spreadsheet. Instead of having the user remember /FR<filename> <return>, etc., you could tell them to simply press F1.

In thinking about turnkey applications one question arises: If the user doesn't know how to load ProKey and the necessary macro file, how will the F1 macro get loaded? Is there some way that a ProKey macro file can be loaded so that the macro definitions are automatically in memory when the user begins?

The answer is yes, and comes partly from the concept of DOS batch files and the PROKEY.COM program. DOS provides a means of automatically executing a number of DOS commands. The PROKEY.COM program has the ability to load a macro file as part of a DOS batch file. To understand the advantages and possibilities involved with batch files, this idea will be explored in detail.

Hard Drive:

The hands-on section that follows is designed for use with a hard disk system. The assumption is made that you are working on a hard disk that has a working copy of Lotus 1-2-3. In addition, the files PKLOAD.COM and PROKEY.COM are also on the hard disk. A path must be open between the directory with Lotus 1-2-3 and the directory that contains the ProKey program. Load the ProKey program.

Floppy Drive:

If you have a floppy disk system you will probably find that these techniques are not very practical. You can perform the same task, but the drive setup gets a bit tricky. After you have booted your computer, place a working Lotus 1-2-3 in drive A. In drive B place a disk with the ProKey files PKLOAD.COM and PROKEY.COM on it. Load the ProKey program.

In addition you should copy the Lotus driver files to the disk in drive B.

copy 123.cnf b: < return >
copy a:??.drv b: < return >

Then open a path to drive A. Enter **path a: \ < return >**
Change the active drive to B. Enter **b: < return >**
You can now run 1-2-3 from the B drive.

Lotus File:

You will also need a Lotus spreadsheet file to work with. The file used in this example is called SAMPLE.WKS. If you have a file you want to use, simply remember to substitute the file's real name wherever you see SAMPLE used in the example.

8.22.   Creating the Batch Program

Suppose that you have a file, 123test.pro, that contains two macros which would allow a novice to make some changes in a 1-2-3 spreadsheet you had designed:

F1 = loads 1-2-3 and a spreadsheet file called REPORT
F2 = prints the spreadsheet, saves any changes, and quits 1-2-3

To create the F1 macro, enter **[Alt/]e[F1]**
   The first step is to load the 1-2-3 program. Enter **123 ‹return›**
   When 1-2-3 loads, it presents a screen that tells the name of the program. A key is pressed when this screen is displayed. In order to include this process in the macro you will need to include another ‹return›. However, there is second issue involved. Following the 1-2-3 ‹return› portion of the macros, the computer will be loading a program, i.e., performing a reading operation from the disk. Many times, when computers read or write to the disk drives, keystrokes entered into macros get lost. As protection from this, a delay will make sure that loading is complete before the next part of the macro is executed. Enter **[Alt/]d2 ‹return›**
   This will insert a two-second delay when the macro is played back.

[If you are working with a floppy drive system that is especially slow, the delay may need to be increased.]

   Continue entering keystrokes: **‹return›**
   At this point, 1-2-3 reads the disk again, checking for the copy protection scheme. Once again it would be wise to enter a delay. Enter **[Alt/]d2 ‹return›**
   Now enter the keystrokes that will load the file: **/frsample ‹return›**
   The macro is now complete. Enter **[Alt Return]**

The next task is to make a macro that prints the spreadsheet, saves the changes if any, and quits the 1-2-3 program. At this moment you should still be at the ProKey Command menu. Enter **e[F2]**

Begin with the keystrokes that will print the worksheet. Enter

/ppr < return > gpq/fssample < return > r/qy < cmd > d2 < return > clear < return >

Complete the macro: **[Alt Return]**

You have created the two macros that you need. To save the macros in a file, enter **w123test.pro < return >**

Clear the memory of macros: **c < return >**

Now you have stored the macros to the disk and are ready to create the batch commands. Exit the ProKey Command menu: **< return >**

8.23. More about Batch Commands

Normally, the only way to load macros into the memory of the computer is to call up the ProKey command menu and use the Read command. Batch files make it possible to implement that loading command directly from DOS. The PROKEY.COM program will perform this task.

The PROKEY.COM program will perform six functions:

prokey <filename>/r	read a file into memory
prokey <filename>/w	store macros to a file
prokey <filename>/m	merge a file into memory
/c	clear the memory
/q	remove ProKey from memory
/i	install ProKey into memory

[Function /i will install ProKey after it has been loaded and suspended. You still must load PKLOAD before you can use PROKEY.COM]

For example, to load the 123test.pro macro file into memory, enter the following command: **prokey 123test.pro/r < return >**

Check to see if the file has been loaded: **[Alt/]l**

You can see the macros listed. Enter **< return > < return >**

You can use the ProKey command to clear macros: **prokey/c < return >**

The macros are cleared from the memory. To check, enter **[Alt/]l**

No macros are listed. Return to the DOS prompt: **<return> <return>**

The advantage of using commands with the PROKEY.COM program is that these commands can be used as part of a DOS batch file.

[If you are not familiar with the concepts of batch files, see Chapter 2.22.]

You can create a batch file with any ASCII word processing program, the DOS program EDLIN, or even with the DOS COPY command. In this example, the DOS COPY command will be used. The disadvantage of COPY is that you cannot go back to previous lines and make corrections. If you are familiar with EDLIN you might want to use that program instead. Enter **copy con: update.bat <return>**

Now enter the batch commands. The first command is used to load the PKLOAD.COM program. Enter **pkload <return>**

The next command is a variation on the PROKEY/R command. In addition to loading the macro file 123.pro, you can tell ProKey to automatically execute one of the macros in that file. This is done by following the command with the name of the macro key that you want to automatically execute.

The key is placed in square brackets, [ ]. Note that the [F1] in the ProKey command means to type the four characters: [F 1]. It does not mean to press the [F1] function key. Also note that you should not press **<return>** at the end of the command. Enter **prokey 123test.pro/r/[F1]**

To save the macro enter **[F6] <return>**

DOS will tell you that the one file has been copied. This means that the text you typed has been stored in a file on the disk. Now create another batch file called CLEAR.BAT. (This step is not absolutely necessary. The CLEAR.BAT will use the ProKey program to clear the macros out of the memory after the program has completed and return the function keys F1 and F2 to their original definitions.)

Create the batch file by entering

copy con: clear.bat <return> prokey/c <return> cls <return>
echo Lotus Update Program Complete

Save the text to a file by entering **[F6] <return>**

DOS will confirm the saving by telling you that one file was copied. You are now ready to execute the batch file. Enter **update <return>**

What is happening? First the Lotus 1-2-3 program loads. Then the macro loads the spreadsheet, SAMPLE. You are now ready to make any necessary changes. Enter **[F2]**

This executes the second macro. The file prints, then saves. Then the macro exits from 1-2-3. The CLEAR.BAT file is executed, removing the macros from the memory and returning the function keys to their normal status. You can run these batch files as many times as you like. The use of ProKey commands in DOS batch files is quite handy. Programs that allow you to access DOS, such as dBASE III, provide an interesting way to combine keyboard programs and applications programs. The section in this chapter on dBASE III illustrates these techniques.

8.24.   Text Files

When you save macros in files, they are stored as ASCII standard text files. This means they can be edited by any of the ASCII standard editing or word processing programs described in Chapter 1. In the previous section you created a macro file called 123test.pro. Because that file is stored as a standard DOS file, you can use DOS commands to examine and edit the file. At the prompt, enter **type 123test.pro <return>**

The screen will display:

```
*
<begdef><f1>123<enter>
<cmd>d2<enter>
<enter>
<cmd>d2<enter>
/frsample<enter>
<enddef>
*
<begdef><f2>/ppr<enter>
gpq/fssample<enter>
r/qy<cmd>d2<enter>
clear<enter>
<enddef>
*
```

What does it all mean? If you look closely you will see that the macros typed into the memory appear as a series of symbols. Let's examine the file in detail. The first line consists of a single character, *. The line is used to mark the beginning of a macro section. You can see that each section is separated by such a line.

The next line begins the actual definition. The symbol < begdef > is the symbol that ProKey stores to show that the text begins a macro definition. The next symbol on that line is the symbol for the key under which the macros will be stored. The remainder of the symbols and letters correspond directly to the keystrokes in the macro. Finally the symbol < enddef > appears. This marks the end of the macro. The pattern repeats for the next macro.

When you examine the pattern of a macro file, you realize that it would be a simple matter to reverse the process and create a macro file by simply typing the characters into a text file. Why would you want to create macros this way? Isn't it simpler to use the recording or interactive mode? In most cases, that would be correct. Interestingly enough, when ProKey was first designed, the only way to create macros was to create text files and load them into the memory.

The main reason to alter a macro file is to take advantage of the editing features found in word processing programs. One prime feature is search and replace. As an example, refer to the macros in the sample file 123TEST.PRO. Suppose that you wanted to add more macros to the list. Many of the macros might use the filename SAMPLE. Macros can be created using a text editor if you conform to the pattern that ProKey uses when it creates a file. As an example, use Edlin to change the 123TEST.PRO file: **edlin 123test.pro < return >**

Enter the LIST command to display the contents of the file: **L < return >**

Edlin lists the text of the file and numbers the lines. What type of editing would be useful? Suppose that you wanted the macro to use the file SAMPLE rather then the file BUDGET. That means that you need to change two of the lines in the file. Enter **6 < return >**

Then enter **[F1]** (3 times)

Type the name of the new file: enter **budget**

Complete the entry by entering **[F3] < return >**

Now change line 10. Enter

10 < return >
[F1]   (6 times)
budget[F3] < return >

To save the file, enter **e < return >**

The revised file is stored on the disk. When you load the macros from 123test.pro they will now work with a file called BUDGET.WKS.

8.25. Other Features and Modes

ProKey has a number of settings that change the way the program operates. One of the most interesting is the one-finger mode.

The one-finger mode is an adaptation of the fact that many of the features of keyboard programs require the use of key combinations such as [Alt /], etc.

ProKey makes it possible to eliminate the need to enter these combinations by holding down the first key while pressing the second. This is possible because of the way in which the keyboard functions. When you press a key combination, the computer records the fact that the [Alt], [Ctrl], or [Shift] key is being pressed down. When the next key is pressed it interprets the character differently than it would if the [Alt], [Ctrl], or [Shift] key had not been held down.

In normal use, if you let go of the [Alt], [Ctrl], or [Shift] key before you press the other key, the computer ignores the [Alt], [Ctrl], or [Shift] and handles the entry as a normal keystroke. When the one-finger mode is active, the pressing of the [Alt], [Ctrl], or [Shift] keys is recorded in the memory of the computer. Even if you let up on the [Alt], [Ctrl], or [Shift] key, the next keystroke will be considered a combination keystroke.

This means that all the key combinations can be accomplished by a sequence of single, one-finger keystrokes. This is very beneficial to people with handicaps. It means that any program can be operated without the need to hold down the [Alt], [Ctrl], or [Shift] keys in combination with other keys.

The one-finger mode is initiated from the ProKey menu, or DOS. To operate the one-finger mode from the menu, enter

[Alt /]o +   (turns on one-finger mode)
[Alt /]o −   (turns off one-finger mode)

and from DOS

prokey/o + **<return>**   (turns on one-finger mode)
prokey/o − **<return>**   (turns off one-finger mode)

When the one-finger mode is active, combination commands are entered sequentially. For example, the normal way to list the macros in the memory is:

[**Alt /**]l (two keystrokes)

In the one-finger mode you would enter

[**Alt**]/l (three keystrokes)

8.26. ProKey's Working Speed

Two other modes are designed to control the way that ProKey types data into an application: the Fast mode and the Disk Wait mode. The Fast mode is concerned with the speed with which ProKey feeds macro keystrokes to the application. Normally, ProKey types macro keystrokes the equivalent of 1,800 words per minute.

However, that speed may be too fast for the application you are working with. If you find that your application is losing keystrokes as the macro is being played back, you should turn off the fast mode. This reduces the speed of the typing by about one-tenth, to approximately 180 words per minute. To operate the Fast mode from the menu, enter

[**Alt /**]f+   (turns on Fast mode)
[**Alt /**]f−   (turns off Fast mode)

and from DOS

prokey/f+ <**return**>   (turns on Fast mode)
prokey/f− <**return**>   (turns off Fast mode)

The default is set to the Fast typing mode. ProKey also allows you to enter a number between 0 and 256 to select some speed between the extremes. For example, entering [Alt /]f128<return> would select a speed about halfway between fast and slow. (Note that the number that you type in is not the actual typing speed, but merely a rating used by ProKey.)

The Disk Wait mode is designed to eliminate the loss of macro keystrokes that occurs in certain applications when the disk drive is being accessed by the program. Turning on the Disk Wait mode causes ProKey to suspend typing when the application accesses the disk. To operate the Disk Wait mode from the menu, enter

[Alt /]k +   (turns on Disk Wait mode)
[Alt /]k −   (turns off Disk Wait mode)

From DOS

prokey/k + < return >   (turns on Disk Wait mode)
prokey/k − < return >   (turns off Disk Wait mode)

The default is to have the Disk Wait mode turned off.

8.27.   Suspending the Program

ProKey allows you to suspend the operation of the program. The purpose is to return the keyboard to normal without removing the macros from memory. When ProKey is suspended you can neither play back nor create macros. However, any macros that are in the memory will remain there and will become active when you turn off the suspension.

The Suspend mode can be controlled from the menu by entering

[Alt /]s +   (turns on the Suspend mode)
[Alt /]s −   (turns off the Suspend mode)

From DOS

prokey/s +   (turns on the Suspend mode)
prokey/s −   (turns off the Suspend mode)

When using DOS commands to change ProKey modes, note that you can change more than one mode at a time. For example, you could turn off both the Disk Wait and Fast modes with this command: **prokey/f − /k − < return >**

8.28.   Changing ProKey

There are two important changes you can make in the way ProKey operates. The first changes the amount of memory that ProKey uses when it loads. The default is for ProKey to set aside four kilobytes (4,096 bytes) of memory for macro recording. Since most macros are short, this is usually adequate.

However, you can change the amount of memory used by ProKey for macros. The minimum amount of memory is one kilobyte, and the maximum is 30 kilobytes. Enlarging the memory allows you to create larger macros. Decreasing the memory frees memory space for other applications. In practical terms, an additional three kilobytes is not likely to make much difference.

It is important to note that the size of ProKey in the memory is set when you load PKLOAD. If you want to change the size of ProKey, you must reboot the computer and load PKLOAD in a with a special parameter.

The parameter is a / followed by a number between 1 and 30 indicating the number of kilobytes of memory you want to allocate—for example, pkload/10<return>. This command would block out a ten-kilobyte block of memory for ProKey.

Another reason to alter the size of the memory area that ProKey occupies is to increase the size of the "type ahead" buffer. The IBM PC uses a 15-character buffer to capture keystrokes as you enter them. The keystrokes are then fed to the application. This means that you can type a maximum of 15 keystrokes ahead of the application you are working with.

If you try to type in more characters after the buffer has been filled, the computer emits a high-pitched squeal. The problem comes up in 1-2-3 when the arrow keys are held down to scroll the display. After a few seconds, keystrokes are being entered faster than 1-2-3 can execute the commands.

Any keystrokes that are entered after the buffer is filled are lost. ProKey can enlarge the typing buffer area to allow you to enter more keystrokes. This allows you to type ahead of the application without losing keystrokes. To enlarge the keystroke buffer area, enter **pkload/t100<return>**

This sets the type ahead buffer at 100 keystrokes. Like the memory size parameter, you can enter the type ahead buffer size only when you first load ProKey. If you want to change the size of the type ahead buffer and you have already loaded ProKey, you must reboot your computer.

[The type ahead buffer will not solve all your problems with applications that take time to complete a command. Many programs cannot accept keystrokes while they are performing certain tasks, such as reading and writing data to and from the disk.

Keystrokes presented by the buffer to the application during these tasks are ignored. dBASE is representative of this problem. Enlarging the keystroke buffer will not solve this problem. However, it will work with 1-2-3. Keystrokes entered into the type ahead buffer with 1-2-3 will eventually be executed.]

If you want to change both the macro memory size and the type ahead buffer size, you must enter a single command with two parameters. The example below sets the macro memory area to five kilobytes and the type ahead buffer to 50 keystrokes. Enter **pkload/5/t50<return>**

8.29. Changing ProKey Commands

The command keystrokes that are used by ProKey can be changed to other keys. There are two reasons to change the command keys in ProKey. The first is to avoid conflicts with programs that also use the same key combinations. The second reason is more personal. You simply might prefer to use a different set of keys to command the program.

The commands can be changed when you load the PKLOAD program. Unlike the memory area command, you can change the ProKey commands at any time, and several times, by issuing consecutive PKLOAD commands. There are eight special ProKey keystroke commands that can be redefined. Each key is associated with a letter that designates which command you want to redefine.

Function of Command	Default Key	Letter Symbol
Begin Macro	[Alt=]	b
End Macro	[Alt-]	e
Variable Field	[Ctrl-]	v
Fixed Field	<Ctrl[>	f
Display Menu	[Alt/]	c
Swap Function	[`]	o
Long Name	[Alt,]	m
Save Macro	[Alt Return]	a

Each key command that you want to redefine is preceded by /x. Then use the letter that corresponds to the command that you assign to a new key, followed by the ProKey name for the key. For example, to redefine the command that displays the ProKey menu ([Alt/]) as the [Home] key, enter **pkload/xc[home]<return>**

Observe that in this command square brackets were used in entering the key name. This is because angle brackets, < >, are used by DOS to indicate redirection of a program's input and output. If you used the an-

gle brackets with this command DOS would display the message: File not
Found.

[The command pkload/xc<home> would indicate to DOS that the program PKLOAD
expected input from a file called HOME. Since there probably isn't a file called HOME
on your disk, DOS tells you that the input file cannot be found.]

As an example, suppose that you wanted to define the [F9] and [F10]
function keys as the begin recording macro and end recording macro keys
respectively. Enter **pkload/xb[f9]/xe[f10]<return>**
Test the command's effect. Enter **[F9]**
The prompt appears at the top of the screen, telling you that ProKey is
ready to define a macro. Enter **[Alt z]**
To end the macro, enter **[F10]**
The prompt disappears, indicating that F10 has terminated the macro.
Keep in mind that the original command keys, [Alt=] and [Alt-], do not
retain their functions when you redefine the command keys.
Unlike the settings for memory size and buffer size, the command key
assignments can be made at any time. You could change the begin and
end macro commands to operate with the [Home] and [End] keys respectively. Enter **pkload/xb[home]/xe[end]<return>**
Now enter **[Home]**
The screen shows the prompt that indicates a macro definition has begun. Enter **[Alt z][End]**
To return the key commands to their primary keys, enter
pkload/xb[alt=]/xe[alt-]<return>

8.30.   Layout

In addition to the PKLOAD and PROKEY programs, the ProKey disk
contains another program, called *Layout.*
The purpose of Layout is to change the position of the keys on the
keyboard. Why would you want to do this? One reason is that you simply
don't like the position of the keys. One common complaint about the
IBM PC keyboard is the position of the [\ |] and the [Shift] key. Layout
gives you a chance to swap those keys.
In addition, the program is supplied with a several layout files that convert your keyboard to an IBM selectric keyboard, an IBM AT keyboard, a
Texas Instruments keyboard, or a Dvorak keyboard.

The Layout program affects the basic relationship between the keyboard and the computer. For this reason the Layout program *must* be loaded before you load ProKey or other utilities.

[As with other utility programs that directly modify memory, Layout may be incompatible with certain other utility programs. Layout is closely dependent on the BIOS supplied with the computer. Some IBM-compatible computers, e.g., the Televideo PC II, will not operate properly with Layout.]

The Layout program works with the special Layout files supplied with the program. You cannot construct a Layout file from scratch. The only way to create a personalized Layout is to modify one of the Layout files that are supplied with the program.

If you want to create a personal Layout but don't want to change one of the existing files you can use DOS to make a copy of a layout file and then use the layout program to modify that copy. For example, one of the files supplied with the program is IBM.LAY. This contains the IBM PC keyboard layout. Use DOS to copy this file. Enter

copy ibm.lay new.lay < return >

Now you have a new file, NEW.LAY, that has the same contents as the IBM.LAY file. Begin the Layout program. Enter **layout < return >**

To illustrate how Layout works, modify the NEW.LAY file. Enter

c < return > new.lay < return >

[If Layout displays the following message it indicates that you have loaded the PKLOAD program before you began working with Layout:

```
        Layout must be installed before anything else.
        Please reboot and run layout before anything else.
```

In order to work with Layout you must reboot your computer and run Layout before you load the PKLOAD program.]

The Layout program presents a screen that looks like this:

```
    This diagram of your current keyboard is for reference:

F1  F2  Esc  !   @   #   $   %   ^   &   *   (   )   -   +   Bsp  NmL  ScL
F3  F4  Tab  Q   W   E   R   T   Y   U   I   O   P   [   ]   Ent  7   8   9
Min
F5  F6  Ctl  A   S   D   F   G   H   J   K   L   ;   '   `        4   5   6
F7  F8  Shl  \   Z   X   C   V   B   N   M   ,   .   /   Shr Prt  1   2   3
Pls
F9  F10 Alt                  Spc                 Cpl     Ins  Del
```

```
      This diagram will display your changes as you make them:

Fl  F2  Esc  !  @  #  $  %  ^  &  *  (  )  -  +  Bsp  NmL  ScL
F3  F4  Tab  Q  W  E  R  T  Y  U  I  O  P  [  ]  Ent  7   8    9
Min
F5  F6  Ctl  A  S  D  F  G  H  J  K  L  ;  '  `     4   5    6
F7  F8  Shl  \  Z  X  C  V  B  N  M  ,  .  /  Shr Prt 1   2    3
Pls
F9  F10  Alt              Spc            Cpl     Ins  Del
```

```
        Press:  Space bar    to change a key.
                Escape key   to cancel changes and restart.
                Enter key    to save your new keyboard.
                q            to quit without saving.
```

The only action that you can take in the Layout program is to swap the position of various keys. Suppose that you wanted to swap the positions of the [Alt] key and the [Shift] key. In order to change the position of the keys you must perform two steps:

1) Change the [Alt] key to the [Shift] Position.
2) Change the left [Shift] key to the [Alt] Position.

To change a key location, begin by entering **<space bar>**
Now type the key that you want to change. Enter **[Alt]**
The Alt symbol on the upper keyboard appears in reverse video. Now you must enter the key that will function as the [Alt] key. The key you want to swap is the left SHIFT key. Enter **[Shift]**
The bottom keyboard now shows two positions for the [Alt] key:

```
            Fl   F2   Esc   !   @
            F3   F4   Tab   Q   W
            F5   F6   Ctl   A
            F7   F8   Alt   \   Z
            F9   F10  Alt
```

Now you must complete step two. Enter **<space bar>**
Enter the key that you want to place on the new keyboard. The key is the left [Shift] key. Enter **[Shift]**
The left [Shift] symbol on the upper keyboard is highlighted. Now enter the key that will function as the [Shift] key. Enter **[Alt]**

The screen now shows:

```
   This diagram of your current keyboard is for reference:

F1  F2  Esc  !  a  #  $  %  ^  &  *  (  )  -  +  Bsp  NmL  ScL
F3  F4  Tab  Q  W  E  R  T  Y  U  I  O  P  [  ]  Ent  7  8  9
Min
F5  F6  Ctl  A  S  D  F  G  H  J  K  L  ;  '  `     4  5  6
F7  F8  Shl  \  Z  X  C  V  B  N  M  ,  .  /  Shr  Prt  1  2  3
Pls
F9  F10  Alt              Spc              Cpl   Ins   Del


   This diagram will display your changes as you make them:

F1  F2  Esc  !  a  #  $  %  ^  &  *  (  )  -  +  Bsp  NmL  ScL
F3  F4  Tab  Q  W  E  R  T  Y  U  I  O  P  [  ]  Ent  7  8  9
Min
F5  F6  Ctl  A  S  D  F  G  H  J  K  L  ;  '  `     4  5  6
F7  F8  Alt  \  Z  X  C  V  B  N  M  ,  .  /  Shr  Prt  1  2  3
Pls
F9  F10  Shl              Spc              Cpl   Ins   Del
```

The lower keyboard shows the new positions of the keys that you have swapped. The process can continue until you have created a keyboard that you want to work with. If you want to abandon the changes, you can press the <Esc> key and the keyboard will return to the original layout.

[To change an individual key back to its original simply enter the same key twice. Example

<space bar>[Alt][Alt]<space bar>[Shift][Shift]

The keys will return to normal.]

In order to save the new keyboard, enter **<return>**

You can now enter the name of the file that you want to create. Enter **new.lay<return>**

Layout then asks you if you want the new layout to become effective immediately. Enter **y**

To test the new layout, load the ProKey program. Enter **pkload<return>**

If all is correct the left [Shift] key will function as the [Alt] key. To activate the macro program, hold down the left [Shift] key and press **=**

The prompt appears at the top of the screen. To terminate the macro hold down the left [Shift] key and press **-**

8.31   Removing and Activating a Keyboard

When a layout file has been loaded, you can return to the normal keyboard by using the QUIT command. The simplest way to issue this command is to enter **layout/q<return>**

The keyboard returns to normal. To reinstall the layout you can use the layout command with the Load parameter. Enter
layout new.lay/l<return>

The new keyboard layout is reinstalled. Keep in mind that when a layout has been installed, you cannot change without rebooting the computer.

[Because you can load a keyboard with a command parameter it is possible to execute a keyboard layout command from a DOS batch file.

Specifically, you can add the command to the AUTOEXEC.BAT file and automatically load the keyboard every time you boot your computer. Note that if you do add a Layout command to the AUTOEXEC.BAT, you will have a hard time changing the layout. Remember that you cannot change a keyboard after it has been loaded; you must reboot. But if you have an AUTOEXEC.BAT that contains the Layout command, then every time you boot the computer, Layout is loaded.

To break this cycle you must stop the AUTOEXEC.BAT command from executing the Layout command by removing the command from the AUTOEXEC.BAT.]

8.32.   Conclusion

The ProKey system is a powerful way to create keyboard macros. The Layout program adds the ability to alter the position of keys. The primary weakness of ProKey is that it is not compatible with SideKick. For users with Sidekick, SuperKey offers a level of compatibility with Sidekick that enhances both programs.

To see how ProKey stacks up with other macro programs, see the comparison in Chapter 12.

9.

SuperKey

SuperKey is a keyboard enhancement program from Borland, the same company that produces Sidekick. As a keyboard program, SuperKey includes most of the functions and features of ProKey. Further, the manufacturer has included some additional functions and features, such as a keyboard locking program, a cut and paste program, pop-up messages, and data security coding.

SuperKey is important if you are a Sidekick user because there are many ways in which it can be used in combination with Sidekick to perform some very useful functions.

9.1. The Program

SuperKey comes on a single floppy disk which contains 33 files taking up 318,464 bytes of disk space. The only file that is absolutely required to operate SuperKey is KEY.COM. It takes up 40,960 bytes, or 40K, of disk space. The other files have the following functions:

KEYDES.COM—This program is a duplicate of the KEY.COM, i.e., the main SuperKey, program. The only difference is that the technique employed by this version of the program to create encrypted data files conforms to the Data Encryption Standard issued by the federal government in order to protect sensitive data. The KEY.COM file uses a method for encryption that is faster than the Data Encryption Standard method. Most users will find that the normal encryption method is quite adequate to protect their files from unauthorized users.

KEY.HLP—This file contains the help screens for the SuperKey program. Note that help screens are not memory-resident. They must be loaded each time help

249

is requested. With the exception of help screens, SuperKey is fully functional without this file.

KEYINST.COM—This program is used to install three aspects of the SuperKey program: 1) screen type, 2) colors, and 3) amount of memory allocated for macros. The default value for memory size is 8,000 characters. The memory can range from 128 bytes (one-eighth of a K) to almost 64K.

LAYOUT.COM—Keyboard layout program. This program allows you to change the position of the keys on the keyboard.

READ-ME.COM—This program is used to display the READ-ME.KEY data file. This file contains updates and information not contained in the printed documentation.

READ-ME.KEY—This is the file read by the READ-ME program.

PCJRINST.BAT—This file modifies the KEY.COM program to operate with the PCJR's keyboard. The JR cannot send the [Alt/] character that is used by SuperKey. The file is modified to work with [Ctrl/] instead.

9.2.   Memory Space

SuperKey takes up about 57K or 58,050 bytes of internal memory when it is loaded. Note that this figure assumes that you are using the standard 8,000-byte memory area for defining macros.

[If you are loading both Sidekick and SuperKey, you *must* always load SuperKey first. Sidekick should always be the last program loaded into memory. If you load SuperKey after Sidekick, Sidekick will disappear from the memory.]

9.3.   Creating Macros with SuperKey

Macro commands can be created with SuperKey in the same three ways that they are created in ProKey:

1. *Interactive Mode.* This mode allows SuperKey to record your keystrokes as you actually enter commands into the computer. For many people the interactive mode is the simplest to work with because the program reacts just as it normally would when commands are entered. All the prompts and the menus appear as they normally do. The only difference is that SuperKey is recording the keystrokes.

2. *Editing Mode.* This mode is usually used to add and delete keystrokes from macros that have been created with the interactive mode. However, it is possible to create macros entirely in the EDIT mode. The EDIT mode can be used to create macros when you do not want to have the program react immediately to the keystrokes as you enter them.

   If the macro invokes printing or sorting commands that take a long time to execute, you might find it simpler to create it in the EDIT mode.

   There is a disadvantage to the EDIT mode: because the program is not running when you enter the keystrokes, menus and prompts that help you remember what to enter will not appear.

3. *Text Files.* Macros can be created and edited by means of ASCII standard text files. These files can be created with programs like Edlin and many word processing programs. (For information about word processing programs and ASCII files see Chapter 1.24.)

Though most of the time you will find that the first two methods, interactive and EDIT, are simpler and faster, there are some instances when text editing has advantages. These involve groups of macros that require extensive editing. Word processing features like search and replace can speed that editing process.

[Sidekick users can use the Sidekick notepad to edit macros files. The notepad produces Standard ASCII text files.]

9.4.   What Keys?

SuperKey can assign macros to almost any key combination you can make on the IBM PC or compatible keyboard. Each key on this keyboard can be used four ways:

1. By itself.
2. Shifted. Hold down one of the two [Shift] keys and press another key.
3. With the [Ctrl] key. Hold down [Ctrl] and press another key.
4. With the [Alt] key. Hold down the [Alt] and press another key.

While all these combinations are potential macro keys, you should probably avoid defining macros for standard typing keys such as a through z, A through Z, 0 through 9, etc. Since most of your typing is done with these keys it is wiser to use combinations like [Alta].

There are some keys and combinations that you cannot define as macro keys. They are:

[Alt] [Ctrl] [Shift] [Caps Lock] [Num Lock] [Scroll Lock] [Shift PrtSc] [Ctrl Esc] ` [Alt-]

9.5.   Setup for Hands-On

To insure that you have the same software setup, the following hands-on sections will utilize a DOS diskette.

Floppy Systems:
Drive A: A copy of your DOS system disk.
Drive B: A copy of the SuperKey program disk.

> To begin, change the drive to drive B. Enter **b:<return>**
> Load the SuperKey program. Enter **key<return>**
> Now change the default drive back to A: by entering **a:<return>**
> Clear the display by entering **cls<return>**

Hard Disk Systems:
Drive A: A copy of your DOS system disk.
Drive C: Use the CD command to make the directory that contains copies of the file from the SuperKey program disk.

> Load the program by entering **key<return>**
> Change the default drive to A. Enter **a:<return>**
> Clear the display by entering **cls<return>**

9.6.   The Interactive Mode

The fastest and most simple way to use SuperKey is to use the interactive mode. This mode records in the memory of the computer any keys that you press while the mode is active. The keystrokes are assigned to a selected key. When that key is pressed, the keystrokes are replayed from the memory.

The interactive mode has three special keys:

1. [Alt=]: Pressing this combination activates the interactive recording mode. The first key pressed after the [Alt=] is entered will be used by SuperKey as the key to which the macro will be assigned.
2. [Alt-]: Pressing this combination terminates that macro recording. You can continue working or immediately play back the macro.
3. [Ctrl Esc]: This is a *very* important combination. Pressing this cancels the playback of a macro. If you accidentally create a looping macro, this is the only way to stop it.

To create a macro, enter **[Alt=]**

SuperKey displays a box on the screen. The box contains a prompt that requests that you enter the key to which the macro will be assigned.

As mentioned previously, macros can be assigned to almost any key or combination, with the exception of a few special keys. However, you should take care not to assign a macro to a key that already has a specific purpose in the application in which you are working. This usually means that keys that type letters, numbers, or special symbols should rarely be used for macros because this will interfere with their normal typing functions.

Also keep in mind any special keys, such as function keys, that have special uses in some applications. For example, in DOS, keys [F1] through [F6] have special functions.

In this case, use the [Home] key: **[Home]**

SuperKey displays the message KEY: <HOME> Text- Press <Alt-> to end.

Next enter the keystrokes **dir<return>**

[When you are working in the interactive mode, your keystrokes will have the same effect that they normally do when you are working with that application.]

When the directory display has completed, turn off the recording mode. Enter **[Alt-]**

You have now created a macro. Test the macro by entering **[Home]**

The keystrokes you recorded are automatically replayed.

9.7. Using the Menu

There is another way to create macros involving the use of the SuperKey menu. To display the SuperKey menu, enter **[Alt/]**

```
┌─────────────────────────────────────────────────────────────────────┐
│ Macros   Commands  Functions   Options    Defaults  Encryption Layout  Setup │
└─────────────────────────────────────────────────────────────────────┘
```

Fig. 9-1. SuperKey Menu.

There are eight options on the SuperKey main menu. The two ways to make selections from them are:

1) *Arrow Keys.* The arrow keys will move the highlight from option to option. If the menu is horizontal, then you use the left and right arrow keys. If the menu is vertical, then you use the up and down arrow keys. When you have highlighted the option you want, select it by pressing <return>. Note that selection requires two actions, highlight and <return>. Highlighting itself is not sufficient.

2) *Type a Letter.* Each menu item has one of the letters in the item capitalized. The letter is usually the first letter. However, on menus where two options begin with the same letter, another letter is used. For example, the eDit command is written that way to indicate that the letter "d" is pressed for that option, not "e". Keep in mind that when you select a menu item by typing its letter, no <return> is necessary.

To cancel a menu, use the <Esc> key. Be aware that the action of the <Esc> key differs with the method you use to enter a menu or submenu. If you select an item by highlighting and pressing <return>, the <Esc> key cancels only the last menu entered. If you enter by typing letters, the <Esc> key cancels all the keystrokes and returns you to your application.

The eight options on the SuperKey main menu are:

Macros. This option allows you to create, edit, save, and recall macros.

Commands. This option allows you to enter a special SuperKey command. There will be more detail about commands later.

Functions. You may have noticed that the the word *Functions* appears in a different shade of video display than do the other options. This is because the functions menu can only be accessed while recording a macro.

Options. Options are special settings that affect the general operation of SuperKey. Options do not directly affect macros.

Defaults. SuperKey defaults are the key combinations you must use to access SuperKey functions. SuperKey is supplied with a default set of command keys, but you can change them at any time.

Encryption. This option enters the data encryption portion of the program.

Layout. This option is used for creating alternate keyboard layouts.

Setup. This option allows you to specify default directories for data and macro files.

When you choose any of these items, you will display a submenu that pops up beneath the item you chose.

In this case you are interested in the Macro menu. Enter **m**

The macro menu is displayed:

```
┌─────────────────────────────────────────────────────────────────────────┐
│ Macros   Commands  Functions   Options    Defaults  Encryption Layout  Setup │
├──────────────────┐                                                        
│ Begin            │                                                        
│  Title           │                                                        
│  Fixed Field     │                                                        
│  Var Field       │                                                        
│  autO-start      │                                                        
│ End              │                                                        
│ cUt and paste    │                                                        
│ eDit             │                                                        
│ Load             │                                                        
│ Merge            │                                                        
│ Clear            │                                                        
│ Save             │                                                        
└──────────────────┘                                                        
```

Fig. 9-2. The Macro Menu.

Notice that some of the options appear in a different video display than do others. This indicates that they are not available at the current moment. For example, Title can only be used when you are actually recording a macro.

When items are set apart like this, SuperKey is indicating that it cannot carry out those functions at the present time. Accessing the same menu under different circumstances will show that different options are available at different times.

The SuperKey menu contains a number of commands that affect the operation of the program. At this point you are interested in the command that will allow you to define a macro. The Begin command creates new macros. Enter **b**

```
┌─DEFINE MACRO─────┐
│ Press key to define │
└─────────────────────┘
```

Fig. 9-3. Select a Key Prompt.

Once again the box appears, asking you to type the key for which the macro will be defined. Enter **[End]**

The message KEY: <END> Text- Press <Alt-> to end appears at the top of the screen. Enter the keystrokes that will define the key: **dir/w <return>**

To complete the macro you can enter **[Alt-]** or use the menu. To use the menu, enter **[Alt/] m**

The macro menu appears. Notice that now all the options with the exception of eDit are available to you. To terminate the macro, enter **e**

The screen clears and you are returned to the system prompt. Now test the macros you have created. Enter **[Home]**

The command is typed and executed. Now test the next one. Enter **[End]**

The macro executes the command stored under it.

```
PRINT     COM     4608  10-20-83  12:00p
RECOVER   COM     2304  10-20-83  12:00p
ASSIGN    COM      896  10-20-83  12:00p
TREE      COM     1513  10-20-83  12:00p
GRAPHICS  COM      789  10-20-83  12:00p
SORT      EXE     1408  10-20-83  12:00p
FIND      EXE     5888  10-20-83  12:00p
MORE      COM      384  10-20-83  12:00p
BASIC     COM    16256  10-20-83  12:00p
BASICA    COM    26112  10-20-83  12:00p
        23 File(s)     28672 bytes free

A:\>dir/w

    Volume in drive A has no label
    Directory of  A:\

COMMAND  COM   ANSI     SYS   FORMAT    COM   CHKDSK  COM   SYS      COM
DISKCOPY COM   DISKCOMP COM   COMP      COM   EDLIN   COM   MODE     COM
FDISK    COM   BACKUP   COM   RESTORE   COM   PRINT   COM   RECOVER  COM
ASSIGN   COM   TREE     COM   GRAPHICS  COM   SORT    EXE   FIND     EXE
MORE     COM   BASIC    COM   BASICA    COM
        23 File(s)     28672 bytes free
```

Fig. 9-4. A Recorded Macro.

The two methods employed to create a macro have one thing in common. As you typed your keystrokes, they were recorded by SuperKey and then passed through to the application. The keystrokes had the same impact on the application as they would when you are not recording a macro.

[In some cases you might notice a slight slowing down of the application.]

However, there might be an occasion when you want to create a macro but not actually execute the keystrokes. You can do this by using the SuperKey edit mode. Begin by displaying the SuperKey menu: **[Alt/]**

Choose macros by entering **m**

Now instead of choosing "b", Begin, enter **d**

The box appears on the screen asking you for the key you want to define. Enter **[Pg Up]**

The screen clears. At the top of the screen you see the following prompt:

```
Key: PGUP        Insert    F1 -Help AltESC-Exit AltC-Copy AltM-Move
```

You are now in the edit mode. [Alt Esc] tells SuperKey that you have completed entering the macro. [F1] displays the help screen. [Altc] and [Altm] are used in advanced macro editing. You will see examples of their use later. The word "Insert" indicates that you are in an insert mode such as you would find in a word processing program. Keystrokes are always added in the insert mode. You cannot "type over" characters.

Pressing the [Ins] key will change the mode to an "overwrite" mode. Pressing it again will return to the "insert" mode.

[The information used to display help screens is not loaded into memory when you load SuperKey. It is stored on the disk in a file called KEY.HLP. In order for SuperKey to find that file when you request help, you must load the program from the same disk and directory that contain the help file. If you do not, SuperKey will function properly except that it will not be able to to find the help files.]

Now enter keystrokes as you would to produce a macro. Enter **cls <return>**

Note that the keystrokes have no direct effect. They are being recorded but not passed to the application. Continue by entering **dir/w <return>**

9.8. Editing Keystrokes

One of the advantages of the edit mode is that because the keystrokes are only recorded, but not passed to the application, you can change your mind about what you have typed. Suppose that you do not want to display a wide directory, but a long directory with a pause. To change the macro you must change the /w to /p. This is very easy in the edit mode. The arrow keys will position the cursor under any of the characters in the macro.

To change a character you can use one of two methods:

1) Use the [Del] key to delete the *w*, for example, and then enter a *p*.
2) Enter the overwrite mode and change the *w* to a *p*.

In this case use the [Del] key. Enter **[Del] p**

The macro has been changed.

[Many programs allow you to delete characters using the <backspace> key as an erasing backspace. In the edit mode of SuperKey the <backspace> key is considered a special key in the same way as the <return> is. If you press the <backspace> key a special symbol, <BKS>, will appear in the macro text.]

9.9. Special Symbols

You may have noticed that SuperKey uses special symbols to denote keys that do not have simple letters, numbers, or characters on them. The symbols appear in a different color video than do the other keystrokes. The change in video is used to suggest that these characters are symbols, not simply character strings.

In this example, <ENTER> is a special symbol used to represent the <return> key.

Special symbols can be entered in two ways. You have seen the first—simply typing the special keys. Interestingly, there is another way. To illustrate the method, remove the **<ENTER>** by entering **[Del]**

Now type in the following characters: **< e n t e r >**

What has happened? At first, when you typed, the characters were displayed as text characters. However, as soon as you completed the text and formed the **<ENTER>** symbol, SuperKey converted the text into a symbol. Also note that the symbol was recognized even though you entered it in lower case letters.

9.10. Saving a Macro in Edit Mode

When the macro is correctly entered, you can save it by first signaling SuperKey that the editing is complete. Enter **[Alt Esc]**

A box is displayed asking whether or not you want to save this macro.

```
┌──EDIT MACRO──────────┐
│Save this macro (Y/N)?│
└──────────────────────┘
```

Fig. 9-5. Save Macro Box.

Enter **y** to return to your application. Test the macro by entering **[Pg Up]**

The macro executes, clearing the screen and displaying a paused directory display. If your directory is longer than a single screen, the display will pause. Press **<return>** until the display is complete.

9.11. More Macro Editing

Macro editing is important for several reasons. The basic reason is that people make typing mistakes. This is as true when you are recording a macro as it is when you are merely trying to type a command or a sentence.

When you make a typing correction while a macro is being recorded, the keystrokes you use to correct the mistake become part of the macro itself.

SuperKey has no way of knowing which keystrokes you want and which ones are mistakes. To see how this happens and how the situation can be corrected, create another simple macro. In this instance you will make a typing mistake on purpose. Begin the macro by entering **[Alt=]**

To choose the [F10], enter **[F10]**

The purpose of this macro is to perform a check disk (CHKDSK) command. But when entering the command you are to make a typing mistake, as follows: **chkddk <return>**

DOS responds with a "Bad command or filename" message. The reason is that the program's name was mistyped. Unfortunately, the recording mode was active. What should you do?

One solution is to stop the recording and start again. Try this method. To stop the recording, enter **[Alt-]**

Now start the recording again. Enter **[Alt=] [F10]**

This time the prompt box is altered a bit.

```
 ─────────────VERIFY──────────
│ Already a macro key. Redefine <F1Ø>-key (Y/N)? │
 ──────────────────────────────
```

Fig. 9-6. Redefine a Macro Message Box.

SuperKey warns you that the key you are about to define as a macro already has been defined. In this case you will want to redefine the macro correctly. Enter **y**

The prompt appears at the top of the screen, telling you that you are currently defining a macro for the [F10] key. Now enter **chkdsk <return>**

To complete the creation of the macro, enter **[Alt-]**

Test the macro by entering [F10] The CHKDSK command is executed.

9.12.   Cancelling a Macro

Once you enter a command to begin the creation of a macro, there is no single key you can press to cancel it. For example, suppose you began to define a macro for a key that already had a macro. As a concrete illustration, enter **[Alt=] [F10]**

SuperKey warns you that a macro already exists for that key. If you wanted to preserve that macro you would enter "N" to tell SuperKey not to redefine the key. Enter **n**

What happens? The macro definition does not get cancelled. Instead, SuperKey displays the DEFINE MACRO box asking you to enter the correct key. But what if you just want to cancel the whole operation?

It would seem logical to press <Esc> to cancel the whole thing. Enter
<Esc>

What happens? Remember that the <Esc> key is one that can be assigned a macro definition by SuperKey. Therefore, <Esc> did not cancel
the command but simply told SuperKey to use the <Esc> key as the
macro key.

Because <Esc> is considered a normal keyboard key, instead of going
directly to the definition mode, SuperKey displays the VERIFY box.

You don't want to redefine <Esc>, so enter **n**

Once again you are confronted with the DEFINE MACRO box. How
can you get out of this cycle? The answer is that you must choose a key
that does not already have a macro and proceed as if you were really going
to define that key. As an illustration you can use [Altz].

[The symbol [Altz] represents the combination keystroke produced when you hold down
the [Alt] key and then press [z].]

Enter **[Altz]**

Now you have gotten beyond the DEFINE MACRO box. However,
you have the problem of having begun the creation of a macro that you
don't really want to create. The solution lies in what you do next. Rather
than normal keystrokes, end the definition by entering **[Alt-]**

Not only does this complete the macro definition process but the macro
is treated as if it never been begun. Entering the [Alt-] as the only keystroke in the macro is called a *null*. Null macros are ignored by SuperKey.

9.13. Clearing a Key

The previous technique also indicates how a macro definition can be removed from a key. Assume that you want to return the [F10] key to its
original function, whatever that might be in the application you are using.
The method is to redefine the key as a null macro.

To illustrate this technique, begin a macro definition by entering
[Alt=] [F10]

You are warned that this key is already a macro key. In this instance
you will want to redefine the key. Enter **y**

Now instead of entering any keystrokes, enter **[Alt-]**

The macro definition that has previously been assigned to [F10] has
been removed. SuperKey now considers [F10] an unassigned key. Test
this hypothesis by entering **[F10]**

Nothing happens because there is no longer any macro definition for that key stored in memory.

9.14.   Revising Macros

Another handy feature is SuperKey's ability to allow you to revise a macro after it has been created. The macro illustrations used in this chapter are short. When you are working with larger macros, it is not as easy or practical to reenter the entire macro in order to correct a mistake. In those cases you will want to simply revise the macro.

To take a look at this procedure, create a macro with an error. Enter

[Alt =] [F10] chkddkl < return > [Alt-]

You now have a macro defined for the [F10] key that does not work because of typing errors. The task is to correct the problem without having to retype the entire macro.

The key to this procedure is the eDit command. The eDit command can be reached only from the SuperKey menu. Enter **[Alt/]**

Select Macro eDit by entering **md**

Choose the key you want to edit by pressing the appropriate combination, in this instance [F10]. Enter **[F10]**

The screen shows the keystrokes.

```
   Key: F10          Insert    F1 -Help AltESC-Exit AltC-Copy AltM-Move
   chkddkl<ENTER>
```

You can now use the editing keys to correct the entry. Position the cursor under the letter "d". Enter **[Del]**

Next place the cursor under the "k". Enter **s**

Finally place the cursor under the "l". Enter **[Del]**

The macro now reads correctly. You now need to save the corrections. Enter **[Alt Esc]**

The EDIT MACRO box appears. Enter **y**

[When the EDIT MACRO box appears, entering "n" does not necessarily eradicate the macro. What does happen is that the macro returns to the way it was prior to editing. The SAVE question posed in the EDIT MACRO box pertains only to the keystrokes added or deleted during editing, not to the entire macro. Thus if you had entered "n" the macro would still be stored as "chkddkl<ENTER>".]

Test the macro by entering [**F10**]

Now the chkdsk works properly. The larger and more complex the macro, the greater the advantage of editing. The next task is to learn how to save the macros you have created.

9.15.   Showing Macros

There is another command that is associated with the process of saving and recalling macros. The command is the "shoW titles" command. Its purpose is to display a list of keys that currently are assigned macros. Like many of the SuperKey commands, you can access this feature through the SuperKey menu or with a special keystroke command.

Menu Command   [Alt/]cw
Keystroke Command   [Alt PrtSc]

Enter [**Alt PrtSc**]

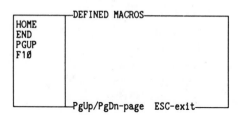

Fig. 9-7. Defined Macro Display Box.

The box displayed lists the keys that currently are assigned macros. If there are more macros defined than can be displayed in the box at one time, the [Pg up] and [Pg Dn] keys can be used to display the additional macros. To cancel the display, enter <**Esc**>

You might have noticed that to the right of the macro listing is an empty display area. This area is used to display data that explains the function of the macro keys. The explanations are called *titles*. SuperKey allows you to assign a one- to 30-character description of the macro as a title. How do you assign these titles? There are two ways to accomplish this:

1) Assign a title as you are defining the macro.
2) Use the eDit command to add a title to an existing macro.

You will learn both methods. The simplest way is to create the title when you create the macro. Try this example. Begin by creating a macro for the [F9] key. Enter

[Alt=] [F9] chkdsk/v<return>

Note that you are still in the interactive recording mode. Before you end the macro with the [Alt-] command, you will want to add a title for this macro. The command to create a title is [Alt']. The ['] character is the one on the key that has ['"] as its upper case not the key with the [~] as upper case. Enter **[Alt']**

A special box appears on screen.

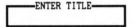

Fig. 9-8. Title Box.

Next enter the title of the macro. Enter
Check Disk — Verbose<return>
   Conclude the macro by entering **[Alt-]**
   Now display the macro titles; enter **[Alt PrtSc]**
   The title appears next to the [F9] key.

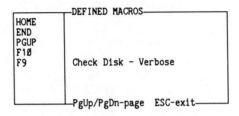

Fig. 9-9. Macro Title Displayed.

To remove the display enter **<Esc>**

[Macros are listed in the order in which they were created.]

Titles can be created at any time during the recording of a macro. You do not have to wait until the end of the macro recording. If you have already thought out the title, you can begin the macro with a title definition.

You can also continue entering keystrokes following the title entry. What does a macro with a title look like in memory? The question can be answered by using the eDit mode to examine the keystrokes in the macro. Enter **[Alt/] m d [F9]**

The screen displays the stored keystrokes:

```
Key: F9          Insert    F1 -Help AltESC-Exit AltC-Copy AltM-Move
<TITLE>Check Disk - Verbose<TITLE>chkdsk/v<ENTER>
```

You can see how SuperKey arranges the title in the macro. The special symbol <TITLE> precedes and follows the title text. Also note that SuperKey has placed the title text at the beginning of the macro even though you entered it after you had entered the macro text.

Looking at this display, the method by which titles can be added to a macro may have already occurred to you. Exit this macro. Enter **[Alt Esc] n**

[Because you simply looked at the macro and made no changes it really doesn't matter whether you say "y" or "n" to the Save prompt.]

The task now is to use the eDit mode to add a title to an existing macro. Choose the [F10] macro. Enter **[Alt/] m d [F10]**

The macro is displayed:

```
Key: F10         Insert    F1 -Help AltESC-Exit AltC-Copy AltM-Move
chkdsk<ENTER>
```

To create a title, begin by entering the title command **[Alt']**

In this mode, the title command does not display a box but simply types the special symbol <TITLE>. Now enter the text of the title:

Check Disk — Normal

Instead of ending the entry with <return>, enter another title command **[Alt']**

The <TITLE> symbol is inserted. Save the macro by entering
[Alt Esc] y

Now display the titles by entering **[Alt PrtSc]**

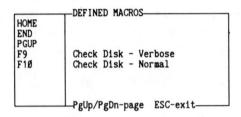

```
                  ┌─DEFINED MACROS───────────────────────┐
        ┌──────┐  │                                      │
        │ HOME │  │                                      │
        │ END  │  │                                      │
        │ PGUP │  │                                      │
        │ F9   │  │   Check Disk - Verbose               │
        │ F10  │  │   Check Disk - Normal                │
        │      │  │                                      │
        │      │  │                                      │
        │      │  │                                      │
        └──────┘  └─PgUp/PgDn-page  ESC-exit────────────┘
```

Fig. 9-10. Titles Displayed.

[You may have noticed that the [F10] macro is now the last one on the list. When a macro
is edited SuperKey treats it as if a new macro were defined. This means that it is now the
latest macro created and thus the last one on the list.]

Clear the display by entering **<Esc>**

From what you have already learned about the way SuperKey treats
text and symbols, you might have guessed that it is not always necessary to
use the [Alt'] command when editing a macro. You could simply type the
<TITLE> symbol. Enter

[Alt/] m d [Home]

To create a title you can type the following:

<title> Directory <title>

Save the macro and display the titles by entering

[Alt Esc] y [Alt PrtSc]

The title for the [Home] macro appears just as if it had been created by
using the [Alt'] command. Clear the display by entering **<Esc>**

9.16. Saving and Recalling Macros

As mentioned previously, macros can work only if they are stored in the internal memory of the computer. However, turning off the computer will erase any information stored in the internal memory. In order to avoid the need to create the macros over again each time the computer is turned off, you need some method of storing the macros.

[In SuperKey, the responsibility for saving macros is on the user. If you create macros but forget to save them, SuperKey does not warn you about their potential loss. Always remember to save any macros, or changes to old macros, before you turn off the computer.]

SuperKey stores macros in standard ASCII DOS text files. Macros created with the interactive and editing modes can be saved by using the SuperKey Command menu. To save the two macros you have created, return to the SuperKey Command menu by entering **[Alt/]**

Choose Macros. Enter **m**

SuperKey has four commands which are concerned with saving and restoring macros:

Save. This command stores all the macros currently in the memory to a specified text file. The macros in the memory are not erased. They remain as they were before the command.

Load. This command loads all the macros stored in a specified text file into the memory. Any macros that are currently in the memory will be automatically erased when you read the macros from the disk.

Merge. This command loads the macros from a file but does not erase the macros currently in the memory of the computer. This feature allows you to combine macros from different files.

If the file being loaded contains a macro for the same key as one currently in the memory, the active macro is erased and the macro being loaded takes its place.

[When you merge macro files, be aware that the total amount of space used by all the macros cannot exceed the space allocated for SuperKey. The default setting is 8,000 keystrokes. If SuperKey displays the message "Macro too long" when you are merging a file, this means that you have run out of room for those macros. The amount of memory area for macros can be changed from a minimum of 128 keystrokes to a maximum of 65,536 keystrokes by using the SuperKey install (KEYINST.COM) program.]

Clear. This command erases all of the macros currently in the memory. Macros erased with clear and not previously saved cannot be recovered.

If you want to clear individual macros use the technique shown previously to create null macros.

To save the macros that are currently in the memory, enter **s**

You need to enter a filename for the macros. Any valid DOS filename will do. Keep in mind that if you do not specify an extension, SuperKey will automatically add .MAC to the end of the filename. Enter **dos < return >**

The macros are saved in a file called DOS.MAC. Saving macros to a file has no effect on the memory of the computer. This means that the macros remain in the memory of the computer exactly as they were before you saved them. Further, any changes that you make in the memory will not appear in the file unless you use the Save command to save a new version of the file.

[You can choose your own extension by entering a full filename with extension. For example, 123.rob might be used to indicate that this file contains macros for Lotus 1-2-3 created by Rob.

If for some reason you wanted to create a file without any extension at all, you should end the filename with a period. Look at the filenames below:

What you enter	*How they appear on the directory*
TEST.XYZ	TEST.XYZ
TEST	TEST.MAC
TEST.	TEST

You might also have noticed that the macros were saved on the A disk. This is because SuperKey uses the active drive and directory as the one to store the macros.

You can change this in two ways. The most direct is to include the full pathname of the place where you want to store the macro file. Examples:

File Specification	*Result*
b:test	Creates a macro file TEST.MAC on the disk in drive B.
c:\sk\test	Create a macro file called TEST.MAC in the SuperKey directory of the C drive.

The other method to specify a particular drive or directory is to use the Setup menu. Enter **[Alt/] s**

The Setup menu appears.

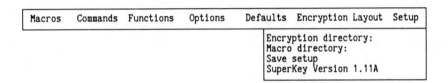

Macros	Commands	Functions	Options	Defaults	Encryption	Layout	Setup

```
Encryption directory:
Macro directory:
Save setup
SuperKey Version 1.11A
```

Fig. 9-11. Setup Menu

The second item on the menu, Macro directory, is where you would specify the directory to be used for saving and loading files. For example, if you wanted to specify the SuperKey directory on drive C you would enter

m c:\sk<return>

[Entering a specification into this part of the menu will control the saving and loading of files *only* for this session. The next time you load SuperKey the value for this specification will again be blank. If you want to maintain consistency from session to session you should use the Save Setup command on the Setup menu. This will ensure that each time SuperKey is loaded, the directory specifications will be set automatically.]

To see what the effect of the Save command is on the disk, enter **[End]**
The directory display appears. You should see the file DOS.MAC on the directory. To examine the file use the DOS TYPE command to display the contents of the file by entering **type dos.mac<return>**
The screen will show:

```
<BEGDEF><END>dir/w<ENTER>
<ENDDEF>
<BEGDEF><PGUP>dir/p<ENTER>
<ENDDEF>
<BEGDEF><F9><TITLE>Check Disk - Verbose<TITLE>chkdsk/v<ENTER>
<ENDDEF>
<BEGDEF><F10><TITLE>Check Disk - Normal<TITLE>chkdsk<ENTER>
<ENDDEF>
<BEGDEF><HOME><TITLE>Directory<TITLE>dir<ENTER>
<ENDDEF>
```

You can see from this display the way in which SuperKey creates a file for macro definitions. In addition to the symbols that appear when you are in the eDit mode, SuperKey adds other symbols:

1) <BEGDEF>—Begin Definition. This symbol is always the first part of a macro definition.
2) <key name>—Immediately following the <BEGDEF> symbol, the SuperKey synonym for the key to which the macro will be assigned is entered.
3) <ENDDEF>—End Definition. This symbol marks the end of the definition for a given key.

9.17.   Clearing the Memory

If you want to remove all the macros from the memory of the computer, you can do so with the Clear command. The Clear command can only be accessed through the SuperKey menu. Enter [**Alt/**] **m c**

What has happened? Enter [**Home**]

Nothing happens because there is no longer any macro definition assigned to that key. Enter [**Alt PrtSc**]

The titles listing is blank, again confirming that the macros have been cleared.

[If you attempt to clear the memory of macros before they have been saved, SuperKey will warn you that you run the risk of losing data. Because you have just saved the macros in memory to a disk file prior to using the Clear command, no prompt was displayed and the clearing took immediate effect.]

Clear the display by entering <**Esc**>

9.18.   Loading Macros from a File

Clearing the memory of macros is not a serious problem when you have saved the macros. To reestablish the macros all you need to do is load the text from the file. When the file is loaded, SuperKey reads the characters in the file as if they were coming from the keyboard. In a sense, a macro file is really a "super" macro that automatically defines a whole group of macros.

[Logically it follows that macros can be created with the use of the interactive or editing modes. All you need do is create a standard ASCII file with a text editor (EDLIN) or a word processor (WordStar Non-Document Mode) that contains the proper sequence of characters to create macros. Use the load command to read the file and the macros are defined in memory exactly the way they would be using other methods. One advantage of this method is that you can create a large number of similar macros using word processing techniques, such as block copying and search and replace. You will learn more about such techniques later in this chapter.]

The Load command will read a macro text file and create from the stored text the macro definitions. In this example you have saved a macro file called DOS.MAC. Now that the memory is clear, you can get the macros back by entering **[Alt/] l**

Now you must enter the name of the file that you want to load: **dos <return>**

[The same logic applies to filenames when you are loading macros as it does when you are saving macros. Entering a filename, such as DOS, tells SuperKey to load a file called DOS.MAC. The drive and directory of the file are assumed to be the active drive and directory unless you specify otherwise. You can specify otherwise by typing in the full pathname along with the filename or using the Setup menu to enter a new default value for drive and directory.

Keep in mind that to load a file without an extension you should place a period at the end of the filename.]

The macros are now once again resident in the memory of the computer. Enter **[Alt PrtSc]**

The list shows the macros have been restored to the memory of the computer. To test to see if they still function correctly, enter **<Esc> [Home] [End]**

The macros function exactly as they did when you first created them.

9.19. Merging Files

The Merge command is a variation on the Load command. When a macro file is read into the memory of the computer with the Load command, SuperKey first clears all the existing macros from the memory. If, however, the Merge command is used to load a file, the macros in the memory, if any, remain and the macros defined by the file being read are added. The merge process can be repeated with any number of macro files. Each time the merging is done, the macros are added to memory without destroying existing macros.

There is one exception. If the file being read contains a definition for a key that is already assigned as a macro key, the new definition being read in will take precedence over the existing macro. This is quite reasonable considering the fact that SuperKey treats a macro file like a "super" macro. Reading in a new definition for a key is very similar to using the [Alt=] command to redefine an existing macro key.

9.20.   Using Commands in Macros

One of the interesting features of a program like SuperKey is that you can create macros to perform all sorts of tasks. One important task in working with a macro program is to save the macros that you create.

As you have learned, this can be done by using the [Alt/] command to gain access to the SuperKey menu and entering the Macro Save command. SuperKey does not provide a single keystroke command to accomplish this very important task. However, you can create a macro of your own that will make this important task faster and easier. Creating a macro that saves macros implies that the keystrokes of which the macro will be composed will be SuperKey commands. This is acceptable to SuperKey.

Suppose that you wanted to save the macros you created by using this text in a file called LESSON.MAC. You will assign this macro to the [Alts] combination. Begin by entering **[Alt=] [Alts]**

You are now in the recording mode. The first keystroke that you enter is the same one that you would enter if you were about to manually save the macros as a file. Enter **[Alt/]**

The SuperKey menu appears, with one minor difference: it is displayed one line lower than usual to allow the SuperKey definition line to be displayed. Enter the command to save the macros:

m s lesson < return >

The SuperKey menu disappears. Complete the macro by entering **[Alt-]**

You might have noticed that when you entered the [Alt/]ms command the disk drive did not spin. Were the macros saved? List a directory and see if the file LESSON.MAC is really on the disk. Enter

dir *.mac < return >

The file is not there. Why not? The answer is that when commands are entered as part of a macro, they are not executed, they are only recorded. The command keystrokes will only be effective when you play back the macro. To test this, enter **[Alts]**

This time the drive did spin and the red light came on, indicating that something was happening to the disk. Check the directory for the file by entering **dir *.mac < return >**

Now the file LESSON.MAC appears. Try the macro again. Enter **[Alts]**

Is something different? SuperKey now displays a box labeled VERIFY on the screen.

```
            ┌──────VERIFY──────────────┐
            │Overwrite A:LESSON.MAC (Y/N)?│
            └──────────────────────────┘
```

Fig. 9-12. Verify Box.

The box indicates that a macro file with the name LESSON.MAC already exists on the disk. You must decide whether or not to overwrite the file. In this example, you would probably choose to overwrite the file each time. Enter **y**

However, you did not anticipate this keystroke when you created the macro. In order for the saving to really be a single keystroke command, you might like to alter the macro to include this new keystroke. Unfortunately, this cannot be done with SuperKey. The VERIFY box will accept input *only* from the keyboard, not from a macro. The reason is that the purpose of VERIFY is to make sure that the user specifically answers the prompt. Thus the program does not allow you to circumvent its safety checks.

9.21.   Delays and Pauses

Up to this point all the macros you have created execute all their keystrokes as quickly as possible when you press the macro key. There are many instances when you might like to create macros that pause at certain points. The pause allows macros greater flexibility in dealing with applications. The pauses can be used to allow you to enter into the macro a piece of information necessary for the completion of the task. Creating macros with pauses allows you to make more generalized macros, i.e., macros that apply to many situations.

There are three types of pauses that can be inserted in macros:

1) *Timed Delays.* A timed-delay pause halts the execution of a macro for a specified length of time. When the time has expired the macro continues to execute. Time delays allow screen displays caused by commands stored in macros to remain on the screen long enough to be read before the rest of the keystrokes execute.

SuperKey can pause a macro and allow you to enter data into the flow of the macro. A pause that allows you to type keystrokes into the application while the macro is executing is called a *field*. There are two types of fields available in SuperKey.

2) *Fixed-Length Entries.* A fixed-length entry is limited to a specific number of characters. If the fixed-length entry is filled, the macro automatically continues executing. This eliminates the need to press <return> at the end of the entry.

[If your entry is smaller than the length of the fixed-length field, a <return> is still needed.]

3) *Variable-Length Entries.* Variable-length entries vary in size. To continue the macros you must enter <return>.

The following section illustrates how pauses work.

9.22.   Delays in Macros

One interesting feature of SuperKey is its ability to insert timed delays into macros. In most simple situations you want a macro to execute as quickly as possible. However, there are situations in which it is advantageous to have a delay inserted between the keystrokes of a macro. Why would you want to create such a delay?

One reason is to pause the screen display to allow the user to read the information displayed by one part of the macros before the next display appears. You could even use the delay to cause a program to load and execute some function after you had left work. For example, you might want to use a telecommunications program to transmit data during the night, when access time is less expensive.

[The original issue of SuperKey contained a type of delay function called a *delay factor*. This function gauges the delay according to the number of times that the application scans the keyboard for user input. This means that the amount of real time paused by the delay factor will vary depending upon which program is running at the time the macro is executed. The delay factor is specified as a whole number between 1 and 999.

Version 1.11A, used in writing this book, contains another type of delay function called *real time delay*. A real time delay uses the system clock to keep track of the length of a delay. A real time delay is specified in hours, minutes, seconds, and hundredths of seconds. This is a more accurate and simpler way to understand types of delay.

In this book, delays will be entered as real time delays. Note that the delay factor is still available in Version 1.11A.]

To illustrate how a delay operates, suppose that you wanted to display the directory of a disk, clear the screen, and run a disk check. A delay would be useful to give you time to look over the directory before the screen is cleared and the next command is executed. Time delays can be entered into macros in both the interactive recording mode and the editing mode. Begin with the interactive mode: **[Alt =]**

The prompt at the top of the screen asks you to press the key you want defined. Enter **[Altd]**

You are now ready to enter the commands for the macro.

9.23.   Nesting Macros

Before you enter any keystrokes, you might have remembered that you have already created macros that perform the tasks you want to do. When this is the case there is no need to enter the keystrokes into the new macro. Instead, you can simply type the macro keys that perform those functions.

Including macros inside of other macros is called *nesting*. SuperKey allows you to nest macros in this manner. The first macro that you will want to use is the [Pg Up] macro that displays a paused directory. Enter **[Pg Up]**

The directory is displayed on the screen. When the screen is filled the listing is paused. But for how long? Normally, DOS will wait until you press a key. But by using a timed delay function you can automatically time the pause.

9.24.   Entering a Function

Time delays, and other special tasks performed by SuperKey, are referred to as *functions*. Functions are similar to commands except that functions can only be used as part of a macro.

[That is why the function menu can only be displayed when you are recording a macro.]

Commands, on the other hand, are independent of macros. For example, [Alt PrtSc] is a command that displays the macros in memory. It can be executed at any time.

A timed-delay function will only have an effect when the macro is played back. When you enter the command to insert a function in a macro, the function has no effect at that moment.

In the case of time delays you can see how practical this distinction between commands and functions is. Suppose you entered a time delay of an hour. If the function took effect immediately, you would have to wait an hour before you could complete the entry of the macros.

To enter a function you must call up the SuperKey menu. Enter [Alt/]

Notice that "Functions" is now displayed in the same video as the rest of the menu options. Enter **f**

KEY: ⟨AltD⟩ Text- Press ⟨Alt-⟩ to end.

Macros	Commands	Functions	Options	Defaults	Encryption	Layout	Setup

```
TEXT               dAte            a
SYS       COM  168 Beep            p
DISKCOPY  COM  257 Clear screen    p
DISKCOMP  COM  218 Delay factor    p
COMP      COM  253 Keyboard lock   p
EDLIN     COM  460 Logged drive    p
MODE      COM  313 Path            p
FDISK     COM  636 Real time delay p
BACKUP    COM  368 Screen off      p
RESTORE   COM  400 screen On       p
PRINT     COM  460 Time            p
RECOVER   COM  230 cUt and paste   p
ASSIGN    COM   89                 p
```

Fig. 9-13. The Functions Menu.

The function that you want to use is the "Real time delay" function. You can select the function by moving the highlight with the arrow key or simply typing the letter of the item. Enter **r**

The ENTER DELAY box appears.

KEY: ⟨AltD⟩ Text- Press ⟨Alt-⟩ to end.

Macros	Commands	Functions	Options	Defaults	Encryption	Layout	Setup

```
TEXT               dAte              a
SYS       COM  168 Beep              p
DISKCOPY  COM  257 Clear screen      p
DISKCOMP  COM  218 Delay factor      p
COMP      COM  253 Keyboard lock     p
EDLIN     COM  460 Logged drive      p
MODE      COM  313 Path              p
FDISK     COM  636 Real tim┌ENTER DELAY┐
BACKUP    COM  368 Screen o│ 00:00:00.00│
RESTORE   COM  400 screen O└───────────┘
PRINT     COM  460 Time              p
RECOVER   COM  230 cUt and paste     p
ASSIGN    COM   89                   p
```

Fig. 9-14. Entering a Time Delay.

Time delays are entered in the format hh:mm:ss.##. The longest time delay that can be entered is 99:59:59.99, or 99 hours, 59 minutes, and 59.99 seconds.

You can use the arrow keys to position the cursor. Enter a time delay of ten seconds. To continue recording the macro, enter **<return>**

Now enter another **<return>**

The rest of the directory is displayed. The next step is to clear the screen. But before you do that, record another delay. Enter

[Alt/] f r 000015 <return> cls <return> [F10]

The macro is complete. Enter **[Alt-]**

To see the result of this macro, enter **[Altd]**

Notice that each part of the macro executes, but there is a timed delay between each part.

9.25. Functions in the Edit Mode

SuperKey functions can be added to a macro when you are in the edit mode. To illustrate how this is done, suppose that you wanted to add some further commands to the [Altd] macro. This requires editing. Enter

[Alt/] m d [Altd]

The edit screen displays:

```
Key: AltD        Insert    F1 -Help AltESC-Exit AltC-Copy AltM-Move
<PGUP><CMD>FR00:00:10.00<CMD><ENTER><CMD>FD000<CMD><CMD>FR00:00:15.00<CMD>cls<EN
TER><F10>
```

The display reveals how a function is entered into a macro. The special symbol <CMD> indicates that a command function is being used. The ten-second delay is entered as <CMD>FR00:00:10.00<CMD>.

To add to this macro, move the cursor to the end of the file using the <right arrow> key.

Your next task is to enter a delay of 15 seconds. Enter **[alt/]**

The SuperKey menu appears. Enter

f r 000015 < return >

Note that the function was entered in exactly the same way as it was in the interactive mode. Enter **cls < return >**

Save the macro by entering **[Alt Esc] y**

Execute the macro by entering **[Altd]**

The macro executes with the delays.

[Some programs, such as dBASE II and III, have a tendency to lose keystrokes when macros execute. This is because when dBASE performs certain operations, typically reading or writing information to or from the disk, it ignores any characters entered on the keyboard. Since characters entered by macros appear to the program to be coming from the keyboard, the program will miss some of the keystrokes in the macro.

You can solve this problem by inserting a delay, of .1 or .2 seconds in between each keystroke. This makes the macro cumbersome to type, but it will eliminate the lost keystrokes and allow your macro to operate properly. If you find that even with these delays keystrokes are lost, increase the time of the delay.]

9.26.   Macros with Entry Fields

Entry fields in macros provide a means by which the user can add information to the macro as it executes. After the information is entered, the macro will continue to execute until the task is complete. The advantage of this type of macro is that you can add a crucial piece of information, such as a filename, to the macro as it executes. As mentioned before, macros with entry fields come in two types:

1. *Fixed-Length Pauses.* A fixed-length pause is used when the response of the user will always be the same number of characters. For example, if you wanted the user to specify a disk drive, you would leave a fixed-length pause of one character, since all drive names are single letters. The advantage of fixed-length pauses is that the macros will automatically continue as soon as the character or characters have been typed. It is not necessary to signal the computer that you have finished by entering a < return >.
2. *Variable-Length Pauses.* The variable-length pause allows the user to enter as many characters as needed while the macro is paused. However, because the computer cannot know for sure when you have finished, the user must type in a < return > to signal SuperKey that the entry is completed.

[The final < return > is not part of the macro and will not be sent to the application. Its only function is to tell SuperKey that a variable field entry is completed.]

Fields can be entered into macros in both the interactive and editing modes.

9.27. A Fixed-Length Field

Fields allow you to create more generalized macros. As an example, if you had three disk drives in your system, A, B, and C, you might create three macros to list the directories of each drive. On the other hand, you could get a similar result by creating a single macro with a pause that would allow you to enter the drive specification. As an illustration of this technique, a macro will be created that will list the directory of any drive.

The first example will use the interactive mode. Enter **[Alt=][F7]**

Begin the macro by typing the directory command: **dir<space>**

The change comes next. Instead of typing the letter of the drive, enter the SuperKey command to create a fixed field pause. The command is a combination of holding down the Ctrl key and pressing the right bracket key,]. Enter **<Ctrl]>**

The prompt at the top of the screen displays:

```
KEY: <F7> Fixed field- Press <Ctrl]> to end.
```

This prompt apprises you that you are entering a fixed field. During this portion of the macro entry process, the interactive recording method is altered slightly.

Any keystrokes that you enter will be passed to the application. However, the keystrokes themselves will not be recorded. What is recorded is simply the number of keystrokes entered. This number will determine the length of the fixed-length field. The longest fixed-length field allowed is 255 characters. In the present case, only one character is needed to stand for the drive letter. For the purpose of creating a fixed-length field macro, it makes no difference what letter you enter. The only factor that affects the macro is the number of keys entered. Enter **a**

To complete the fixed-field entry, enter the SuperKey command for fixed field: **<Ctrl]>**

Enter the remainder of the macro: **:<return>[Alt-]**

Test the macro by entering **[F7]**

The letters "dir" appear. Then the FIXED FIELD box appears on screen.

[The purpose of the Fixed Field box might not be obvious. Why doesn't SuperKey just let you type the character in at the cursor position? The answer is that SuperKey has some advanced features that work with fields. These features allow you to control entry and data formats when fields are used.

In order to implement these features, SuperKey intercepts your field entries so that they can be analyzed or formatted before they are passed to the application.]

Enter **a**

The macro completes its playback and the directory of drive A is displayed. Try the macro again. Enter **[F7]**

Once again, the macro pauses for your entry. This time enter a different drive letter (B if you have a floppy system, C for a hard disk system).

9.28.   How Fixed Fields Are Recorded

Before you go on to create macros with variable-length fields, it might be instructive to examine the way the fixed-length field macro you just created is stored in the memory. Enter **[Alt/] m d [F7]**

The screen shows:

```
Key: F7            Insert     F1 -Help AltESC-Exit AltC-Copy AltM-Move
dir <FFLD> <FFLD>:<ENTER>
```

The <FFLD> symbol represents a fixed-length field. Note that the number of spaces between the symbols indicates the length of the field. In this instance, there is a single space.

Exit the display by entering **[Alt Esc] n**

9.29.   Variable-Length Fields

Variable-length fields are required when it is not possible to know in advance the number of characters that need to be entered into a macro. As an example, you will create a macro that will search the disk for files that are of certain specifications. The method employs the use of the CHKDSK and FIND commands.

The macros will execute a special form of the CHKDSK command using the /V option. The FIND command will be used to filter the filenames to select those that contain certain characters. Look at the following command: chkdsk/v I find"TXT"

This command would find all the files that had the letters TXT in their filenames or extensions. The I is the vertical line character found on the same key as the backslash character, \.

[Similar results can be obtained with a DIR *.TXT command with two exceptions. First, the *.TXT will select only files with TXT as the extension. The CHKDSK command will select files in which the characters appear in any part of the filename or extension, such as NEWTXT.DOC or TXT.COM. Second, the DIR command will search only one directory at a time. The CHKDSK command will examine all the files on the disk no matter what directory or subdirectory they appear in.]

Since this command is awkward to type, it is a perfect candidate for a macro. In addition, since the characters you are searching for will vary with each use of the command, it will require a variable-length field pause. Like fixed-length pauses, variable-length pauses can be entered from the interactive and the recording modes.

This time, begin with the interactive mode. Enter **[Alt =] [F8]**

Begin to enter the keystrokes for the macro. Enter **chkdsk/v I find"**

Next you need to tell SuperKey to pause for the entry of a variable-length field. The command to enter a pause for a field of variable length is Ctrl- (Hold down Ctrl and press the dash key). Enter **< Ctrl- >**

As with the fixed-length field command, when it is entered in the interactive mode the variable-length command displays nothing on the screen. What should you enter next? In the case of a variable-length field it really doesn't matter. The fixed-length field counted the number of keystrokes entered in the field. This is not the case with variable-length fields. In this case there is no need to enter anything at all. You can simply enter another variable-field command. Enter **< Ctrl- >" < return >**

The CHKDSK command will execute. No filenames will be displayed because you didn't actually enter any characters between the quotation marks. Complete the macro by entering **[Alt-]**

Now replay the macro by entering **[F8]**

The macro pauses after the first quotation has been displayed. Now enter the characters to match. Remember they *must* be entered as upper case characters. Enter **BAS**

To tell SuperKey to continue with the replay of the macro, enter **< return >**

SuperKey completes the command. Any files on the disk that contain the letters BAS are listed.

9.30. Multiple Fields

It is possible to create a macro that pauses several times during the play-back. Suppose that you want to be able to select different drives to be checked with the CHKDSK command. The macro would have to pause twice, first for the drive letter and then for the characters to match. This time you will use the SuperKey command menu to create the macro. Enter

[Alt=] [Shift F8]

Begin by entering the CHDKSK command:

chkdsk/v <space>

Now insert a fixed-length field for a single character. In this instance, instead of using the command keystroke for a fixed-length field, use the SuperKey menu. Enter

[Alt/] m f . <Ctrl]>

You can use the menu to enter fixed- or variable-length fields. You will probably find the keystroke commands to be much faster. Now enter the FIND filter: **: l find"**
Now insert the variable field command: **<Ctrl-> <Ctrl->**
Finally complete the macro. Enter **"<return> [Alt-]**
Play back the macro by entering **[Shift F8]**
The first pause is for the drive letter. The fixed-field box appears. Enter **a**
Note that because the field was fixed-length, no return was necessary. The macro plays back more keystrokes and then pauses again. Enter (up-per case letters) **CO <return>**
The command then lists the file, if any, on drive A that contains the letters *CO*.

9.31. Data Entry Control

One feature found in SuperKey and not found in the other keystroke macro programs discussed in this book is its ability to control the data entered into the macro fields. SuperKey allows you to specify the characters that may be entered into field by type. SuperKey recognizes the following types of data:

1. N—Numeric Only. If this type of data is specified, only numbers 0 through 9 and math symbols, such as decimal points, plus signs, and minus signs, will be accepted.
2. U—Upper Case Only. This data type accepts only letters A through Z. If lower case letters are entered, they are converted to upper case. All other characters are ignored.
3. L—Lower Case Only. This data type is exactly like U expect that the roles of upper and lower case letters are reversed.
4. A—Alphabetical Only. This data type allows you to enter A through Z and a through z. All other characters are ignored.

Data entry control is established when the character type symbols are inserted between the fixed- or variable-field symbols in a macro. The characters can be entered by editing existing macros or by entering the characters during the creation of a macro in the interactive mode. Be aware that in order to use the interactive mode to create fields with data control characters, the FORMAT FIELDS option must be ON when you create the macro. You will see an example of this later on.

To begin, it will be simpler to eDit a macro that already exists. The macro assigned to the [F8] key is the one that uses the CHKDSK command to search the file directory for filenames that contain certain characters.

When you used [F8] previously, you were warned that the text characters *must* be entered in upper case. This macro would be easier to use if you created an entry control that converted any lower case entries to upper case.

The process begins with the eDit command. Enter **[Alt/] m d [F8]**

The screen shows the macro as it was created. The <VFLD> symbols indicate the existence of a variable length field in this macro.

```
chkdsk/v|find"<VFLD><VFLD>"<ENTER>
```

Your task is to enter the data type character you want between the <VFLD> markers. Move the cursor to the beginning of the second <VFLD> character. It is here that you want to enter the character type. Entering data type control characters into a variable field is quite simple.

In this example you can simply enter "u" to specify only upper case characters: **u**

Note that the data entry control character can be entered as an upper or lower case character. SuperKey will interpret either character the same way. You have now restricted the entry in this field to upper case characters.

[You can enter more than one data control character in a variable length field. Look at the macro below:

<VFLD>ul<VFLD>

There are two data entry control characters. The "u" specifies that the first character be upper case only. The "l" restricts the rest of the field to lower case only. Because the length of a variable-length field can differ each time, SuperKey assumes that the last data control character in the field controls the entry type for the remainder of the field.

If you enter any other character other than n,u,l, or a, SuperKey will consider it an indication that any character is acceptable. The macro below has two data control characters entered into the variable field. The first is a "u". The second is an "x". Inasmuch as "x" is not one of the special control characters, SuperKey will allow you to enter any keyboard character into the remainder of the field.]

Save the macro by entering **[Alt Esc] y**

Now execute the macro. Enter **[F8]**

Something different happens this time. Previously, when a variable field was encountered, no special entry box was displayed. However, when you specify a data entry control character, SuperKey displays a VARIABLE FIELD entry box.

This time enter the characters in lower case in order to test the effect of the data entry control character inserted in the variable field. Enter **sys<return>**

Observe how the data entry control feature works. The characters that you type are entered into the entry box as lower case letters. When SuperKey passes the characters to the application, the characters are converted to upper case. Try the macro again. Enter **[F8]**

Test the data entry control by typing in a non-alphabetic character. Enter **123**

What happens? Nothing! Because of the data entry control the numeric characters are ignored. Now enter **b1a<return>**

Pay attention to the fact that the letters "b" and "a" are accepted while the number "1" is ignored. The macro proceeds and finds the file specified.

9.32.   Data Control in Fixed Fields

Data entry control characters function in fixed-length fields in much the same way as they do in variable-length fields. The only exception is that in a fixed-length field each data entry control character controls the entry of only one character.

This time you will insert the data entry control characters as you create the macro. The purpose of the macro will be to list the directory of the disk alphabetically sorted and with a pause. To accomplish this you need to use the SORT and MORE filter commands along with the DIR command.

Normally, SuperKey is indifferent to the specific character entered in the fixed field. SuperKey only records the number of characters typed. However, if you desire to enter the characters in one of the data entry control characters (a,u,l,n) you *must* turn on the Format fields option. This is the first option that you have encountered. The default value for this option is OFF, i.e., characters entered in variable or fixed fields during macro creation are not recorded. Turning the option on will allow the data entry control characters you type to be recorded as part of the macro. To change an option, display the menu by entering [Alt/] o

```
 Macros   Commands  Functions   Options    Defaults  Encryption Layout   Setup
                                Arrow keys      OFF
                                Bottom line     OFF
                                Command stack   ON
                                Format fields   OFF
                                Keyb. click     OFF
                                One finger      OFF
                                Playback delay    Ø
                                proTect delay   OFF
                                sUspend         OFF
                                disk Wait       OFF
                                Save options
```

Fig. 9-15. Options Menu.

The current setting for Format fields is OFF. Enter **f**

SuperKey returns you to the application. To check to see if this really turned on the Format fields option enter [Alt/] o

You can see that Format fields is ON. Enter <Esc>

Begin the macro by entering [Alt=][Alts]

Type in the beginning of the command by entering **dir<space bar>**

At this point you will need to set up a fixed-length field that will allow you to enter the drive specification. This entry should be restricted to alphabetical characters. DOS does not care if the letter is upper or lower case, so the A data entry control character will be sufficient. Begin the fixed field by entering **<Ctrl]>**

Next enter the data entry control character for this field: **a**

End the fixed-length field. Enter **<Ctrl]>**

Complete the entry of the macro by entering

: | sort | more<return> [Alt-]

The More filter pauses the display. Enter **<return>**

The display is completed. You now have a macro that should contain a fixed-length field of one character that will accept only a letter. Test this macro by entering **[Alts]**

Enter **1**

SuperKey does not accept the number. Try again by entering **!**

The exclamation point is also ignored because it is not part of the alphabet. Now enter the letter

b   (floppy drive systems)

c   (hard drive systems)

SuperKey accepts the letter and completes the macro. Press **<return>** until the display has been completed.

9.33.   Advanced Formats and Functions

Now that you have learned some of the basic techniques of macro creation, you might be interested in the variety of formats and functions that SuperKey can use in macros.As macros get more complex, they begin to serve purposes that go beyond simply saving keystrokes when entering commands. Macros can aid in filling out long strings of data that contain many special functions and fields.

In most cases you will use macros like this with specific applications, such as spreadsheets and word processing. In order to make these examples as general as possible, the application used will simply be the DOS COPY command which creates a text file. This is roughly equivalent to simple word processing. Hopefully you will be able to use the principles illustrated here with a broad variety of applications.

9.34. Alignment within Fields

The following applies to fixed fields only. When a fixed field is several characters long you may find that the entry placed in the field does not fill up the entire field. Because fixed-length fields have a specific length, any characters not entered from the keyboard will automatically be filled with a "fill" character.

The fill character is usually a <space>. That is the SuperKey default value, though you can specify a different character if you desire.

Fill characters can be added to a field in three ways. Depending upon where the fill characters are placed, the alignment of the characters you typed in will vary.

1. Left Adjusted. If the fill characters are added to the right of the text, the text is considered "left" aligned. This is the default alignment.
2. Right Adjusted. If the fill characters precede the entered characters, the text is said to be "right" adjusted. To create right adjusted text you enter an "r" as the data entry control character.
3. Center Alignment. The entered text is centered if the fill characters are added evenly before and after the entered characters. Of course, this may vary by a character if the number of fill characters is an odd number. To create center adjusted text you must enter "c" as the data entry control character.

To illustrate the use of these alignment data entry control characters, you will create a special macro, [Alte]. Begin by entering **[Alt=] [Alte]**

The first step is to use the macro to create a text file. Remember you *must* have the Option Format fields turned ON to create this macro. If you have been following these examples, it should currently be turned on.

[To check, enter **[Alt/]o**. If Format field is ON, press <**Esc**>; if it is OFF, enter **f**]

Enter the following:

copy con: example < return >
The text below illustrates the use of alignment formats. < return >
< return > < return > **Left Adjusted** < tab >

Now you want to create a fixed data field with a length of ten characters: **< Ctrl] >**

Since left alignment is the default, there is no special alignment data
entry control character to enter. Enter

x (ten times)

Complete the field by entering **< Ctrl] >**

Next enter more text: **< return > Right Adjusted** < tab >

The next task is to create an example of a right aligned field. Create the
field by entering **< Ctrl] >**

To make the field right aligned you must enter the data entry control
character **r**

It is important to remember that the "r" used to indicate the alignment
characteristic of the field does not count as one of the characters that
determine the length of the field. This means that you still must follow the
"r" with ten characters in order to define this field as a ten-character field.
Complete the field by entering **x** (ten times) **< Ctrl] > < return >**

Finally, create a center adjusted field. Enter

Center Adjusted < tab > **< Ctrl] >** cx   (nine times)
< Ctrl] >

The next stage in the macro is to save the file, clear the screen, and type
out the results. Enter **< return > [F6] < return >**

The screen should look like this:

```
A>copy con: example
The text below illustrates the use of alignment formats.

Left Adjusted   xxxxxxxxx
Right Adjusted  rxxxxxxxxx
Center Adjusted cxxxxxxxxx
^Z
        1 File(s) copied
```

Complete the macro by entering

cls < return > type example < return > [Alt-]

Now try out the macro. Enter **[Alte]**

The first pause is for the left aligned text. To make the comparison obvious you will enter the same text in each field. Enter

hello < return > hello < return > hello < return >

The text will look like this:

```
A>type example
The text below illustrates the use of alignment formats.

Left Adjusted    hello
Right Adjusted          hello
Center Adjusted       hello
```

9.35.   Changing the Fill Character

The fill character need not be a <space>. To change the fill character used in the field enter **[Alt/] d**

This displays the defaults menu. Here SuperKey lists the default values for command keys and special options.

```
┌──────────────────────────────────────────────────────────────────────────┐
│ Macros   Commands  Functions   Options   Defaults  Encryption Layout  Setup │
└──────────────────────────────────────────────┬─────────────────────────────┘
                                               │ Begin macro    Alt=         │
                                               │ Title          Alt'         │
                                               │ autO-start     Alt'         │
                                               │ End macro      Alt-         │
                                               │ Menu           Alt/         │
                                               │ Fixed field    Ctrl]        │
                                               │ Var field      Ctrl-        │
                                               │ cUt and paste  Alt]         │
                                               │ beGin block    B            │
                                               │ sKip macro     '            │
                                               │ stoP           CtrlESC      │
                                               │ shoW titles    AltPRT       │
                                               │ Command stack  Alt\         │
                                               │ Decimal point  .            │
                                               │ deLimiter      ,            │
                                               │ fill cHaracter <SPACE>      │
                                               │ help sYstem    F1           │
                                               │ Arrow keys                  │
                                               │ Save defaults               │
                                               └─────────────────────────────┘
```

Fig. 9-16. The Defaults Menu.

To change the fill character, type **h**
Make the new fill character a period. Enter **.**
Now run the macro. Enter

[Alte]hello < return > hello < return > hello < return >

The screen shows this:

```
A>type example
The text below illustrates the use of alignment formats.

Left Adjusted   hello.....
Right Adjusted  .....hello
Center Adjusted ..hello...
```

9.36. Numeric Formats

Another way in which data entry can be formatted is through the use of special numeric formats. Numeric formats are concerned with comma and decimal places.

[As with field alignment macros, the FORMAT FIELD option must be turned ON when you enter the following macro.]

The formats operate with both variable-length and fixed-length fields. To see how they operate, you will create another macro. Begin by entering

[Alt =][Altn]
copy con: numbers < return >
The text below shows numeric formats. < return >
< return > < return > Variable Fields < tab > < tab >

Now create a variable field by entering **< Ctrl- >**
You can indicate two things for a numeric variable-length field:

1) **,**   A comma tells SuperKey to add commas to the numbers.
2) **.#**   A period followed by # signs indicates the number of decimal places that should be displayed. If fewer numbers are entered, the places are padded with zeros.

Enter **,.## < Ctrl- >**

Now tab over further to create another field. Enter

<tab> <tab> <Ctrl-> ,.#### <Ctrl-> <return> <return>

Next you will create examples of fixed-length fields. Enter

Fixed Fields <tab> <tab> <Ctrl]>

With fixed-length fields it is necessary to enter a # for each numeric position that you want to use. The following field will have four digits with a comma and two decimal places. Enter

#,###.## <Ctrl-> <return>

Now create another fixed field. Enter

<tab> <tab> <tab> <Ctrl-> #,###,###.# <Ctrl->

Complete the macro by entering

<return> [F6] <return> cls <return> type numbers <return> [Alt-]

Test the macro by entering **[Altn]**
For the sake of comparison, enter the same number into each field:

12345.67 <return> (four times)

The screen will look like this:

```
A>type numbers
The text below shows numeric formats.

Variable Fields          12,345.67                    12,345.6700

Fixed Fields             1,234.67
                                          ..12,345.6
```

Notice the effect of the various formats on the numbers entered. The second field padded the decimal places with two zeros. The fixed fields are more restrictive. The first fixed field allowed only four integers. The

"5" was ignored. The second fixed field was large enough for seven integers. Because you only entered five numbers, the left side of the field was filled with the fill character, currently a period.

9.37. Advanced Editing Techniques

SuperKey has two special commands that are available in the eDit mode that can help you create macros by combining macros that have already been created. For example, you now have two macros, [Alte] and [Altn], that demonstrate the use of formats in fields. It might be desirable to make a single macro that demonstrates both techniques.

You might think that you would have to rerecord the keystrokes to accomplish this. Not so! The goal is to create a new macro, [Altf], that combines the techniques shown in both macros. Begin by entering the edit mode.

[Alt/] m d [Altf]

SuperKey has two commands that copy the keystrokes assigned to one macro into the macro you are editing. They are:

[Altc]—This copies the keystrokes of a selected macro into the one you are editing. The macro from which the keystrokes are copied is unaffected.
[Altm]—This command performs precisely as the [Altc] does with the exception that the macro from which the keystrokes are copied is deleted from memory.

[Altc] is a safer command than [Altm].The task is to combine the functions of two macros into a single macro. First copy the keystrokes from the [Alte]. Enter **[Altc]**
The COPY MACRO box is displayed. Enter the macro that you want to copy. Enter **[Alte]**
The entire [Alte] macro is copied.
Before you add the [Altn] macro, it is necessary to consider if any keystrokes need to be added or deleted from the macro before you combine it with another macro. In this case move the cursor to the [F6] symbol near the end of the macro. The cursor is moved here because the [F6] is

used to close the file. In this example, you will want to add more key-strokes to the file before you close it.

If you enter the [Altc] command at the current cursor position, the keystrokes will be copied beginning at that position. Enter **[Altc] [Altn]**

The keystrokes from the [Altn] macro are combined with the key-strokes already in the macro.

Since all the keystrokes are part of a single file, you should delete the text *copy con: numbers* using the [Del] key. One final trimming operation is necessary to make the macro coherent. Once again move the cursor to the <F6> symbol. Delete the keystrokes <F6><ENTER>cls<ENTER>type numbers<ENTER>. When you are done, the next <F6> symbol should be at the cursor position. The macro keystrokes will look like this:

```
Key: AltF         Insert    F1 -Help AltESC-Exit AltC-Copy AltM-Move
copy con: example<ENTER>The text below illustrates the use of alignment formats.
<ENTER><ENTER>Left Adjusted<TAB><FFLD>          <FFLD><ENTER>Right Adjusted<TAB>
<FFLD>R          <FFLD><ENTER>Center Adjusted<TAB><FFLD>C          <FFLD><ENTER>
<ENTER>The text below shows numeric formats.<ENTER><ENTER>Variable Fields<TAB><T
AB><VFLD>,.##<VFLD><TAB><TAB><VFLD>,.####<VFLD><ENTER><ENTER>Fixed Fields<TAB><T
AB><FFLD>R#,###.##<FFLD><TAB><ENTER><TAB><TAB><TAB><FFLD>R#,###,###.#<FFLD><ENTE
R><F6><ENTER>cls<ENTER>type example<ENTER>
```

Save the macro by entering **[Alt Esc] y**

Now run the macro by entering **[Altf]**

Fill in the fields with the following: **super<return>** (three times)

Now the macro continues with the numeric format section. Enter **999.9<return>** (four times)

The screen will look like this:

```
A>type example
The text below illustrates the use of alignment formats.

Left Adjusted    super.....
Right Adjusted   .....super
Center Adjusted  ..super...
```

Numeric formats will appear as follows:

```
Variable Fields        999.90            999.9000

Fixed Fields           ..999.90
                       ......999.9
```

9.38.   Cut and Paste

Another unique feature of SuperKey is called Cut and Paste. It allows you to capture characters displayed anywhere on the screen as macro keystrokes. This is a tremendously powerful command. A simple example will illustrate how it works. First clear the screen. Enter
cls < return > chkdsk < return >

[If you have been following along, you might have used the [F10] key to perform the check disk.]

Suppose that you wanted to transfer the numbers displayed on the screen by the CHKDSK command to some other program, perhaps a word processing program or spreadsheet. Normally you would have to type them in. Cut and Paste allows you to capture the data on the screen directly.

The command to begin a screen capture (Cut) starts by entering **[Alt/] m u**

A dialog box is displayed. Press the key with which the text you are about to capture will be associated. In this example, enter **[Altc]**

A modified cursor is blinking at the top of the screen. You can now position the cursor to the upper left-hand corner of the block of text you want to capture. The Cut process works by highlighting a rectangular area of the screen.

Move the cursor down three lines. To begin the highlighting, enter **b**

The cursor now becomes a highlight. Move down six more lines. Then use the right arrow to widen the highlight until all the numbers are highlighted. The process is completed by entering **< return >**

Notice that the Cut command does not actually cut out the text from the screen. It merely copies the text. The screen display is undisturbed. The data that was highlighted has been converted into a keystroke macro.

There is no hurry to Paste the text into an application. Like the other macros, the keystrokes will be available when you need them. It might be interesting to examine the macro. Enter **[Alt/] m d [Altc]**

The lines have been converted into text keystrokes ending with <return> characters.

[In SuperKey all lines end with a <return>. Depending upon the application you are pasting into, this may prove to be a disadvantage. If the application is a word processing program, then the <return> characters are appropriate in most cases. This would also be the case with data base programs like dBASE III, since field entries are usually ended with <return>s. However, if the application is a spreadsheet like 1-2-3 or Multiplan, ending each entry with a return would cause each number to overwrite the previous number entered. Unlike most word processing or data base programs which move from line to line or field to field with <return>s, the spreadsheets mentioned require <arrow> key entries to move to new cells.

There is an exception. SuperCalc 2 and 3 use a system whereby the entry of data with a <return> automatically advances the cursor to the next cell. Sidekick's cut and paste function allows you to suppress the ending <return> character. The pasting is done one line at a time. Each time the macro key is pressed, one line is typed. You can then add any keystrokes necessary before you type the next line.]

Pasting is really playing back the macro that was created when the capturing (Cut) was done. Exit the editing mode by entering **[Alt Esc] n**

To demonstrate how the macro plays back, use the EDLIN program to create a file called FIGURES. Enter **edlin figures <return> i <return>**

Now play back the keystrokes assigned to [Altc] by entering **[Altc]**

The numbers are typed into the lines of the text file. To save this enter **[Ctrlc]e <return>**

9.39.   Functions in Macros

The next topic is how to use some of SuperKey's special functions in macros. You were introduced to the time delay function. This, however, is a closer look at some of the other functions that can be performed with SuperKey. Functions can only be accessed through macros. When a macro is recorded, the function does nothing until the macro is played back. This suggests that to use functions effectively, you should create simple macros that reveal exactly how functions behave.

In addition to the delay functions, SuperKey has the following capacities:

System's Data. There are four functions that can be used to enter data about the status of the computer system. They are:

L—Logged drive. This function enters the letter corresponding to the active drive at the time the macro is executed. It always returns a single character.

P—Path. This function returns a string of keystrokes corresponding to the active directory at the time the macro is executed.

A—dAte. This function returns a string of ten keystrokes that correspond to the system's date. The date is returned in the form mm/dd/yyyy.

T—Time. This function returns a string of keystrokes that correspond to the system's time at the time when the macro is executed. The time is an eight-keystroke string in the form hh:mm:ss.

All four of these functions have one thing in common: their values can be different each time they are executed.

Audio:

B—Beep. This function causes a tone to be sounded through the computer's speaker. The pitch and the duration of the tone can be specified.

Video. The following functions perform special video actions:

C—Clear Screen. This function clears the screen much in the same way that the DOS command CLS does.

S—Screen Off. This function differs from the clear screen function in that the current screen information is simply suppressed. The screen is merely blanked until a Screen On function is issued.

How does a Screen Off function affect commands that would normally place information on the screen? The commands function normally in all respects except that you do not see any data they may send to the screen. When the Screen On function is used to turn on the screen display, the information displayed is that which you would see following any commands that have taken place while the screen was turned off.

O—Screen On. Turn on the screen display.

U—cUt and paste. This function performs in a similar manner to the cut and paste command. The function allows you to create a cut and paste action during a macro.

The function differs slightly from the cut and paste command in that instead of assigning the cut text to a macro key, the cut text is immediately passed to the application. The effect is that the text highlighted during the cut session is pasted into the macro that is executing at that time. An example of how to use this function will follow later in this section.

K—Keyboard lock. This feature allows you to lock your keyboard from unauthorized inputs. The keyboard lock function allows you to specify a special sequence of keystrokes that will unlock the keyboard. The keyboard lock feature can only be defeated by rebooting the computer.

To understand better how these functions can be utilized, you can create some simple macros that take advantage of these features.

The macro that you will create will produce a special text file using the COPY command. However, in this macro you will use the special function to add system's information to the file. Begin by engaging the macro recording mode. Enter **[Alt =][Alt F10]**

The first step is to create a text file using the EDLIN command. Enter **edlin sample < return > i < return >**

The next step is to begin entering the text. The purpose of this text will be to illustrate how functions can add systems information to text. Enter

This file was created on
< space bar >

Now use a SuperKey function to place the date into the text. Enter **[Alt/] f**

Remember that dAte is selected by entering A, not D. Enter **a**

Did the date appear? The reason it did not is that functions do not execute while you are recording the macro. In this aspect they are an exception to the way keystrokes function in the interactive mode. Functions only have an effect when they are played back. One of the reasons for this is that some functions, such as time delays and keyboard lock, alter your ability to operate the computer. If they took immediate effect when you entered them, you might never be able to complete the macro.

You can see that using functions requires you to imagine what the effect of the function will be when the macro is played back. The need to visualize the future impact of commands is the kind of thinking that is required for programming. With a little practice you will find that it is not too difficult to create complex macros using functions.

Now continue entering text:

. < return > < return >

The current time is < space bar >

Now enter the time function. Enter **[Alt/] f t**

Continue the text entry:

. < return > < return >

Now enter

The screen will now go blank for 10 seconds. < return >

The task now is to use the screen off and screen on functions. To time the action of the screen on and screen off commands, use another function discussed previously, the real time delay. Before you blank the screen, you should place a delay in the macro. Why? Because you want to leave time for the user to read the message before you blank the screen. Enter

[Alt/] f r 000015 < return >

Now turn the screen off. Enter

[Alt/] f s

Now place the ten-second delay into the macro. Enter

[Alt/] f r 000010 < return >

The next step is to turn the screen back on. But before you enter that function, enter some additional text. What should happen is that the text will be typed onto the screen while the screen is blank. When the screen is turned on, the additional text will appear as part of the screen display. This illustrates how screen output is handled while the screen display is off. Enter

This text was typed while the screen display was OFF. < return >

Now issue the function that will turn the screen display on. Enter
[Alt/] f o

[Take care that you do not end a macro with the screen display set OFF. Since the screen ON function is available only during macro execution, you will find it difficult to correct this mistake. In theory you can create and execute a macro to fix this situation, but you will have to do it blind, i.e., without screen display. If you are working with Screen OFF functions it might be a good idea to create a simple Screen On macro to save yourself if you make the mistake of leaving the screen OFF. Example: [Alt =][Alto][Alt/]fo[Alt-]]

Next insert the drive and pathname. Enter

The current disk drive is < space bar > [Alt/]fL
, and the directory is < space bar > [Alt/]fp. < return >

Next, add some sound to the macro. Enter

Pay attention![Alt/]fb

The DEFINE BEEP box appears. There are three numbers that you need to enter:

1) The starting frequency number.
2) The ending frequency number.
3) The duration of the tone in hundredths of seconds. Thus, if you enter 100, the tone would last one second.

Frequency or pitch is entered as the number of Hertz. A Hertz is a measure of the frequency of a sound wave. One Hertz is equal to one cycle (wave) per second. For example, 260 Hertz is approximately middle C. 525 Hertz is approximately high C. If you wanted the tone to slide though a scale from middle C to high C you would enter 260 as the starting frequency and 525 as the ending frequency. To slide down a scale simply reverse the starting and ending numbers.
Enter **260 < return > 525 < return > 100 < return**
Now you are ready to save the EDLIN file. Enter

[Ctrlc]e < return > type sample

This is probably a good place to clear the screen. Begin with the SuperKey menu command: **[Alt/]f**
Next, select the clear screen function. You can use the arrow keys to highlight your choice or simply enter **c**
Now complete the macro by entering **< return > [Alt-]**
The macro is complete. Now execute the macro. Enter **[Alt F10]**

The macro will execute each of its functions in the order in which you entered them. When you are done the screen will look like this:

```
This file was created on 12/28/1985.

The current Time is 13:44:31.

The screen will now go blank for 10 seconds.
This text was typed while the screen display was OFF.
The current disk drive is A, and the directory is \.
Pay attention!
```

[If you execute the macro again, the file SAMPLE will increase in size because the ED-LIN command adds the text each time.]

If you have trouble with the macro, below is the [Alt F10] macro as it would appear in the eDit mode.

```
edlin sample<ENTER>i<ENTER><CMD>FC<CMD>This file was created on <CMD>FA<CMD>.<EN
TER><ENTER>The current Time is <CMD>FT<CMD>.<ENTER><ENTER>The screen will now go
blank for 10 seconds. <ENTER><CMD>FR00:00:15.00<CMD><CMD>FS<CMD><CMD>FR00:00:10.
00<CMD>This text was typed while the screen display was OFF.<ENTER><CMD>FO<CMD>T
he current disk drive is <CMD>FL<CMD>, and the directory is <CMD>FP<CMD>.<ENTER>
Pay attention!<CMD>FB00260 00525 00100<CMD><CtrlC>e<ENTER>type sample<CMD>FC<CMD
><ENTER>
```

9.40.   A Cut and Paste Macro

Using the cut and paste function inside a macro is an unusual technique. As you will see, the macro you are about to create will raise a problem that requires an interesting solution.

The idea is to use the cut and paste function to select a DOS command from a list of commands displayed on the screen.

Step #1. Clear the screen.
Step #2. Display a text file that lists the commands in DOS.
Step #3. Use the Cut and Paste function to highlight the command you want to execute. The function will then type out the text to DOS, and in so doing execute the command.

First you must make the text file. Since cut and paste works from data on the screen, the text file must display exactly the command words you want on the screen. Use the EDLIN program to create the file.

edlin commands < return > i < return >
Highlight the command you want to execute. < return > < return >
Dir < return > Chkdsk < return > Format a: < return > Edlin < return >
[Ctrlc]e < return >

The file is now created. Now for the macro. Enter
[Alt =][Altp]type commands
This would be a good place to clear the screen before you enter the
< return > Then only the text of your command file would appear for the cut and paste. Enter **[Alt/] f c < return >**
Next enter a cut and paste function. Enter **u**
Complete the macro by entering **< return > [Alt-]**
Now execute the macro. **Enter [Altp]**
The screen appears as a blank. What is wrong? The answer is that the commands are not executing in exactly the order you anticipated. The cut and paste function is operating before the text is displayed on the screen. The cursor is positioned for cut and paste but there isn't anything to cut.

What happened to the text in the COMMANDS file? Why isn't it on the screen? How did the cut and paste function get to execute before the text was displayed?

The answer to all these questions reveals a problem that will occur from time to time when you use macros with certain applications. SuperKey is memory resident. When a macro is executed, the program attempts to send the keystrokes stored in the macro to the computer as quickly as possible.

While speed is generally desirable, a problem will arise when the application cannot complete a task quickly enough to be prepared to receive the next keystrokes from the macro. In this instance the problem is caused when the DOS command TYPE accesses the disk to read the contents of the file commands. As it happens, TYPE always reads the file first and then displays the contents. The delay caused by the disk access slows down the display of the text on the screen. SuperKey is still executing keystrokes from the macro.

The result is that the cut and paste function takes place before DOS has had a chance to display the text on the screen. Another symptom of the same problem is when keystrokes are dropped as the macro is replayed. Before you can find the solution you need to release the computer from its confused state. Enter <return>

Notice that now the computer catches up and displays the text. The only problem is that the cut and paste has been terminated by the last <return> you entered.

9.41. Playback Delays

There are two options in SuperKey that deal with problems caused by playing back the keystrokes too quickly. These options are found on the options menu. Enter [Alt/] m

The options are:

P—Playback Delay. You can enter a number from 0 to 999. The number indicates the delay factor. The larger the number, the longer the time between each keystroke that is played back.
W—Disk Wait. This option stops the playback of keystrokes whenever the disk drives are active.

To solve a playback problem you can use either or both of these commands. In this case the best choice is the Playback delay. How do you know which to use? You don't! When a problem occurs you must experiment to see if the problem can be solved by delays. Enter p

SuperKey displays a BOX. Enter the number that you want to use as a delay factor. Once again, experience and experimentation are your best guides to which number to use. Enter 75 <return> <Esc>

Now execute the macro again. Enter [Altp]

Notice how much more slowly the keystrokes are replayed. However, this time the text is displayed when the cut and paste takes place. To cut and paste, move the cursor down to the Chkdsk. To begin a text selection, enter b

Use the <right arrow> to highlight the word "Chkdsk". Then enter <return>

The function takes the highlighted text and pastes it into DOS as a command.

9.42.   Options in Macros

SuperKey options can be programmed as part of macros, just like commands and functions. Now that you know of the need to use the playback delay, you can create a macro that turns on the delay, executes the [Altp] macro, and then resets the delay to zero. Enter

[Alt =][Alty][Alt/]o p 100 < return > [Altp] < return > [Alt/] o p 0 < return > [Alt-]

Now enter **[Alty]**

When the cut and paste cursor appears at the top of the screen, highlight Chkdsk again.

When the macro ends, the playback delay should be reset to zero. Test this by running one of the other macros: **[Alt F10]**

The macro executes at normal speed.

9.43.   Keyboard Locking

The keyboard lock feature is another function that can only be accessed as part of a macro. To create a keyboard lock macro, enter

[Alt =][Altl][Alt/] f c [Alt \ ] f k
Away from my desk, be back in a minute[Alt-]

Now execute the macro. Enter **[Altl]**

The ENTER LOCK-KEYWORD box appears. You can now enter a code which will be used to unlock the keyboard: **abc < return >**

SuperKey asks you to confirm the password by typing it again. If you do not correctly confirm the password, you will return to the ENTER LOCK-KEYWORD display. Enter **abc < return >**

The keyboard is locked. Enter **[Alt =]**

No response, even to a SuperKey command. The only characters that will unlock the keyboard are the ones that you entered to lock it. Therefore, make sure you remember the password or you will have defeated your own purpose. Enter **abc < return >**

The keyboard is now unlocked.

9.44. Display Macros

A display macro is different from the other type of macro that you have been working with up until now. The purpose of a display macro is not to record and play back sequences of keystrokes but to create a pop-up display of your own design. A display macro allows you to create a display message, text, or even menus, without having to create computer programs to do so.

These display macros can be used with any application. One use might be to create your own help screens. The TRANSPARENT option provided with Version 1.11A of SuperKey allows you to create menus with display macros.

Another difference is that display macros cannot be created in the usual macro creation modes. The only way to create a display macro is to make an ASCII text file that contains the proper SuperKey commands.

You can use any text editor or word processor that will produce an ASCII file. If you have Sidekick, the notepad is excellent for this purpose.

In this example, you will use the DOS editor, EDLIN. To begin, clear the memory of all existing macros. Enter **[Alt/] m c**

The basic form of a display macro is the <BEGDISP> instruction. This instruction is followed by a minimum of seven items. They are:

1. Key Symbol. This tells SuperKey which key will be assigned the display macro.
2. Beginning Column. This is a number between 1 and 78 which indicates the column in which the upper left-hand corner of the display macro frame will appear.
3. Beginning Row. This is a number between 1 and 25 which indicates the row in which the upper left-hand corner of the display macro frame will appear.

   [If the number zero is entered for the column, row, or both, SuperKey performs a special type of placement. The placement of the upper left-hand corner of the frame is not based on an absolute screen location, but on the current screen position of the cursor when the macro is executed.

   SuperKey refers to this technique as "pop-up" placement. If only the row or only the column is zero, then the zero component varies while the other component always appears at the column or row specified.

   The effect of "pop-up" placement is quite dramatic because your attention is usually focused at the cursor location anyway.]

4. Width in Columns. This number indicates the width in columns of the display macro frame.

5. Length in Rows. This number specifies the length in rows that the display macro frame will extend.
6. Period. Frame definitions *must* be followed by a period to be understood by SuperKey.
7. <ENDDEF>. Remember that in addition to other special elements, display macros (like all macros) must end with a <ENDDEF> symbol. As you will see, the <ENDDEF> need not immediately follow the frame definition. All that is necessary is that there be one following the last commands.

To illustrate, create a couple of simple display macros. Enter **edlin frames.mac<return>i<return>**

The first entry will create a frame beginning at row 10, column 10, that is 20 columns wide and 15 columns long. Take care to enter the period where it is supposed to be entered. Enter

<begdisp> <alta> 10,10,20,15. <enddef> <return>

Now enter another

<begdisp> <altb> 10,1,40,5. <enddef> <return>

Save the file by entering

[Ctrlc]e <return>

Now that the display macros have been defined as text, you can use the Load command to transfer them into the memory. Enter

[Alt/] m l frames<return>

Try the display macros: **[Alta]**
The only key that will clear the display is <Esc>: **<Esc>**
Now display the other frame: **[Altb]<Esc>**

9.45.   Adding Text to Frames

Obviously, just displaying frames is of little practical value. SuperKey allows you to add text to the frames. Begin by deleting the FRAMES.MAC file. Enter **del frames.mac**

Now use edlin again: **edlin box.mac < return > i < return >**

Begin by entering a command that will create the basic frame. If you want a title for the macro, you *must* place the < TITLE > command in the first line of the macro. Enter

< begdisp > < f10 > 10,8,40,12. < title > Display Macro < title > < return >

Now enter the following text:

This text is used to explain < return >
something to the person using < return >
the computer. < return >
< return >
The text appears in the frame < return >
created by the display command. < return >
< enddef > < return >

Save the macro. Enter **[Ctrlc] e < return >**
Load the macro into the memory. Enter **[Alt/] m l box < return >**
Check the titles by entering **[Alt Esc]**
The [F10] macro is labeled Display Macro. Enter **< Esc >**
Display the macro by entering **[F10] < Esc >**

9.46. Auto Display

SuperKey will allow you to create a macro that will display as soon as it is loaded. The symbol < AUTO > must be placed in the first line of the macro. Enter **[F3] < return >**

To make a change in line 1, enter **1 < return > [F3]**

Enter **< auto > < return >**

9.47. Pages

SuperKey will also allow you to create display macros that contain more text than can be displayed within the frame at one time. The [Pg Up] and [Pg Dn] keys will scroll through the text.

You can create definite page breaks in the text by inserting <ctrlL> characters. Enter

5 < return > < CtrlL > < return > e < return >

Load the macro by entering **[Alt/] m l box < return >**
This time the macro displays as soon as it is loaded. Also notice that only part of the text is displayed in the box. Enter **[Pg Dn]**
The next part of the text is displayed. Enter **[Pg Up]**
To remove the macro display enter **< Esc >**

9.48. Video Attributes

SuperKey allows you to specify special video display attributes for the text contained in a display macro.

<Ctrlb> = bold
<Ctrld> = enhanced

[The effect of the attribute depends upon the type of video display being used.]

To see how this works, change the macro by entering

[F3] < return > 5i < return >

Type in the symbol for bold display. Enter

< Ctrlb > Press Pg Dn For More . . . < Ctrlb > < return >
< return > [Ctrlc]

Now an example of the other type of video: enter

8i < return > < Ctrld > End of Text < Ctrld > < return >
[Ctrlc]e < return >

Load the macro by entering **[Alt/] m l box < return >**
When you have inspected the macro, exit by pressing **< Esc >**

9.49. Display Macros as Menus

So far, the display macros you have created function only as display items. Any keystrokes entered while a display macro is active are interpreted as only part of the display macro. None of the keystrokes are passed to the application.

Version 1.11A of SuperKey includes a new macro command called Transparent. The symbol for this command is <TRANSP>. Like <TITLE> and <AUTO>, <TRANSP> must appear in the first line of the display macro.

Its function is to allow keystrokes that are entered while a display macro is on the screen to be passed through to the application. Without the transparent feature, you would have to press <Esc> to terminate the display macro before you could enter keystrokes. With a transparent macro, the keystroke entered is passed through. If the keystroke passed though is assigned a SuperKey macro function, then the macro will execute.

The result is that you can create a menu of commands using a display macro. In addition to using the transparent command in the display macro, you must include the macros to which the menu will refer in the same file as the display macro. This will create a working menu.

As an example, the hands-on section below will create a menu with two options, list a sorted directory, or check the disk. Begin with the EDLIN command to create a text file. Enter

edlin menu.mac < return > i < return >

The first macro must be the display macro. Enter

< begdisp > < altm > 0,0,30,10. < AUTO > < TRANSP > < return >

The first line defined the display frame's dimensions. The 0,0 was used as the location for the upper left corner of the display frame. SuperKey will then vary the location of the frame, depending upon the current cursor location at the time the macro is invoked.

In addition, the line included the <AUTO> and <TRANSP> commands. Notice that a <TITLE> command was not entered this time.

The next portion of the macro contains the text that will be displayed in the frame. Enter

<return>
Press [F9] to list a sorted directory.<return>
<return>
Press [F10] to check disk statistics.<return>
<return>
Press <Esc> to exit menu.<return>
<enddef> <return>

In order to complete a working menu you will need to create macros for the [F9] and [F10] keys that will execute the functions designated to them by the text in the display frame. Enter

<begdef> <f9>cls<enter>dir | sort | more<enter> <enddef> <return>
<begdef> <f10>cls<enter>chkdsk *.*<enter> <enddef> <return>

Save the file by entering **[Ctrlc]e<return>**
Now load the macro. Enter **[Alt/] m l menu<return>**

```
Press [F9] to list a sorted di

Press [F10] to check disk stat

Press  to exit menu.
```

Fig. 9-17. Menu Display Macro.

Test the macro by entering **[F9]**
The display macro disappears and the directory is listed. When the display pauses, press any key to continue.
Display the menu again by entering **[Altm]**
This time test the other macro by entering **[F10]**
Display macros allow you to customize menus for any application or situation in which you find that your productivity would be improved by macro use. The display macro combines most of the skills you have learned already and places them into a coherent visual format.

9.50. Submenus

It might have already occurred to you that it may be possible to create a menu within a menu by including more than one display macro in a file. Suppose that you wanted to add a third option to the existing menu, one that would not execute a command but display a different menu.

This is a perfectly acceptable idea. You can see how this works by adding some additional information to the MENU.MAC file you just created.

Enter **edlin menu.mac < return >**

Before you enter new text, use the L, list command, to display the contents of the file as they now exist. Enter **l < return >**

The file looks like this:

```
1:*<begdisp><altm>0,0,30,10.<AUTO><TRANSP>
2:
3: Press [F9] to list a sorted directory.
4:
5: Press [F10] to check disk statistics.
6:
7: Press <Esc> to exit menu.
8: <enddef>
9: <begdef><f9>cls<enter>dir|sort|more<enter><enddef>
10: <begdef><f10>cls<enter>chkdsk *.*<enter><enddef>
```

First, insert a new line for the submenu. Enter **7i < return >**
Enter

Press [F8] for more selections. < return > < return > [Ctrlc]

Now add a macro definition for [F8] making it a display macro. Enter

13i < return > <begdisp> <f8> 1,1,25,10. <transp> < return > < return >
This is a submenu. < return >
It could include more commands. < return >
Press [Altx] to return < return >
to the main menu. < return >
<enddef> < return >

There is one last macro to define. If [Altx] is assigned [Altm] then instead of exiting, the submenu will return to the main menu. Enter **<begdef> <altx> <altm> <enddef> <return>**

Save the file by entering **[Ctrlc] e<return>**

Now load the macro. Enter

[Alt/] m l menu<return>

Test your macro by entering **[F8]**

The submenu appears. Enter **[Altx]**

The main menu reappears. SuperKey provides a means of creating a network of menus and prompts that can enhance almost any program you work with.

9.51. Batch Commands

The advantages of programs like SuperKey that alter and expand the function of the keyboard lead logically to the design of Turnkey applications. Turnkey refers to the use of generalized programs like 1-2-3 or dBASE as specific applications. When an application like dBASE or 1-2-3 is used as a Turnkey program, the user is less aware of the general nature of the program. They are usually only interested in the specific job that they do with the computer.

The purpose of Turnkey applications is to allow someone to use a complex program and accomplish a task by using macro functions prepared in advance. With macro functions, tasks that might take considerable time and knowledge can be executed by anyone who knows what macro keys to press.

For example, you might create a macro for the F1 key that loads a Lotus 1-2-3 spreadsheet. Instead of having the user remember /FR<filename> <return>, etc., you could tell them to simply press F1.

In thinking about Turnkey applications, one question might occur to you: If the user doesn't know how to load SuperKey and the necessary macro file, how will the F1 macro get loaded? Is there some way that you can automatically load a SuperKey macro file so that the macro definitions are automatically in memory when the user begins?

The answer is yes. The answer comes partly from the concept of DOS batch files and the KEY.COM program. DOS provides a means of automatically executing a number of DOS commands. The KEY.COM program has the ability to load a macro file as part of a DOS batch file.

To understand the advantages and possibilities involved with batch files, this idea will be explored in detail.

Hard Drive:
The hands-on section that follows is designed for use with a hard disk system. The assumption is that you are working on a hard disk that has a working copy of Lotus 1-2-3. In addition, the file KEY.COM is also on the hard disk. A path *must* be open between the directory with Lotus 1-2-3 and the directory that contains the SuperKey program.

Floppy Drive:
If you have a floppy disk system you will probably find that the techniques are not very practical; you can perform this same task, but the drive setup gets a bit tricky. After you have booted your computer, place a working Lotus 1-2-3 in drive A. In drive B you will place a disk with the SuperKey file KEY.COM on it.

In addition you should copy the Lotus driver files to the disk in drive B.

copy 123.cnf b:<return>
copy a:??.drv b:<return>

Then open a path to drive A:

path a:\ <return>

Change the active drive to B:

b:<return>

You can now run 1-2-3 from the B drive.

9.52.   The Spreadsheet File

You will also need a Lotus spreadsheet file to work with. The file used in this example is called SAMPLE.WKS. If you have a file you want to use simply remember to substitute the file's real name wherever you see SAM-PLE used in the example.

9.53. Creating the Batch Program

Assume that you had a file, 123test.mac, that contained two macros which would allow a novice to make some changes in a 1-2-3 spreadsheet you had designed.

F1 = loads 1-2-3 and a spreadsheet file called REPORT
F2 = prints the spreadsheet, saves any changes, and quits 1-2-3

[SuperKey needs to be loaded into the computer in order to perform the following tasks.]

To create the F1 macro, enter **[Alt/] m d [F1]**

The first task for the macro is to load the 1-2-3 program. Enter **123 < return >**

When 1-2-3 loads, it presents a screen that tells you the name of the program. You must press a key when you see this screen. In order to include this process in the macro, you will need to include another < return >. However, there is second issue involved. Following the 123 < return > portion of the macro, the computer will be loading a program, i.e., performing a reading operation from the disk. Many times, when computers read or write to the disk drives, keystrokes entered into macros get lost. As protection from this problem, a delay will make sure that the loading is complete before the next part of the macro is executed. Enter **[Alt/] f r 000002 < return >**

This will insert a two-second delay when the macro is played back.

[If you are working with a floppy drive system that is especially slow, the delay may need to be increased.]

Continue entering keystrokes. Enter **< return >**

At this point, 1-2-3 reads the disk again, checking for the copy protection scheme. Once again it would be wise to enter a delay. Enter **[Alt/] f r 000002 < return >**

Now enter the keystrokes that will load the file. Enter **/frsample < return >**

Finally, enter a command that makes the macro an auto start macro. Enter **< auto >**

The macro is now complete. Enter **[Alt Esc] y**

The next task is to make a macro that prints the spreadsheet, saves the changes if any, and quits the 1-2-3 program. At this moment you should still be at the SuperKey command menu. Enter **[Alt/] m d [F2]**

Begin with the keystrokes that will print the worksheet. Enter

/ppr < return > gpq/fssample < return > r/qy
[Alt/] f r 000002 < return > clear < return >

Complete the macro. Enter **[Alt Esc] y**

You have created the two macros that you need. You need to save the macros in a file. Enter **[Alt/] m s 123test.mac < return >**

Clear the memory of macros. Enter **[Alt/] m c**

Now you have stored the macros to the disk and are ready to create the batch commands.

9.54.   Batch Execution

Normally, the way to load macros into the SuperKey memory is to use the SuperKey command [Alt/]ml. If this were the only way to accomplish that task, there would be no way to create the Turnkey systems you desire with SuperKey. Fortunately, this is not the case.

The customary way to load the SuperKey program is to enter **key < return >**

However, the KEY command can accept parameters. The parameters can be used to carry out almost all of the commands, options, defaults, etc., that you would typically perform from the SuperKey menus. The entire scope of parameter commands will be discussed later in this chapter. Right now you will be concerned chiefly with parameters that carry out the functions of the commands on the Macros menu.

[If you are unfamiliar with the concept of command parameters see Chapter 1.14.]

The structure of the parameters emulates the commands used in SuperKey. For example, if the SuperKey command to clear all macros is [Alt/]mc, then the equivalent batch command would be KEY /MC.

One tricky part is that if the parameter requires the name of a file, then the filename precedes the parameter. In this example, you will want to load a macro file called 123TEST.MAC as a parameter. (The .MAC is not necessary because SuperKey will assume that file extension.)

The command would be KEY 123TEST/ML. Again, remember that the filename precedes the parameters. Test the command by entering
key 123test/ml < return >

The file is loaded into memory. To check to see if this really happened, enter **[Alt PrtSc]**

You can see the macros listed. Enter **< Esc >**

You can use the SuperKey command to clear macros. Enter
key /mc < return >

The macros are cleared from the memory. To check, enter **[Alt PrtSc]**

No macros are listed. Return to the DOS prompt. Enter **< Esc >**

The advantage of using commands with the KEY.COM program is that these commands can be used as part of a DOS batch file.

[If you are not familiar with the concepts of batch files, see Chapter 2.22.]

You can create a batch file with any ASCII word processing program, the DOS program EDLIN, or even with the DOS COPY command. This example will use the DOS COPY command. The disadvantage of COPY is that you cannot go back to previous lines and make corrections. If you are familiar with EDLIN you might want to use that program instead.

Enter

copy con: update.bat < return >

Now enter the batch commands. The first command is used to load the SuperKey program, and in addition, to load the macro file 123TEST.MAC.

key 123test/ml < return >

To save the macro, enter

[F6]
< return >

DOS will tell you that one file has been copied. This means that the text you typed has been stored in a file on the disk.

Now create another batch file called CLEAR.BAT. (This step is not absolutely necessary.) CLEAR.BAT will use the SuperKey program to clear the macros out of the memory after the program has completed and return the function keys F1 and F2 to their original definitions.

Create the batch file by entering

copy con: clear.bat<return>
key /mc<return>
cls<return>
echo Lotus Update Program Complete

Save the text to a file by entering

[F6]
<return>

DOS will confirm the saving by telling you that one file was copied. You are now ready to execute the batch file. Enter

update<return>

What is happening? First the Lotus 1-2-3 program loads. Then the macro loads the spreadsheet, SAMPLE. You are now ready to make any necessary changes. Enter

[F2]

This executes the second macro. The file prints, then saves. Then the macro exits from 1-2-3. The CLEAR.BAT file is executed, removing the macros from the memory and returning the function keys to their normal status.

You can run these batch files as many times as you like. The use of SuperKey commands in DOS batch files is quite handy. Programs that allow you to access DOS, such as dBASE III, provide an interesting way to combine keyboard programs and applications programs.

9.55.   The Command Stack

SuperKey includes another feature that is related to DOS commands, called the Command Stack. When you enter a command at the system's prompt, DOS does not forget the command. Instead, DOS saves the command in a special area in the memory. The command is remembered until you issue another command. This feature allows you to recall the last command that you entered. If you want, you can reissue the command.

This is a useful feature, but it is limited to the last command entered. SuperKey extends the DOS command memory to include the last 256 keystrokes entered at the system's prompt. This means that you can recall and execute any of the commands entered in the last 256 keystrokes. The command stack can be accessed by entering alternate backslash or [Alt/]cc.

To display the command stack enter **[Alt\]**

The screen will show the COMMAND STACK display.

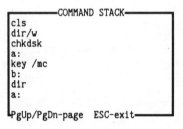

Fig. 9-18. Command Stack.

The commands are listed such that the last command given is listed first. The highlight in the box can be positioned to select any of the commands displayed. The [Pg Up] and [Pg Dn] keys will display additional screens. Pressing <return> will pass the highlighted keystrokes to DOS as if they had been reentered.

9.56. Sidekick

If you have Sidekick, SuperKey provides a special command to include Sidekick functions into SuperKey macros. For example, suppose that you wanted to create a macro that displayed the Sidekick date calculator. Enter

[Alt =]
[F10]
[Alt/]
c
s
[F3]
[Alt-]

Press <**Esc**> to exit Sidekick. Now test the macro by entering

[F10]

The calculator is displayed.

[When Sidekick is accessed by SuperKey, it is the same as if you had accessed Sidekick manually from the keyboard. This means that if you had already used Sidekick, the settings would still be active when the macro is executed.

One important consideration is the way you exit Sidekick. The macro shown above assumes that when Sidekick is called up the main Sidekick menu will appear. However, if you had previously used Sidekick and exited with [Ctrl Alt] rather than <Esc>, when the macro calls Sidekick, the last function used will appear instead of the main menu. Keep this in mind when you design macros with Sidekick included.]

Another interesting blend of SuperKey and Sidekick is to create a macro that will copy the displayed screen into the Sidekick notepad using the Sidekick Import text feature. Begin by defining a macro, [Alti]. Enter

[Alt =]
[Alti]

Now call Sidekick. Enter

[Alt/]
c
s

Choose the notepad function. Enter

[F2]

Use the Sidekick notepad command to position the cursor to the end of the notepad file. This is to make sure that the data you are about to import does not conflict with any data already in the notepad. Enter

[Ctrlq]
d

Now enter the import commands:

[F4]
[Ctrlk]
b

Use the arrow keys to highlight the entire screen. Then enter

[Ctrlk]
k
[Ctrlk]
c

The screen image is copied into the notepad. Now leave Sidekick. Enter

<Esc>

Conclude the macro by entering

[Alt-]

Now replay the macro by entering

[Alti]

The import function executes automatically capturing the screen data into the Sidekick notepad.

Another combination of features is to use the SuperKey DOS commands to run Sidekick functions from batch files.

For example, suppose you wanted to capture a screen display as part of a batch file. Normally there would be no way to execute a Sidekick command as part of a batch. But SuperKey solves that problem. The macro you just created is a good example.

Modify the macro to be an auto-execute macro. Enter

[Alt/] m d [Alti] < a u t o > [Alt Esc] y

Now save the macro in a file. Enter

[Alt/] m s side ‹ return ›

With this setup you can issue a DOS level command to run a Sidekick function. The following command assumes that the KEY.COM program is in the default drive. Enter **key side/ml ‹ return ›**

The screen is captured as part of a DOS level command. You can then use a batch file to implement this action.

9.57.   Other Features and Modes

SuperKey has a number of settings that change the way the program operates. The following section will describe these functions and options. Many of the options are toggles that are set either ON or OFF.

Most of these features can be implemented in three ways:

1) *From the Command Mode.* This is the most usual way to enter commands, options and defaults. Commands are entered by using the SuperKey menus. For example, to set the Format Fields function ON, enter **[Alt/]of**.

2) *From Macros.* Options, defaults, and commands can be set as part of keystroke macros. Defaults and options can be included in macros in exactly the same way that functions and SuperKey commands are included. Like functions, option or default settings included in macros do not take effect when you enter them. They only come to life when the macro is played back.

   If the option is a toggle command then you must enter a + to turn the function ON or a − to turn the function off. For example, to create a macro to set the Format Fields option On, enter **[Alt =] [Altf] [Alt/]of + [Alt-]**. To implement the macro enter **[Altf]**.

3) *Load as a DOS Command.* The majority of the options and defaults can be set as DOS by using the KEY command with the specified parameters. Toggle options are set using a + for On and a − for OFF. For example, if you wanted to set the Format Fields option ON you would enter **KEY /OF +** .

SuperKey has the following options displayed on the Options menu ([Alt/]o):

A—Arrow Keys. This option allows you to reposition the arrow keys to other keys or combinations on the keyboard. The default is OFF, meaning that the arrow keys function normally.

B—Bottom Line. This option displays the SuperKey prompt line at the bottom of the screen rather than the top of the screen. The default is OFF, i.e., the prompt line appears at the top of the screen.

C—Command Stack. This option controls whether or not SuperKey will record the DOS keystrokes. The default setting is ON, i.e., recording DOS keystrokes.

F—Format Fields. This option should be on if you want to record formatting keystrokes within variable or fixed fields. The default is OFF, i.e., field format characters not recorded.

K—Keyboard Click. This option generates a clicking sound whenever a key is pressed to simulate the audio feedback found on typewriters. The default value is OFF, i.e., no clicking.

O—One Finger. The one-finger mode is an adaptation to the fact that many of the features of keyboard programs require the use of key combinations such as [Alt /], etc. SuperKey makes it possible to eliminate the need to enter these combinations by holding down the first key while pressing the second. This is possible because of the way that the keyboard functions. When you press a key combination the computer records the fact that the [Alt], [Ctrl], or [Shift] key is being pressed down. When the next key is pressed, it interprets the character differently than it would if the [Alt], [Ctrl], or [Shift] keys had not been held down. The default setting is OFF.

P—Playback Delay. This option controls the speed at which keystrokes recorded in macros are played back. The delay factor is a number between 0 and 999. The default value is zero, i.e., no delay.

T—Protect Delay. This feature is used to turn off the screen display if you do not enter a keystroke within a specified number of minutes. The purpose is to prevent screen "burn in" caused by displaying the same screen for too long. The default is OFF.

U—Suspend SuperKey. SuperKey allows you to suspend the operation of the program. The purpose is to return the keyboard to normal without removing the macros from memory. When SuperKey is suspended you can neither playback nor create macros. However, any macros that are in the memory will remain there and will become active when you turn off the suspension. The default setting is OFF, meaning that SuperKey is active.

W—Disk Wait. The function of disk wait is similar to the playback delay. The disk wait suspends the playback of keystrokes while the disk drive is active.

S—Save Options. This command saves a copy of the current setting on the options menu. The next time you load SuperKey, the options will be set as they were when you issued the Save command.

9.58. Changing SuperKey Defaults

There are two important changes you can make in the way SuperKey operates. The first is to change the amount of memory that SuperKey uses when it loads. The default is for SuperKey to set aside 8,000 bytes of memory for macro recording. Since most macros are short, this is usually quite adequate.

However, you can change the amount of memory used by SuperKey for macros. The minimum amount of memory is 128 bytes. The maximum is 64 kilobytes (65,536 bytes) of memory. Enlarging the memory allows you to create larger macros. Decreasing the memory frees memory space for other applications.

It is important to note that the size of SuperKey in the memory is set when you load KEY. If you want to change the size of SuperKey, you must use the SuperKey install program, KEYINST.COM, to change the memory size allocation and then reboot the computer and load KEY again.

The second change is to change the command keystrokes that are used by SuperKey. There are two reasons to change the command keys in SuperKey. The first is to avoid conflicts with programs that also use the same key combination. The second reason is more personal. You simply might prefer to use a different set of keys to command the program.

Unlike the memory area command, you can change the SuperKey commands at any time. Bring up the menu by entering **[Alt/] d**

The default keys that are supplied with SuperKey are:

Begin macro	[Alt =]	Title	[Alt']
autO-start	[Alt `]	End macro	[Alt-]
Menu	[Alt/]	Fixed field	<Ctrl]>
Var field	[Ctrl-]	cUt and paste	<Alt]>
beGin block	b	sKip macro	`
stoP	[Ctrl Esc]	shoW titles	[Alt PrtSc]
Command stack	[Alt \]	Decimal point	.
deLimiter	,	fill cHaracter	<space bar>
help sYstem	[F1]	Arrow keys	[F7][F8][F9][F10]

The last item on the menu is used to Save any changes that you want to make permanently in the default menu. To leave the menu as it is, enter **<Esc>**

Changes can be made in any of the three usual ways. For example, suppose that you wanted to change the Begin macro and End macro command keys to [Home] and [End]. You can do this

1) By using the SuperKey menus. Enter **[Alt/] d b[Home] [Alt/] d [End]**
2) By including the menu commands in a macro. The following keystrokes will create a macro that change the command keys:

   [Alt=] [Altk] [Alt/] d b [Home] [Alt/] d [End] [Alt-]

   Execute the macro by entering **[Altk]**
3) By using parameters with the KEY command from DOS. At the DOS prompt enter **key /db[home]/de[end] <return>**

[Observe that in this command the square brackets were used in entering the key name. This is because the angle brackets, < >, are used by DOS to indicate redirection of a program's input and output. If you used the angle brackets with this command, DOS would display the message "File not found".

The command key /db<home>/de<end> would indicate to DOS that the program KEY expected input from a file called HOME. Since there probably isn't a file called HOME on your disk, DOS tells you that the input file cannot be found.]

9.59. Encryption

Most microcomputer programs produce data files that store information in a standard manner. This allows the data to be accessed quickly and easily. However, this also means that anyone who is familiar with the computer can access the data, even though they do not have the program, by using DOS commands or utilities like Norton Utilities (see Chapter 3).

SuperKey includes a feature that allows you to code data files for security purposes. This feature is used to convert normal data files into encrypted files. These files cannot be used or accessed unless they are decrypted. The process is protected by a password.

As an example of the use of this encryption feature, you can use the file READ-ME.KEY that is supplied with the SuperKey program. Make sure that a copy of this file is on the disk in the default directory or drive.

The file is an ASCII standard file. You can display its contents by typing **type read-me.key<return>**

The goal of the encryption program is to prevent unauthorized people from gaining access to this data. Begin by bringing up the SuperKey menu. Enter **[Alt/] e**

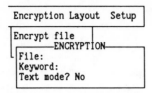

Fig. 9-19. Encrypt Menu.

There are two options:

1) Encrypt File.   Convert a data file to a coded file.
2) Decrypt File.   Convert a coded file back into a normal file.

Enter **e**

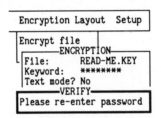

Fig. 9-20. Encrypt Options.

There are three decisions that you must make when encoding a file:

1. *File.* Specify the name of the file to cipher. You can enter any valid DOS filename. Remember that if a file has an extension, you must specify it. There are no default extensions in the encryption command.

   If you want to use a DOS wildcard to select a group of files, that is also permitted. For example, *.mac would select all the files with a MAC extension on the disk for encoding.
2. *Keyword.* The keyword is the password. A file can only be encrypted if the correct keyword is entered during the decoding process. The password can be up to 30 characters in length. Needless to say, you must take care to remember the password or your data will be lost forever.
3. *Text Mode?* SuperKey has two modes of use in coding files:

Text Mode = NO. If NO is entered for text mode, the coding copies over the file or files selected with the coded file. The newly coded file occupies the same disk space as the uncoded file did. Once a file has been coded in the non-text mode, the original data can only be accessed after it has been successfully decoded. The non-text mode is the usual way of using the program when you want to safeguard files on the disk.

Text Mode = YES. If the text mode is selected, then the coding creates a new file that is a coded version of the original. The original file is unchanged. The text mode is used when you want to make a secure copy of a file for transmission to another computer via modem.

There is also a technical difference between the non-text and text coding method. The non-text method creates a binary file much like the contents of a program file. The text method creates a text file in which the contents appear to be all upper case letters, A to Z.

The text file takes up more disk space than does a non-text version of the same coded file.

[If you use the text mode and then use the DOS DEL or ERASE commands to remove the original uncoded file, you have not protected your data. The reason is that even after a file has been erased, the data is still on the disk. Programs like Norton Utilities can access this data.

To completely erase the contents of a file you need to use a program such as the one provided with the Norton Utilities program, called WIPEFILE.COM. This program writes zeros over an old file. This will prevent unauthorized recovery of the data.]

Enter the name of the file: **read-me.key < return >**

Now enter the keyword. Enter **password < return >**

Note that the letters you type are not displayed, only asterisks appear in the box. SuperKey now asks you to reenter the keyword as a confirmation. Enter **password < return > < return >**

A box displaying the word "encrypting..." appears. When the process is complete, you are returned to the menu. Exit SuperKey by entering **< Esc >**

Now try to use the TYPE command. Enter **type read-me.key < return >**

The screen shows only a scramble of graphics characters. To return the file to its normal state you must use the Decrypt option.

[A file must be decoded in the same mode that it was encoded in. This means that if the file was encrypted in the NON-TEXT mode, you *must* select the NON-TEXT mode for decryption. The same applies to file coded in the TEXT mode.]

To decode a file, enter

[Alt/] e d read-me.key <return> password <return>
password <return> <return>

Test the file by entering **type read-me.key <return>**

The text appears as it did before the encryption process was used.

[SuperKey is supplied with two versions of the main program. They are KEY.COM and KEYDES.COM. The only difference is that the KEYDES.COM uses an encoding process that conforms to the Federal Data Encryption Standard (DES). The KEY.COM encodes files using a method developed by Borland.

The KEYDES.COM provides a marginally more secure file, but it takes longer to operate than does the method employed by the KEY.COM program.

Menus and commands are identical for both programs.]

9.60. Layout

In addition to the KEY.COM program, the SuperKey disk contains another program called LAYOUT.COM

The purpose of Layout is actually to change the position of the keys on the keyboard. One common complaint about the IBM PC keyboard is the position of the [\ |] and the [Shift] keys. Layout gives you a chance to swap those keys.

In addition, the program is supplied with a layout file that converts your keyboard to a Dvorak keyboard.

The Layout program affects the basic relationship between the keyboard and the computer. There are two parts to working with Layout:

1) Use the LAYOUT.COM program to create a layout file.
2) Use the Layout option on the SuperKey menu to load the layout.

The Layout program can be used to modify an existing Layout file or create a new layout from scratch. As a short illustration of how Layout works, you can create a new layout.

Begin the Layout program. Enter **layout <return>**

You are asked to enter the name of a layout file. Since you want to create a new layout file, enter a new name: **mykeys.lay <return>**

Layout displays a message telling you that since the file MYKEYS.LAY is a new file, the IBM PC/XT layout will be used as a default. Enter **<return>**

The layout program presents a screen that looks like this:

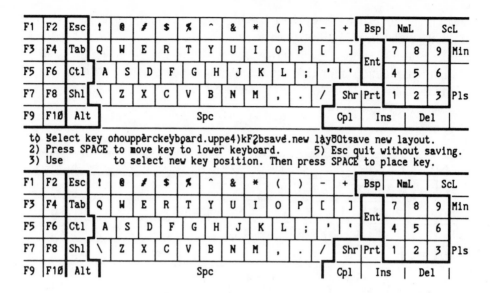

Fig. 9-21. Layout Screen.

The only action that you can take in the Layout program is to swap the position of various keys. The upper keyboard shows the current position while the lower keyboard will reflect any changes in the layout.

Suppose that you wanted to swap the positions of the [Alt] key and the [Shift] key. In order to change the position of the keys you must perform two steps:

1) Change the [Alt] key to the [Shift] Position.
2) Change the left [Shift] key to the [Alt] Position.

First, use the arrow keys to highlight the [Alt] key on the upper display. To change a key location, begin by entering **<space bar>**

Now type the key that you want to change. Use the arrow keys to move the highlight on the lower keyboard to the Left [Shift] key. Enter **<space bar>**

The Alt symbol on the upper keyboard appears in reverse video. The bottom keyboard now shows two positions for the [Alt] key. Now you must enter the key that will function as the [Alt] key. The key you want to swap is the left SHIFT key. Move the highlight on the upper keyboard to the left [Shift] key. Enter **< space bar >**

The bottom keyboard now shows two positions for the [Alt] key. One is highlighted and blinking. Move the highlight down to the position formerly used by the [Alt] key. Enter **< space bar >**

The screen now shows:

F1	F2	Esc	!	@	#	$	%	^	&	*	(	)	-	+	Bsp	NmL	ScL
F3	F4	Tab	Q	W	E	R	T	Y	U	I	O	P	[	]	Ent	7 8 9	Min
F5	F6	Ctl	A	S	D	F	G	H	J	K	L	;	'	`		4 5 6	
F7	F8	Shl	\	Z	X	C	V	B	N	M	,	.	/	Shr	Prt	1 2 3	Pls
F9	F10	Alt			Spc										Cpl	Ins	Del

1) Use   to select key on upper keyboard.   4) F2 save new layout.
2) Press SPACE to move key to lower keyboard.   5) Esc quit without saving.
3) Use   to select new key position. Then press SPACE to place key.

F1	F2	Esc	!	@	#	$	%	^	&	*	(	)	-	+	Bsp	NmL	ScL
F3	F4	Tab	Q	W	E	R	T	Y	U	I	O	P	[	]	Ent	7 8 9	Min
F5	F6	Ctl	A	S	D	F	G	H	J	K	L	;	'	`		4 5 6	
F7	F8	Alt	\	Z	X	C	V	B	N	M	,	.	/	Shr	Prt	1 2 3	Pls
F9	F10	Shl			Spc										Cpl	Ins	Del

Fig. 9-22. Swapped Keys.

The lower keyboard shows the new positions of the keys that you have swapped. The process can continue until you have created a keyboard that you want to work with. If you want to abandon the changes, you can press the < Esc > key and the keyboard will return to the original layout.

[To change an individual key back to the original, simply enter the same key twice. Example: **< space bar >** (two times)
The keys will return to normal.]

In order to save the new keyboard, enter **[F2]**

To test the new layout you use the SuperKey menu. Enter **[Alt/] l l mykeys < return >**

Now try out the new keyboard. If all is correct the left [Shift] key will function as the [Alt] key.

To activate the macro program, hold down the left [Shift] key and then press = . The prompt appears at the top of the screen. To terminate the macro hold down the left [Shift] key and press -

The left [Shift] functions as the [Alt] key. Test the other end of the swap by holding down the **[Alt]** key and typing. The characters will be upper case.

9.61. Removing and Activating a Keyboard

When a layout file has been loaded, you can return to the normal keyboard by using the Layout Clear command. Layout commands can be entered as batch commands also. Enter **key /lc < return >**

The keyboard returns to normal.

9.62. Conclusion

The SuperKey system is a powerful way to create keyboard macros. The Layout program adds the ability to alter the position of keys. For a comparison of SuperKey with other macro programs see Chapter 12.

10.

Recall

Another interesting program that is designed along the lines of ProKey and SuperKey is Recall. It duplicates many of the functions described in detail in the chapters on ProKey and SuperKey, but it also provides some features that cannot be found in other programs. Even though Recall is not as well known as ProKey or SuperKey, it is worthy of consideration.

This chapter will describe how Recall works and how it differs from the other programs explained in Part 3.

10.1   Vital Statistics

The Recall program is provided with a number of demonstration files. The program itself is a single command file that takes up about 43 kilobytes of disk space. When loaded, the program occupies 33 kilobytes of internal memory.

10.2.   Macro Creation

Recall creates macros in a manner similar to the other programs described. Recall differs from the other programs in that its macro definitions are created in a mode that combines the features of the two modes used by SuperKey and ProKey.

With SuperKey and ProKey, you can create macros in one of two modes, interactive and editing. In the interactive mode, the keystrokes are passed to the application as you enter them and the program records your keystroke for later playback. The primary advantage of this mode is that you get to see exactly what effect the keystrokes will have as you enter them into the macro.

On the other hand, the interactive mode does not provide an immediate means by which errors can be corrected. If you make a typing mistake and attempt to correct the error, the macro recording mode records the keystrokes used to make the typing correction. Every time the macro is played back the error will be made and corrected again.

The editing mode is different from the interactive mode in two respects. First, any keystrokes entered are not passed to the application. Second, all the keystrokes in the macro are displayed as symbols. The advantage of this mode is that you can use editing keys to add or eliminate keystrokes from the macro. The disadvantage is that, because your keystrokes are not being passed to the application as you type them, it is more difficult to imagine the effect that they will have on that application.

Recall attempts to bridge the two methods by providing a macro creation mode in which your keystrokes are passed to the application but are displayed simultaneously.

In addition, in Recall, you can switch between interactive recording and editing modes. This enables you to make corrections while you are creating the macro.

How is this accomplished? Suppose that you wanted to create a macro that assigned to the [Home] key the DIR command. (This illustration was used in the chapters on SuperKey and ProKey.)

Like the other programs, Recall begins with a command keystroke that turns on the macro creation mode. In this case the keystroke is **<Alt[>**

Next, you enter the key to be redefined, for example, [Home]. What happens next is that the a highlight appears across the center of the screen. At the same time the cursor remains in its proper position within the application—in this case, next to the DOS prompt.

The highlight contains R I [< Hme >] I . This indicates that the [Home] key is being redefined. As you enter your keystrokes—in this example, dir < return >—the keystrokes are passed to the application but also appear in the highlight. For example, **R I [< Hme >] I dir < Ent >**

What if you had made a typing error? For example, suppose instead of the correct keystrokes you had entered **R I [< Hme >] I dor < Ent >**

In SuperKey and ProKey you would have to complete the recording and enter another mode to correct the typo. In Recall you simply press **[Scroll Lock]**. You are now in an edit mode. You can correct the keystrokes in the macro recording as well as in the application.

Entering **[Scroll Lock]** again places you back into the recording mode. You can move back and forth between modes as much as you require. The idea is that you can actually get the macro right the first time instead of having to choose between starting all over again or saving the macro and editing it later.

Another feature of Recall is that, when you begin to define a macro, the program displays the simulated keyboard. You can then see which keys have already been used for macros.

10.3. Fields

Like SuperKey and ProKey, Recall also allows the user to create input fields with macros. Recall supports both variable- and fixed-length fields. However, once again there are some interesting and pleasant differences in the implementation of input fields.

One useful difference is related to the fact that Recall provides for simultaneous recording and editing modes. In SuperKey and ProKey, if you forget to include a field in a macro you must change modes completely in order to add the field. In Recall all you need do is use the [Scroll Lock] key to access the edit line that appears on the screen as you enter keystrokes. Once on the edit line, you are free to create a field or fields at any position in the macro you desire.

To create a field, you enter **[Altf]**. This brings up a pop-up menu that helps you define the field. The first item selects the type of field, fixed length or variable length. Unlike other programs, the length of a fixed-length field is selected by entering a number instead of typing characters.

The next three features are ones that are not found in SuperKey or ProKey:

1. *Save Field Entry*. This option allows you to automatically record the data entered into a field as another macro. For example, suppose that you had a macro called [Altc] that copied a file to another disk. If that macro contained a field which was used to allow you to specify the file to be copied, a save option would automatically record the entry in that field as another macro, [Altf] perhaps.

   The macro could be made to also delete the file after it was copied. With SuperKey and ProKey you would have to create a second field and enter the filename again. But with Recall you could simply reference [Altf], which would contain the name of the file.

The save field option allows you to pass a single parameter to a number of macros. This provides a logical link between groups of macros.

2. *Message.* This option is so useful and logical it is surprising that other macro programs do not have it. The message allows you to create a screen prompt that will appear when the macro encounters the field command.

The message is text that is entered into the macro but is not passed to the application. This feature is very powerful and adds a tremendous amount to the ease of use of macros that require user input.

3. *Terminator.* In SuperKey and ProKey all field entries are terminated with a <return>, with the exception of fixed fields that are completely filled by the entry. Recall allows you the option of terminating a field entry with some other character of your choice. For example, you might wish to use the <tab> key to terminate the entry.

10.4.   Debugging Macros

Another feature of Recall is its ability to replay macros one keystroke at a time. This is called the *single step* mode. The single step mode is designed to help you find bugs and inconsistencies in your macros.

Recall usually replays the macros in the "R"-replay mode. You can switch Recall into the single step mode by entering **[Alt\]<return>**

When you call a macro, the edit line appears on the screen. Recall does not automatically pass the keystrokes to the application. Rather it waits until you give it a specific signal. This is done by pressing the [+] on the numeric keypad.

Each time the plus sign is pressed, Recall passes one of the keystrokes in the macro to the application. The [Scroll Lock] key allows you to move between the replay and edit modes.

This enables you to have full control of the playback of the macro and find and correct any problems in the macro. The other programs do not have the ability to step through the macros one keystroke at a time. They either replay the entire macro or enter an edit mode.

Recall contains a number of features concerning the use of fields that improve the handling of user inputs into macros a great deal.

10.5.   Menus

While the features already mentioned are interesting, the most significant feature of Recall is its ability to create user menus.

SuperKey and SmartKey feature "display" macros which have limited menu ability. ProKey does not have this ability. Recall's menu ability has a number of beneficial and practical advantages.

1. *Menus are created interactively.* In SuperKey, the creation of menus (display macros) cannot be accomplished in the interactive recording or editing modes. The only way to create this sort of macro is to use a text editor or word processing program to create a text file that contains the codes and symbols that create the menu. Then the menu must be loaded into the SuperKey program to be displayed.

   This creates two disadvantages. First, you must exit the application you are working with in order to create a text file. Second, you cannot see what the menu will look like until you have completed the macro and loaded the file into SuperKey.

   With Recall the menu is created interactively in about the same way that you create a macro. There is no need to exit the application you are working with in order to create a text file.

   In addition, Recall displays the menus on the screen as you create them. You can see how the final menu displays will appear as you make them.

2. *Menus directly implement macros.* With SuperKey and SmartKey, the relationship between the items displayed in the menu and the macro commands with which they are associated is indirect. In SuperKey, you write the display macro, and then a series of macros related to the text are displayed in the window.

   Recall allows you to enter the macro commands as you create the menu items.

3. *Highlight selection in menus.* Recall's menu structure allows the user to select menu items by using a highlight that can be positioned to any item in the menu. If an item is highlighted and the <return> key is pressed, the macro associated with that menu item will be executed. The result is that you can create a series of menus that operate like the type of menu structures used in many popular programs, such as Lotus 1-2-3.

4. *Menus used as part of a larger macro.* Another advantage of the Recall system is that because menu's are created interactively, they can be used as part of macros that contain other types of keystrokes. In SuperKey, it is more difficult to combine menus with other macros. Recall makes it simple to create menus as parts of other macros as well as menus as parts of menus, i.e., submenus.

For example, suppose that you wanted to create a menu that would provide the user with DOS commands, such as directory listings and disk checks. First you might create the basic macros using the interactive recording mode. You might create the following macros:

Macro	*Keystrokes*
[Alta]	dir < return >
[Altb]	dir/w < return >
[Altc]	dir/p < return >
[Altd]	chkdsk < return >
[Alte]	chkdsk *.* < return >
[Altf]	chkdsk/v < return >

Your goal would be to create menus that would implement these commands. With Recall you would begin as you would with a normal macro. The following command will begin creation of a macro: **< Alt] > [F10]**

To make the macro a menu macro, place Recall into its edit mode and enter **[Altm]** to begin creating a macro using the following keystrokes: **[Scroll Lock][Altm]**

Recall now displays a box in the upper left-hand corner of the screen. The box will become the menu display. You would then enter the text of the menu item. You can create 23 items on a menu. Each item is restricted to a 27-character string of characters. For example, you might enter **Normal Directory**

The next step is to associate the menu line with a macro command. This is equally simple. Enter **< tab >**

Now enter the macro key, in this case **[Alta]**

Next you would want to add another item to the menu. This is done simply by entering **+**

The box is extended by a line. You can now enter another menu item, for example, **Wide Directory < tab > [Altb]**

The process can continue for as many as 23 items on a menu. You might choose to divide the macros into two menus. [F10] might contain macros [Alta–c], the directory commands, while another macro, [F9], might contain macros [Altd–f], the check disk commands.

Finally you might make another menu macro that allows you to select from the two menus, [F9] and [F10].

10.6.   Conclusion

Recall is a program that is more limited in scope than SuperKey and SmartKey. It concentrates on keystroke macros and on creating interactive menus that implement those macros. Unlike SuperKey, Recall does not have many special functions. It does allow for delays in macros but does not supply some of the other specialized functions found in SuperKey. Options like keyboard lock and data encryption are not found in Recall.

However, Recall does perform well in the areas that it is designed to cover. The combination of editing and interactive macro creation is very helpful.

The menu creation is outstanding. If you are interested in creating pop-up menus for application programs, Recall has outstanding features.

For a detailed comparison of features, see Chapter 12.

11.

SmartKey

The final program in the keyboard enhancement section of this book is SmartKey. SmartKey is produced by the same company that created SmartPath, discussed in Chapter 6.1.

SmartKey generally covers the same ground as ProKey, SuperKey, and Recall. Of course, SmartKey implements the same functions in a different way than do the other programs. This chapter looks at SmartKey and its strongest features.

11.1. Vital Statistics

The disk contains 16 files that occupy 159,744 bytes of disk space.

```
SKSETUP.COM     SMARTKEY.COM    SKBATCH.COM     DVORAKEY.COM
CRYPTOR.COM     D.COM           PK2SK.COM       PCKEY.COM
LOTUS.DTX       DBASE.DTX       MENU.DTX        MENUDEMO.DTX
WORDSTAR.DTX    SAMPLE.DTX      COMMANDS.DTX    README.1ST
```

The main program is SMARTKEY.COM It is the only file that is absolutely necessary to operate the macro portion of the SmartKey program. When loaded into the computer, SmartKey takes up about 32 kilobytes of memory.

The other programs supplied with SmartKey are:

SKSETUP.COM—This program is used to install new defaults in the SmartKey program.

SKBATCH.COM—This program allows you to circumvent the SmartKey menu and execute SmartKey commands from DOS.

339

PCKEY.COM—This program is used to modify the keyboard setup of your computer. It allows you to reassign keys like the LAYOUT programs in SuperKey and ProKey. In addition, it implements key click, screen blank, and other keyboard-related functions.

DVORAKEY.COM—This program is a special form of the PCKEY program. It is used to convert the PC keyboard to a Dvorak keyboard.

CRYPTOR.COM—This program is used to create encrypted files for security purposes.

PK2SK.COM—This program has a special function. It is used to convert ProKey macro files into SmartKey macro files.

D.COM—Utility for listing a file's directory. The program creates a listing that looks like this:

```
ANSI    .SYS  2k | CONFIG .SYS  1k | MENU    .MAC  1k | SAM    .    0k
ASSIGN  .COM  1k | DISKCOMP.COM  3k | MODE    .COM  4k | SIDE   .MAC  1k
COMP    .COM  3k | GRAPHICS.COM  1k | RESTORE .COM  4k

Total of 149k bytes in 39 files, 5k bytes remain available
```

11.2. Macro Creation

SmartKey's approach to basic macro creation is a bit different from the other programs. SuperKey, ProKey, and Recall all provide an obvious "recording" mode. Macro creation begins with a begin macro command and the recording continues until the end macro command is issued.

SmartKey, on the other hand, requires that you access the SmartKey menu to begin any of the SmartKey functions, including the RECORD mode. In addition, SmartKey designates two special keys:

1) SMART KEY—This key is used to gain access to the main SmartKey menu. The default key for the Smart key is the plus sign located on the numeric key pad. The symbol for that key is K + .

2) Super SHIFT—The super SHIFT key is initially assigned to the minus key on the numeric keypad. The symbol for this key is K − .

The purpose of the Super SHIFT key is to enlarge the number of macro assignments that can be made. For example, most macro programs allow you to define macros for [Shift], [Ctrl], and [Alt] combinations of keys. The Super SHIFT key doubles the number of definable keys by adding another layer to the key definition. For example, SuperKey would allow you to define macros for the following keys:

[F10] [Shift F10] [Ctrl F10] [Alt F10]

SmartKey with the Super SHIFT key adds four more possible definitions:

[SS] [F10] [SS] [Shift F10] [SS] [Ctrl F10] [SS] [Alt F10]

Macro creation begins by entering the SMART key, [k +]. SmartKey displays a window at the top of the screen. You can choose to define a key or bring up the SmartKey menu.

SmartKey has the same abilities to record keystrokes, edit macros, and save and recall macros from text files as you find in the other programs.

One unusual command is the UNDO command. SmartKey allows you to change your mind about alterations you may have just made in an existing macro. UNDO returns the macro to its previous version. SuperKey performs the same type of function when you leave the edit mode and must decide to save or reject changes you made during the editing of the macro.

11.3.   Buffer Recording

As long as SmartKey is present in the computer memory, it is recording keystokes. It creates a buffer area in the memory that retains the last 64 keystrokes entered, with the exception of keystrokes entered in SmartKey.

The recording takes place automatically. To use these keystrokes you can command SmartKey to transfer the contents of the buffer to a macro key. Once this is done you can replay the keystrokes by entering the macro key.

Of course, you will seldom want to replay all 64 keystrokes arbitrarily. Once the buffer contents have been assigned to a macro key, you can use the editing commands to eliminate commands you do not want.

The buffer is also a quick way to create a simple macro. The buffer can be cleared at any time by entering **[Ctrl Scroll Lock]**

To create a macro simply enter the **[Ctrl Scroll Lock]** before you type. The keystrokes you type will be the first ones stored in the buffer. You can then copy them to a macro key and thus create a macro.

11.4. Lists

SmartKey provides a direct method of listing the macros defined in memory. This is a feature that is not found in other programs. In the other keystroke programs you can display the contents of a single macro at a time. SmartKey enables you to scroll through the definitions of all the macros in memory.

For example, enter

[k+]	(Smart Key)
[k+]	(Smart Key)
L	(List)
A	(All)

This command will display not simply the macro keys but all the keystrokes assigned to those keys.

In addition, SmartKey contains a direct command to print out the macros and their keystrokes. In the other programs a list of the contents of macros can only be acquired by saving the macros in memory to a disk text file. Then the text file must be printed using a word processor or DOS printing commands. The command below will print out a list of all the macros and their keystrokes directly from memory.

[k+]	(Smart Key)
[k+]	(Smart Key)
L	(List)
P	(Print)

The advantage of these commands is that you do not have to leave your application in order to get a screen or printer listing of the macros.

11.5. Editing Features

In addition to the usual editing techniques, SmartKey includes commands that are found in SuperKey. They are commands that Copy a defined macro to another key or Move a macro definition to another key.

11.6. Captured Fields

SmartKey also has a feature that duplicates one found in Recall. This feature is used to capture the input made into an input file so that the data can be passed to other macros or repeated in the application at another time.

This means that the data entered into an input field, a filename, for example, can be used again in that macro or another macro without having to require the user to reenter the data.

11.7. DOS Functions

Another useful series of commands available in SmartKey are DOS commands that can be executed without having to leave the application you are working in. The commands available are:

Chdir—Change active disk directory. This command performs the same function as the DOS command CD.

Directory—This command lists the contents of the directory. You can specify a particular drive or directory. The command displays a directory that looks like the type displayed by the DOS command DIR/W.

Erase—Deletes a file from the disk.

Rename—Renames a file.

Type—Displays the contents of a file. This command is similar to the DOS type command and therefore should be used to display the contents of ASCII text files only.

11.8. Special Functions

SmartKey provides special functions similar to those found in SuperKey and ProKey. These functions are used to:

1) Enter the system's time and date into a macro.
2) Create a timed delay in the macro playback.
3) Alter the speed at which the keystrokes in a macro are replayed.

11.9.   Keyboard Lock

Like SuperKey, SmartKey also has the ability to lock the keyboard so that unauthorized persons cannot enter anything into the computer while you are away from it.

The primary difference between SuperKey and SmartKey in this instance is that SuperKey requires you to write a macro in order to lock the keyboard, while SmartKey allows you to lock the keyboard directly from the SmartKey menu.

With SmartKey all you need to do to lock the keyboard is enter

[k +]	(Smart Key)
[k +]	(Smart Key)
o	(Options)
l	(Lock)

Enter your code letters and the keyboard is automatically locked.

11.10.   Windows and Menus

If you are interested in creating macros that can be used as display windows and menus, SmartKey has a number of interesting features that enhance your ability to do so.

SmartKey falls somewhere between SuperKey and Recall in the way that it accomplishes windows and menus. SuperKey requires that "display" macros be created in a text editor. There are some disadvantages to this, in that you must leave your application and call up a word processor or text editor. It also means that you must load the macro from a file into the memory before you can see the results of the macro.

On the other hand, Recall displays the menus as you construct them. The Recall system is very visual and immediate.

Like Recall, SmartKey allows you to create display window macros as you would a normal macro in the edit mode. The entry is not as immediate as Recall. With SmartKey you enter the keystrokes and see them recorded. Then when the macro is defined, you can display the results immediately.

The actual contents of a SmartKey window closely resemble the type of information you would enter into a SuperKey text file. The main difference is that the definition process in SmartKey begins from the SmartKey menu.

To begin a window macro, select a key to assign a macro to in the usual manner. Instead of entering keystrokes, use the Smart key **[k +]** to access the Commands menu. Select the Window option.

SmartKey will ask you the line and column location for the upper left-hand corner of the window. Any text that follows will be displayed within the window. The window will initially display the text exactly as it is typed. If you have entered <return>s, the display will be on different lines. SmartKey does not display a frame around the display text.

In addition, you can add the following special features to windows:

1. *Window Frame.* SmartKey will draw a highlighted double-line frame around the text if you include the [PgUp] and [PgDn] keystrokes in the window macro. The frame will be set to a size of 16 lines by 40 columns unless specified otherwise.
2. *Window Size.* You can specify the window size by entering [Alth] followed by a number specifying the height in lines and/or [Altw] followed by a number specifying the width in columns.
3. *Title.* A title is text that appears on the top line of the window frame. A title can be added to a window by entering [Altt] followed by the title text. The entry is terminated by a <return> character.
4. *Sound.* A tone is sounded when the window is displayed if you included [Ctrlg] characters in the text.

   [[Ctrlg] is the BELL character in the ASCII coding system.]

5. *Graphics.* SmartKey windows will display the full IBM character set. You can enter these characters by using the [Alt] key in combination with the numbers on the numeric key pad.
6. *Colors and Attributes.* SmartKey makes it possible for you to select the video attributes or colors of the text and frame in a display window. The function keys control the colors or attributes.

Key	Foreground Color	Monochrome Attribute
[F1]	Black	Reverse
[F2]	Blue	Underline
[F3]	Green	
[F4]	Cyan	
[F5]	Red	
[F6]	Magenta	
[F7]	Brown	
[F8]	White	
[F9]	Bright	Bright
[F10]	Normal Intensity	Normal Intensity

Key	Background Colors
[Shift F1]	Black
[Shift F2]	Blue
[Shift F3]	Green
[Shift F4]	Cyan
[Shift F5]	Red
[Shift F6]	Magenta
[Shift F7]	Brown
[Shift F8]	White

7. *Ending Character*. Menus can be ended with several types of functions. The most common type of ending is a fixed length field of a single character. If you specify a length of 0 for the fixed input field, the keystroke will not be passed to the application. If you make it a length of 1, then the keystroke is remembered and passed to the application.

You can also end the window with a timed delay. If this is used in place of the input field, the display will remain on the screen for a specified period of time.

11.11.   Making Windows Menus

SmartKey has an interesting approach to creating menus. The technique is designed to create menus that assign macro values to the ten function keys, [F1] through [F10]. The process begins with the creation of a window display as described in the previous section. The only difference in the macro comes at the very end. Instead of ending the macro with a fixed input field, a special "menu" command is entered.

The menu command contains the name of a macro. This macro also has a special purpose. It does not contain keystrokes as would an ordinary macro. The *linking* macro contains a list of up to ten existing keystroke macros. The linking macro assigns the existing keystroke macros consecutively to the ten functions keys.

For example, suppose you had defined the following macros to perform DOS functions:

[Altd] = dir
[Altc] = chkdsk
[Altf] = format a:
[Altw] = dir/w

Your goal would be to create a menu to implement these commands. First you would create a window display that would show the user which keys would perform which functions.

Press F1 for a Normal Directory
Press F2 for a Wide Directory
Press F3 to Check the Disk
Press F4 to Format a Disk

At the end of the window macro you would enter a macro name that would serve as the linking macro between the keystroke macros you had already created and the key assignments indicated in the window display. Call that macro [Altl]. You place a special command at the end of the window macro, for example

[K+]   (Smart Key)
c   (Command)
m   (Menu)
[Altl]   (Name of the linking macro)

Once you have selected a macro to serve as a link between the menu and the actual macros that contain keystrokes, you need to assign the existing macros to the function keys.

This is done by defining the linking macro, in this illustration [Altl]. [Altl] will not contain ordinary keystrokes. Instead it will contain a series of special commands. These are called *expand commands*. The expand commands link the macros they mention with functions 1 through 10 consecutively. In other words, the macro mentioned in the first expand command in the file will be assigned to [F1], the next command will be assigned to [F2], and so on.

An expand command is entered like this:

[K+] (Smart Key)
c   (Command)
e   (expand)
[Altd]   (name of the existing keystroke macro)

Entering this command as the first entry into the [Altl] macro assigns the keystrokes in the macro [Altd] to the [F1] key.

[The macro assigned to a function does not have to exist when you assign it. You could, for example, assign [Altx] to [F1] and then later define the actual keystrokes for [Altx].]

When the window macro is displayed, the linking macro assigns the keystroke macros to the function keys. Pressing any of the function keys executes the macro to which the linking macro has assigned them.

When the menu display disappears, the function keys return to their previous state. Thus the menu command makes a temporary assignment of macros while the menu is displayed.

11.12.   Submenus

The SmartKey system makes possible the creation of networks of submenus that can return to the main menu.

Submenus are created when one of the macros called by the menu is itself a menu.

If you want the menu to return to the previous menu, the last command in the lowest level of the submenu should be an expand command that calls the function key that was used to access the submenus. For example, if [F2] is used to access a series of submenus, terminating the submenu with an expand command for [F2] will redisplay the main menu.

11.13.   Menus in Macros

Menus and submenus can be used as part of macros that enter keystrokes. For example, you could create a macro that would type a business letter. Normally you would use input fields to allow you to enter variable data into the letter.

The menu system allows you to store standard paragraphs as macros and use a menu display to select the paragraphs to use. When the menu is finished, the macro can continue typing the fixed text.

11.14.   Batch Commands

SmartKey has the ability to execute some functions as DOS commands. These functions are:

1. Load a macro file into memory
2. Clear the memory of macros
3. Save the current macros to a file
4. Merge a file with the macros in memory
5. Kill SmartKey, remove it from memory

These functions are about the same as those found in ProKey and Recall, but are much more limited than those found in SuperKey.

11.15. PCKEY

SmartKey is provided with an additional program called PCKEY. PCKEY should be run before you load SmartKey.

The program provides a number of specialized functions:

1. *Keyboard Layout.* PCKEY functions like the Layout programs in ProKey and SuperKey, and to a lesser degree the Swap function in Recall. You can change the placement of keys on the computer keyboard with this program. A special version is provided that converts the keyboard to a Dvorak keyboard.
2. *Type Ahead.* The type ahead buffer of the IBM PC is expanded to 128 characters.
3. *One-Finger Mode.* Key combinations can be entered by consecutive rather than simultaneous entry.
4. *Screen Blank.* This feature is similar to one found in SuperKey. Its purpose is to protect your screen from "burn in" caused by leaving the same display on the screen for hours. A delay of between 1 and 9 minutes is specified. If there has been no activity for the specified time period, the screen will blank until a key is pressed.

11.16. File Encryption

SmartKey also is furnished with a program called Cryptor. The function of cryptor is to create a coded version of a file that conforms to the DES (Data Encryption Standard) of the federal government. SuperKey has a similar feature.

Cryptor creates a binary file that protects your file from unauthorized access. The same program operates to uncode a file. Cryptor detects whether or not the file specified is coded or uncoded.

Cryptor has an option which erases the original input if you enter Y.

The SmartKey manual says that the erasing will destroy the original file. However, in testing the program it seems that the erasing done by Cryptor is the same as would be done by the DOS DEL command. This means that the original file can still be recovered by using a utility program. Norton Utilities was able to immediately recover the test file. This means that in order to have a secure disk you *must* use a utility like the WIPEFILE or WIPEDISK programs supplied with Norton Utilities.

11.17.   Conclusion

SmartKey is a strong contender in the keystroke macro area. The Super SHIFT idea expands the number of keys that can be assigned macros. While there doesn't seem to be a shortage of keys to define, you may find that the Super SHIFT allows you to use your favorite keys more often. Many users like to assign the macro keys mnemonically, e.g., directory = [Altd]. The Super SHIFT allows you to use the [Altd] key again for another command that begins with the letter "d".

The strongest feature in SmartKey is its window and menu functions. If you are interested in creating background menus and command structures to enhance software programs, you will find SmartKey an outstanding program to use for this purpose.

12.

Keystroke Enhancement Programs: A Comparison

The largest part of this book has been dedicated to keyboard enhancement programs. The reason is that, while many maneuvers contribute to productivity, the slowest process in working with computers is entering the data and the commands from the keyboard. The keyboard program plays a crucial role in increasing productivity. Four programs have been covered in this part of the book:

ProKey
SuperKey
Recall
SmartKey

In this chapter these programs will be compared and rated as to their features and functions.

12.1. Overall Programs

All of the macro programs described have additional features besides the basic function of creating macros. The broadest of the programs is

SuperKey. In terms of macro creation, it has the largest number of features, functions, and options. But this is not to say that it has all of the features found in other programs.

The topic is quite complex. In hopes of simplifiying it, we shall list features and compare the programs discussed in the book, feature by feature.

1) **Macro Keys**. The programs usually can define macros for the same number of keys. The exceptions are generally keys like [Alt], [Ctrl], and [Shift]. SmartKey provides a feature that doubles the number of keys available.

2) **Macro Modes**. There are several ways to define macros:

a) *Interactive Recording*. Keystrokes are passed to the application as you record the macro. ProKey, SuperKey, Recall, and SmartKey.
b) *Editing Macro Symbols*. Macro keystrokes are presented as character and symbol strings. ProKey, SuperKey, Recall, and SmartKey.
c) *Loading Text Files*. Macros can be created by using a text editor to create an ASCII text file and loading that file into the macro program memory. ProKey, SuperKey, Recall,and SmartKey. (Recall features a macro creation mode that combines the characteristics of both the editing and interactive modes. Pressing [Scroll Lock] toggles you between the modes.)
d) *Cut and Paste*. SuperKey provides a means by which a macro is created by highlighting existing text on the screen.
e) *Copy and Move Macros*. SuperKey, Recall, and SmartKey.

3) **Macro Titles**. Once you have created a macro or two, you might need to review the macros or add descriptive names:

ProKey. Macros can be listed by entering the main menu and using the L command. The macro key and the keystrokes appear. You can create a description for the macro key. The description command is separate from the macro creation commands. If a description exists, it is listed instead of the keystrokes. There is no direct means of printing these lists.

SuperKey. The advantage with this program is that the macro list can be displayed on the screen with a single keystroke [Alt PrtSc]. The disadvantage is that you cannot display the keystrokes of a macro unless you enter the edit mode. SuperKey allows you to create titles for macros as part of the macro creation or edit process. No direct means of printing macros.

Recall. This program displays a model of the keyboard with keys assigned macros highlighted. No direct means of printing macros.

SmartKey. This program has the most complete means of listing macros on screen and to the printer. The program does not allow descriptive names for macros.

4) **Input Fields**. Input fields make it possible for the user to insert information into a macro as it is being played back. Typically, this information is not part of the macro but is passed to the application.

a) Fixed-Length Fields. ProKey, SuperKey, Recall, and SmartKey.
b) Variable-Length Fields. ProKey, SuperKey, Recall, and SmartKey.
c) Format Data Input in Fields. SuperKey only.
d) Save Input Data for recall. Recall and SmartKey.
e) Display prompt for field. Recall only.
f) Change field terminator. Recall only.

5) **Functions**. Functions are special actions that can be performed during the playback of the macro. Functions perform actions independent of the application during which the macros are played back.

a) Timed Delays inserted in macros. ProKey, SuperKey, Recall, and SmartKey
b) Insert System Time and Date in macros. SuperKey and SmartKey.
c) Playback Speed Variation. ProKey, SuperKey, Recall, and SmartKey.
d) Lock keyboard from unauthorized entry. SuperKey implemented through a macro. SmartKey allows you to select this option through its command menu.
e) DOS commands, access through memory. SmartKey only.
f) Redefine command keys. SuperKey though menus, in macros or from DOS level commands. ProKey, but only by entering a DOS-level command. SmartKey enters commands mostly from menus but allows you to redefine Smart and Super Shift keys temporarily or permanently through setup program.
g) Guarded Macro. ProKey only. Protects macro from being overwritten by incoming macros loaded from a file.
h) Protect Screen. Blank-in active screen. SuperKey from menu, macro, or DOS command. SmartKey through supplemental program.
i) Auto-Start Macro. ProKey, SuperKey, Recall, and SmartKey can automatically run a macro when the program is loaded using a batch command. SuperKey will store an AUTO command in the macro itself. Auto macros in SuperKey execute when loaded from menu commands as well.

6) **Operational Modes**. These modes affect the way the overall operation of the program and the computer work.

a) One-finger typing. ProKey, SuperKey, and Recall. SmartKey through a supplemental program.
b) Keyboard Click. SuperKey and SmartKey through supplemental programs.
c) Command Buffer. SuperKey records only DOS-level commands. Reentry is performed by selecting commands from a display. SmartKey records all non-

SmartKey commands in a buffer. Reentry of the commands is accomplished by transferring the keystrokes to a macro key, then using the macro to type the keystrokes.

d) Suspend operation, keyboard functions normally, macros saved in memory. ProKey and SuperKey.

e) Type Ahead Buffer. SuperKey and SmartKey create an automatic 128-keystroke keyboard buffer. ProKey allows you to select buffer size from 0 to 256 characters.

f) Single Step Playback. Recall only.

7) **Change Keyboard Layout**. ProKey, SuperKey, and SmartKey use supplemental programs to create layout. SuperKey loads and clears layouts while running. ProKey and SmartKey require rebooting to change existing layout. Recall allows key swaps while program is active.

8) **Data Encryption**. SuperKey provides file security coding from menus. SmartKey uses a supplemental program. SmartKey provides DES standard encryption. SuperKey has two programs, one for DES, the other for a faster encoding system.

9) **Pop-up User Displays and Menus**. SuperKey, Recall, and SmartKey all provide systems for user displays and menus.

a) Definition. SuperKey only creates display macros by loading text files. Recall displays the pop-up windows as you create them. SmartKey uses an edit mode to create window displays. The SuperKey system is the most cumbersome. Recall is the most immediate and visual.

b) Titles. SmartKey allows a title to be printed on the frame border. SuperKey and Recall only allow text within the window.

c) Cursor movement in window. Recall only.

d) Link macros to window items. Recall has the most direct method of linking macros to window items. SmartKey allows the creation of a linking macro that temporarily assigns macros to function keys. SuperKey has no direct linkage.

e) Window size. SuperKey and SmartKey are limited to screen display size. Recall creates windows 27 characters by 23 lines maximum.

10) **Batch/DOS Command Processing**. Program Commands that can be executed from DOS or Batch files:

a) Load macro file. ProKey, SuperKey, Recall, and SmartKey.

b) Merge macro file. ProKey, SuperKey, and SmartKey.

c) Save macros in memory. ProKey, SuperKey, and SmartKey.

d) Clear memory. ProKey, SuperKey, and SmartKey.

e) Kill program. ProKey, SuperKey, and SmartKey.

f) Change Modes. ProKey and SuperKey.
g) Change command keys. ProKey and SuperKey

12.2.   Ratings

This area is a bit subjective.

1) *Overall Features.*
   Outstanding—SuperKey offers the widest variety of features and supplemental programs. Another big plus is its ability to use Sidekick in macros.
   Good—SmartKey provides a good package of features.
   Fair—Recall and ProKey are more limited. ProKey is strictly concerned with keyboard issues.
2) *Macro Definition Ability.*
   Outstanding—ProKey, SuperKey, Recall, and SmartKey.
3) *Batch Processing.*
   Outstanding—ProKey and SuperKey.
   Fair—Recall and SmartKey.
4) *Menus and Displays.*
   Outstanding—Recall and SmartKey.
   Good—SuperKey.

Part 4.
Background Utilities

13.

Background Utilities

This chapter introduces another type of utility, called the background utility. To understand what these programs are and how they were developed you have to look back into the evolution of computers and software.

The history of personal computers has been one of steady growth in the internal and external memory of the computers. Only a few years ago the basic microcomputer was equipped with 16K internal memory and a cassette tape as the external storage device. As the capacity of the computer's memory increased, programmers began to design applications that would make use of the greater capacity of the machines.

Whenever a more powerful machine is developed, it is usually ahead of its time, because the current crop of software is designed for a less powerful machine. New machines offer new capacities, but it is up to the programmers to actually put those capacities to practical use.

When the IBM PC arrived, it brought with it the potential for a large internal memory. Before the IBM PC, most of the popular computers were limited to 64K or less internal memory. The IBM PC has a capacity of 640K, about ten times as much internal memory as earlier machines. The problem is that the potential of the machines was far ahead of the software uses for all that memory.

13.1. Ramdisks and Spoolers

The first utility programs to make use of the additional internal memory of the PC were programs that used the memory as a substitute for hardware devices, such as disk drives and print buffers.

Ramdisks, or electronic disk drives, weren't really disk drives at all. They were software programs that used part of the internal memory of the computer as if it were a disk drive. Information could be read and written to this area of the memory as though it were an actual disk.

The advantage of this arrangement was performance. Information written to a part of memory functioning as a disk drive would perform approximately a hundred times as fast as a typical floppy disk. This was a great advantage to programs that would read and write often, such as dBASE II.

Ramdisks had one major disadvantage. Like all internal memory areas, turning off the computer would destroy the contents of a ramdisk. To save the data, the contents would have to be transferred to a disk before the computer was turned off. Even so, the use of the ramdrive would greatly improve the performance of many programs.

Spoolers, or buffers, were another popular use of internal memory. The purpose of these programs was to free the computer to do something else while printing was taking place. Because printers work so slowly compared to computers, printing directly from a program would often tie up the computer for an extended length of time.

When an area in the memory was set aside as a spooler, the program would send its output to the memory area, not directly to the printer. As with the ramdisk, the memory would absorb the printout at a high rate of speed. The computer would be free for other functions. In the meantime, the printer would be fed data from the buffer area until the printing was completed.

Not surprisingly, these programs were often sold as part of the package when users bought expansion boards for their computers. The makers of memory expansion boards, such as AST, found it a good selling point to provide some ready-made uses for the memory their expansion cards provided.

Utilities such as ramdisks and spoolers suggested the concept of programs that operated in the background of the main application. Background utilities share the main memory of the computer with other applications. They make sense because computers with large internal memories are available at a relatively low cost.

The programs presented in Part 4 represent an extension of the logic suggested by those basic types of background programs. As you will see, the amount of creativity applied by the makers of these programs explains why they are in the most rapidly expanding area of the market.

13.2. Vdisk

The ramdisk has finally achieved the status of being part of the operating system. With the release of the 3.0 and 3.1 versions of PC DOS, IBM has supplied their users with a ramdisk program. The ramdisk is provided in the form of the VDISK.SYS device driver. You can create a ramdisk by adding a command to your CONFIG.SYS file. Example:

DEVICE = VDISK.SYS 256

Remember that, in addition to adding the above command to the CONFIG.SYS file, you must also copy the VDISK.SYS into the root directory of the boot drive.

14.

Sidekick

The best-known of the background programs is Sidekick. Sidekick is based on the premise that many computer users have more memory in their computers than they need to run most of their applications.

Further, Sidekick assumes that it would be handy to have an electronic version of some standard desktop accessories in your computer. For instance, Sidekick provides the user with the electronic equivalent of a notepad, a calculator, a calendar, an appointment book, a personal telephone directory, and even a table of ASCII code values for those users who know what ASCII is all about.

What makes Sidekick so interesting is that these items are immediately available to the user whenever they are desired, no matter what application or program is running in the computer.

14.1.   The Sidekick Program

Sidekick is provided on a single disk. The program is sold in a copy-protected and an unprotected version. The maker, Borland, indicates that it prefers to sell unprotected programs, and the future may see Sidekick sold only in the unprotected version.

The version of Sidekick used for this book is version 1.56. The disk contains nine files that take up a total 271,360 bytes of disk space. The files are:

README.COM	16,074 bytes
SK.COM	39,515 bytes
SKN.COM	34,009 bytes

SKC.COM	28,049 bytes
SKM.COM	17,642 bytes
SK.HLP	53,632 bytes
NOTES	1,783 bytes
PHONE.DIR	1,393 bytes
READ-ME.SK	13,458 bytes

As with most programs, not all the files are required to operate the program.

The SK.COM file contains all the functions of Sidekick with the exception of Help. If you want to have on-screen help displays, you will need to add the file SK.HLP to your working disk, either hard or floppy. Note that, as usual, the help screens take up a good deal of space. (In this case they take up more than the program itself.)

Three other files, SKN.COM, SKC.COM, and SKM.COM, are additional versions of the Sidekick program. Because Sidekick is loaded into the memory of the computer and remains there while other programs operate, Sidekick decreases the amount of memory available to those programs.

The main Sidekick program stored in the file SK.COM will take up about 63K of memory. If you want to load a limited version of Sidekick, you can use less memory but you must give up some features. The table below shows how the different versions of Sidekick function.

Filename	in K	in Bytes	Available
SK.COM	63K	64,176	Notepad, Calculator, Calendar, Dialer and ASCII table
SKN.COM	54K	55,120	Notepad, Calculator, Dialer, and ASCII table. Calendar omitted.
SKC.COM	42K	42,992	Calendar, Calculator, Dialer, and ASCII table. Notepad omitted.
SKM.COM	25K	25,120	Calculator and ASCII table only.

[The notepad function can vary in size depending upon the amount of text you want to store in the memory at any one time. The default size of the notepad is 4K or 4,096 bytes. The figures shown in the above table assume that the notepad portion of the program is set at the 4K size.]

The files SKINST.COM and SKINST.MSG are used to alter certain aspects of the Sidekick program. It is not necessary to modify Sidekick before you use it. The program is set with default values that will allow you to operate it as it is supplied. The SKINST.COM program is used to alter the default settings for:

1. Screen type—allows you to specify the type of screen display with which you are working.
2. Notepad commands—allows you to alter the commands used in the notepad, (word processing), area of Sidekick. Sidekick is installed with a set of commands similar to those used in WordStar. You can program the notepad to respond to different key combinations using this program.
3. Notepad size—allows you to increase or decrease the amount of memory used for the notepad. The default value is 4K, 4,096 bytes. The notepad size can range from 1,000 to 15,000 bytes.
4. Right margin—allows you to specify the default value for the right margin in the notepad. The default is 65.
5. Dialer—allows you to select a modem for use with the automatic dialing feature.
6. Colors—allows you to select color combinations for the various displays of Sidekick. If you have a monochrome screen, Sidekick allows you to select the video attributes, such as normal and reverse video, that can be displayed on a monochrome display.
7. Activate commands—allows you select combinations of Ctrl, Alt, and Shift that will activate Sidekick. The default settings allow Sidekick to be activated by using Ctrl-Alt or Left Shift-Right Shift combinations.

The files README.COM and READ-ME.SK are used to store information about the program that is not printed in the manual. Manufacturers often provide last-minute information on problems or changes in the form of README files. Borland also provides a program that displays the data on the screen.

NOTES and PHONE.DIR, are sample files used with the notepad and the dialer respectively. They are not necessary and function only as examples.

14.2.   Using Sidekick

In getting ready to use Sidekick, you should follow the basic procedures explained in Chapter 1. If you have a floppy drive system, you should make a backup copy of the Sidekick program files. If you have a hard disk system, you should copy the files to an appropriate directory. (If you have a \DOS directory on your drive, that would be a good place for the Side-kick program.)

Once you have prepared your disks, you are ready to begin.

SETUP
Drive A: Copy of MS DOS system disk.
Drive B: Copy of Sidekick disk
Drive C: Change to directory that contains Sidekick files

Floppy System: Change active drive to B. (B:<return>)
Hard Disk : Change active drive and directory to the directory containing the Sidekick files.

Using Sidekick is different from using a normal application by virtue of the fact that Sidekick will remain in memory as other programs are loaded and unloaded. In order to use Sidekick at any time, you must first load the program before you load any applications.

The Sidekick program is loaded by typing the name of the program, SK, SKN, SKM, or SKC, at the system's prompt.

Enter **sk<return>**

When the program loads, it displays information about the amount of memory used and the amount of memory left over.

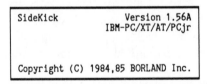

```
┌─────────────────────────────────────────┐
│ SideKick              Version 1.56A      │
│                     IBM-PC/XT/AT/PCjr     │
│                                           │
│                                           │
│ Copyright (C) 1984,85 BORLAND Inc.        │
└─────────────────────────────────────────┘


Full System

524288 bytes total memory
460688 bytes were free
385504 bytes free
```

Fig. 14-1. Memory Allocation Display.

In the illustration, the full Sidekick program was loaded into a 512K computer. You can see that the Sidekick program takes up about 63K of the memory of the computer. The important fact is that this computer still has about 376K left for programs.

You can now run your word processor, data base, spreadsheet, or other programs. The Sidekick program will be in the memory, ready to work when you need it.

14.3. Activating Sidekick

To use Sidekick, you would enter the key combinations that will suspend your application and activate Sidekick. All versions of Sidekick will respond to the combination of the Ctrl and Alt. Version 1.5 will also respond to the use of the shift key. Enter **[Ctrl Alt]**

In the center of the screen is the Sidekick menu.

```
SideKick Main Menu

F1    Help
F2    NotePad
F3    Calculator
F4    caLendar
F5    Dialer
F6    Ascii-table
F7    Setup
Esc   exit
```

Fig. 14-2. Sidekick Menu.

There are three ways to select one of the items on the menu:

1. Use the arrow keys to move the underline in monochrome or the highlight in color to the option you desire and press **< return >**
2. Press the Function key that corresponds to the item you want to select. For example, [F2] selects the notepad.
3. Press the combination of Alt and the upper case letter in each selection.

Alt/h selects HELP
Alt/n selects NOTEPAD
Alt/c selects CALCULATOR
Alt/l selects CALENDAR
Alt/d selects DIALER
Alt/a selects ASCII
Alt/s selects SETUP

The position of the menu on the screen display can be changed. To change the position enter **[Scroll Lock]**

If you look at the bottom right corner of the screen, you will see the word SCROLL LOCK appear. Now press **<left arrow>**

The menu box is moved one column to the left. Enter **<up arrow>**

The menu box moves up one row. You can use the arrow keys to move the menu box to any position on the screen. When you are done, enter **[Scroll Lock]**

The words SCROLL LOCK disappear from the lower right-hand corner of the screen. The arrow keys will now move the highlight within the menu box instead of the entire box itself.

To exit from the menu and return to your application, enter **<Esc>**

Sidekick returns you to the exact position in the application where you were when you activated the program.

14.4. Help

Sidekick provides an on-screen help display that explains the functions and commands of the program. Help is context sensitive. This means that the help screen that appears when you press the F1 key will depend upon where in the Sidekick program you are at the time. Sidekick will attempt to display the most appropriate help screen for the task you are working on.

It is important to note that the Sidekick help screens are not part of the memory-resident program. The help displays are stored in a file called SK.HLP.

SK.HLP takes up 53,632 bytes of space on the disk. If you want to use the help screens, the file must be present on one of the disks in the system. If you are using a floppy drive system, this means you must make sure that one of the drives contains the file SK.HLP.

Further, you must take care in loading the Sidekick program so that Sidekick can find the help file. Sidekick makes the assumption that the drive and directory that are active when the program is loaded will be the drive and directory in which the Sidekick help file can be found.

In a floppy drive system, if you intend to store the SK.HLP file on a disk in drive A, then A must be the active drive when you load Sidekick.

If you do this, Sidekick will remember where to find the help file, even if you later change the active drive to B.

In hard disk systems, you must take the same precaution only if you must consider the active subdirectory as well. Suppose that you store the files SK.COM and SK.HLP in a directory called \DOS. The directory \DOS *must* be active when you load Sidekick if you want to be able to use the help screens.

Note that making a directory active requires you to use the DOS command Change Directory (CD). For example:

cd\dos<return>
sk<return>

By using the above commands, Sidekick will be able to find the help files it needs, even if you subsequently change active directories.

DOS allows you to use the PATH command to load SK without using the Change Directory command. While this method will load Sidekick it will not correctly set up Sidekick to find the help file. For example:

path\dos<return>
sk<return>

This method will load Sidekick, but when you ask for help, Sidekick will not be able to find the SK.HLP file.

If you feel you do not want or need the Sidekick help files, there is no need to have the SK.HLP file in the system. All the functions of Sidekick, except for help, are memory resident and do not require the help file. If you are concerned about disk space, as users of floppy systems are, then it makes sense to eliminate the help screens and open up more disk space for your applications files.

14.5. The Calculator

To explore exactly how Sidekick works, you will begin with the simplest of the functions and work towards the more complex ones. Enter the command to activate Sidekick. Enter **[Ctrl/Alt]**

The Sidekick menu appears. To activate the calculator, enter **[F3]**
The calculator appears in the upper right-hand corner of the screen.

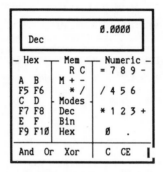

Fig. 14-3. Sidekick Calculator Display.

The calculator functions like a typical pocket calculator. In addition the calculator features:

1. Display modes for binary, decimal, and hexadecimal numbers. The calculator displays BIN, DEC, or HEX in the number window to indicate which mode it is in.
2. A single-number memory function.
3. The ability to copy a number from the calculator display into the application with which you are working.

[To make entry simpler, Sidekick automatically places the numeric keypad on the IBM PC into the the NUM LOCK mode. This means that you can enter numbers into the calculator without having to press the NUM LOCK key.

You can also use the number keys on the top row to enter numbers. Sidekick will allow entry from both sets of keys.

If you have already used the NUM LOCK key in your application, it will remain locked while working with Sidekick.]

Start with a simple example. Enter **25+4=**
The calculator shows the answer. To clear the calculator, enter **c**
The calculator is reset to zero. Arithmetic can be performed on the calculator just as you would on a normal calculator. The only difference is that the multiplication sign used on a computer is the *. For example, to multiply 6.25 times 4, enter **6.25*4=**
The answer appears in the window. To clear the calculator, enter **c**

14.5.1. Using the Memory
with the Calculator

The calculator has the ability to store a single number in its memory. This is a common feature in pocket calculators and is recreated in Sidekick. The memory is used to store a number that will be needed in future calculations. Suppose that your monthly mortgage payment was $977.18 on a fixed-rate 30-year mortgage at 12% for $95,000. How much of your first mortgage payment is applied towards the principal?

Begin by figuring out what 1/12 of 12% is. Enter **.12/12 =**

Store that figure into memory. Enter **m +**

The number is added to the memory. Clear the display by entering **c**

Enter the amount of the loan: **95000**

Multiply that by the number in the memory. Enter **m***

Clear the display: **c**

Now subtract the number in the memory from the monthly payment. Enter **977.18 − mr =**

The figure $21.18 is the amount applied towards the principal in the first monthly payment.

To clear the memory, enter **mc**

14.5.2. Mode Changes in Calculator

The calculator has the ability to display numbers in either decimal, binary, or hexadecimal number formats.

The default display is decimal. Conversion between number systems is more useful to programmers than to the average user. However, there are times when you might want to perform arithmetic in some system other than decimal. As a simple display, enter **b**

The display is now in binary. Enter **1 + 1 =**

The display shows not 2 but 10. The number 10 is equal to 2 in decimal. To confirm this enter **d**

The display switches to decimal. The value appears as 2. Enter **100**

Switch to binary. Enter **b**

The figure 1100100 appears. Note that all numbers in the binary mode are expressed as ones and zeros. Binary arithmetic recognizes only those two numbers.

In contrast, the hexadecimal systems includes 16 numbers. The number are 0 through 9 and A, B, C, D, E, and F. Enter **h**

The display shows 64. 64 is the hexadecimal equivalent of 100 in the decimal system. Enter **d250**

Change to hex. Enter **h**

The screen shows FA. FA may look like a word but it is really a hexadecimal number. If you are new to computers, you may not see the need for such conversions. Don't worry. If the need does arise, you have Sidekick to help you out.

Clear the calculator and return to decimal mode. Enter **cd**

14.5.3. Programming Keys

One of Sidekick's most interesting features is the ability to enter the number displayed on the calculator directly into the application.

There are two advantages to this feature:

1. It saves time and improves accuracy.
2. By programming different keys with different numbers, you can recall a variety of numbers when you are working in your application.

[The program option is provided in the later versions of Sidekick. If you have early versions, 1.1 for example, you may not have this option. In versions that do provide this feature a "p-paste" command will be displayed at the bottom left-hand corner of your screen when the calculator display is active.]

Begin with a simple example. Calculate the number of feet in three miles. Enter **5280*3 =**

Suppose that you wanted to use that number in your application. To program a key with the number, enter **p**

The next key or combination that you press will indicate to Sidekick which key you want to program. You can program any key, but it makes sense to avoid programming keys or combinations that already serve a purpose in the application you are working with. You can use Shift, Ctrl, or Alt combinations to avoid programming needed keys.

For example, if you were working in WordStar you would want to use Alt combinations, since many of the Ctrl keys are already used by WordStar.

In this example, enter **[Alt m]**

This means that whenever you press [Alt m] the number will be typed.

You can program more than one key at a time. For example, you might clear the calculator and enter a new calculation. Enter **c 5280/3 =**

Now store that number as [Alt y]. Why "y"? Since the number 1,760 represents the number of yards in a mile, y might be appropriate. Enter **p [Alt y]**

You can continue to program keys until you have completed your calculations. To enter these numbers into an application, you must exit Sidekick.

14.6. Leaving a Sidekick Application

When you have completed your work in Sidekick and want to return to the application in which you were working, you will find that there are two methods:

1. <Esc>—The <Esc> key will cancel one Sidekick display at a time. For example, if the calculator and the calendar are displayed, then two <Esc> keys will return you to your application.
2. Deactivate—If you enter the Sidekick activate or deactivate command, either Ctrl Alt or Shift Left-Shift Right will immediately return you to your application.

The deactivate method has two advantages over the <Esc> key. First, it's quicker because it takes only a single keystroke. The more Sidekick displays on the screen, the more times you would have to press <Esc>.

Second, when you activate Sidekick again you will return to the exact spot in Sidekick where you left off. If you exit by using the <Esc> key, when you activate Sidekick again you will return to the menu box.

If you want to shift between Sidekick and your application, the deactivate command jumps between your application and the Sidekick program without having to use the Sidekick menus.

To see the difference, exit the calculator by using the <Esc> key. Enter **<Esc>**

To return to the calculator, enter **[Ctrl Alt] [F3]**

Notice that because you exited Sidekick with the <Esc> key, when you activated the program again with the [Ctrl Alt], you brought up the Sidekick menu. Now try the deactivate method. Enter **[Ctrl Alt]**

You return to your application. Enter **[Ctrl Alt]**

You return to the calculator display of Sidekick.

[The number on the calculator displays and all programmed keys remain as they were no matter how you enter or leave the Sidekick display.]

Return to the application you are working in. Enter **[Ctrl Alt]**

Remember you have two keys programmed, [Alt y] and [Alt m]. To enter the contents of the keys into the application, enter **[Alt m]**

The number 63360.000 is typed into the application.

[The entry of numbers into an application must fit the expectations and conventions of the application. If you enter a number at the DOS prompt and press <return>, nothing much will be accomplished.

Also note that entering programmed numbers into programs like 1-2-3 still requires you to enter any characters like <return> that are necessary to terminate the entry.]

Enter **<return>**

Now try the next number. Enter **[Alt y]**

Sidekick types 1760.000 for you. Enter **<return> [Alt m]**

The number 63360.000 is typed again. This is important. Once a key has been programmed to type a number by the Sidekick calculator, it will retain that number until you reboot the computer or return to the calculator and clear all the programmed keys.

14.6.1. Clearing Programmed Keys

Once keys have been programmed to type numbers, that programming will remain in place until you specifically clear those keys. To clear the keys you must return to the Sidekick calculator. Enter **[Ctrl Alt]**

The calculator appears on the screen. Enter **p**

Instead of typing the key you want to program, enter **c**

All the keys that had numbers programmed into them have been cleared. The keyboard will function normally again. Exit the calculator. Enter **<Esc>**

14.7. The Calendar

Another feature that Sidekick provides is a calendar. The calendar not only displays the months and days but includes an appointment calendar as well.

To bring up the calendar, enter **[Ctrl Alt] [F4]**

The calendar is displayed. The day that is displayed when you call up the calendar is determined by the DOS system's date. The initial date in this case is 11/7/85.

Nov		7		1985		
Sun	Mon	Tue	Wed	Thu	Fri	Sat
27	28	29	30	31	1	2
3	4	5	6	7	8	9
10	11	12	13	14	15	16
17	18	19	20	21	22	23
24	25	26	27	28	29	30
1	2	3	4	5	6	7

Fig. 14-4. Calendar Display.

The arrow keys will change the display in the following ways:

<up arrow>   displays the same day and month, next year
<down arrow>   displays the same day and month, previous year
<left arrow>   displays the same day and year, previous month
<right arrow>   displays the same day and year, next month

Enter **<up arrow>**
The year is increased by one, in this example 11/7/86. Enter **<down arrow> <down arrow>**
The year is decreased by two, in this example 11/7/84. Enter **<left arrow>**
The month changes to October. Enter **<right arrow> <right arrow>**
The date is now 12/7/84. Enter **<up arrow>**
In this example, you are now on 12/7/85. For the sake of consistency, make your date 12/7/85. The rest of this section will assume that you are starting from that point.

14.8.   Entering an Appointment

After you have selected a date you can enter an appointment into the calendar. Enter **<return>**
The appointment calendar for 12/7/85 appears.

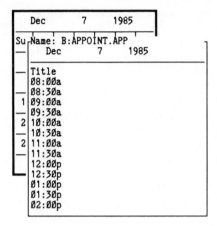

Fig. 14-5. Appointment Calendar.

14.9. Entering Appointments

Once you have displayed the appointment calendar, you can leaf through the appointment calendars for other days or make entries into the respective daily calendars. In this case you will want to enter an appointment for 9:00 A.M. Move the cursor to the correct time slot by entering **<down arrow>** (three times)

> Enter **Walter La Fish Meeting <return>**

Sidekick allows you to enter a 26-character note for each slot on the appointment calendar. Next enter a lunch date for that same day. Enter the following:

<down arrow> (seven times)
Lunch with Tom <return>

You have now entered two appointments into the calendar. Next you will want to enter an item into the appointment calendar for another date. To change the day's calendar display, use the <left arrow> and <right arrow> keys. The <left arrow> changes the display to the previous day, in this case, 12/6/85. The <right arrow> changes the displayed calendar to the next day, in this case 12/8/85. Enter **<right arrow>**

The appointment calendar display shows a new blank sheet for the date of 12/8/85. Continue using the <right arrow> until the date is 12/24/85. Note that when you move from day to day the highlight returns to the top line of the appointment calendar. This line is called TITLE.

The title line is used to give the date a special name. The most obvious way to use TITLE is to enter special days, such as holidays or birthdays. In this case you will give December 24th a special name. Enter **Christmas Shopping<return>**

Use the <down arrow> to move to the 10:00 A.M. slot. Enter **Stores Open<return>**

There is a small trick to removing an entry. Suppose that you realize that the stores open at 9:00 on December 24th. Enter **<up arrow>**

The cursor is positioned at the end of the entry line. In order to remove the entry you must use the Backspace key. Do *not* use the <left arrow> key. If you use the <left arrow> you will move the calendar to the previous day. Enter **[Backspace]**

Use the Backspace key to erase the entry. Now enter **<up arrow>**

What happens? The entry is restored. Sidekick requires that you end with a <return> to actually remove an entry from a date. This is a little safety feature. Try this again. Enter the following:

<down arrow>
[Backspace]   (until the characters are gone)
<return>
<up arrow>

This time the line remains blank. Move the highlight to the 9:00 A.M. slot with the <up arrow>. Enter **Stores Open<return>**

When you are done making entries, enter **[Esc]**

Note that when you exit the appointment calendar mode by pressing [Esc], Sidekick will then record your entries into a disk file. What file will be used?

The answer is that Sidekick defaults to a file called APPOINT.APP. If an APPOINT.APP does not already exist in the active drive, Sidekick will create it.

[Appointment calendar files are organized by the default settings of Sidekick. The first rule is that all appointment calendar files are stored in the root directory of the active drive. Sidekick does this in order to help you be consistent about finding the correct file each time you call up the appointment calendar.

The appointment calendar presents a practical problem for floppy drive users that the calculator does not. Because appointments accumulate over a period of time, they must be stored on disk. The only way to keep ongoing appointments is to place the same disk in the machine every time the appointment calendar is used.

Users with fixed hard disks will not encounter this problem because the hard disk cannot be removed and is always present. However, hard drives are almost always broken into a series of directories. But because the calendar always stores its data in the root, it does not matter what directory you are working in; when you call the appointment calendar, you will always get the same file.

If for some reason you desire that the appointment calendar files be stored on some directory other than the root, you can specify this in the SETUP section of Sidekick.]

14.10. Multiple Calendars

The Sidekick appointment calendar is capable of recording appointments for several different people. The simplest way to accomplish this is to use the NAME, [F3], command. For example, you might want to create appointment calendars for John and Marcia.

To record these new appointments, you must display the calendar. If you are working along with this book, you have the date 12/24/85 displayed.

[If you do not have the calendar displayed, enter **[Ctrl Alt] [F4]**]

The NAME, [F3], command allows you to change to a specific appointment calendar file. If the filename that you enter does not already exist, Sidekick will create it. Enter **[F3]**

The cursor shifts to the top of the appointment calendar's display. The program displays the words New Name:. You can now enter the name of the appointment calendar file.

The simplest way to use the appointment calendar is to use the name or initials of the person as the name of the calendar. However, you can choose to enter any valid DOS filename.

The advantage to using names is that Sidekick will automatically assign an APP extension to the file. This makes it simple to locate and identify the files as belonging to the appointment calendar.

[The names of the files are restricted by the DOS filename conventions. The most important of these are that the names cannot exceed eight characters and cannot include spaces.]

Enter **john < return >**
Sidekick creates a new calendar file called JOHN.APP on the root directory of the active drive. Enter **Christmas Eve < return >**
Now create a calendar for Marcia. Enter the following:

[F3]
Marcia< return >

Now the calendar is using a file called MARCIA.APP. Once again the screen shows a blank calendar, because Marcia's calendar file does not yet contain any appointments. Enter: **The night before Christmas< return >**

Now that you have several calendars, you may want to switch back and forth among them. You can have Sidekick display a list of the calendars. Enter **[F3]**

Instead of entering the name of the calendar, enter **< return >**

Fig. 14-6. Appointment Calendars.

All the files that have the APP extension are displayed in a box at the top of the screen. You can use the arrow keys to move the cursor to the name of the appointment calendar that you want to use. You can now see the advantage of allowing Sidekick to add the APP extension to each filename.

Move the cursor to JOHN.APP, then enter **< return >**

John's appointment calendar appears. Enter **[F3] < return >**

Move the cursor to the file name APPOINT.APP. Enter **< return >**

You have returned to the original appointment calendar file.

[If you want to remove the files JOHN.APP and MARCIA.APP, this can be done from the DOS prompt by using the DEL command. e.g., DEL MARCIA.APP< return >.]

14.11.   Printing Calendars

Finally, it would be useful to be able to obtain a printed copy of the appointments entered into the calendar. Sidekick provides two means of doing this:

[F2]   print a specified range of dates
[F4]   print all dates that contain appointments

When Sidekick prints calendars, it prints one page for each calendar day that contains at least one entry. Any dates that do not contain any entries are not printed. Each page will contain only the appointments for a single day. If you want to print more than one day on a page, see the next section.

To print a specified range, enter **[F2]**

You must now enter six numbers. They stand for:

1. Number of first month
2. Number of first day of the month
3. Number of the first year
4. Number of the last month
5. Number of the last day of the month
6. Number of the last year

Note that year values must be the full numeric value of the year, i.e., 1985, not 85. Enter

12 < return >
1 < return >
1985 < return >
12 < return >
31 < return >
1985 < return >

Sidekick prints the calendar.

To print the entire calendar, enter **[F4]**

14.12. Deleting Entries

If you use the appointment calendar feature extensively, you will probably want to delete dates from the calendar. The purpose of deleting is to make it simple to print appointments. For example, if at the end of every week or month you delete your old appointments, you can enter the [F4], PRINT ALL command and get a listing of all your upcoming appointments.

[If you want to use old appointments as a reference, you should not delete them. Once deleted they cannot be recalled.]

To delete entries, enter **[F5]**

As with the [F2], PRINT, command you must enter six numbers that specify the range of dates to purge. Enter the following:

1 <return>
1 <return>
1985 <return>
12 <return>
31 <return>
1985 <return>

The entries for the entire year are purged. Notice that Sidekick does not ask you to confirm the deletions. Therefore make sure that you really mean to delete the data before you press the [F5] key.

Exit Sidekick by entering **<Esc> <Esc>**

14.13. Printing More Than One Day on a Page

The normal method of printing calendars prints one day's appointments on each page. Sidekick prints all the appointments for a given date and then issues a form feed character.

A *form feed* is a software instruction that tells the printer to skip to the top of the next form. This is the same operation that you manually perform when you take your printer off line and press the FORM FEED or TOF button.

Form feeds are logical commands. What this means is that when a command to feed a form is entered, the printer looks at the definition of form size held in the printer's memory. Most printers automatically assume that your paper is 11 inches long, (66 printed lines). This setting is built into the printer or selected when you set the DIP switches in your printer.

Each Sidekick appointment calendar day can contain up to 28 entries. Because each day will print on a separate, 66-line page, most of the page will be blank. In order to conserve paper, you can get more than one day's items on a page if you change the form size setting in the printer to something smaller than 11 inches.

From a practical point of view, you would want to set the page length to a number of lines that divides evenly into 66. For example, you might want to set the page length to 22 or 11 lines. This would print three or six days, respectively, on one 11-inch sheet.

The length you choose depends upon how many entries you make in the calendar for any one day. If you never have more than ten entries you would be safe in choosing 11 lines per page. Remember that you have to allow for an extra line because Sidekick prints the date at the top of the calendar.

There are two problems with adjusting the form size:

1. Sidekick does not have the ability to issue printer control commands. You must use some other application to create a simple program that will set the page size properly.
2. Not every printer uses the same commands to set the form size.

In the next section, you will learn about programs that will set up some popular printers for different size forms. The programs will be written in BASIC and dBASE III. Since all MS DOS computers come with BASIC, the BASIC version is the most universal.

To create a BASIC program, you must place the disk with the BASIC.COM program on it into the computer. For floppy disk users this would usually be a copy of your MS DOS systems disk. Hard disk users will usually find the file on their hard disk. Many dealers store BASIC in a directory on the hard disk called DOS. Hard disk users can gain access to the DOS directory by entering CD\DOS.

Once BASIC is in place, enter **basic <return>**

The OK prompt appears. This tells you that you have loaded the BASIC language. The program needed to set the form length is usually only one line long. Most printer manuals list the codes needed to change the form length. However, they are usually in the form of "Escape" sequences. For example, the Epson manual tells you that to change the form length you enter ESC "C" N. This means that you must send to the printer the ASCII characters that represent the ESC key, the letter C and a numeric value equal to the number of lines on a page.

This can get a bit confusing for many people. In BASIC the function CHR$(27) represents the Escape key, CHR$(67) the letter C, and CHR$(11) a numeric value of 11. The numbers are called the decimal equivalent of the ASCII name.

This strange process of conversion can be aided by Sidekick. Sidekick has a built-in ASCII value table. For example, if you didn't now what the decimal number of the ASCII code of ESC was, you would call up the Sidekick ASCII table. Enter **[Ctrl Alt] [F6]**

Sidekick displays the ASCII table.

```
D  H Ch    Ctrl Mem
0  00        ^@  NUL
1  01        ^A  SOH
2  02        ^B  STX
3  03        ^C  ETX
4  04        ^D  EOT
5  05        ^E  ENQ
6  06        ^F  ACK
7  07        ^G  BEL
8  08        ^H  BS
9  09        ^I  HT
10 0A        ^J  LF
11 0B        ^K  VT
12 0C        ^L  FF
13 0D        ^M  CR
14 0E        ^N  SO
15 0F  *     ^O  SI
```

Fig. 14-7. ASCII Table.

The table shows five different ways of expressing the same ASCII value:

D = decimal value of the character
H = hexadecimal (base 16) value of the number
Ch = character displayed by the IBM PC for the ASCII character
Ctrl = the Control Combination used to produce the ASCII character
Mem = the mnemonic name for the character. For example, the mnemonic for
   the Escape key is ESC.

To display more of the table, enter **<right arrow>**

Look down the right-hand column and locate the line on which you see the mnemonic ESC. You can see from this table that the Escape key, mnemonic name ESC, has the value of 27.

How about the letter C? Enter **<right arrow>** three times.

The table displays more values.

```
D  H  Ch     D  H  Ch
64 40  @    80 50  P
65 41  A    81 51  Q
66 42  B    82 52  R
67 43  C    83 53  S
68 44  D    84 54  T
69 45  E    85 55  U
70 46  F    86 56  V
71 47  G    87 57  W
72 48  H    88 58  X
73 49  I    89 59  Y
74 4A  J    90 5A  Z
75 4B  K    91 5B  [
76 4C  L    92 5C  \
77 4D  M    93 5D  ]
78 4E  N    94 5E  ^
79 4F  O    95 5F  _
```

Fig. 14-8. More ASCII Values.

This display is a bit different. Characters 33 and above in the ASCII system do not have Ctrl or mnemonic values. The reason is simply that these values are directly related to normal keyboard characters. You can see from the table that the letter C has a decimal value of 67.

The ASCII table is probably not an everyday tool for most users. However, it can be quite handy to have when you are working with printers.

14.14.   Program to Change Form Length

Below are sample programs for Epson and Diablo printers in BASIC.

EPSON

If you have an EPSON printer or one that emulates an EPSON, enter

10 lprint chr$(27);chr$(67);chr$(11) <return>

The last chr$() entry actually specifies the number of lines to set the form length. For example, if you wanted 22-line pages you would change the entry to

10 lprint chr$(27);chr$(67);chr$(22) <return>

DIABLO

If you have a DIABLO printer or one that emulates a DIABLO, enter

10 lprint chr$(27);chr$(12);chr$(11) <return>

As with the Epson, the last chr$() entry actually specifies the number of lines to set the form length. For example, if you wanted 22-line pages you would change the entry to

10 lprint chr$(27);chr$(12);chr$(22) <return>

If you have a different printer, check your manual for appropriate codes. If you need to find the ASCII values for the codes you can use the Sidekick ASCII display.

To make the program automatically exit BASIC, add another line. Enter **20 system <return>**

When you have entered the program, you must save it on the disk. Enter **SAVE"CALFORM <return>**

This creates a file CALFORM.BAS on the disk. To exit BASIC, enter **system <return>**

Check to see if the file has really been saved. Enter **dir a:*.bas <return>**

The directory listing should show the file. Whenever you want to set up your printer for printing the calendar, you can execute the program by entering **basic calform <return>**

The printer is now ready for Sidekick printing.

If you have dBASE II or dBASE III you can create a similar program in dBASE that will have the same effect. First load dBASE. When the period prompt appears, enter the following:

modify command calform <return>

Enter the following command for EPSON:

set print on < return >
? chr(27) + chr(67) + chr(11) < return > < return >
set print off < return >
quit < return >

Enter this command for DIABLO:

set print on < return >
? chr(27) + chr(12) + chr(11) < return >
set print off < return >
quit < return >

When the program is entered, save the file by entering **[Ctrl w]**

Exit dBASE by entering **quit** < return >

Execute the program before you print the calendar by entering **dbase calform** < return >

To return the printer to the default setting for form length, you can create another program to set it back to 66 lines. However, there is a much simpler method. Just turn the printer off and then on again. When you do this the printer reads the settings indicated by the DIP switches and returns automatically to the default, 66 lines.

14.15. The Dialer

The Dialer program combines two special functions:

1. Data File. The dialer has the ability to search a file for specific information.
2. Auto-dialer. The dialer also has the ability to work with autodial modems like the Hayes 1200 model to automatically dial phone numbers through the computer.

Depending upon the way you work with your computer, you may want to use the Dialer for one or both of these functions.

The dialer is meant to serve as an electronic Rolodex-file. Each entry in the dialer file consists of one line of text not to exceed 78 characters in length.

The Sidekick program comes with a file called PHONE.DIR. Its only purpose is to demonstrate to you how the dialer works.

The dialer will work with almost any standard ASCII text file. You can create such a file with the DOS commands COPY and EDLIN, with word processing programs that create text files (e.g., WordStar non-document mode), with spreadsheets like 1-2-3, or databases like dBASE II and III.

While the name *dialer* suggests that the data file contains names and phone numbers, there is no requirement that the file should contain such information.

The dialer will read any standard file and display the first 78 characters. In addition it will search the file to locate a specific entry. Sidekick allows you to enter a key of up to ten characters to locate. The searches are conducted in two ways:

1. Initial Search—This search always begins with the first character on each line and searches for a match.
2. Search All—This search looks at all 78 characters on each line and searches for a match at any position on the line.

Initial Search is faster than Search All. To take advantage of the rapid search you can begin each line with a short code or "initials" to signify the entry on that line. Setting unique codes allows you to search a large directory very quickly.

The Search All option works more slowly but allows you to locate items based on information other than that which begins the line.

To see how this works, you will create a phone file from scratch. It really isn't very hard at all.

SETUP
Floppy and Hard Disk Users:
Sidekick loaded in memory
Drive A: Copy of MS DOS diskette

Make sure that the current drive is drive A. Enter **a:<return>**
You can use the EDLIN program to create a text file. Enter **edlin phone.dir<return>**
An * will appear. Enter **i<return>**
The screen will show 1:*. You can now enter some data. In this example you will create a phone list.
If you have a modem and want Sidekick to automatically dial the number for you, it is necessary to create the text according to a specific

format. This format is:

<code> <number> <comments>

The *code* is the initials or code you want to use for the quick search option.

The *number* is the telephone number of the person or place. Phone numbers must follow a few simple rules:

1. They must contain a special character that identifies them as phone numbers. The usual characters are -, (, or). The Sidekick install program allows you to change these characters if for some reason you need to use others. The following are examples of numbers that Sidekick will recognize:

   (215)-453-8903
   234 678-8903
   234-675-8634
   (202) 546-9090

2. Including characters **T** or **P** in the phone number tells Sidekick to use Tone or Pulse dialing. The characters can be embedded into the phone number so that part of the number can be dialed with tone and the remainder with pulse.
3. An @ sign embedded in the number will tell Sidekick to pause the dialing. The @ sign makes it possible to use the Sidekick dialer with special long distance carriers. For example, many long distance carriers require you to call a local access number and then wait for a tone and enter a special code, followed by the number you want to call. Suppose that your local access number is 666-9000. Your personal code is 123999. The number you want to dial is 212-245-6400. You could enter the number as

   666-9000@123999212-245-6400

   When Sidekick dials this number it will pause after 666-9000 has been dialed. When you hear the tone, pressing <return> will cause the remainder of the numbers to be dialed.

Enter

WL 568-9527 Walter La Fish Consolidated Chemical Corp.<return>
SS 678-9000@111999-212-245-6400 Simon & Shuster (Using MCI)<return>
DT 657-5858 Dr. Dale Tucker<return>
Tom 546-9087 Accountant<return>
LAW 654-9084 George and Chick<return>

To save this file, enter

[Ctrl c]
e < **return** >

Now that you have created a phone list you can see how the dialer works.
Enter **[Ctrl Alt] [F5]**

```
WL 568-9527 Walter La Fish Consolidated Chemical Corp.
SS 678-90000111999-212-245-6400 Simon Shuster (Using MCI)
DT 657-5858 Dr. Dale Tucker
Tom 546-9087 Accountant
```

Fig. 14-9. Dialer Display.

The phone list appears in the dialer window. You can move from one
entry to another by use of the arrow keys. Enter < **down arrow** >
    The highlight moves to the next name. Enter < **down arrow** >
    The highlight is now on Dr. Tucker. You can position the highlight by
using the search capacity of the dialer. You can begin by using the the
initial search. Enter **[F5]**
    Enter the initials that you want to search for. Enter **law** < **return** >
    The highlight is moved to the first line that contains the initials LAW.

[The search is not sensitive to differences in cases of letters. This means that that law, Law,
LAW, and laW will all be considered as the same initials.]

    The words SEARCH ACTIVE appear at the top of the window. The
< up arrow > and the < down arrow > keys will continue the search in their
respective directions. Enter < **down arrow** >
    The highlight falls on a blank at the end of the file. Enter
< **up arrow** > < **up arrow** >
    The highlight falls at the beginning of the file. To turn off the search
option, enter **[F7]**
    The words SEARCH ACTIVE disappear from the border of the win-
dow. The < up arrow > and the < down arrow > keys will now simply move
from line to line.
    The full search option allows you to search for character groups that do
not occur at the beginning of the line. Enter **[F6] mci** < **return** >

The highlight falls on the line that contains the letters MCI. Terminate the search by entering [F7]

When the highlight is on a line, pressing **<return>** will dial the number.

[If you have a modem, you must use the Sidekick install program, SKINST.COM, before you can dial. If you have not installed a modem into Sidekick and you attempt to dial, you will get this message:

```
Sidekick not installed for modem. Press Esc to continue or F1 for help
```

To correct this problem you must use the install program and then reboot the computer and reload the Sidekick program.]

To exit the dialer program, enter **<Esc>**

14.16.   Creating a Phone List with dBASE III

If you have a large phone list and also have a data base program like dBASE III, you can prepare a phone directory file for Sidekick. dBASE offers a variety of features that make it simple to enter data and sort it into the proper order. This section is designed to explain how data stored in a dBASE III file can be used to create a phone list file that will work with the Sidekick dialer program. It also illustrates the principle of interchanging data among programs by using ASCII outputs.

This section assumes some familiarity with dBASE III. The procedure begins with a dBASE III file. Below is the structure of a typical file.

Field	Field name	Type	Width	Dec
1	FIRST	Character	10	
2	LAST	Character	20	
3	COMPANY	Character	20	
4	ADD	Character	30	
5	CITY	Character	20	
6	ZIP	Character	5	
7	PHONE	Character	14	
8	REMARK	Character	15	
** Total **			135	

The file includes more data than is needed for the phone dialer. This is because the file was originally designed as a client data file. You will see how to select only the data you want for the dialer file.

The assumption is further made that you have entered the data in the file already. Now you are ready to transfer the data to the Dialer.

Begin by placing your data base file in use. My example file is called CLIENTS. Enter **use clients < return >**

The technique demonstrated here takes advantage of the report generator supplied with dBASE III. The report generator is used to create column reports. Usually these reports are printed on a printer. However, dBASE contains an option that allows you to send the column report not to the printer but to a disk file. This output to a disk file is exactly what is needed to create a file that the Dialer can read.

The first step is to design the form of the report. To create a report, enter **create report phones < return >**

dBASE displays the first screen. The top part of the screen is used for setting the headings for the report. You will not need headings, so this section can be ignored. The bottom of the screen contains information about the width of the lines to be printed. The default values appear as:

Page width (# chars):	80
Left margin (# chars):	8
Right margin (# chars):	0
# lines/page:	58
Double space report? (Y/N):	N

You will need to change these. First change the page width to 78 characters. That is the maximum allowed in the dialer. Next change the left margin setting to zero. The bottom should look like this:

Page width (# chars):	78
Left margin (# chars):	0
Right margin (# chars):	0
# lines/page:	58
Double space report? (Y/N):	N

After you have made those changes enter **[PgDn] [Pg Dn]**

You are now ready to enter the contents of the first column of this report. What should that be? Remember that the dialer uses the leftmost columns for the rapid search command. You will want to place the initials of the people on your list in those columns. This might be a problem, since you did not enter the initials as part of the data base. However, dBASE III has functions that can solve this problem. The SUBSTR( )—substring—function allows you to select part of a field. In this case, you will use the substring function to select the first characters of the first and last names to form the initials. Enter the following into the field contents area:

substr(first,1,1) + substr(last,1,1) < return >

No column heading is necessary. Enter **c[Pg Dn]**

    The next column will contain the person's name. The TRIM( ) function is used to eliminate trailing blanks. Enter the following:

trim(first) + " " + last < return >
[Pg Dn]

The next column is the phone number. Enter **phone < return > [Pg Dn]**

    Finally you can add the remarks field. Enter
remarks < return > [Pg Dn]

    To complete the entry of the report, enter **< return >**

    The next step is optional. If you want the list to be alphabetized, you can use the INDEX command to order the file. The following command will alphabetize the file on last name and first name. Enter

index on last + first to phones < return >

Now you are ready to create the file for the dialer. Enter

report form phones to file phone.dir plain noeject < return >

dBASE III has created the PHONE.DIR file for you from the data stored in your client file.

[The PHONE.DIR file must be stored in the active disk and directory when the Dialer is called up. This means that you may have to copy the Dialer file to another disk or directory in order to use it.]

    When you activate the Dialer, the list created by dBASE III will appear in the window.

[The report form automatically adds four heading lines at the top of the file when a report is created, even if you do not specify a heading. Therefore, you will see four blank lines at the top of the file.

The lines do no harm, but you may find them annoying. You can use the Sidekick notepad to eliminate those lines.

Bring up the notepad. Enter **[F3]** **phone.dir<return>**

This loads the PHONE.DIR file. Remove the four top lines. Enter **[Ctrl y]** (four times)

Save the file. Enter **[F2]**

The file will now appear in the dialer with no blank lines.]

14.17. The Notepad

The notepad is a word processing program that can be called up in a window just like the other Sidekick functions. The notepad is designed to function in a similar manner to WordStar.

[Unlike WordStar, the notepad writes ASCII-compatible files only. The document mode of WordStar will alter the text by changing some of the letters. This means that if you read into the notepad a file created in the document mode of WordStar, the text will appear to have all sorts of funny graphics characters embedded in it. In other words, WordStar can read a Sidekick notepad file but not necessarily the other way around.]

The Sidekick notepad can read and write ASCII-compatible files. In addition, you can perform the standard editing functions that comprise the common standard for word processing programs. The notepad provides:

1. Basic Editing—The ability to type text, automatically wrap around line endings, insert and delete characters in the text.
2. Block Functions—You can mark a section of the text as a block. This block can be moved, copied, deleted, or written as a separate ASCII file.
3. Search and Replace—You can search for a certain group of characters and replace them with another group of characters.

These functions are implemented in a similar manner to the command structure used in WordStar.

In addition, the notepad will perform some functions and features not found in WordStar:

1. Sort—The notepad will perform an ascending sort (lowest to highest) for numbers and an alphabetical sort for text on a specified block of text.
2. Graphics—The notepad will display all 255 IBM characters. WordStar and other programs will display only the standard text characters.

[Even though the notepad displays all 255 characters, this does not mean that you will be able to print them out. Most printers do not have the full IBM character set (including graphics) built into them. This is particularly true of daisy wheel printers. Note that most wheels have only 96 spokes, and therefore only 96 different characters to print.

If you want to print all the characters that you see on your screen you will need a printer that supports "the full IBM character set." Another alternative is to use the graphics mode provided by some dot printers and special utility programs that duplicate the IBM character set.]

3. Import and Export—This is probably the most valuable of the notepad's functions. The notepad can be used to copy part or all of the screen display into the notepad as a text file. This means that information displayed by a program, even messages or menus, can be copied into an ASCII file. The text can be used with word processing programs, edited, and printed.

Also, the notepad can transfer text marked as a block in the notepad to another application as if you had manually typed the keystrokes yourself. This feature allows you to feed data from one application to another by using the notepad to copy and then feed the information.

[The import feature is available on most versions of Sidekick. The export or paste feature requires Sidekick Version 1.56 or newer.]

The notepad has a dual character. It is filled with enough useful and interesting features to function as a word processing program for letters, memos, and other business tasks. On the other hand, because it functions in the background of other programs and imports and exports data, the notepad has fascinating possibilities as a way to integrate data between programs by quickly creating ASCII text out of screen displays.

The following section will explore both characteristics of the notepad.

14.18.   Notepad as Word Processor

The Sidekick notepad allows you to enter a word processing environment no matter what application you are working on at the time. The notepad is a bit different from the other Sidekick modes in that it functions very much like a typical microcomputer application with the exception that it can pop-up from the background whenever needed.

The prime advantage of the notepad as a word processor is that there is no need to close the application you are working on in order to word process. The notepad is designed to function like WordStar.

There are two reasons why WordStar is an appropriate model for the notepad. First, WordStar still has the largest installed base among microcomputer word processing programs. This means that many users will already be familiar with the concepts and commands of WordStar. Second, the aim of the notepad is to produce a generic text file that can be used as widely as possible with other programs. Word-Star, with one notable exception, stores only the keystrokes you type in the text file. The formatting commands, such as margins, are shown on the screen but are not stored as part of the file. This is exactly the aim of the notepad.

Bring up the notepad. Enter **[Ctrl Alt] [F2]**

The notepad appears as a box that covers the bottom half of the screen.

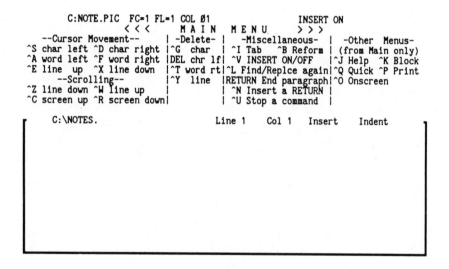

Fig. 14-10. Notepad Display.

The notepad immediately searches the correct disk and directory (drive A, root directory) for a file called NOTES. If that file cannot be found, Sidekick creates the file. There must always be a file in use by the notepad. While the default is always called NOTES, it is possible to use any valid DOS filename for a notepad file.

Because you probably don't have a NOTES file on your DOS disk, Sidekick creates the file and displays an empty notepad.

The top border to the window contains special information. It is called the status line because it displays information about how the text in the window is being entered.

The status line displays three types of information:

1. The leftmost display indicates the name of the disk file that is associated with the text in the window. There must always be a filename in the the notepad border. The default value is a file called NOTES in the active directory. If no NOTES file is found, then Sidekick will create one.
2. Cursor position. The center section of the status line displays the current line and column position of the cursor in the text.
3. Mode Indicators. The right portion of the line is used to display the mode indicators for Sidekick. There are three modes that are used in the Sidekick notepad:

   a. INSERT. When the word *Insert* is exhibited, any characters typed are added to the text. You cannot type over characters when you are in the Insert mode. When Insert is not exhibited, you can type over characters that have already been entered. When Sidekick loads, the Insert is automatically activated.
   b. INDENT. The word *Indent* on the status line indicates that Sidekick is in the auto-indent mode. This mode is used to create special margin effects, such as outlines. When not displayed, Sidekick begins all new lines at the left edge of the window. When Sidekick loads, the Indent mode is automatically activated.
   c. GRAPH. The word *Graph* on the status line indicates that Sidekick will display all 255 IBM graphics characters. When not displayed, only the standard 128-character ASCII codes will be displayed. The default mode for Sidekick is non-graphics.

How much can the notepad hold? The default value for the notepad size is 4,096 characters. Each character that you type, including spaces and carriage returns, counts as a character. This limitation means that you can type up to 4,096 characters before you have to save the file. However, there is no reason why you cannot have many files of 4,096 characters apiece.

The size of the notepad file can be adjusted in the Sidekick install program to be between 1,000 and 15,000 characters. To make this change you must reboot the computer and reload Sidekick. Using the install after Sidekick has been loaded will not affect the size of the file in memory.

Like the other Sidekick displays, the notepad's position can be adjusted by using the arrow keys after the Scroll Lock has been pressed. Enter **[Scroll Lock] <up arrow>**

The display moves one line up. Return the window to its original position. Enter **<down arrow> [Scroll Lock]**

Unlike the other Sidekick displays, the size of the notepad display can be changed. F9 will allow you to expand the notepad window, while F10 will contract the window. The largest window is 22 lines by 78 columns. Enter the following:

[F9]
<up arrow>
<up arrow>
<up arrow>
<up arrow>
[F9]

To contract the window, enter the following:

[F10]
<down arrow>
<down arrow>
<down arrow>
<down arrow>
[F10]

[The width or length of the notepad window does not affect the width of the line or the number of lines that you can type. The width is determined by the right margin setting. The total number of lines is determined by the size of the notepad file.

If the width of the margin is greater than the width of the notepad window, the display will scroll horizontally right and left as you enter text.]

To learn more about the notepad and its word processing functions, enter the following text. Do not worry about ending the lines; Sidekick will automatically break the lines for you.

Experience does not err, it is only your judgment that errs in
promising itself results which are not caused by your
experiments.

Notice that when you typed the quote from Leonardo da Vinci the notepad broke the lines for you. This is called wraparound typing. The notepad uses a line length of 65 characters as standard.

14.19.   Basic Editing

The basic editing set of any word processing program consists of three types of commands:

1. Commands that move the cursor.
2. Commands that delete text.
3. Commands that insert text.

Sidekick has a full set of commands that accommodate most of the operations of WordStar. They are:

Move one character left	[Ctrl s]	
Move one character right	[Ctrl d]	
Word left	[Ctrl a]	[Ctrl right arrow]
Word right	[Ctrl f]	[Ctrl left arrow]
Line up	[Ctrl e]	
Scroll up	[Ctrl w]	
Scroll down	[Ctrl z]	
Page up	[Ctrl r]	[Pg Up]
Page down	[Ctrl c]	[Pg Dn]
To left on line	[Ctrl q]s	[Home]
To right on line	[Ctrl q]d	[End]
To top of page	[Ctrl q]e	[Ctrl Home]
To bottom of page	[Ctrl q]x	[Ctrl End]
To top of file	[Ctrl q]r	[Ctrl Pg Up]
To end of file	[Ctrl q]c	[Ctrl Pg Dn]
To end of file & insert date/time	[Ctrl q]o	

To beginning of block	[Ctrl q]b	
To end of block	[Ctrl q]k	
To last cursor position	[Ctrl q]p	

INSERT and DELETE

Insert mode on/off	[Ctrl v]	[Ins]
Insert line	[Ctrl n]	
Delete line	[Ctrl y]	
Delete to end of line	[Ctrl q]y	
Delete right word	[Ctrl t]	
Delete char under cursor	[Ctrl g]	[Del]
Delete left character	[Ctrl h]	

BLOCK COMMANDS

Mark block begin	[Ctrl k]b	[F7]
Mark block end	[Ctrl k]k	[F8]
Mark single word	[Ctrl k]t	
Hide/display block	[Ctrl k]h	
Copy block	[Ctrl k]c	
Move block	[Ctrl k]v	
Delete block	[Ctrl k]y	
Read block from disk	[Ctrl k]r	
Write block to disk	[Ctrl k]w	
Sort block	[Ctrl k]s	
Print block	[Ctrl k]p	

MISCELLANEOUS COMMANDS

Save note file	[Ctrl k]d	[F2]
Paste block	[Ctrl k]e	
Cut and paste		[F4]
Tab	[Ctrl i]	\<tab\>
Repeat last find	[Ctrl l]	
Control character prefix	[Ctrl p]	
Reformat line	[Ctrl b]	
Set right margin	[Ctrl o]r	

Find	[Ctrl q]f
Find & replace	[Ctrl q]a
Auto tab on/off	[Ctrl q]i
Restore line	[Ctrl q]l
Read date and time	[Ctrl q]t
Graphics on/off	[Ctrl q]g
Cancel Command	[Ctrl u]

[Sidekick does not provide a block column as does WordStar.]

Enter **[Ctrl q] r**
The cursor moves to the beginning of the text. Enter **[End]**
The cursor moves to end of the line. Enter **[Ctrl q] d**
The cursor moves to end of the text.

14.20.   Inserting and Deleting

The notepad follows the basic design of WordStar. When you begin, the notepad is automatically placed in the *Insert* mode. As described above, the insert mode means that any typing that you do adds characters to the text. You can't type over characters that have already been entered. It also implies that as you type, the notepad will adjust any characters to the right or below the point of entry.

The insert mode can be turned into a *typeover* mode by using the [Ins] key or [Ctrl v] combination.

Insert mode on/off	Ctrl-V	Ins
Insert line	Ctrl-N	
Delete line	Ctrl-Y	
Delete to end of line	Ctrl-Q-Y	
Delete right word	Ctrl-T	
Delete char under cursor	Ctrl-G	Del
Delete left character	Ctrl-H	D

Move to the beginning of the text. Enter **[Ctrl q] r**
Enter the following text:

The following is a quotation from the Italian artist Leonardo da Vinci.
< return >
< return >

Notice how the text was automatically inserted. The text below and to the right of the new text was moved down as the new text was added.

14.21.   Saving the Text

When you enter text into the notepad, the text is stored in the internal memory of the computer. It is not automatically transferred to a disk file. This means that you must specifically command Sidekick to save the text if you do not want it to be lost when you turn your computer off. The [F2] function key in the notepad transfers the contents of the notepad to a file on the disk. Enter **[F2]**

When the text is saved, the data in the notepad is not changed in any way. The only thing changed by the save command is that there is now a text file with the same data on the disk.

[If you make changes in the notepad after you have saved, you must keep in mind that you must enter another save command to save the revised notepad text.]

14.22.   Reforming Text

When text is removed from a paragraph, it is necessary to reform the text in order to get the line lengths properly adjusted. Sidekick does not automatically adjust the lines; you must enter a special command to tell Sidekick to do so.

As an example, remove the first four words of the second paragraph. Enter **[Ctrl t]** four times.

Now remove the letter *i* and replace it with the letter *I*. Enter **[Ins] I [Ins]**

Note that the lines are out of adjustment. To get the line lengths adjusted, enter **[Ctrl b]**

14.23.   Other Editing Commands

The Sidekick notepad will perform search and replace functions. This allows you to make mass replacements. For example, suppose that you wanted to change the word *your* to the word *one's*. Enter **[Ctrl q] a**

Enter the word to search for: **your < return >**
Next enter the word to replace it with: **one's < return >**
The last entries are the search and replace options. The options are:

w—Only whole words will be considered a match.
g—Global, search from the beginning of the document despite the cursor's current location.
n—No prompting, replace all automatically.

In this case, enter *g* and *w* for a global search that looks for only the whole word *your*. If the letters *your* appear as a part of a larger word, they will not be selected. Enter **gw < return >**

The cursor moves to the first word *your*. The status line asks REPLACE [Y/N]. Enter **y**

The swap is made and Sidekick finds the next match and asks the same question. Enter **y**

14.24.   Changing the Right Margin

The right margin setting determines the length of the line that can be typed in the notepad window. The line length can be a maximum of 255 characters. The default value is 65 characters.

The command [Ctrl o] r is used to set the right margin. For example, suppose that you wanted to change the right margin setting to 45. Enter the following:

[Ctrl o]
r
45 < return >

What has happened? The answer is that nothing has changed in the text at all. Changing the margin will affect only the following:

1. Any text that is entered after the margin has been changed.
2. Paragraphs that are reformed with the [Ctrl b] command.

Move the cursor to the beginning of the text. Enter **[Ctrl q] r**
Reform the text. Enter **[Ctrl b]**
The lines are reformed within the new margins.

When changing the margins, you must reform each paragraph with a [Ctrl b] command separately. This is exactly the same as in WordStar.

14.25. Indents

One of the most interesting features of the Sidekick notepad is its ability to create indented text. When the Indent mode is active, you can create indented paragraphs or reform old text into indented paragraphs. The Indent mode is automatically activated when Sidekick loads.

Move the cursor to the beginning of the text again. Enter **[Ctrl q] r**

The trick to creating an indent is to indent the first line with spaces. Enter **<space>** five times.

Now reform the paragraph. Enter **[Ctrl b]**

The paragraph is now indented on the left as well as the right.

You can type a paragraph that begins with an indent. Move to the bottom of the text. Enter **[Ctrl q] d**

Create an indent by typing spaces. Enter **<space>** (ten times)

Now enter the following text:

This text is indented ten characters on the left and has a line length of 45 characters. <return>

You can see that the text is formed to fit the indent and the right margin setting. When you press <return>, the cursor moves to the next line but remains at column 10. To turn off the indent and put the cursor back in column 1, enter **<return>**

14.26. Opening a New Notepad File

Sidekick allows you to create text files with names other than NOTES. The [F3] function key creates a new file. Enter **[F3]**

Sidekick displays a message. The message indicates that there have been changes or additions made to the text in the notepad that have not been saved. When a new file is started, all the text is removed from the memory. That means that you must decide to either save or abandon what you have already typed. Enter **y**

The text is saved. You can now enter a new filename or pick one from the file directory.

[The file directory can be activated by entering a DOS wildcard or an empty filename. For example, if you used the backspace key to erase the current filename and pressed <return>, Sidekick would open a window above the notepad and display the file in the active directory. The arrow keys can be used to position the cursor to the file you want to use. Pressing the <return> will load that file.

If you want to be more selective. you can enter a DOS wildcard, e.g., NOTES*. This would display only files that begin with the letters N-O-T-E-S.]

Enter **newfile<return>**

The new filename appears at the top of the Sidekick window. The notepad is cleared of all text and the cursor is at the top of the window. You are now ready to create a new notepad document. Enter the following text:

This file is created with the Sidekick notepad.<return>

Save this notepad text. Enter **[F2]**

14.27.   Recalling a File

Now that you have more than one file, you can load files that already exist by using the [F3] key. Although the command is called NEW FILE, it can be used to load the text of existing files into the notepad.

[You can load any standard text file into the notepad. It does not have to be a file that was created with Sidekick. Examples of the types of files you might load are DOS batch files, word processing files that are in standard ASCII format, or data files from programs that store data in ASCII format.]

The file PHONE.DIR that you created for use with the Sidekick Dialer is a standard ASCII file. You can load that file into the notepad and make additions and changes to it. The Sidekick notepad can replace EDLIN as an editor. The notepad and EDLIN produce the same type of files, ASCII text files.

Enter **[F3]**

Type in the name of the file. Enter **phone.dir<return>**

The notepad is filled with the data from the PHONE.DIR file.

14.28.   Selecting Filenames

Sidekick allows you to select the file that you want to use from a directory display. Enter **[F3]**

Sidekick displays the last filename entered. In this case it is NEWFILE. Instead of entering the name of the file that you want to load, you can get Sidekick to display a directory of files. First you must remove the filename that is currently on the line. *Use the <backspace> key to remove the filename.*

Now enter **<return>**

Sidekick now displays a second window above the notepad. The window is filled with the names of the files stored on the disk. Your cursor is positioned in the window at the first filename.

[You can display a directory window for directories or drives other than the active drive and directory. This is done by entering a drive specification and/or a path. Drive specifications consist of a letter followed by a colon. Pathnames are preceded and followed by a backslash character. Examples:

b: (selects drive B)
\123\   (selects the 123 directory on the current drive)
c:\123\   (selects the 123 directory on the C drive)

You may also use DOS wildcard symbols to specify a limited group of files to be displayed. Example:

notes*.*   (displays only files that begin with NOTES)]

The arrow keys will position the cursor to different filenames. The window displays 25 filenames. If there are more names on the disk, the [Pg Up] and [Pg Dn] keys will display the next or previous group of files.

Position your cursor to the NOTES file. Enter **<return>**

The NOTES file is loaded into the notepad.

14.29.   Combining Files

You can combine files by using the [Ctrl k]r command. This command reads the contents of a disk file into the notepad *without* erasing the text that is in the notepad. The effect is to combine the two files into a single notepad entry.

The files are combined based on the position of the cursor at the time you enter the READ A FILE command. For example, the cursor is currently at the beginning of the file. If you entered the command now, the text from the other file would be placed at the beginning of this file. To add the text at the end, you would move the cursor to the end of the document first, then enter the READ command.

In this case, read the text into the beginning of the file. Enter **[Ctrl k] r**

Sidekick needs to know the name of the file that you want to add to the notepad text. In this example you will want to display only the files on the disk that begin with the letter N. Enter **n*<return>**

Notice that the directory window contains only files that begin with N. Move the cursor to NEWFILE. Enter **<return>**

The text of the NEWFILE file is added to the text already in the notepad. Observe that the text is shown in a different video display than the rest of the text. This is because when text is added with the READ command, it is automatically marked as a block. You can now use the block commands to move, copy, or delete the marked text:

Move a Block   [Ctrl k]v
Copy a Block   [Ctrl k]c
Delete a Block   [Ctrl k]y

To leave the text as it is and remove the block marking, enter **[Ctrl k] h**

14.30.   Import and Export of Text

In the previous section you saw how the notepad functioned as a word processing program. The notepad's function as a word processor is important. As a result of it, you do not have to quit the application you are working in to make or revise notes. Except for the fact that the notepad is a memory-resident, pop-up program, the functions described could be found in any word processing or text editing program. The notepad itself emulates the functions of WordStar.

However, the notepad can be used to perform some unusual functions that cannot be duplicated by word processing programs. The functions are the importing and exporting of data. These functions allow you to do the following:

1. *Capture Screen Displays.* The IMPORT function enables you to capture the information displayed at any time on the screen and store it in the notepad. The text can then be saved as a notepad file.

   [The notepad can capture text information only in the notepad. The text includes all the IBM low-resolution graphics characters, such as lines and boxes. Any character displayed on a monochrome monitor can be captured.

However, you cannot capture data displayed in high-resolution graphics mode. An example of high-resolution graphics is the charts drawn by 1-2-3. These displays are bit-mapped graphics and cannot be captured as text. Microsoft Windows has a Clipboard function that will capture bit-mapped images from the high-resolution screen. Of course, you need a special graphics-based word processor, like Microsoft Write, to print the captured image.

Be aware that some screen displays can have an odd effect when they are captured in the notepad. Screen displays that use ASCII characters below the space character (31 or lower) will have unexpected results when they are imported into the notepad. Some programs display these characters on the screen.

Some common examples are the ruler line display in MultiMate and the hexadecimal display of Norton Utilities. If you attempt to capture these displays, you will find that the captured product will not function like a text file. For example, the musical note character is the ASCII character 13, which stands for a carriage return. When the musical note is captured in a text environment like the notepad, it has the same effect as if someone had pressed the return key.

Other characters such as the double bracket, < < or > >, that appear on the ruler lines of MultiMate and DisplayWrite word processors, will not appear in the text when imported to the notepad.

Programmers often display these characters on the screen to make special displays and menus that stand out from the usual text characters. If you try to capture a display and encounter missing or distorted characters, this is usually the reason.]

2. *Export Text to an Application.* The notepad can send a block of ASCII text from the notepad into the application that you have running.

The power of this feature comes from the fact that there are many ways to get text into the notepad. The text can simply be typed into the notepad, or loaded from a file or captured from a screen display.

The combination of Import and Export allows you to integrate data from applications that do not normally have methods of exchanging information.

To learn more about import and export and their potential uses, begin with a simple example.

14.31. Importing Data

Begin by creating a new notepad file. Enter **[F2] [F3] import < return >**

The next step is to deactivate Sidekick. Why? When you use the import function, you first have to get the data that you want to capture on the screen. To deactivate Sidekick enter **[Ctrl Alt]**

Clear the screen. Enter **cls < return >**

Now enter a command that will create a screen display. Enter **chkdsk < return >**

The display on the screen may represent data that you want to capture for use at some other time, perhaps with another program. To begin the capture process bring up the Sidekick notepad. Enter **[Ctrl Alt]**

The notepad window is displayed in the bottom half of the screen. Enter the import command: **[F4]**

The notepad window disappears. What has happened? Are you out of Sidekick and back in DOS? The answer is no. You are still in Sidekick. How can you tell?

There are two signs. The first is that the bottom line of the screen still shows the Sidekick commands for the notepad. The second is the position of your cursor. The cursor is not in the position that you left it in when you left DOS. It has been placed at the top of the screen. You are free to move the cursor in any direction.

The arrow keys will move the cursor freely in any direction. Enter **<down arrow>** three times.

The cursor should now be on the first line of the data displayed by the CHKDSK command. It is here that you want to begin the capture of the data. The command that begins data capture is [F7]. Enter **[F7]**

[The command issued by the [F7] key can be duplicated by entering [Ctrl k]b. This is the command that marks the beginning of a block.]

The space at the cursor position appear in reverse video. Enter **<down arrow>**

What happens? The highlight expands to cover two spaces.

Use the **<down arrow>** key to move the cursor to the bottom of the text displayed by the CHKDSK command.

Now enter **<right arrow>**

The highlight expands horizontally.

[What happens if you expand the highlight too far? Moving the cursor in the opposite direction will contract the highlight. If you want to abandon the entire process, press <Esc> and you will return to the Sidekick notepad immediately.]

You can highlight more than one column at a time. Enter **[Ctrl right arrow]**

The highlight jumps ten spaces to the right. The combination of [Ctrl] and the left or right arrow keys helps to contract or expand the highlight horizontally. Enter **[Ctrl right arrow]** three times.

This should highlight all the text displayed by the CHKDSK command. To complete the marking process, enter the END block command: **[F8]**

[The END block command can be entered as **[Ctrl k]k**]

The notepad window returns just as you left it. Where is the text to be imported?

The answer is that it is being held in the memory of the computer waiting to be inserted into the notepad. Why isn't it inserted automatically?

The purpose of not automatically writing the highlighted text is to allow you a chance to position your cursor to the spot in the notepad that you want the text inserted at. As with the READ command, [Ctrl k]r, the text is inserted at the cursor position.

In this example, the notepad is empty. However, you could enter some text before you import that data from the screen. You might want to record the time and date that this data was captured.

14.32.   Time Stamping

The Sidekick notepad offers a command that automatically writes the system's time and date into the text. Enter **[Ctrl q] t**

Sidekick types the time and date into the file. Enter **<return>**

This moves the cursor to the next line. Time stamping is a very useful function because it helps keep track of when files were created or updated.

[The notepad has another command that performs a similar function. The command [Ctrl q]o writes the time and date, but does so at the end of the notepad text. The [Ctrl q]t command places the time and date at the cursor position.]

Now copy the text from the screen. The command to copy the text is the COPY block command, [Ctrl k]c. Enter **[Ctrl k] c**

Sidekick jumps back to the normal screen display. The cursor flashes as it scans the screen. Then the notepad window returns. Sidekick then enters the text into the notepad. Notice that the cursor position is at the beginning of the block that was copied.

This is very important. If you want to import more text, you *must* remember to move the cursor to the end of the text.

14.33.   About Imports

Importing data is a quick and handy way to capture data that appears on the screen. Many programs display information on the screen in formats that are not included in the program's printouts. Without Sidekick, the only way to obtain a printed copy would be to to use the screen dump (Shift PrtSc) command.

The import function offers several advantages:

1. It is faster than printing the data.

2. You can import only the portion of the screen you need.
3. The data can be stored in a text file and printed later. You can store many screens in a single notepad file. You are only limited by the total number of characters the notepad can hold. The default is 4,096, but that can be changed with the install program.

[Text captured from the screen usually uses up more memory than text typed directly into the notepad because all the blank space imported counts as space characters. For example, if you highlighted a full screen, 24 lines by 80 columns, the copied text would use up 80 times 24, or 1,920 bytes of memory space, even thought many of the characters are spaces.]

4. The data can be edited and the time and date entered by using the [Ctrl q]t command.
5. By combining import and export techniques, Sidekick can be used to transfer data between applications. One good example is capturing data from the screen and exporting it to the Sidekick calculator.

14.34.   Exporting Data

Sidekick can not only import data, i.e., duplicate data displayed on the screen in the notepad, but also export data, i.e., copy data displayed in the notepad into some other application.

Combined with the import feature, this gives the Sidekick notepad a new dimension. The notepad can now function by way of transferring data from one application to another by means of storing it in the notepad.

Currently you have the text from the CHKDSK display in the notepad window. Suppose that you wanted to perform some calculations using the numbers that you copied into the notepad.

The export feature saves the trouble of typing the numbers again. You can use the export feature to directly enter the numbers into the Sidekick calculator.

For example, the first number shown on the CHKDSK display is the total number of bytes on the disk. How many sectors of 512 bytes each are contained on the disk? To find the answer you could use the Sidekick calculator. You can now use the notepad to directly input the number on the screen into the calculator.

The first step is to mark the text that you want to copy as a block. Move the cursor to the beginning of the number by entering **[Ctrl f]**

Mark the beginning of the block: **[F7]**

Move the cursor one word to the right. Enter **[Ctrl f]**
Mark the end of the block. Enter **[F8]**
You have now selected the data to be transferred.

14.35.   Pasting a Key for Export

In order to transfer the marked text to an application, you select a key to be programmed with the selected text. The process resembles the technique used to paste the value in the calculator into an application.

The command to export data is [Ctrl k] e. Enter **[Ctrl k] e**

Sidekick displays `Press key to paste with:`. The key you type now will later be used to copy the selected text into the application. In selecting a key or key combination, keep in mind that you do not want to conflict with any functions already assigned to that key. Alternate key combinations are usually a safe bet. Enter **[Alt e]**

Next you must decide whether you want the text to be stored as a block or a series of lines. (This distinction applies only to text that covers more than one line.)

The distinction between block and line concerns the way export treats the ends of the lines. In BLOCK mode, the lines are automatically ended with a carriage return character. The entire block is typed automatically when you press the assigned key.

The LINE mode is a bit different. When the key assigned to paste the text is pressed, only the first line of the block is typed. No <return> is typed at the end of the line. To get the next line typed you must press the assigned paste key again.

The purpose of the line mode is to allow you to paste text into applications more selectively. By pausing after each line, Sidekick gives you the opportunity to type characters or move the cursor in between pasted lines.

In this example choose LINE mode. Why? Because the <return> at the end of the line is not needed in the calculator. Enter **l**

The [Alt e] combination is set to paste the number into an application when it is needed.

The next step is to bring the Sidekick calculator up on the screen. To bring up another Sidekick application while one is already on the screen, hold down the [Alt] key for a few moments.

The Sidekick menu appears. Enter **[F3]**

[If the calculator is not clear, clear it by entering **C**]

To paste the number, enter **[Alt e]**

[When you are typing an alternate key combination while in Sidekick, take care that you do not hold down the [Alt] key too long before pressing the other key. If you do, Sidekick will think that you want to look at the Sidekick menu, and will display it. If this happens, just press <Esc> and retype the combination without the delay.]

The number is entered into the calculator display. Complete the calculation by entering: **/512 =**

The answer, 708, appears in the calculator display. This tells you that there are 708 data sectors on a double-sided disk.

Now that the number is assigned to the [Alt e] key, you can use it over and over again. Enter a new calculation. Enter the following: **c [Alt e]/1024 =**

The number 354 appears in the calculator display. This number tells you the number of kilobytes of data that can be stored on a double-sided disk. It is an interesting fact that a 360K disk actually only has room for 354K of data after formatting.

Now you can paste data in the other direction. Enter **p [Alt n]**

This assigns the number in the calculator display to [Alt n]. Return to the notepad. Enter **<Esc>**

Move the cursor to the bottom of the notepad file by entering **[Ctrl q] c <return>**

Now you have two stored numbers to type with. Enter the following:

There are
[Alt n]
bytes on a disk.
<return>

14.36. Pasting a Column of Numbers

Importing and Exporting data is a fascinating topic. The advantages of using these features range from saving typing time to improving the accuracy of your entry. As an example, return to CHKDSK display.

```
362496 bytes total disk space
 22528 bytes in 2 hidden files
266240 bytes in 37 user files
 73728 bytes available on disk

524288 bytes total memory
416896 bytes free
```

It seems logical that if you add up the number of bytes in hidden files, user files, and empty space, the total should be the same as the total number of bytes. To check this, you can use the import command to grab the numbers off the screen. Then use the export command to pass those numbers to the calculator.

Begin by importing the numbers. Enter **[F4]**

Move the cursor down three lines by entering **<down arrow>** (three times)

Begin marking the block. Enter **[F7]**

Extend the highlight to the right by entering **<right arrow>** (eight times)

Now extend the highlight down by entering **<down arrow>** (three times)

You should now have four numbers highlighted. Complete the block by entering **[F8]**

Copy the highlighted text into the notepad. Enter **[Ctrl k] c**

The next task is to export the figures to the calculator. Mark the numbers as a block. Enter **[F7]**

Move the cursor to the end of the notepad file by entering **[Ctrl q] c**

Mark the end of the block by entering **[F8]**

[When defining a block of text to export, you should consider whether or not the block is to be pasted in the line or block mode. If the line mode is going to be used, the END BLOCK marker should be at the end of the last line of the block.]

```
{Begin Block}    362496
                  22528
                 266240
                  73728{End Block} <———Correct for LINE pasting
```

Positioning the block marker that way avoids an extra line when the lines are being pasted.

If the text is meant to be pasted in the BLOCK mode, you would usually want to mark the end of the block on the line below the last line of the text.

{Begin Block}   362496
                   22528
                  266240
                   73728
{End Block} ⟵— Correct for BLOCK pasting

Positioning the marker in this manner ensures that the block ends with a carriage return.]

Now store the block for exporting. Enter **[Ctrl k] e**

You can use [Alt e] (e for export) again. Note that using [Alt e] again erases the previous block pasted with that key. If you had wanted to preserve the text you could have used another key combination. Enter **[Alt e]**

Now choose the mode to paste the block with. In this case you will want to use the LINE mode. The reason is that you will want to enter the arithmetic operation, $+, -, *$, or $/$ following each number. The LINE mode will allow you to do so. Enter **l**

Now bring up the calculator. Press down the **[Alt]** key. When the menu appears enter **[F3]**

Clear the calculator. Enter **c**

Now begin entry of the numbers using the export key. Enter **[Alt e]**

The first number, 362496, is entered. Now enter the subtraction sign:

—

Enter the rest of the calculation:

[Alt e]

—

[Alt e]

—

[Alt e]

=

The figure on the calculator display shows zero. This indicates that the figures balance. The import and export features of the program demonstrate the power that can come from the simplest commands.

14.37.   Conclusion

Sidekick was the first program of its type. It still remains an outstanding value. One of the most important factors in using Sidekick is that it is now one of a family of products from Borland (SuperKey and Turbo Lightning are the others) that work together to improve the productivity of your computer.

If you want to see how Sidekick stacks up against the other background utilities discussed in this book, see Chapter 18.

15.

Spotlight

Spotlight is a background utility program marketed by Lotus Development Corporation, makers of 1-2-3 and Symphony. The program consists of six background functions. They are:

NOTEPAD—This is a pop-up word processing program designed for documents that require limited typing such as memos or notes.
CALCULATOR—This program emulates the functions of a pocket calculator.
APPOINTMENT BOOK—This program provides an electronic appointment book and calendar.
PHONE BOOK—This program serves as a phone book. It can call the phone numbers stored in it, when a modem is attached to the computer system.
INDEX FILE—This program functions as an index card file for storing all types of data.
FILER—This program allows the user to perform DOS functions while operating an application.

15.1. Copy Protection

Spotlight is the only program in this book that is furnished in a copy-protected version only. Lotus Development Corporation copy protects all of its software. Version 1.1 of Spotlight does allow you, however, to transfer Spotlight to a single hard disk.

[For a full discussion of copy protection see Chapter 1.]

Another major difference between Spotlight and the other background programs is that Spotlight is not totally memory resident. When you call for one of its functions, Spotlight reads information about the function from the disk.

15.2. Notepad

The notepad is a simple word processing program that can be accessed while other aplications are running. To call up the notepad, enter **[Shift Alt n]**

```
 Erase  File  Print  Abandon  Quit




                           -1-

 Note Pad                  1-Ø3-86   2:54p
```

Fig. 15-1. Spotlight Notepad.

Like all Spotlight applications, the window is divided into three sections:

TOP. The top section contains the command menu. Each choice represents an action that can be performed. The QUIT command returns you to the application you were working with, or to the last previous Spotlight application, if you are using more than one at a time.

CENTER. The center section is the contents area. This area usually contains the data or text that the application is concerned with. Data entries are made in the contents area.

BOTTOM. The bottom of the window is a status display. The status display indicates the name of the application and the current system's date and time.

15.3. Window Position

The placement of the window on the screen can be changed. To change the location of the window, enter **[Scroll Lock]**

The bottom of the window displays a prompt that indicates that you can use the arrow key to reposition the window. When you have placed the window, turn off the movement mode by entering **[Scroll Lock]**

The notepad is a window display that allows you to enter text into a page that is 14 lines long and 40 characters wide. Each notepad entry can have up to eight pages. [Pg Up] and [Pg Dn] will flip through the pages. After page 8 the notepad returns to page 1.

The notepad will create wraparound text as you type. However, you must manually advance to the next page. When you have filled the current page the notepad will beep, but it will not go on to the next page automatically. You must enter the [Pg Dn] command.

15.4. Using the Menu

The notepad begins with the cursor in the contents area. In order to move into the menu area, enter **<esc>**

You can select a command by one of two methods:

1) Highlight the command you desire and then press **<return>**
2) Press the letter key that corresponds to the first letter of the menu command that you want to use. For example, to perform Erase, press E. Note that no <return> is necessary when you type the letter of the command.

Many commands have subcommands. For example, when you use the erase command the menu display changes.

The <Esc> key is used to move backwards one menu. For example, when you are in the Erase Submenu, pressing <Esc> takes you back to the main notepad menu. When you are at the main notepad menu, pressing <Esc> returns your cursor to the contents area.

There are five commands in the notepad menu. They are:

ERASE
Erase Page—Erases the currently displayed page.
Erase All—Erases all pages.

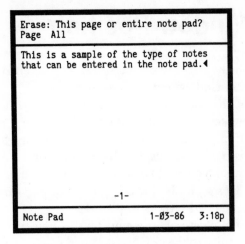

Fig. 15-2. Erase Submenu.

FILE
File Page—Stores text on the current page to a DOS file.
File All—Stores the text on all pages to a DOS file.

PRINT
Print Page—Sends the text on the screen to the printer.
Print All—Prints all the pages.

ABANDON
Exits the notepad without saving any changes made in the text.

QUIT
Exits the notepad. Spotlight automatically saves any data.

Spotlight uses a default file called NOTEPAD.DAT.

15.5.   How the Data Is Saved

The notepad creates a DOS text file in ASCII format. The file is always a four-kilobyte file. Any text that is not filled with typing is stored as blank spaces. The file, therefore, is padded with blanks. The notepad does not insert carriage returns at the end of lines that were wrapped around.

The notepad is limited. It can create files, but it cannot reload files after they have been saved except for the default file NOTEPAD.DAT.

[Using DOS, you can change the name of an existing file to NOTEPAD.DAT. When Spotlight loads, it will use that file.]

15.6. Help

In any of the Spotlight applications, pressing the [F1] key displays the help window.

15.7. Help Window

The help window displays text that explains the commands and functions of the various elements of Spotlight. The QUIT command returns you to the function with which you were working.

15.8. Calculator

The calculator emulates the operation of a pocket calculator. It will perform addition, subtraction, multiplication, and division. It also operates with a percentage key and a one-number memory. The calculator can also store a constant.

The calculator can be accessed by entering **[Shift Alt c]**

The calculator uses the numeric keypad keys and the following special keys:

<Backspace>	= CE/CA Clear Entry/Clear All
[	= M − Memory Subtract
]	= M + Memory Add
'	= MR/C Memory Recall/Clear
`	= % Percent
<return>	= Equals

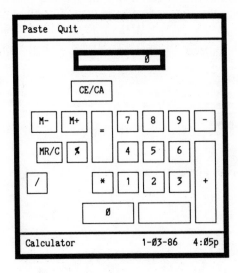

Fig 15-3. Calculator Display.

15.9.   Calculator Menu

The calculator menu has only two commands:

PASTE. The Paste command transfers the number currently in the calculator
display window to the application you are currently working with. When Paste
is used, the calculator display is terminated and the number is immediately
entered at the position of the cursor in the application you are working with.
(Note that the next time you use the calculator all previous entries will be
forgotten.)

QUIT. Exit calculator. This also clears the calculator of all data.

15.10.   The Appointment Calendar

The appointment calendar is one of the more sophisticated of Spotlight's
applications and is used just like an appointment book.

Use **[Shift Alt a]** to display the appointment calendar.

```
Calendar  Weekly  Today  Insert  Delete  Recall
Alarm  Note  Options  MkWkly  Print  File  Quit

              Friday, January 3, 1986


         6:00a
         7:00
         8:00
         9:00
        10:00
        11:00
        12:00p
         1:00
         2:00
         3:00
         4:00
         5:00
         6:00
         7:00
         8:00

Appointment Book              1-03-86    4:21p
```

Fig. 15-4. The Appointment Book.

The appointment calendar displays the appointment page for today, based on the system's date. The cursor also moves to the hour closest to the hour of the day indicated by the system's time.

For each item on the calendar display, you can enter a 44-character note (for example, a sales meeting).

The calendar display can be moved by the following keys:

[Pg Up]   Next day.
[Pg Dn]   Previous day.
[Home]   First appointment, current day.
[End]   Last appointment, current day.

15.11. Appointment Calendar Commands

The appointment calendar has a variety of commands governing a number of facilities that make it useful.

```
┌─────────────────────────────────────────────────┐
│ Calendar  Weekly  Today  Insert  Delete  Recall  │
│ Alarm  Note  Options  MkWkly  Print  File  Quit  │
├─────────────────────────────────────────────────┤
│              Friday, January 3, 1986             │
│                                                  │
│         ───────────────────────────────────      │
│        5:00a                                     │
│        6:00                                      │
│        7:00                                      │
│        8:00                                      │
│        9:00                                      │
│       10:00                                      │
│       11:00                                      │
│       12:00p                                     │
│        1:00                                      │
│        2:00                                      │
│        3:00                                      │
│        4:00   Sales Meeting 4:15, Room 217       │
│        5:00                                      │
│        6:00                                      │
│        7:00                                      │
├─────────────────────────────────────────────────┤
│ Appointment Book            1-03-86    4:29p     │
└─────────────────────────────────────────────────┘
```

Fig. 15-5. Meeting Listed on Calendar.

```
┌─────────────────────────────────────────────────┐
│ View  Weekly  Today  Discard  Quit               │
├─────────────────────────────────────────────────┤
│                   S   M   T   W   T   F   S      │
│        1985  December  8   9  10  11  12  13  14 │
│                   15  16  17  18  19  20  21     │
│                   22  23  24  25  26  27  28     │
│                   29  30  31                     │
│                                1   2 ▶ 3◀  4     │
│                   5   6   7   8   9  10  11      │
│        1986  January  12  13  14  15  16  17  18 │
│                   19  20  21  22  23  24  25     │
│                   26  27  28  29  30  31         │
│                                            1     │
│                   2   3   4   5   6   7   8      │
│        1986  February  9  10  11  12  13  14  15 │
│                   16  17  18  19  20  21  22     │
│                   23  24  25  26  27  28         │
│                                            1     │
│                   2   3   4   5   6   7   8      │
│        1986  March  9  10  11  12  13  14  15    │
├─────────────────────────────────────────────────┤
│ Appointment Book            1-03-86    4:36p     │
└─────────────────────────────────────────────────┘
```

Fig. 15-6. Calendar View.

- CALENDAR. This command displays a generalized calendar view. Today's date is highlighted. The arrow keys will move to different days. The [Pg Up] and [Pg Dn] keys will move the cursor one month forward or backwards.

  When you have selected a date, you can return to the appointment calendar view by entering **<Esc> <return>**

- CALENDAR DISCARD. This command is used to purge all appointments entered into the calendar before a specified date, i.e., the date where the cursor is located when in the calendar display mode.

- TODAY. The Today command works in the appointment calendar and calendar displays. It returns your cursor to today's date immediately.

- WEEKLY. This is one of the most powerful commands in the appointment calendar. The Weekly command allows you to make a single entry that will repeat each week. Suppose that you have scheduled a sales meeting every Friday at 11:00. Instead of marking the meeting each Friday, you could create a weekly entry by entering **<Esc> w**

  The weekly meeting calendar appears.

```
View  Calendar  Today  Insert  Delete  Recall
Alarm  Quit

  Sunday

  Monday

  Tuesday

  Wednesday

  Thursday

  Friday

  Saturday



Appointment Book              1-03-86    5:13p
```

Fig 15-7. Weekly Meeting Display.

Move the cursor to the line for Friday. To enter a weekly appointment, use the Insert command. Enter

\<Esc>
i
11:00
\<return>
Sales Meeting Conference Room \<return>

Now you have entered not just one meeting but a meeting for every Friday on the calendar. To check, return to the calender mode and display a Friday. You will see the meeting already entered. Note the character on the left side. This indicates that this entry is a weekly entry.

```
Calendar  Weekly  Today  Insert  Delete  Recall
Alarm  Note  Options  MkWkly  Print  File  Quit

           Friday, January 10, 1986
_____

        6:00a
        7:00
        8:00
        9:00
       10:00
   T   11:00  Sales Meeting -Conference Room
       12:00p
        1:00
        2:00
        3:00
        4:00
        5:00
        6:00
        7:00
        8:00
_____
Appointment Book           1-03-86    5:19p
```

Fig 15-8. Weekly Entry.

- MKWKLY. This command is a special form of the weekly meeting command. It is used to convert a one-time meeting entry into a weekly meeting entry. To use this command, place the cursor on the entry for the meeting you wish to convert. Enter **\<Esc> m**

  The meeting is now a weekly meeting. Note that using the conversion technique differs from the Weekly command in that the meetings begin at the date where the conversion was used, not at today's date. This is an advantage if the weekly meetings are not scheduled to start until some months in the future.
- INSERT. The Insert command allows you to place into the appointment calendar a time that is not one of the specific times displayed. Suppose that on

January 8th you have a 1:45 P.M. appointment. You can insert that into the calendar for that day. Enter

<Esc>   (access menu)
i   (insert command)
1:45   (time of the meeting)
<return>

The calendar will now show the inserted appointment.

```
+----------------------------------------------------------+
| Calendar  Weekly  Today  Insert  Delete  Recall          |
| Alarm  Note  Options  MkWkly  Print  File  Quit          |
+----------------------------------------------------------+
|                Thursday, January 9, 1986                 |
|          _____          |
|                                                          |
|            7:00a                                         |
|            8:00                                          |
|            9:00                                          |
|           10:00                                          |
|           11:00                                          |
|           12:00p                                         |
|            1:00                                          |
|       T    1:45   Reminder                              |
|            2:00                                          |
|            3:00                                          |
|            4:00                                          |
|            5:00                                          |
|            6:00                                          |
|            7:00                                          |
|            8:00                                          |
+----------------------------------------------------------+
| Appointment Book              1-03-86    4:46p           |
+----------------------------------------------------------+
```

Fig 15-9. Appointment Inserted.

- DELETE. Removes inserted entries from a calendar.
- RECALL. Recall functions with DELETE. When a calendar appointment is deleted, the text of the appointment entry is not lost completely. It is stored in an area of the memory that can be recalled by using the RECALL command.

  The RECALL command is useful for moving the time of a meeting. This is done by using DELETE to take the entry out of one time slot. The cursor is positioned to another time and/or day. Then RECALL can be used to place the text into a new spot in the calendar. Note that the RECALL command buffer is only one deletion deep, i.e., only the last deletion can be recalled.
- ALARM. One of the most useful of the features provided by background utilities is the alarm feature. The alarm sounds at a specified time. When you make an entry in the appointment calendar, you can add an alarm to it. When the

time arrives, Spotlight will sound an alarm no matter what application you are working in.

Alarms are saved as part of the appointment calendar. Therefore, alarms can be entered for future days and times. Note that when you load the computer after turning it off, you need to run a special program provided with Spotlight called REFRESH. This program causes Spotlight to read the appointment calendar and reset any alarms that have been stored there.

You can also adjust the time at which the alarm rings. If you have an 11:00 meeting, you might enter the alarm as 11:00. If you wish to be reminded 15 minutes early, you can program Spotlight to sound the alarm at quarter to eleven.

- NOTE. The note command is used to place a special title at the top of the daily display. For example, you might want to mark down your spouse's birthday. Enter <**Esc**> **n**

Spotlight asks for the text of the note. Whatever you type is displayed at the top of the calendar.

```
┌─────────────────────────────────────────┐
│ Calendar  Weekly  Today  Insert  Delete  Recall │
│ Alarm  Note  Options  MkWkly  Print  File  Quit │
├─────────────────────────────────────────┤
│           Saturday, May 10, 1986          │
│             Carolyn's Birthday            │
│      ──────────────────────────────       │
│        6:00a                              │
│        7:00                               │
│        8:00                               │
│        9:00                               │
│       10:00                               │
│       11:00                               │
│       12:00p                              │
│        1:00                               │
│        2:00                               │
│        3:00                               │
│        4:00                               │
│        5:00                               │
│        6:00                               │
│        7:00                               │
│        8:00                               │
├─────────────────────────────────────────┤
│ Appointment Book          1-03-86   5:05p │
└─────────────────────────────────────────┘
```

Fig. 15-10. Daily Note.

- PRINT. Prints the contents of the days displayed to the printer. You can also enter a number that will print a number of days in advance. The default value is to print one day.
- FILE. File is really a special version of the PRINT command. The main difference is that FILE sends the calendar information to an ASCII text file. This

can be used by other programs that read standard DOS text files, such as word processing programs.

Note that FILE is not used to save the appointment calendar. That is done automatically when you QUIT.

- OPTIONS. The options menu allows you to select custom features for the appointment calendar:

  1) Meetings. The calendar display can be changed from hourly meetings, to meetings every 15 minutes or every half hour. You can choose 12-hour or 24-hour displays. The Appointment Only mode displays only those items for which appointments have been filled in.

  2) Alarm. The alarm can be set to ring ten minutes in advance of the scheduled meeting and sounds every minute thereafter.

  3) Printer. Used to enter printer customization codes, e.g., for compressed printing.

  4) Hour. Sets the first hour displayed at the top of each calendar page. The default is 6:00 A.M.

- QUIT. Exits the appointment calendar and automatically saves any changes.

15.12. Phone Book

Spotlight also offers a personalized phone book. If you have a modem you can actually use the phone list to dial numbers automatically.

The phone book can be called up by entering **[Shift Alt p]**

```
┌─────────────────────────────────────────────────────────┐
│ View-card  New· Delete  Goto  Search  File  Print        │
│ Alternate  Telephone  Quit                               │
├─────────────────────────────────────────────────────────┤
│ Kamrin, Terry    Drugs                   415-987-9476    │
│ La Fisk, Walter                          415-987-2727    │
│ Ornas, Eric    Computer Tech Support     415-876-3833    │
│ Robbins, Chet    Photo Finishing         415-425-2992    │
│                                                          │
│                                                          │
│                                                          │
├─────────────────────────────────────────────────────────┤
│ Phone Book                            1-Ø3-86    5:54p   │
└─────────────────────────────────────────────────────────┘
```

Fig. 15-11. Phone Book Display.

The phone book has two views. The *index view* is displayed when you call up the phone book. Each person in the phone book is listed as a single line in the table. You can see seven names at one time, but the phone list can contain 500 names. In addition, you can have up to 36 different phone lists.

The *card view* displays an entire file card of information about the person. This can contain the address and other pertinent data. To display a person's card, use the highlight to indicate the person you desire to display. Then enter **<Esc> v**

The card is displayed.

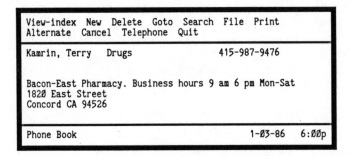

Fig. 15-12. Card View.

15.13.   Phone Book Features and Commands

The phone book has commands in three areas.

1) *List Maintenance*. These commands are used to add, remove, and update the data in the phone book.

   VIEW. Switches between CARD view and INDEX view. Editing can be performed only in the CARD view.
   NEW. Adds new cards to the file.
   DELETE. Removes a card from the file.
   ALTERNATE. Selects an alternate phone book. The phone books are named with a single letter or digit, i.e., A–Z and 0–9. The default is phone book 0.
   PRINT. Prints the contents of the highlighted card or all the cards to the line printer.

FILE. Creates a DOS text file out of the contents of the highlighted card or the entire card file. The file can then be accessed by programs that read DOS text files.

2) *Searching Commands*. These commands are used to locate a particular card.

GOTO. Performs a sequential search for specified characters. The search tries to match the first character in the search string with the first character in the card entry. For example, if you entered the letters *eric*, Spotlight would not find a match on the card for this person:

```
Ornas, Eric   Computer Tech Support   415-876-3833
```

GOTO tries to match the first characters on the line. Using "or" would have been correct. The case of the letters is not important.

SEARCH. This command searchs the entire card to find a match for the search criterion. This is called a "substring" search because if the search text appears anywhere in the text stored on the card, it will be tagged. Take care not to use too loose a criterion when performing this type of search. For example, "er" would match "Terry", "Eric", or "Walter", whichever came first.

3) *Auto-Dialing*. These commands are used to dial the number entered into the card. The features explained here are not covered in the Spotlight manual but can be found on the help screens for the program. The program assumes that you are using a Hayes or Hayes-compatible modem.

If you have a Hayes or Hayes-compatible modem, use the Telephone command to access an autodialer and call a number in your current phone list. Enter <**Esc**> **t** and the Telephone menu appears.

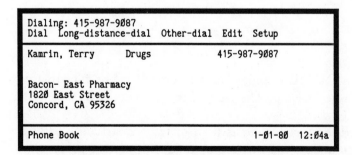

Fig. 15-13. Telephone Menu.

Spotlight will perform three types of dialing: regular, long distance, and other. What makes these modes different are the setups for each of the types.

When using a modem you need to send certain codes before sending the phone number. These codes are easily put in a setup string. You can save three setup strings in Spotlight.

15.14. The Filer

The Filer is a program that allows you to access DOS file management commands without having to leave the application in which you are working.

The Filer is accessed by entering **[Shift Alt f]**

```
┌─────────────────────────────────────────┐
│ View  Up Home  Sort  Other...  Delete    │
│ Copy  Rename  Mkdir  Paste  Quit         │
│                                          │
│                  A:\                      │
│ ANSI      SYS     1664  10-20-83  12:00p  │
│ ASSIGN    COM      896  10-20-83  12:00p  │
│ BACKUP    COM     3687  10-20-83  12:00p  │
│ CHKDSK    COM     6400  10-20-83  12:00p  │
│ COMMAND   COM    17792  10-20-83  12:00p  │
│ COMMANDS           83  12-28-85   2:18p  │
│ COMP      COM     2534  10-20-83  12:00p  │
│ CONFIG    SYS       22   1-01-80  12:00a  │
│ DISKCOMP  COM     2188  10-20-83  12:00p  │
│ DISKCOPY  COM     2576  10-20-83  12:00p  │
│ EDLIN     COM     4608  10-20-83  12:00p  │
│ EXAMPLE            262   1-01-80   7:15a  │
│ FDISK     COM     6369  10-20-83  12:00p  │
│ FIND      EXE     5888  10-20-83  12:00p  │
│                                          │
│ Filer                    1-01-80   1:00a  │
└─────────────────────────────────────────┘
```

Fig. 15-14. Filer Display.

The RENAME command is a command in the filer that would have made sense in DOS. The RENAME command will rename an existing directory.

The PASTE command is used to transfer a file or pathname to the application. This can save typing time and increase accuracy.

The filer commands are:

VIEW. Change displayed disk or directory.

UP. Move one level up, used with subdirectories only.

HOME. Return to the active directory.

SORT. Sort the display of files by date/time last modified, size, or extension. Note SORT does not change the order of the files stored by DOS. It only changes the display listing. To permanently change a directory, you need to use the Norton Utilities program DS (Directory Sort).

DELETE. Erase highlighted file or (empty) directory.

COPY. Make a copy of the highlighted file.

RENAME. Change the name of the highlighted file or directory.

PASTE. Quit Filer and type the highlighted filename or pathname into the application.

MKDIR. Create a new subdirectory in viewed directory.

OTHER. Includes these additional commands:

a) REREAD. Redisplays the contents of viewed directory. Updates the display after changes to the DOS directory.

b) INFO. Displays summary information about viewed directory, including bytes left on the disk.

c) CHDIR. Change DOS definition of current directory.

d) FORMAT. Format a diskette.

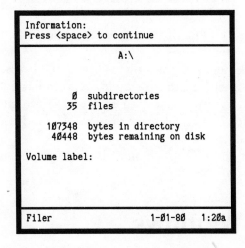

```
Information:
Press <space> to continue

                   A:\


        Ø  subdirectories
       35  files

   107348  bytes in directory
    40448  bytes remaining on disk

Volume label:




Filer                    1-Ø1-8Ø   1:2Øa
```

Fig. 15-15. Disk Info Display.

15.15.   Index Card File

The Index Card File is a card file program for storing indexed lists of information. The Index Card File is a general version of the Phone Book and uses most of the same commands. Use the Index Card File to keep a record of dates of business conversations, business expenses, or a list of things to do.

When you call up the Index Card File for the first time, you are on a blank index card with 12 lines.

Fig 15-16. Blank Card File.

Like the phone book, the card file will hold 500 cards. You can create 36 card files using single letters or numbers to indicate the file.

Once you have created some card entries, you can view the file as an alphabetized index or as single-card displays. The index displays the first line of each card.

The SEARCH and GOTO commands act the same as they do in the phone list program.

15.16.   Windows

Spotlight can layer its applications on the screen. This means that while using one Spotlight application you can call up another.

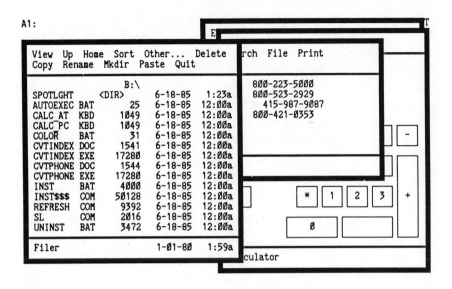

Fig. 15-17. Multi-layered Applications.

15.17.   Conclusion

The main problem that you have to resolve with Spotlight is copy protection. Version 1.1 allows you to copy a program to your hard disk, which is a vast improvement over previous versions. Spotlight actually compares quite well to other programs of this type. The weakest part of the system is the notepad, which is limited in functions and cannot read in old files.

The calculator is not very sophisticated, but it does what most users would need from a pocket calculator. One nice touch is the visual feedback given whenever you press a key (the key blinks).

The two outstanding features of Spotlight are the Calendar and the Filer. The Calendar programs in Sidekick and DeskSet are not nearly as developed and subtle as Spotlight's. The entry of weekly meetings and alarms is duplicated somewhat in DeskSet, but the Spotlight implementation is much more coherent and usable.

The Filer provides DOS access when your application does not. While DeskSet has some of these features, the Spotlight Filer is much more powerful and simple to use.

The phone book and index programs are well conceived.

Generally speaking, Spotlight provides a very good set of background utility functions. The 1-2-3-like menus provide a common command structure that makes learning the system rather easy.

If you need strong notepad functions, this program is not adequate. However, if DOS access and appointment calendars are important, this program is superior. Also note that Sidekick will run quite comfortably with Spotlight if you load Spotlight first. You can have the best of both for a little more cash.

16.

DeskSet

DeskSet is a group of programs that provide a number of background utilities. DeskSet differs from Sidekick in that each of the background functions is designed as a separate application. They can be used one at a time or in any combination that you wish.

The design of DeskSet allows you to load selected background functions that fit your needs and your computer memory. Remember that when working with background utilities, the ability to manage the amount of memory used is important. The memory must allow for the operating system, application, data, and background utility to be active, all at the same time.

16.1. What DeskSet Offers

DeskSet is comprised of the following programs. Each program is stored in a single file on the disk. It can be called up by a single keystroke. The programs are summarized below.

Program	Size of File	Memory Used	Key Command
POPCLIP.COM	14,449	16,000	[Altb]
POPALARM.EXE	14,573	14,000	[Alta]
POPANY.EXE	15,264	variable	[Alt F10]
POPCALC.EXE	16,619	18,500	[Altc]
POPDATE.EXE	31,360	31,000	[Altd]
POPDOS.EXE	21,632	21,000	[Altu]
POPFCALC.EXE	31,083	30,000	[Altf]
POPNOTE.EXE	24,392	25,000	[Altn]
POPVOICE.EXE	15,291	17,000	[Altv]
POPMODEM.EXE	29,440	30,000	[Altm]

Two other applications are supplied with DeskSet. These are not background utilities but actual programs. They are expanded versions of the pop-up telecommunications programs POPMODEM and POPVOICE. They are run from DOS like any other application.

VOICE.EXE	58,288
MODEM.EXE	65,936

As you can see, many of the programs duplicate functions found in other programs of this type, such as Sidekick and Spotlight. DeskSet also has some features that are unique to this program. DeskSet offers a sophisticated telecommunications program that will function both as a primary (foreground) program, or in a more limited version as a background utility.

The usual functions of calendar, notepad, and calculator are implemented in a different manner than in Sidekick. You will learn in detail in this section exactly what DeskSet has to offer.

16.2. Notepad

Notepad is a simple text program that allows you to enter notes into a text file while you are using other applications. The notepad is called up by entering **[Altn]**

The notepad can contain 100 lines of text, each line 35 characters in width. The window is restricted to the display size. However, you can change the position of the window on the screen by moving the display with the [Ctrl left arrow] or [Ctrl right arrow] combinations. The notepad has the usual editing commands for inserting and deleting text.

The window also displays a feature called the *menu bar*. The menu bar is located on the right edge of the window. It contains a listing of special commands that are used in the window.

Commands in the menu bar can be executed in one of two ways:

1. Press the function key.
2. Use the [+] and [−] keys on the numeric keypad to change the highlight in the menu bar. Then use [Ctrle] to execute the highlighted command.

The notepad has the following commands:

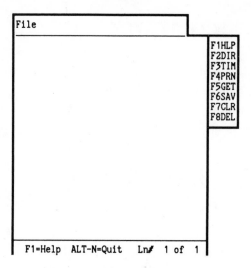

Fig. 16-1. Notepad Window.

[F1]—HLP—Help. The help command is noteworthy because, unlike Sidekick, all of the DeskSet applications load their help screens into memory. This means that the background application does not need to access a disk file in order to display help. This is an advantage for a floppy disk system, since help is not dependent upon the presence of any particular file. On the other hand, the help data takes up memory space. You will find that DeskSet's help screens are terse but useful.

[F2]—DIR—Directory. This command displays a directory of the all the notepad files on the disk. Notepad files are recognized by a PAD file extension.

[F3]—TIM—Time. This command displays the system's current time and date in the box at the bottom of the window. It does not place the time and date into the notepad text as is done in Sidekick.

[F4]—PRN—Print. This is a unique feature of DeskSet. It allows you to print the contents of the notepad without having to leave the notepad or your application. The Sidekick notepad cannot print.

[F5]—GET—Get a File. This command retrieves a notepad file from the disk.

[F6]—SAV—Save. This command saves the text in the notepad to a disk file. Notepad files are ASCII files.

[F7]—CLR—Clear. Clears the notepad of text. Sidekick does not have a command to do this. You can only clear the notepad in Sidekick by deleting the text or opening a new file.

[F8]—DEL—Delete File. This command deletes a file from the disk directly from the notepad.

16.3.   Calculators

DeskSet is supplied with two background calculators. One emulates the functions of a common pocket calculator. The other is a more complex program that provides a number of sophisticated functions for performing financial and statistical calculations.

16.4.   The DeskSet Pocket Calculator

This calculator is a simple calculator program. The calculator can perform addition, subtraction, multiplication, and division. It also contains a percent key. Like the other DeskSet applications, help is available for the calculator from data that is memory resident.

When the calculator is displayed, the keys on the numeric keypad are automatically placed into a number lock position.

The DeskSet calculator has some useful and interesting features:

1. Tape Simulation. As calculations are entered, DeskSet displays the inputs and outputs as a tape. This simulates the way a tape is produced by a printing calculator.

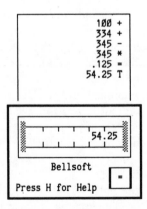

Fig. 16-2. Calculator Tape Display.

The current total always appears on the calculator display.

2. Printing. The normal way to display the tape is on the screen. However, the P command toggles the calculator in a printing mode. In this mode any data that is displayed on the screen is also sent to the printer. This enables you to get a printed copy of the data input and output from the calculator.

   The printing function can be turned off and on whenever you desire by pressing P. The P is a toggle command.

3. Memories. The calculator features a memory function. Numbers can be placed in the memory and recalled as part of calculations. DeskSet has not one but ten memory cells. Typing a number, 0–9, along with the memory commands selects one of the ten memory areas to work with.

4. Change Colors. If you have a color screen display you can change the color of the calculator display by entering [Ctrlc]. In Sidekick and Spotlight, color can be changed only through a special program that installs colors for all applications.

5. Feed number. The [Altf] command exits the calculator and returns you to the application which is running. In addition, the number currently displayed on the calculator is typed into the application at the current cursor position. This is the same technique as used in Spotlight.

   [Sidekick stores the number as a keystrokes macro in a selected key. The value is not fed to the application until you press the selected key. In DeskSet the feeding is immediate.]

6. The DeskSet calculator retains the value stored in it until it is cleared. The value remains even when you return to number your application. This is the same as Sidekick. Spotlight clears the calculator each time you return to your application.

16.5. The Financial Calculator

The Financial Calculator continues where the calculator ends, and contains all of its functions. It adds a number of special commands and functions that enable the user to perform intricate financial and statistical calculations.

Pressing "h" displays a large help panel.

Note that the help screen for the financial calculator remains displayed while you enter calculations.

In addition to the basic arithmetic operations found in the calculator, the financial calculator adds the following operations:

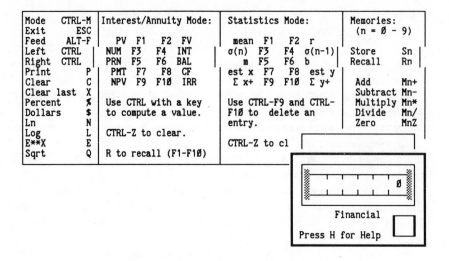

Fig. 16-3. Financial Calculator.

N—Natural logarithm of the displayed value.
L—Base 10 logarithm of the displayed value.
E—E raised to the power indicated by the displayed value
Q—The square root of the displayed value.

16.6.   Special Modes

The **[Ctrlm]** command toggles the financial calculator through a sequence of five modes. The first four of these modes are listed below. (The fifth mode is discussed later in this section.)

1. Normal. This mode performs the basic calculations, plus the exponential functions.
2. Interest
3. Annuity (Begin)
4. Annuity (End)

When the financial calculator is in any of the modes above, the following meanings are assigned to the function keys:

F1   Present Value
F2   Future Value
F3   Number of Periods
F4   Rate of Interest
F5   Principle Amount
F6   Balance
F7   Payment per Period
F8   Cash Flow
F9   Net Present Value
F10   Internal Rate of Return

[The assumption is made that the user possesses an understanding of the mathematical concepts inherent in financial calculations. These concepts are derived from the more general problem of finding the sum of a geometric series. For users not familiar with these concepts, an explanation is beyond the scope of this book. A full discussion of the concepts can be found in my book *Understanding and Using Multiplan* (Bowie, MD: Brady Communications Company, 1985).]

In any given situation, some of the values are known and others need to be calculated. The purpose of the function keys is to store the given values in a calculation. Hold down the [Ctrl] and press the function key that represents the value you want to find. The advantage of the financial calculator is that the relationship between the items is known to the calculator.

For example, suppose that you wanted to find out what the monthly payment would be on a loan. You would need to load three values into the function key registers: the present value of the money you wanted to borrow, the monthly rate of interest, and the number of payments that will be made.

First you would store the amount you want to borrow in F1. Enter **3500 [F1]**

Then the interest rate. Enter **18.5/12 [F4]**

Note that the monthly interest was the annual rate, 18.5%, divided by 12. Finally, enter the number of payments to be made: **12*2 [F3]**

This means 12 payments a year for two years. Since F7 is the monthly payment, to find the monthly payment, enter **[Ctrl F7]**

The financial calculator displays the answer, $162.72, in the display window and on the tape.

16.6.1   Statistical Mode

In this mode the meanings of the function keys change to the following:

F1   arithmetic mean
F2   coefficient of correlation
F3   number of elements
F4   degree of freedom
F5   slope
F6 y intercept
F7   estimated x value
F8   estimated y value
F9   sum of x
F10   sum of y

[The assumption is made that the user possesses an understanding of the statistical concepts inherent in the listed functions. Again, a discussion of the concepts is beyond the scope of this book. For users not familiar with these concepts please refer to *Understanding and Using Multiplan* as mentioned above.]

The calculator functions a bit differently in this mode than in the financial modes. The keys used most often are F9 and F10. They are used to enter a list of values. The F9 key adds values to the X group (independent) and the F10 key adds values to the Y group (dependent).

When the variables have been entered, the function keys can be used to find statistical values. Pressing F2 calculates the r value that shows how closely the groups are mathematically related. F5 and F6 calculate the values m and b to complete the slope intercept formula $y = mx + b$.

[The financial calculator has a user-definable invocation key. Normally the financial calculator is accessed by entering [Altx]. However, this can be changed by loading the program with a special parameter. Enter **popfcalc I = 46 < return >**

This will make the invocation key [Altc]. The number 46 is the number of the [Altc] combination in the extended character codes available on the IBM PC. Note the numbers are *not* the ASCII codes. They are an additional coding system provided by DOS. A listing can be found in the Financial Calculator manual.]

16.7.   Date Calendar

The Date Calendar is a pop-up desk calendar. The calendar is called up by entering **[Altd]**

```
      Dec 1985        |      Jan 1986       |      Feb 1986       |F1HLP
  S  M  T  W  T  F  S | S  M  T  W  T  F  S | S  M  T  W  T  F  S |F2MON
                      |                     |                     |F3GET
  1  2  3  4  5  6  7 |          1  2  3  4 |                   1 |F4SAV
  8  9 10 11 12 13 14 | 5  6  7  8  9 10 11 | 2  3  4  5  6  7  8 |F5SET
 15 16 17 18 19 20 21 |12 13 14 15 16 17 18 | 9 10 11 12 13 14 15 |F6PRN
 22 23 24 25 26 27 28 |19 20 21 22 23 24 25 |16 17 18 19 20 21 22 |
 29 30 31             |26 27 28 29 30 31    |23 24 25 26 27 28    |
                      |                     |                     |
Month=F2   Files=F3,F4    Set=F5    Print=F6  |        F1=Help ESC=Exit
```

Fig. 16-4. Calendar Display.

The calendar initially displays a three-month period, with the current month in the center. Today's date appears as a flashing number. In addition, any special dates, such as holidays, are marked in reverse video.

The arrow keys will change the calendar display. The left and right arrows will move the calendar backwards or forwards a month. The up and down arrows will move the calendar backwards or forwards a year.

There are six special commands listed in the menu bar on the right side of the display.

- [F1]—Help. This command displays the memory-resident help screen.
- [F2]—Month. Pressing [F2] changes the screen display so that the month in the center of the display is expanded.

			Jan 1986			
Sun	Mon	Tue	Wed	Thu	Fri	Sat
			1 New Years	2	3	4
5	6	7	8	9	10	11
12	13	14	15 ML King BD	16	17 Meeting 4	18
19	20	21	22	23	24	25
26	27	28	29	30	31	

Fig. 16-5. Full Month Display.

In this mode it is possible to see the messages entered for individual dates. The messages are ten characters long and appear within the box for each date.

If a date contains more messages than can be displayed in the box, pressing *m* reveals those messages. The arrow keys still change the display one month or year. You can return to the original display by pressing <**Esc**>

- [F3] and [F4]—See below.
- [F5]—Set Messages. One of the primary reasons for using the calendar is to input messages of your own. The [F5] key allows you to make entries into the calendar. The entries come in two forms:

List. These are messages that are entered for one specific date at a time. Entering [F5] L displays the screen that allows you to enter a message for a particular date.

The screen shows the entry for Passover supplied with the program. To create a new entry, enter **[Ins]**

You can make three entries for each message. The first is a ten-character entry that is the text of the message. The next is the date in which that message will appear. You can make a third entry, which is a second date where the same message will appear. The second date is optional.

In addition to adding new messages, the [Pg Up] and [Pg Dn] keys will display the existing messages. They can be changed or removed if you do not want them to appear on the calendar.

DeskSet is supplied with dates for Passover, Easter, Mother's Day, Memorial Day, Father's Day, Labor Day, Yom Kippur, Thanksgiving, Hanukkah, Election Day, and Rosh Hashana.

```
┌──────────────────────┬─────────────────┬───────────────────────┐
│ Set Calendar Date    │ 03/29/83 04/17/84│      Jan 1986         │
│                      │ 04/06/85 04/24/86│  S  M  T  W  T  F  S   │
│                      │ 04/14/87 04/02/88│                       │
│ Message [Passover  ] │ 04/20/89 04/10/90│              1  2  3  4│
│                      │ 03/30/91 04/18/92│  5  6  7  8  9 10 11   │
│ 1st Date 04/19/81    │ 04/06/93 03/27/94│ 12 13 14 15 16 17 18  │
│                      │ 04/15/95 04/04/96│ 19 20 21 22 23 24 25  │
│ 2nd Date 04/08/82    │ 04/22/97 04/11/98│ 26 27 28 29 30 31     │
│                      │ 04/01/99   /  /  │                       │
├──────────────────────┴─────────────────┴──────────┬────────────┤
│ Fields=TAB,BACKTAB  Lists=PgUp,PgDn,INS,DEL,END    │F1=Help ESC=Exit│
└────────────────────────────────────────────────────┴────────────┘
```

Fig. 16-6. List Message Entry.

Cycle. These are messages that are entered for a repeating cycle of dates, for example, a spouse's birthday.

Enter **[F5]** **C** to display the cycle entry screen.

```
┌─────────────────────────┬──────────────────────┬──────────────────────┐
│ Set Calendar Cycle      │      Jan 1986        │      Feb 1986        │
│                         │ S  M  T  W  T  F  S  │ S  M  T  W  T  F  S  │
├─────────────────────────┤                      │                      │
│ Message [New Years ]    │          1  2  3  4  │                   1  │
│                         │  5  6  7  8  9 10 11 │  2  3  4  5  6  7  8 │
│ Start Date 01/01/00     │ 12 13 14 15 16 17 18 │  9 10 11 12 13 14 15 │
│                         │ 19 20 21 22 23 24 25 │ 16 17 18 19 20 21 22 │
│    Cycle   1y           │ 26 27 28 29 30 31    │ 23 24 25 26 27 28    │
├─────────────────────────┴──────────────────────┴──────┬──────────┬────┤
│ Fields=TAB,BACKTAB  Cycles=PgUp,PgDn,INS,DEL           │ F1=Help  │ ESC=Exit │
└───────────────────────────────────────────────────────┴──────────┴────┘
```

Fig. 16-7. Cycle Entry Screen.

The display shows the entry for New Year's Day. To create a new cycle, enter **[Ins]**

To create a cycle message you must enter three items. The first is the ten-character message to be displayed on the date. Next is the first date on the calendar for which the message should appear. The last item is a code that tells DeskSet what type of cycle you want to enter.

A cycle code consists of two items. The first is a one- or two-digit number. The number represents the frequency of the message in a given cycle.

The second is a letter which represents a type of cycle. DeskSet recognizes:

y = yearly
q = quarterly
m = monthly
w = weekly
d = daily

For example, if you enter the code "1w", the cycle would repeat the message once a week starting with the date specified in the Start Date area. If you enter "2w", this tells DeskSet to repeat the message once every two weeks. Entering a code "3d" would tell DeskSet to repeat the message once every third day.

If you don't enter a number, DeskSet assumes you want the number 1. This setup gives you a remarkable flexibility in entering cyclic reminders.

● The [F3] (Get Message) and [F4] (Message) Files—These two commands are listed here because they are related to the message entered into a calendar. The messages are not part of the POPDATE.COM program. Rather, they are stored in a file called DATES.DAT. Each time the calendar program is loaded, it attempts to load the DATES file.

[When POPDATE is loaded, it's assumed that the DATES.DAT file is stored in the active directory and disk. If not, the program will display a message DATES.DAT file not read. This means that the calendar will operate without any messages.

To correct the situation, change the directory and/or disk to the correct one and use the [F3] command to load the file.]

The [F4] key is used to save any changes or additions made to the calendar. Remember that if you make changes they must be saved in the DATES.DAT file if they are to appear when you load the calendar the next time. Otherwise they will be lost when the computer is turned off.

[You can create and use other calendar files besides DATES.DAT. The trick is to use DOS to create a copy of the DATES.DAT file. Then the [F3] command loads that file into the memory.]

- [F6]—Print. DeskSet prints out calendars for requested dates. There are three options to be filled in when printing.

First you must enter the beginning and ending months to be printed. The DETAILS option controls the type of printing to be done. If DETAILS is "n" then a 12-month calendar is printed on each page for each year specified. If DETAILS is "y" then each page contains an expanded monthly display that includes messages.

Entering the [Altf] Feed Date command exits the date calendar and feeds the current date into the application. For example, if the system's date is 01/10/86, then [Altf] will feed January 10, 1986 to the application. Note Desk-Set only feeds the system's date.

16.8.   Alarms

The POPALARM program creates a background program that functions as an alarm clock. To display the Alarm menu, enter **[Alta]**

The alarm has six command functions:

[F1]—Help.
[F2]—Optional Time Display. This command allows you to set a time display mode that appears in whatever application you are working. The time appears in the upper left corner of the screen.

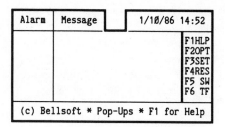

Fig. 16-8. The Alarm Menu.

```
┌──────────┬──────────┬──┬──────────────────┐
│ Alarm    │ Message  │  │ 1/10/86 14:52    │
├──────────┴──────────┴──┴─────────────┬────┤
│                                      │F1HLP│
│                                      │F2OPT│
│                                      │F3SET│
│                                      │F4RES│
│                                      │F5 SW│
│                                      │F6 TF│
├──────────────────────────────────────────┤
│ (c) Bellsoft * Pop-Ups * F1 for Help     │
└──────────────────────────────────────────┘
```

```
┌────────────────┬───┬──────────────────┐
│ Option setting │ F │ 1/10/86 15:05    │
├────────────────┴───┴─────────────┬────┤
│        Display the time:  M      │F1HLP│
│                                  │F2OPT│
│        N - Never                 │F3SET│
│        M - Each minute           │F4RES│
│        H - Each hour             │F5 SW│
│        C - Constantly            │F6 TF│
├──────────────────────────────────────┤
│ Press selection or RETURN or ESC     │
└──────────────────────────────────────┘
```

Fig. 16-9. Time Display Options.

There are four options for time display:

N—never, no time display during the application.
M—display the time every minute. The time appears on the screen for five seconds and disappears.
H—display the time once every hour.
C—display a running clock constantly.

In addition you can choose an audio reminder of each hour. Choosing "h" sounds a tone each hour, while "c" creates a modified tone that sounds like a chime. You can also change the system's date and time.

[F3]—Set Alarms. This option creates an alarm that sounds at a specified time. There are two parts to the alarm. First is the time the alarm should be sounded; then a message can be added. The message reminds you of the reason for which the alarm was sounded.

[Time is entered on a 24-hour clock.]

You can specify six active alarms at one time. DeskSet will order the alarms consecutively. When the time arrives, DeskSet will automatically pop up the Alarm menu and sound a series of tones.

[F4]—Reset. This option clears out existing alarms.

[F5]—Stopwatch. This option allows you to time events as if you have a stop watch. Pressing [F5] followed by the <space bar> produces a stopwatch display.

```
┌──────────────────────┬─────────────────────┐
│   Stopwatch          │  1/10/86  15:28      │
├─────────┬──────────┬──────────┬─────────────┤
│  Start  │   Stop   │ Elapsed  │F1HLP        │
│         │          │          │F2OPT        │
│         │          │          │F3SET        │
│         │          │          │F4RES        │
│00:00:00 │00:00:25  │00:00:25.7│F5  SW       │
│00:00:00 │00:00:31  │          │F6  TF       │
├─────────┴──────────┴──────────┴─────────────┤
│ SPACE=lap  C=Clear  or  RETURN  or  ESC     │
└─────────────────────────────────────────────┘
```

Fig. 16-10. Stop Watch Display.

Pressing <space> again creates a *lap* display. A lap display is the intermediate time elapsed. You can display six laps at any one time.

[F6]—Time Feed. This feature is similar to the read time delay feature found in keyboard macro programs. It allows you to specify a DOS command sequence that will execute at a specified time. This allows you to execute a command, such as running a modem program, when you are away from the computer.

16.9. Batch Processing

The alarm program does not maintain settings from session to session. However, you can load a predefined set of alarms by creating a DOS text file with a text editor or word processing program. For example, a text file called SETTINGS.ALR might contain:

a = 10:00 "staff meeting"
a = 13:15 "call home"

The file will automatically set the two alarms if you load the alarm program followed by a parameter. For example,

popalarm @settings.alr ‹return›

16.10.   DOS Access

The POPDOS program is designed to allow access to DOS commands even though you are working in an application. Entering **[Altu]** will display the DOS window.

There are ten commands in the menu bar for DOS:

[F1]—Help.
[F2]—Change Directory. This command allows you to enter a new directory for display.
[F3]—Directory. The directory command lists current directory files in the display window. You can enter a DOS wildcard specification to select particular files for display.

```
┌──────────────────────────────────┐
│ Dir  B:\                          │
│                              ┌────┴─────┐
│  Dir of a:*.*                │F1HELP    │
│ AUTOEXEC BAT     128   4-29-85   7:49a│F2CD      │
│ CHKDSK   COM    6400   4-29-85   7:49a│F3DIR     │
│ COMMAND  COM   17792  10-20-83  12:00p│F4XDIR    │
│ CORRSTAR OVR   59392   4-29-85   7:50a│F5DEL     │
│ FORMAT   COM    6912   4-29-85   7:50a│F6COPY    │
│ FORMAT   FMT     384   6-18-85  11:30a│F7REN     │
│ INTERNAL DCT   35584   4-29-85   7:50a│F8TYPE    │
│ JOHN     APP      31  11-07-85   1:31a│F9PRNT    │
│ MAILMRGE OVR   13568   4-29-85   7:50a│FØCHKD    │
│ STARINDX COM    1920   4-29-85   7:50a└──────────┘
│ STARINDX OVR   40192   4-29-85   7:50a│
│ WC       EXE   12288   4-29-85   7:50a│
│ WS       COM   45056   4-29-85   7:50a│
│ WSMSGS   OVR   29056   4-29-85   7:50a│
│ WSOVLY1  OVR   41216   4-29-85   7:50a│
│                                       │
│ Press F1 for help.                    │
└───────────────────────────────────────┘
```

Fig. 16-11. DOS Directory Displayed in Window.

[F4]—Extended Directory. This command is a variation on the Directory command. It is of use mainly with disks that contain text or data files. It displays the filename and the first 28 bytes of the file. If the file is a binary program file, the display is generally meaningless. However, with text files the display is useful to identify the contents of the file.

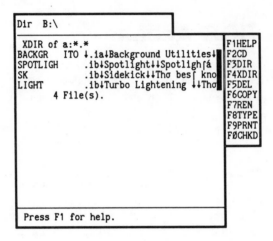

Fig. 16-12. Extended Directory Display.

[F5]—Delete. This command allows you to remove files from the disk.

[F6]—Copy. This command duplicates the DOS command COPY. It allows you to transfer data to different disks or directories.

[F7]—Rename. This command allows you to change the name of data files. Note that you cannot change the names of directories.

[Xtree and Spotlight allow you to change the names of directories, which cannot be performed by DOS.]

[F8]—Type. Displays the contents of a file on the screen.

[F9]—Print Operations. This command is not a simple duplication of DOS commands. In fact, it contains some unique features. Using Print displays a submenu of commands:

1. [F2]—File. This command prints the contents of a file.
2. [F3]—Typewriter. This is a special command that allows you to use your printer as a typewriter. Enter [F3] to display a typewriter emulation screen. Any characters that you type will be sent to the printer immediately.

[Dot matrix printers will not print a line until you have pressed <return>. Daisy wheel printers will usually type each character as it is entered.]

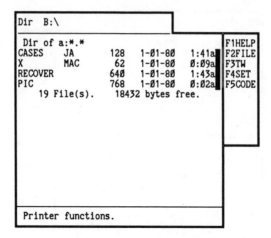

Fig. 16-13. Print Submenu.

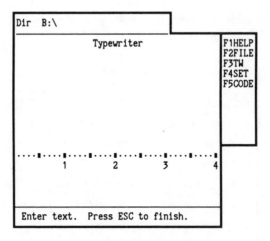

Fig. 16-14. Typewriter Mode.

The text you type is also displayed on the screen. The screen display will scroll to the right if you type a line that is wider than the window.

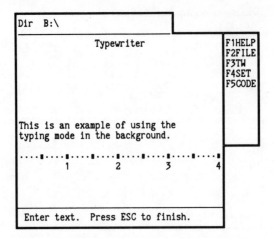

Fig. 16-15. Text Entered into Typewriter.

3. [F4]—Set Printer Attributes. This option displays a number of settings that can be used to change the print characteristics on the IBM graphics printer.

   The commands will also work with all Epson and Epson-compatible printers.

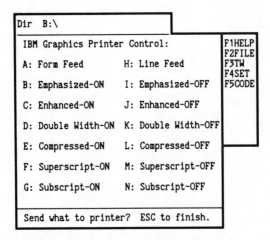

Fig. 16-16. Printer Control Options.

By pressing the letters you can set up compressed print, double width, or other print combinations. The settings will remain in the printer so that the application you are working with prints with those characteristics. Option A,

Form Feed, issues a command to the printer to feed the remainder of the page (ASCII code 12).

[Some programs, such as WordStar, send an *initialization* string before each printing. The initialization will clear all existing print characteristics from the printer, defeating the purpose of the printer control code. Thus you cannot use these commands to affect printing in programs like WordStar.

On the other hand, many programs, e.g., Lotus 1-2-3, dBASE III, do not send such strings. The printer control codes will work with these programs.]

4. [F5]—Control Codes. This option is useful if you have a printer that does not respond to the same control codes as does an IBM graphics or Epson dot printer. The control codes that work with your printer are described in one fashion or another in your printer manual.

The entry of codes must be done by using the ASCII decimal values for the codes that must be sent. For example, suppose that you are using a daisy wheel printer. The manual tells you that the code for bold print is <Esc> "E" 1. You need to use an ASCII table to find the decimal value of those characters.

[Sidekick provides an ASCII table as part of its background functions.]

The values in question are

<Esc>	027
E	069
1	001

Then you would enter the numbers in the display area:

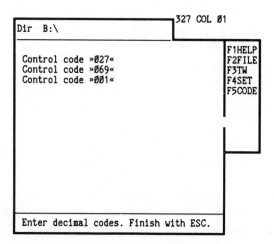

Fig. 16-17. Codes Entered.

Pressing <Esc> sends the sequence to the printer.

The Print commands in DeskSet are very helpful in getting outputs the way you want them when you want them.

[F10]—Check Memory and Disk. Using this command displays the same information as a CHKDSK command. However, with DeskSet you do not need to have the DOS file CHKDSK.COM present in order to get this information.

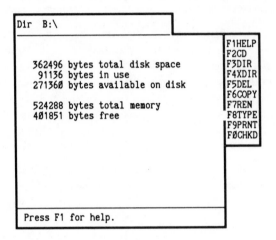

Fig. 16-18. Disk and Memory Check.

[Altf] can be used to feed the current time and date into the active application. The format is mm/dd/yy hh:mm.

16.11. Clipboard

The Clipboard is used to capture screen displays and feed this text to applications. The Clipboard allows you to cut and paste data from one application to another.

[The Clipboard can be used only for text information. Screen displays that are created by high-resolution bit-mapped graphics cannot be handled by the Clipboard or Sidekick's notepad. Only the Clipboard function in Microsoft Windows can perform this function.]

The Clipboard is activated by entering **[Altb]**

When this is done, the screen display presented by the application you are working with is cleared. The Clipboard presents a blank screen with the exception of the line at the bottom of the screen.

To transfer data into the Clipboard you use the **[F3]** command. When you enter [F3] the screen displayed by the application returns, with the exception of the bottom line.

[You can capture text from all but the last line on the screen with the Clipboard.]

The cursor now is displayed as a block on the screen.

[The cursor that is used by your application is temporarily disabled. The Clipboard cursor is independent of the cursor used by your application. After you leave the Clipboard your cursor position in your application will be as before.]

To capture screen data you must move your cursor to the upper left-hand corner of the area you want to clip. To begin a block, press **[F5]**

Moving the cursor now will highlight a rectangular area. The highlight shows the area to be clipped. When the area is completely covered, enter **[F6]**

You return to the Clipboard display. The block appears as an outline. You can change the relative position of the block within the Clipboard display with the arrow keys. When you are satisfied with the position, entering **[Ctrli]** places the text into the Clipboard.

Exiting the clipboard with **<Esc>** returns you to your application. The text remains stored in the memory of the computer until you turn your computer off or perform a warm boot.

You can clip several items from the screen into the Clipboard as long as the size of the items can fit into a single 80-column by 24-line display.

16.12. Pasting Data from the Clipboard

Once you have placed the data into the Clipboard, you can then transfer all or part of the text to an application. Because the text can be stored indefinitely, you can change applications, disks, files, etc. When you have reached a point where you want to insert the text in the Clipboard into the application you have run, you can recall the display by entering [Altb] once again.

You can decide to transfer all or part of the display. The [F5] and [F6] commands allow you to specify a block of text within the Clipboard display, just as they did with the text from the application.

The [Altf] command feeds the text to the application. After you enter [Altf], DeskSet allows you to specify the character with which the lines will be ended.

This is a very useful feature. In most cases a <return> is the proper character. Suppose, however, that you were transferring a column of numbers into a spreadsheet program. Lotus 1-2-3 requires you to terminate the entry with a directional arrow, or else all the numbers will be entered in the same cell.

The DeskSet option allows you to compensate for the needs of the program into which the data is being fed. Feeding data does not remove the data from the Clipboard. Therefore, you can use the Clipboard to feed the data repeatedly into the same or different applications.

Note that the Clipboard cannot directly save its contents to a disk file. You must use some application, such as the EDLIN text editor, to capture the data if you want it saved.

Also note the fact that the Clipboard cannot directly print its contents. This can be done only through an application.

16.13. Voice and Modem

These two programs are used to access your modem directly from an application. The Voice program, [Altv], is primarily an autodialing program. It is used to dial numbers through your modem. It stores three phone numbers and the proper modem codes to dial those numbers.

Modem, [Altm], is a broader telecommunications program that can be used for accessing remote data bases. It can also be used to dial and access a remote source. The size of the window can be expanded to allow you to view more dialog. You can also specify a file into which data received can be downloaded.

As with other DeskSet applications, the modem program can be used to feed information received into the application that is currently running.

16.14. PopAny

The PopAny program is more general than the other programs in DeskSet. Memory sections are allocated to run a program without having to download the application you are working in.

For example, the notepad is a simple program. You might feel the need to run a full word processing program like WordStar in the middle of some other application. The key to using PopAny is to allocate enough memory space for the application or applications you want to run. For example, dBASE II and WordStar will run in 128 kilobytes of memory. To create a PopAny command that will run those programs, enter **popany <return>**

The program will ask you for the amount of memory you want to reserve for a PopAny application. Enter **128 <return>**

Now you can proceed to perform the application you want to work with, e.g., Lotus 1-2-3.

[When PopAny is used, the amount of memory available to other applications is reduced by the amount of memory allocated to PopAny, even if you never use PopAny to load an application. Therefore there will be less memory available to programs like 1-2-3.]

When you want to run WordStar or dBASE II, you do not need to exit 1-2-3. Rather you can simply enter **[Alt F10]**

PopAny displays a modified DOS prompt.

[When PopAny is invoked it reloads the DOS command interpreter stored in the file COMMAND.COM in the drive and directory from which it was originally loaded when the computer was booted. If you have removed the disk with the COMMAND.COM file from that drive, you will not be able to continue.

PopAny will display the message Insert COMMAND.COM in drive A. Place a disk with the correct version of COMMAND.COM on it into the drive and press any key.]

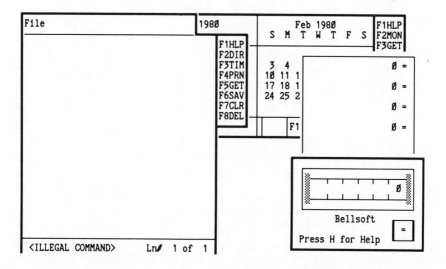

Fig. 16-19. Multiple Windows in DeskSet.

You can now start a new application. For example, enter **ws<return>**

When you exit the application running in PopAny, the computer will immediately return to the application that was run originally from DOS.

PopAny gives you the ability to make almost any application a background application.

16.15.   Conclusion

DeskSet offers a variety of features. Its main difference from Spotlight and Sidekick is its concept of loading each application separately. This provides users with a greater degree of flexibility.

Like the other, more unified background programs, DeskSet can be used with multiple windows open.

Chapter 18 contains a comparison of the features found in the three background utility programs discussed in Part 4.

17.

Turbo Lightning

Turbo Lightning is an exciting productivity tool that contains two types of programs that work together, a spelling correction program and a synonym finder. The combination of these two programs creates an environment in which a writer can be much more productive.

17.1. Vital Statistics

Turbo Lightning comes supplied on three disks:

1) *System Disk.* There are nine files that take up 357,376 bytes of disk space.

LIGHT.COM	34,672
LIGHT.HLP	19,584
LIGHT.TRN	1,152
FLP-DISK.DIC	108,544
FLP-THES.DIC	161,792
AUXI.DIC	3
RAM1.DIC	16,384
READ.ME	10,524
README.COM	427

LIGHT.COM is the main Turbo Lightning program. This file is used to load the Turbo Lightning system. Once the program has been loaded the file need not be available. If you have a floppy disk system, you might want to change disks following the loading of the program.

461

LIGHT.HLP contains the Turbo Lightning help file, and is optional. Turbo Lightning uses the file only when you request help. It is not stored in memory.

LIGHT.TRN contains the dictionary of words with transposed letters.

FLP-DISK.DIC is the smaller version of the dictionary for floppy disk systems. This file is not used with hard disk systems.

FLP-THES.DIC is the thesaurus for floppy disk systems. This file is not used with hard disk systems.

AUXI.DIC contains the auxiliary dictionary. The dictionary is empty initially, but will hold words that you wish to add. The maximum size for an auxiliary dictionary is 2,000 characters, or about 300 words. You can create any number of auxiliary dictionaries. These files are ASCII text files.

RAM1.DIC contains the 6,000-word RAM spelling dictionary. Turbo Lightning loads this dictionary of the most commonly misspelled words into the memory of the computer.

READ.ME contains information not included in the manual.

README.COM is a program that displays the READ.ME text.

[README.COM performs a similar function to TYPE | MORE. You can use README with any text file. Simply enter README followed by the name of the file you want displayed and the program will display your file instead of the READ.ME file.]

2) *Install and Supplemental Files Disk.* This disk contains eight files that occupy 135,168 bytes of disk space.

RAM2.DIC	29,184
RAM3.DIC	38,912
INSTALLH.BAT	1,024
KEYBOARD.MAC	1,075
LIGHTINS.COM	58,507
ENVI.COM	1,539
LIHARD.BAC	1,024
LIHARD.BAT	1,024

RAM2.DIC contains the 12,000-word RAM spelling dictionary. Use depends on the amount of RAM in your computer. If you have extended memory installed in your computer, you can use that space to store the Turbo Lightning dictionaries. Files stored in RAM space are accessed more quickly than are files stored on disk.

RAM3.DIC contains the 16,000-word RAM spelling dictionary. Use depends on the amount of RAM in your computer.

INSTALLH.BAT is the hard disk installation program.

KEYBOARD.MAC is a SuperKey macro used to toggle between Screen and Keyboard modes in the WordStar environment. The SuperKey program is needed to implement this file.

LIGHTINS.COM is the Turbo Lightning installation program.

ENVI.COM is used to automatically load an environment and accompanying auxiliary dictionary of your choice as part of a DOS batch file.

LIHARD.BAC contains data used by the INSTALLH.BAT program. You will not directly utilize this file.

3) *Hard Disk Files*. This disk contains two files that take up 343,040 bytes of disk space. This disk contains the files that should be used when you work with Turbo Lightning on a hard disk.

```
DISK.DIC          179,712
THES.DIC          162,304
```

DISK.DIC contains the complete dictionary.
THES.DIC contains the standard thesaurus.

When Turbo Lightning is loaded, it takes up 83,344 bytes of internal memory. To use Turbo Lightning you must have enough memory left over to run the application you want to use. For example, WordStar 3.31 requires 131,072 bytes of memory to run.

17.2. Automatic Proofreading

There are two main functions in Turbo Lightning. The first is the proofreading function. Turbo Lightning differs from most spelling check programs in the following ways:

1) Turbo Lightning does not wait until you ask it to check a word. In its automatic proofreading mode, the text is checked as you enter it.
2) Turbo Lightning is not tied to any particular program. It can perform its operations in almost any word processor, spreadsheet, or other computer application.
3) Turbo Lightning works by using pop-up menus or special HOT command keys. You can change the command keys to any keys that you feel comfortable with.

17.3.   The Main Menu

The Turbo Lightning main menu contains the basic area in which the program operates. To display the main menu, enter **[Shift F8]**

The main Turbo Lightning menu is shown below. The application running is WordStar 3.31.

```
┌─────────────────────────────────────────────────────────────────┐
│ Environment  Word-check  Full-screen-check  Thesaurus  Setup  Options │
└─────────────────────────────────────────────────────────────────┘
 ^S char left ^D char right |^G  char  | ^I Tab   ^B Reform | (from Main only)
 ^A word left ^F word right |DEL chr lf| ^V INSERT ON/OFF   |^J Help  ^K Block
 ^E line  up  ^X line down  |^T word rt|^L Find/Replce again|^Q Quick ^P Print
      --Scrolling--         |^Y  line  |RETURN End paragraph|^O Onscreen
 ^Z line down ^W line up    |          |  ^N Insert a RETURN |
 ^C screen up ^R screen down|          |  ^U Stop a command  |
 L----!----!----!----!----!----!----!----!----!----!----!--------R
 Easy  Dos It is really a system of menus that interact  with  the
 user to guide them through the use of DOS.  The DOS command menus
 are provided with the system.                                    <
                                                                  <
 In  addition  Easy Dos It allows you to create menus of your  own
```

Fig. 17-1. Main Menu.

There are six functions on the menu. Environment, Options, and Setup pertain to how Turbo Lightning operates. Word-check, Full-screen-check, and Thesaurus are operations that affect the application you are working on.

The menu can be exited by pressing <Esc>. You can select an option in one of two ways:

1) Use the arrow keys to highlight the option you want to work with and press <return>.
2) Type the first letter of the option that you want to use. Note that when you type the letter no <return> is necessary.

17.4.   Word Check

The Word-check option checks the spelling of a word. To choose the Word-check enter **w**

```
┌─────────────────────────────────────────────────────────────────┐
│ Environment  Word-check  Full-screen-check  Thesaurus  Setup  Options │
└─────────────────────────────────────────────────────────────────┘
^S char left │A: Check word at cursor│ ^I Tab   ^B Reform │ (from Main only)
^A word left │B: Check last bad word │ ^V INSERT ON/OFF  │^J Help  ^K Block
^E line  up  └───────────────────────┘ ^L Find/Replce again│^Q Quick ^P Print
      --Scrolling--          │^Y line  │RETURN End paragraph│^O Onscreen
^Z line down ^W line up  │         │ ^N Insert a RETURN │
^C screen up ^R screen down│         │ ^U Stop a command  │
L----!----!----!----!----!----!----!----!----!----!----!--------R
choice that will run the program that you have on you hard disk.        <
                                                                       <
These  custom made menus can also perform specialised tasks  such
as backing up data files,  erasing backup files etc.  Easy Dos It
accepts lists of DOS commands and executes them  from  user
designed menus.  In some senses the program  coordinates  batch
files.  However, to the person using the system, all signs of DOS
```

Fig. 17-2. Word-check Menu.

There are two words with which Turbo Lightning is concerned. The first is the word found at the cursor position. The cursor need not be at the beginning of the word; Turbo Lightning considers a word as all the characters from one space to another. It also considers punctuation marks as indicators of word endings. If you forget to leave a space between two words, Turbo Lightning will consider the text as one large word.

The other word is the *last bad word*. This option has meaning only if you are entering text and the auto-proof mechanism has detected a word entered incorrectly. In that case the "last bad word" will be the one that was last entered incorrectly. If you are reviewing text that has been entered previously, the "last bad word" is assumed to be the word at the cursor location. Turbo Lightning beeps whenever it encounters a word that is misspelled.

17.5.   Using Commands

Most of the time you will not use the Turbo Lightning menu. Instead, Turbo Lightning provides command keys, a much faster way to issue commands. Command keys are entered while you are working in your application. If you are looking at the menu, return to the application by entering **<Esc>**

The two command keys that duplicate the Word-check menu options are:

[Alt F10] = check last bad word
[Alt F9]   = check word at cursor position

In the illustration below, the cursor is positioned on a misspelled word, "specialised". The check word command is entered:

[Alt F9]

Turbo Lightning checks its dictionary and displays a list of words that are close in sound to the word misspelled.

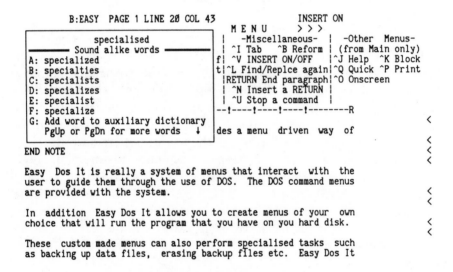

```
     B:EASY  PAGE 1 LINE 20 COL 43              INSERT ON
                                   M E N U      > > >
          specialised            | -Miscellaneous- | -Other Menus-
   ──────── Sound alike words ────── |  ^I Tab  ^B Reform | (from Main only)
   A: specialized               f| ^V INSERT ON/OFF  |^J Help  ^K Block
   B: specialties               t|^L Find/Replce again|^Q Quick ^P Print
   C: specialists               |RETURN End paragraph|^O Onscreen
   D: specializes               |  ^N Insert a RETURN |
   E: specialist                |  ^U Stop a command  |
   F: specialize                --!----!----!----!--------R
   G: Add word to auxiliary dictionary
      PgUp or PgDn for more words   ↓ |des a menu  driven  way  of
                                                                    <
   END NOTE                                                         <
                                                                    <
   Easy  Dos It is really a system of menus that interact  with  the
   user to guide them through the use of DOS.  The DOS command menus
   are provided with the system.                                    <
                                                                    <
   In  addition Easy Dos It allows you to create menus of your  own
   choice that will run the program that you have on you hard disk.  <
                                                                    <
   These  custom made menus can also perform specialised tasks  such
   as backing up data files,  erasing backup files etc.  Easy Dos It
```

Fig. 17-3. Corrections Listed.

[The placement of the box on the screen varies according to the cursor location. If you use Superkey and user display macros, you can take advantage of this cursor-sensitive location by using 0,0 as the address for the upper left corner of the display window.]

Note that the term *sound alike words* is used to describe the words displayed. This indicates that Turbo Lightning uses a phonetic technique to analyze the word misspelled.

Turbo Lightning looks at three things when it checks a word. The first part of the check determines if the word is one of a list of commonly misspelled words. This list is held in the memory of the computer. If your

word is not one of these, then Turbo Lightning uses the phonetic value of
the word and the length of the word to find substitute words.

Turbo Lightning lists the substitute words. If Turbo Lightning finds
more words than can fit into the window, you can scroll through the list
by using the [Pg Up] and [Pg Dn] keys. In this example, Turbo Lightning
found these six words:

```
A: specialized
B: specialties
C: specialists
D: specializes
E: specialist
F: specialize
```

When Turbo Lightning analyzes the misspelled word, it attempts to
rank the suggested spellings according to how close they are to the misspelled word.

There is always one item that ends each list. It is:

```
G: Add word to auxiliary dictionary
```

This option is included for words that are not in the normal dictionary but
are spelled correctly. This includes technical terms, proper nouns, etc.

When you choose G, the word under suspicion is added to the auxiliary
dictionary file. By default, Turbo Lightning uses a file called AUXI.DIC.
Turbo Lightning allows you to create and use as many auxiliary dictionaries as you need. Each dictionary is limited to 2,000 characters. The total
number of words is determined by the length of the individual words.

When the "Sound Alike" box appears, you can select the spelling you
want by the same two methods used in the other Turbo Lightning displays; either enter the letter of your choice or use the arrow keys to highlight the line and press <return>.

In this case you would enter <**return**>

Turbo Lightning retypes the word with the correct spelling.

[Turbo Lightning only enters the correct text. If the text is shorter or longer than the
original spelling, Turbo Lightning does not perform tasks like reforming the text. If you
are using a program like WordStar that does not automatically reform text after an edit,
you must remember to reform the paragraph in order to get the correct line ending justification. This is not a problem in programs that automatically reform text, such as Word or
WordStar 2000.]

17.6.   Full Screen Checks

In addition to working word by word, Turbo Lightning has another mode of operation. This mode consists of a check that scans the entire screen display for misspelled words. There are two reasons that you might want to use the full screen mode:

1. The data was entered without Turbo Lightning to check the spelling while it was being entered.
2. You turned off the Turbo Lightning auto-proof function. Because Turbo Lightning beeps at every word not found in the dictionary, you might find that your train of thought is interrupted by the need to correct your spelling. Turbo Lightning allows you to turn off the auto-proofing.

[The command to toggle the auto-proof mode is:

[Alt F8]   (Display Turbo Lightning menu)
o   (Options menu)
a   (Auto Proof, Item A)

The command key to perform that function is [Alt F5]. The Full-screen-check menu can be displayed by entering [Alt F8]f.]

The menu for Full-screen-check is shown below.

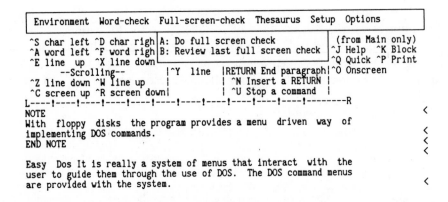

```
 Environment  Word-check  Full-screen-check  Thesaurus  Setup  Options

^S char left ^D char righ A: Do full screen check          (from Main only)
^A word left ^F word righ B: Review last full screen check ^J Help  ^K Block
^E line  up  ^X line down                                  ^Q Quick ^P Print
     --Scrolling--        |^Y line    |RETURN End paragraph|^O Onscreen
^Z line down ^W line up   |           |  ^N Insert a RETURN |
^C screen up ^R screen down|          |  ^U Stop a command  |
L----!----!----!----!----!----!----!----!----!----!----!--------R
NOTE                                                                  <
With floppy disks the program provides a menu driven way of
implementing DOS commands.                                            <
END NOTE                                                              <
                                                                     <
Easy Dos It is really a system of menus that interact with the
user to guide them through the use of DOS.  The DOS command menus
are provided with the system.                                        <
```

Fig. 17-4. Full-screen-check.

17.7. Sound Alike Words

Suppose that once again you checked the word at the cursor position, now the correctly spelled word "specialized". Entering [**Alt F9**] displays a box confirming that the word is correctly spelled.

```
               ┌─────────specialized──────────────────┐INSERT ON
               │Spelling Confirmed Press F2 for Sound Alike Words│> > >
               └──────────────────────────────────────┘ous- │ -Other Menus-
   ^S char left ^D char right │^G char  │ ^I Tab   ^B Reform │ (from Main only)
   ^A word left ^F word right │DEL chr lf│ ^V INSERT ON/OFF  │^J Help  ^K Block
   ^E line  up  ^X line down  │^T word rt│^L Find/Replce again│^Q Quick ^P Print
     --Scrolling--            │^Y line   │RETURN End paragraph│^O Onscreen
   ^Z line down ^W line up    │          │ ^N Insert a RETURN │
   ^C screen up ^R screen down│          │ ^U Stop a command  │
   L----!----!----!----!----!----!----!----!----!----!--------R
   NOTE                                                                    <
   With  floppy  disks  the program provides a menu  driven  way  of
   implementing DOS commands.                                             <
   END NOTE                                                               <
                                                                          <
   Easy  Dos It is really a system of menus that interact  with  the
   user to guide them through the use of DOS.  The DOS command menus
   are provided with the system.                                         <
                                                                          <
   In  addition  Easy Dos It allows you to create menus of your  own
   choice that will run the program that you have on you hard disk.      <
                                                                          <
   These  custom made menus can also perform specialized tasks  such
```

Fig. 17-5. Confirmation Display.

In addition to confirming the spelling, Turbo Lightning offers you a chance to list words that sound like the selected word. This is useful if you think the word you want sounds like the word you typed. This kind of error is called a malapropism. To get a display of the sound alike words, enter [**F2**]

Turbo Lightning displays the group of words closest in sound to the selected word "specialized" (see Fig. 17-6).

To see the next group of words, those that are not quite so close in sound, enter [**Pg Dn**] (see Fig. 17-7).

You can continue using the [Pg Up] and [Pg Dn] keys to scroll though the words. If you desire to make a substitution in the text, type the letter corresponding to the word you want to use. If you decide against making an exchange, enter <**Esc**> (see Fig. 17-8).

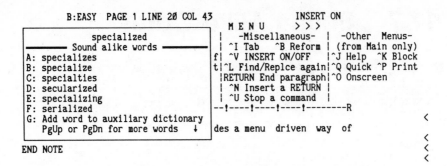

Fig. 17-6. Sound Alike Words.

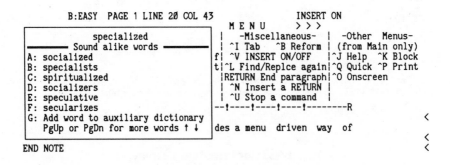

Fig. 17-7. Next Group of Words.

```
Environment  Word-check  Full-screen-check  Thesaurus  Setup  Options

            A: Do full screen check
            B: Review last full screen check
```

Fig. 17-8. Full-screen-check Menu.

To exit enter **<Esc>**

Of more practical use are the command keys that begin the screen checks:

[Alt F8] = perform a full screen check

[Alt F7] = review last screen check

Enter the following to perform a Full-screen-check: **[Alt F8]**

Turbo Lightning displays a special cursor that indicates how the program is scanning the screen. When Turbo Lightning encounters a word that is not in the dictionary, it highlights the word.

When the term *Full-screen-check* is used that is exactly what is meant. Turbo Lightning does not distinguish between the various elements of a screen display when it scans. This means that prompt line and menu displays will also be checked for spelling.

[The Full-screen-check can have some unusual results. Suppose that you are using a program like Sidekick that pops up windows with information in them. You can use Turbo Lightning to check the screen even though windows are displayed. The trick is to call up the window, for example the Sidekick notepad, and then call Turbo Lightning. Enter

[Ctrl Alt]   (Sidekick Menu)

[F2]   (notepad display)

Then call Turbo Lightning. Enter **[Alt F8]**

Turbo Lightning will check the application in the top half of the screen and the Sidekick notepad in the bottom. Turbo Lightning knows about Sidekick and adjusts to its presence on the screen. Be aware that you might find some problems with Sidekick.

First, you cannot use the Sidekick command to return to the application while Turbo Lightning is displaying the the Full-screen-check. Move the cursor in any direction and then enter **[Ctrl Alt]**

Second, the environment setting used for the application you are working in may or may not be the proper one for making replacements in the Sidekick notepad. For example, if you are working in WordStar, the environment setting is the same for the notepad. However, other programs are not. Environment settings are discussed later in this section.]

You can now see the words that Turbo Lightning thinks need to be checked. How do you check them? The answer is that you use your cursor to indicate the word to check and use the **[Alt F9]** command to check the word.

When you begin to move the cursor, the highlights disappear. The program is meant to work this way. You may have forgotten which words were highlighted, but [Alt F7], review last screen check, is used to review them. Enter **[Alt F7]**

The highlights reappear. The smart way to work with this program is to decide at this point the word you want to check. Then, after you correct that word, use **[Alt F7]** to inspect the rest of the highlighted words.

What happens if you change the screen display by scrolling the text to the next line or screen of text? The answer reveals something interesting about Turbo Lightning. If you change the text by scrolling to another screen and enter [Alt F7], Turbo Lightning will highlight only the words on that screen which were also highlighted on the previous screen.

You can see how Turbo Lightning is working. When the Full-screen-check is used, Turbo Lightning stores a list of the incorrect words in the memory of the computer. When another screen is displayed and an [Alt F7] issued, Turbo Lightning highlights any words on the screen that match the list currently in the memory as a result of the last Full-screen-check.

Turbo Lightning does not check the screen for new misspelled words. For that you need to enter [Alt F8]. However, the situation is not without its interesting points. Suppose that you were writing about computers and used the term "DOS". Turbo Lightning would highlight the word during a Full-screen-check. If you scrolled down a screen and entered [Alt F7], Turbo Lightning would highlight all the instances of "DOS". Rehighlighting is faster than performing a Full-screen-check again.

17.8. Capitalization

One detail you might not have thought about is how does Turbo Lightning deal with capitalization in words. It would ruin the effect of a program like Turbo Lightning if the program made the correct replacement but failed to capitalize the word properly.

Most words are stored in the dictionary as lower case words, with the exception of words that always begin with upper case letters, like "English". Look at the following list of words:

a. histery
b. Histery
c. HISTERY
d. hisTery

Since the word "history" is stored in all lower case letters, checking the spelling of word "a" would cause Turbo Lightning to display the following:

```
┌──────────────────────────────────────────┐
│               histery                      │
│  ───────── Sound alike words ─────────     │
│ A: history                                 │
│ B: hostelry                                │
│ C: hosiery                                 │
│ D: hinters                                 │
│ E: holster                                 │
│ F: heisted                                 │
│ G: Add word to auxiliary dictionary        │
│    PgUp or PgDn for more words    ↓        │
└──────────────────────────────────────────┘
```

Fig. 17-9. Lower Case Display.

However, if you checked the spelling of word "b" you would get this:

```
┌──────────────────────────────────────────┐
│               History                      │
│  ───────── Sound alike words ─────────     │
│ A: History                                 │
│ B: Hostelry                                │
│ C: Hosiery                                 │
│ D: Hinters                                 │
│ E: Holster                                 │
│ F: Heisted                                 │
│ G: Add word to auxiliary dictionary        │
│    PgUp or PgDn for more words    ↓        │
└──────────────────────────────────────────┘
```

Fig. 17-10. First Letter Capitalized.

If all the letters in the word are capitalized, Turbo Lightning would suggest the following:

```
┌──────────────────────────────────────────┐
│               HISTERY                      │
│  ───────── Sound alike words ─────────     │
│ A: HISTORY                                 │
│ B: HOSTELRY                                │
│ C: HOSIERY                                 │
│ D: HINTERS                                 │
│ E: HOLSTER                                 │
│ F: HEISTED                                 │
│ G: Add word to auxiliary dictionary        │
│    PgUp or PgDn for more words    ↓        │
└──────────────────────────────────────────┘
```

Fig. 17-11. All Capitalized.

What would happen if word "d" was checked?

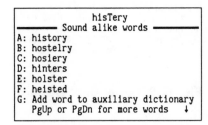

```
                    hisTery
         ——————— Sound alike words ———————
         A: history
         B: hostelry
         C: hosiery
         D: hinters
         E: holster
         F: heisted
         G: Add word to auxiliary dictionary
            PgUp or PgDn for more words    ↓
```

Fig. 17-12. Capital in Word Ignored.

The capital inserted into the middle of the word was corrected.

17.9.   The Thesaurus

Another productivity tool provided by Turbo Lightning is the Thesaurus. This option displays a list of words with similar meanings. You can find a synonym list by entering the menu command **[Alt F8]t**

You can also use the command key, **[Alt F6]**

The Thesaurus uses the word at the current cursor location as the word to match. For example, suppose that you corrected the spelling of the word "histery" but still weren't satisfied with the word. Enter **[Alt F6]**

Turbo Lightning displays a list of words that have similar meanings (see Fig. 17-13).

You can choose to replace the word in the text with any one of the words on the list. This can be done by highlight and <return> or by simply typing the letter that corresponds to the word you want to use. Pressing <Esc> returns you to the text with no change.

Sometimes the words on the synonym list aren't just right either. One course of action is to select one of the words on the list as a substitute. Then use the Thesaurus to check the newly substituted word for synonyms. For example, suppose you accepted word "d". Enter **d**

Now check for synonyms for "story". The Thesaurus will display another list of words (see Fig. 17-14).

Perhaps you like word "k". Enter **k**

Turbo Lightning makes the substitution. You could continue the process by asking for a list of synonyms for "account" (see Fig. 17-15).

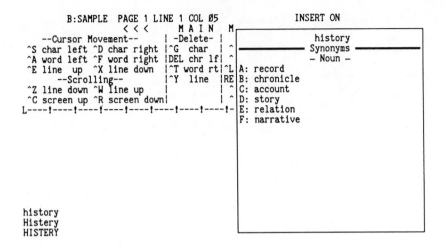

```
B:SAMPLE  PAGE 1 LINE 1 COL Ø5              INSERT ON
          < < <      M A I N   M┌─────────────────────────┐
  --Cursor Movement--   | -Delete- |  |        history      │
^S char left ^D char right |^G  char  |  ^│────── Synonyms ──────│
^A word left ^F word right |DEL chr lf|  ^│       – Noun –       │
^E line  up  ^X line down  |^T word rt|^L│A: record            │
    --Scrolling--          |^Y  line  |RE│B: chronicle         │
^Z line down ^W line up    |          |  ^│C: account           │
^C screen up ^R screen down|          |  ^│D: story             │
L----!----!----!----!----!----!----!----!-│E: relation          │
                                          │F: narrative         │
                                          │                     │
                                          │                     │
                                          │                     │
                                          │                     │
history                                   │                     │
Histery                                   │                     │
HISTERY                                   └─────────────────────┘
```

Fig. 17-13. Thesaurus Display.

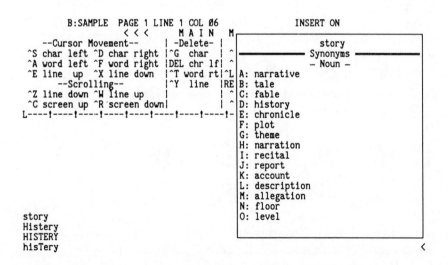

```
B:SAMPLE  PAGE 1 LINE 1 COL Ø6              INSERT ON
          < < <      M A I N   M┌─────────────────────────┐
  --Cursor Movement--   | -Delete- |  |         story       │
^S char left ^D char right |^G  char  |  ^│────── Synonyms ──────│
^A word left ^F word right |DEL chr lf|  ^│       – Noun –       │
^E line  up  ^X line down  |^T word rt|^L│A: narrative         │
    --Scrolling--          |^Y  line  |RE│B: tale              │
^Z line down ^W line up    |          |  ^│C: fable             │
^C screen up ^R screen down|          |  ^│D: history           │
L----!----!----!----!----!----!----!----!-│E: chronicle         │
                                          │F: plot              │
                                          │G: theme             │
                                          │H: narration         │
                                          │I: recital           │
                                          │J: report            │
                                          │K: account           │
story                                     │L: description       │
Histery                                   │M: allegation        │
HISTERY                                   │N: floor             │
hisTery                                   │O: level             │
                                          └─────────────────────┘
                                                              <
```

Fig. 17-14. Synonym List for "story".

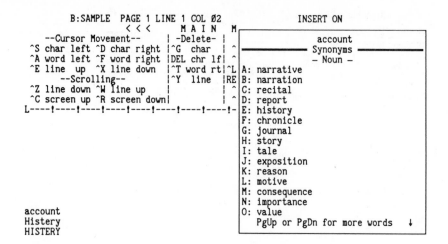

Fig. 17-15. Synonyms for "account".

The Thesaurus feature is a wonderful way to expand your writing vocabulary and add variety to your writing. Using the right word makes your correspondence more precise and comprehensible. The Thesaurus alone is worth the price of Turbo Lightning.

The best part of Turbo Lightning is that you are not restricted to a particular program. Without Turbo Lightning, you might face a choice of buying a word processor that contains a Thesaurus, like WordPerfect, and giving up using your old program, e.g., WordStar. Turbo Lightning eliminates the need to make this choice. Some people use a number of programs, including several word processors. Turbo Lightning means that they can use the Thesaurus with any of these programs, including non-word processing programs like dBASE and Lotus 1-2-3.

[There are some issues involved with making Turbo Lightning work properly with a variety of programs. See Chapter 17.16 for details.]

17.10. Words Not in the Thesaurus

It may happen that the word that you want to change is not found in the Thesaurus. For example, if the word "environments" were checked, Turbo Lightning would display:

```
B:SAMPLE  PAGE 1 LINE 1 ┌─────────────────environments──────────┐
             < < <      M │ Not in Thesaurus - Press F2 for Close Words │
  --Cursor Movement--     │ -De└───────────────────────────────────────┘
^S char left ^D char right │^G  char  │ ^I Tab   ^B Reform │ (from Main only)
```

Fig. 17-16. Word Not in Thesaurus.

Don't give up. Many times words are not found because they are only a part of a word that is in the Thesaurus. For instance, Turbo Lightning may miss a match because of a suffix that is added to the word. Such an example might include a word with an "s" at the end.

In order to deal with this problem, Turbo Lightning will display words that are found in the Thesaurus that are close to the spelling of the selected word. Enter **[F2]**

```
c┌────────────────────────────────────────┐
 │                environments            │
 │        ── Close words with synonyms ── │
 │ A: entice                              │
 │ B: entire                              │
 │ C: entitle                             │
 │ D: entrance                            │
 │ E: entreat                             │
 │ F: entry                               │
 │ G: enumerate                           │
 │ H: envelop                             │
 │ I: environment                         │
 │ J: envy                                │
 │ K: ephemeral                           │
 │ L: epicure                             │
 │ M: epidemic                            │
 │ N: episode                             │
 │ O: epoch                               │
 │ P: equal                               │
 │    PgUp or PgDn for more words ↑ ↓     │
 └────────────────────────────────────────┘
```

Fig. 17-17. Close Words Listed by Thesaurus.

Note that Turbo Lightning always places the word that is closest to the word in the center of the list, usually word "I". This allows you to see the word on either side of the word in the text. In this case to select word "I", enter **i**

Turbo Lightning then searches for that word in the Thesaurus and displays:

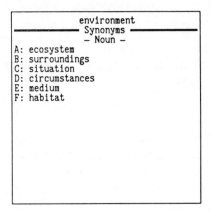

```
┌─────────────────────────────┐
│         environment         │
│━━━━━━━━━ Synonyms ━━━━━━━━━━│
│          – Noun –           │
│ A: ecosystem                │
│ B: surroundings             │
│ C: situation                │
│ D: circumstances            │
│ E: medium                   │
│ F: habitat                  │
│                             │
│                             │
│                             │
│                             │
│                             │
│                             │
└─────────────────────────────┘
```

Fig. 17-18. Synonyms for "environment".

If you want to replace the word in the text, select the word from the list that you think is the most analogous to the word you used. <Esc> leaves the text unchanged.

If you do make a substitution, be aware that that you must manually add any suffixes that the word requires, such as "s" or "ing". Turbo Lightning types the word exactly as it appears on the list.

[If you are unsure of the proper spelling with the suffix added, you could use the [Alt F9] command to check the word and then use [F2] to list sound alike words. Turbo Lightning will usually have the form of the word you are looking for on that list.]

17.11.   Expanding the Dictionary

Suppose that your last name is "Lafish". It might be a good idea to add the word to the Turbo Lightning dictionary. To do so, use the **[Alt F9]** command, Word-check. Turbo Lightning will tell you that the word is not in the dictionary (see Fig. 17-19).

You need to use option "g" to add the name to the auxiliary dictionary. Enter **g**

Turbo Lightning now needs to know the capitalization of the word. In this example, the correct response is "b".

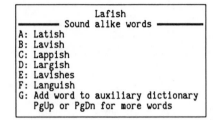

```
┌────────────────────────────────────────┐
│                Lafish                  │
│ ───────── Sound alike words ────────── │
│ A: Latish                              │
│ B: Lavish                              │
│ C: Lappish                             │
│ D: Largish                             │
│ E: Lavishes                            │
│ F: Languish                            │
│ G: Add word to auxiliary dictionary    │
│    PgUp or PgDn for more words          │
└────────────────────────────────────────┘
```

Fig. 17-19. "Lafish" Not Found.

17.12. Making Turbo Lightning Work with Your Software

Turbo Lightning is a flexible system that can be tailored to your own personal computer system, software, and working habits. Turbo Lightning allows you to specify the dictionary files to use. Enter **[Shift F8]s**
The setup menu appears.

```
┌──────────────────────────────────────────────────────────────────┐
│ Environment  Word-check  Full-screen-check  Thesaurus  Setup  Options │
│          ┌──────────────────────────────────────────────┐         │
│          │ A: Auxiliary dictionary file name AUXI       │         │
│          │ B: Disk dictionary file name       DISK       │         │
│          │ C: Thesaurus file name             THES       │         │
│          │ D: Save Setup/Options/Environment             │         │
│          └──────────────────────────────────────────────┘         │
└──────────────────────────────────────────────────────────────────┘
```

Fig. 17-20. Setup Menu.

Option "d" is used to make a copy of the file setup on the disk so that it will be the same each time you load Turbo Lightning. If you change a, b, or c, but do not perform d, the changes are temporary. The next time Turbo Lightning is loaded the file setup will go back to the defaults.

17.13. Key Commands

Turbo Lightning allows you to specify the key that will implement the Turbo Lightning functions. Enter **[Shift F8]o**

```
┌─────────────────────────────────────────────────────────────┐
│ Environment  Word-check  Full-screen-check  Thesaurus  Setup  Options │
└─────────────────────────────────────────────────────────────┘
                          ┌──────────────────────────────────┐
                          │ A: Auto proof          ON        │
                          │ B: Confirm window      ON         │
                          │ ───────────── Hot Keys ───────────│
                          │ C: Main menu           ShftF8     │
                          │ D: Last bad word       AltF1Ø     │
                          │ E: Check word          AltF9      │
                          │ F: Screen check        AltF8      │
                          │ G: Review screen       AltF7      │
                          │ H: Thesaurus           AltF6      │
                          │ I: Toggle auto proof  AltF5       │
                          │──────────────────────────────────│
                          │ Turbo Lightning vers. 1.ØØA       │
                          └──────────────────────────────────┘
```

Fig. 17-21. Options Menu.

The first two items control the modes of Turbo Lightning. The other options allow you to change the command keys to keys that you prefer. For example, many WordStar users do not work with the function keys. You can make Turbo Lightning a one-finger program by switching [Alt F10] to [F10].

To change a key, press the letter of the key you want to change. Type in the key you want to use for that function.

To make the changes permanent from session to session, use the Setup Save command on the Setup menu.

17.14. Environments

Turbo Lightning knows how to work in so many programs because it has a special file that contains the data necessary for it to adjust to the differences in programs. The Environment option on the Turbo Lightning menu comes installed for 13 different programs.

Change environments by selecting the letter of the program that you want to use.

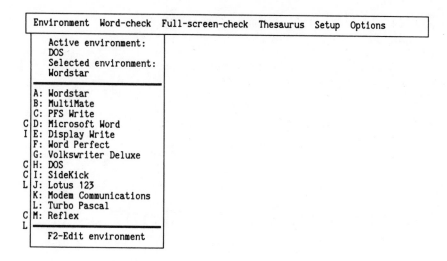

Fig. 17-22. Environment Menu.

[If you change programs often, you might use a macro program like SuperKey to enter the change environment command with a single keystroke.

For example, using SuperKey, the following command would create a macro that would change the environment to 1-2-3:

[Alt=]
[Alt1]
[Shift F8]
e

j
[Alt-]

From this point on, pressing [Alt1] will change the environment to the 1-2-3 environment.

You can also load a special dictionary and change the environment when you run a program by creating a DOS batch file. ENVI.COM is a program that changes environments and loads dictionaries into Turbo Lightning from DOS. Turbo Lightning must be loaded first. Then run ENVI.COM. The program takes one or two parameters:

1) A letter that corresponds to an environment on the environment menu. For example, J stands for 1-2-3.
2) The second parameter, which is optional, is the name of an auxiliary dictionary you want loaded. For example, the command **envi j 123 <return>** would select environment J and load the dictionary 123.DIC. Note Turbo Lightning assumes that dictionaries end with a DIC extension. If this is not the case, you must specify the extension as well.

Creating a batch file with a text editor or word processing program can combine the ENVI command with DOS commands required for running the program. The following example uses the DOS program EDLIN to create a batch file:

edlin run123.bat <return>	(Start EDLIN text editor)
i <return>	(insert lines into batch file)
cd\lotus <return>	(change DOS directory to \LOTUS)
envi j 123 <return>	(Select environment J and dictionary 123)
lotus <return>	(Run 1-2-3 program)
cd\ <return>	(Change directory to root following 1-2-3)
envi a auxi <return>	(reload environment A and AUXI dictionary)
[Ctrlc]	(End line entry)
e <return>	(Save file)

The batch file can be executed by entering: **run123 <return>**]

17.15. New Environments

If the environment for the program you want to use is not listed on the Environment menu, you must change the setting on one of the existing environments to work correctly with your program.

As an example, create environment specifications for two programs, WordStar 2000 and Framework II.

[Programs that operate in the graphics mode, as does Framework II when running on a color graphics computer, cannot use Turbo Lightning to its best ability. Turbo Lightning will operate if you switch it from the screen mode to keyboard. This allows Turbo Lightning to check spelling only as the text is entered. The Full-screen-check and Thesaurus functions do not work. If you run Framework II on a monochrome screen, you can follow the instructions below.]

17.16. Framework II and Turbo Lightning

To begin the process of creating an environment for a new piece of software, bring up the environment menu (Fig. 17-23). Enter **[Shift F8]e**

In order to create a new environment, you will have to revise one of the setups already shown, one that is for a piece of software you will not use. For example, G is set for Volkswriter. Move the cursor so that it highlights item G. Enter **[F2]**

There are 16 options that you must fill out correctly for Turbo Lightning to work with your software.

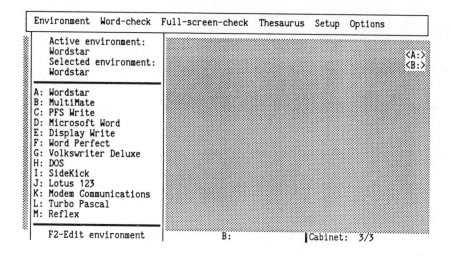

Fig. 17-23. Environment Menu.

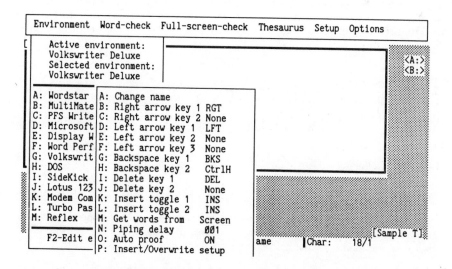

Fig. 17-24. Environment Settings.

The first item is the name of the environment. Enter **Framework II <return>**

The name for item G is now Framework II. Return to the editing mode by entering **[F2]**

Now you must change the actual settings so that Turbo Lightning will know what commands to use for Framework II.

17.17. Arrow Keys

Settings B through F tell Turbo Lightning which keys to use for cursor movement. The settings are currently:

B: Right arrow key 1   RGT
C: Right arrow key 2   None
D: Left arrow key 1   LFT
E: Left arrow key 2   None
F: Left arrow key 3   None

These settings are correct for Framework II. You don't have to make any changes.

[Some programs like WordStar or Sidekick Notepad have more than one way to move the cursor. That is the purpose of having second and third arrow key definitions.]

The next group of entries, G through L, tells Turbo Lightning the editing keys to use with Framework II.

G: Backspace key 1   BKS
H: Backspace key 2   CtrlH
I: Delete key 1   DEL
J: Delete key 2   None
K: Insert toggle 1   INS
L: Insert toggle 2   INS

Options G, H, I, and J are the same in Framework II as in Volkswriter.

[[Ctrlh] is a standard key command for an erasing backspace in most operating systems. Although it does not mention it in the Framework II manual, [Ctrlh] and the <Backspace> key perform the same function.]

However, options K and L are not correct for Framework II. In Framework II the [Ins] key is used to access the menu bar. The command to toggle the insert mode is [Ctrle]t (EDIT Typeover). This creates a problem. Turbo Lightning only allows room for a single keystroke for each option. Framework II requires two keystrokes. The problem can be solved by using a Framework II macro.

This means that you will enter the macro key into Turbo Lightning and create a Framework II macro to link Turbo Lightning to the correct keystrokes.

[Framework II differs from Framework when it comes to macro creation. Framework II has macro creation built into its menu structure. Framework requires that you load the Library file and use its facility for creating macros. The solution shown here will work for Framework as well as for Framework II, but Framework users will have to remember to load the Macro Library frame in order to create a macro or use a Framework formula to create the macro.]

Enter **k[AltT]**

This sets the insert toggle for [AltT]. Later you will need to create a macro, [Altt], that issues the [Ctrle]t command.

Return to the edit mode, enter **[F2]**

Option L should become blank. Enter **L<return>**

Return to the edit mode, enter **[F2]**

The next option is *M: Get words from*. There are two settings: screen or keyboard. Programs that operate in the graphics mode must use the keyboard setting. In this case, screen is correct.

Next is *N: Piping delay*. This option creates a delay in the typing of keystrokes by Turbo Lightning. If the application seems to lose characters, then you need to enter a longer piping delay. The current delay is fine for Framework II.

Next is *O: Auto proof*. This should be set on.

Finally the last setting is *P: Insert/Overwrite setup*. Enter **p**

There are five options that tell Turbo Lightning how the software works. The correct option for Framework is A. Enter **a**

Now select Framework II as the environment you want to work in. Enter **<return> <Esc>**

To complete the installation, create a Framework II macro. Enter

[Ctrlc]	(Create Menu)
m	(Create a Macro)
[Altt]	(Macro key)
[Ctrle]	(Edit menu)
t	(Toggle Typeover Mode)
[Ctrl Scroll Lock]	(End Macro Recording)

[If you want to permanently save the macro, you should save the revise library frame at the end of the Framework session. Framework will automatically prompt you when you exit.]

Test the macro, enter [**Altt**]

Now you can use Turbo Lightning with Framework II.

17.18.   WordStar 2000

If you are using WordStar 2000 instead of WordStar, you can change the environment setup of WordStar to the correct setup for WordStar 2000. Below are the environment listings. The left is WordStar. The right is how the setup should read for WordStar 2000.

```
WORDSTAR ENVIRONMENT                    WORDSTAR 2000 ENVIRONMENT

A: Change name                          A: Change name
B: Right arrow key 1 RGT                 B: Right arrow key 1 RGT
C: Right arrow key 2 CtrlD               C: Right arrow key 2 CtrlD
D: Left arrow key 1   LFT                D: Left arrow key 1   LFT
E: Left arrow key 2   CtrlS              E: Left arrow key 2   CtrlS
F: Left arrow key 3   BKS                F: Left arrow key 3   None
G: Backspace key 1    DEL                G: Backspace key 1    BKS
H: Backspace key 2    None               H: Backspace key 2    None
I: Delete key 1       CtrlG              I: Delete key 1       DEL
J: Delete key 2       None               J: Delete key 2       None
K: Insert toggle 1    INS                K: Insert toggle 1    INS
L: Insert toggle 2    CtrlV              L: Insert toggle 2    CtrlV
M: Get words from     Screen             M: Get words from     Screen
N: Piping delay       002                N: Piping delay       002
O: Auto proof         ON                 O: Auto proof         ON
P: Insert/Overwrite setup                P: Insert/Overwrite setup
```

Fig. 17-25. WordStar and WordStar 2000 Environments.

There are three changes you need to make in the key specifications. They are:

WordStar		*WordStar 2000*	
F: Left arrow key 3	BKS	F: Left arrow key 3	None
G: Backspace key 1	DEL	G: Backspace key 1	BKS
I: Delete key 1	CtrlG	I: Delete key 1	DEL

Finally you have to change the P setting. Enter **p**

In this case, choose E. This option requires you to show Turbo Lightning where on the screen the insert indicator is displayed. You now must place the cursor on the first character of the insert/overtype display. When you are there press <**return**>

Next Turbo Lightning wants to know if the current display on the screen indicates insert or overtype. If it is insert, which is the usual Word-Star 2000 mode, enter **I**; If overtype, enter **O**

Turbo Lightning is now ready for work with WordStar 2000.

17.19. Saving the Changes

To make the changes in the environments permanent, you must remember to use the Setup Save command. When you do, the new environments will be recalled whenever you use Turbo Lightning.

17.20. Conclusion

Turbo Lightning is an exciting, fun-to-use program that increases the productivity of anyone who uses it. Turbo Lightning was created to be part of a growing family of productivity add-ons. The future will show how the potential of Turbo Lightning will be developed.

Turbo Lightning has the added advantage of working with a wide variety of programs. This means that you do not have to give up using software that you like in order to use Turbo Lightning.

18.

Comparing the Background Utility Programs

The three programs discussed in Part 4 are excellent examples of the way programs can fill in the gaps left by the major applications. Each product approaches the task in about the same way. Yet there is enough variation for people with slightly different needs or styles of work to be attracted to one or another. This chapter is a comparison of the features and functions of the three programs.

18.1. Basic System Design

Sidekick and Spotlight share the concept of loading all the applications as a unit. Sidekick allows variation by providing several versions of programs, each of which uses a different amount of memory to load different combinations of features.

Sidekick is completely memory resident with the exception of the help files and data files used by the applications. Spotlight needs to load the programs from the disk as you call them.

Spotlight is the only copy-protected program among the three.

DeskSet is the most radical departure, in that each of its applications is really an individual program. They are even sold separately. The advantage here is that you can load just the applications that you need at any one time.

Also note that DeskSet uses memory-resident help screens, unlike Sidekick.

18.2.   Notepads

All three programs provide a notepad of some sort. Sidekick is by far the leader in this respect. The weakest notepad is Spotlight, although DeskSet is closer to Spotlight than Sidekick.

The Sidekick notepad is superior because it is almost a full-featured word processor. The majority of the commands used in WordStar function in the Spotlight notepad. These include such features as block copy and move, search and replace, and reading and writing files to the disk.

Oddly, DeskSet has one feature that Sidekick does not. Sidekick will not directly print out the contents of the notepad, since it contains no printing commands. The files created by the Sidekick notepad must be printed by some other program.

Sidekick can create fairly large files in the notepad. The text can be typed at full width rather than at the limited window sizes displayed in Spotlight and DeskSet.

Spotlight is considered the weakest because not only does it lack the sophisticated command structure of the Sidekick notepad, but it can only save files, not retrieve them.

The Sidekick notepad also serves another function. It has the ability to perform cut and paste operations. Spotlight has no facility for this type of operation, in which text is copied from a screen display and stored in the notepad. DeskSet does duplicate the function with its clipboard program. There are some significant differences, however.

First, Sidekick can directly save data captured from the screen. The DeskSet Clipboard cannot save the text. It must feed the text to another application which can then create the text file. Also the clipboard can only hold one screen full of information at a time. The notepad can capture as many screens as the notepad file size will allow. Since the Sidekick notepad file size can get as large as 64 kilobytes, this is a considerable advantage.

The Clipboard has the ability to move blocks around in a more flexible manner than the Sidekick notepad, because Sidekick cannot create vertical blocks.

On balance, Sidekick's advantages outweigh those of DeskSet's Clipboard.

Pasting or feeding the text from the notepad or clipboard to an application is also an area of comparison. Both programs feed selected text to an application. With both, one can select all or part of the text for feeding.

In Sidekick you can select by horizontal blocks only. DeskSet allows rectangular blocks. Sidekick stores the text to be fed to the application as a macro in a specific key. The advantage is that the text is not immediately transferred when you return to your application. Instead, you can work on the application and use the macro key to play back the text whenever you need it.

Another advantage of Sidekick is that, because the text is stored as a macro, you can define a number of blocks of text to different keys and paste each one when you want it. The DeskSet system allows only one block at a time to be defined.

Finally, the line ending characters can be controlled when the feeding or pasting is done. Sidekick has two options, <return> or none. If "none" is selected, feeding pauses until the macro key is pressed again. DeskSet allows you to specify the ending character. DeskSet has the advantage if you need only a single character at the end of each line. Sidekick has the advantage if you need to enter more than one keystroke between lines of pasted text.

In general, the Sidekick notepad is the strongest of all the programs. Much of the Sidekick system is built around the notepad. This is not the case with DeskSet and Spotlight.

18.3.   Calculators

All three of the programs provide screen calculators. The weakest of the programs in this regard is Spotlight. Its calculator is quite simple. Its only special feature is the paste command which transfers the value in the calculator to the application. The Spotlight calculator is much larger than the others and features a positive visual feedback when a key is pressed that makes it easy to use. Note that among the three programs only the Spotlight calculator clears its value every time you return to the application. The other programs retain the value until specifically cleared.

Sidekick offers a slightly broader calculator. In addition to the normal features, Sidekick has modes for binary and hexadecimal numbers. It also has logical functions. Perhaps the most useful of the features of the Sidekick calculator is how it pastes numbers from the calculator into applications. Unlike DeskSet or Spotlight, Sidekick assigns values to keys as macros. This means that you can store a series of values into different macro keys and replay them all into your application. DeskSet and Spotlight feed the calculator value immediately into the application. You cannot adjust the application or the cursor position. Sidekick allows you to select the moment for transfer by storing the values in macro keys.

In other areas, the calculator features of DeskSet are by far the most advanced. DeskSet offers a tape simulation that is quite helpful. DeskSet also is the only program that allows you to print directly from the calculator. While Sidekick and Spotlight provide a single memory cell, DeskSet provides ten memories.

In addition, DeskSet provides the financial calculator, which has a whole range of special financial and statistical calculation abilities built in.

If you use the calculator feature, DeskSet is clearly superior in this area. However, many of the calculator functions are duplicated in popular spreadsheet programs.

18.4. Calendars

The calendar programs are probably the closest in sophistication of all the applications. Sidekick provides a full appointment calendar, as does Spotlight. DeskSet allows you to enter short messages that display on the calendar. DeskSet cannot be used as an appointment calendar.

The main limitation of the Sidekick calendar is that is does not provide repeating entries. Both Spotlight and DeskSet have provisions for making repeating or cyclical dates for meetings. DeskSet has the most sophisticated entry system, but it is not really designed to function as a full appointment calendar. You can enter messages that repeat daily, weekly, monthly, quarterly, or yearly.

DeskSet is also useful because it will print calendar displays that can be used as disposable wall calendars.

The Spotlight program provides an interesting feature in the calendar. It allows you to specify alarms to remind you of appointments.

DeskSet also contains a separate program called Alarm that duplicates the ability to sound alarms. The main difference is that Spotlight can store an alarm in the calendar for weeks in advance. The DeskSet alarm is meant to be entered only for the current day.

18.5.   DOS Access

Sidekick does not provide DOS access as a background utility. This feature is provided by Spotlight and DeskSet. Its advantage is that you can perform tasks like copying and deleting files without having to exit your application.

The Spotlight features duplicate DOS commands for DIR, COPY, RENAME, DEL, CHDIR, FORMAT, and MKDIR. In addition, Spotlight will paste the name of a file, disk, or directory into an application.

DeskSet offers roughly the same features, but does not include formatting. DeskSet does offer some unique printing features. The DOS program allows you to print a file from the background memory. In addition, you can enter a typewriter mode which allows you to type directly on your printer. Also included is the ability to send special codes to your printer to set up print features. All this can be done from the background without having to disturb your application.

18.6.   Telecommunications

Spotlight and Sidekick will autodial phone numbers stored in a data file. The Sidekick feature is the simplest and fastest to use. Spotlight uses a card file system for the phone list. Each entry into the phone list can be expanded into an entire file card containing seven lines of text for each person.

The DeskSet equivalent is the Voice program. Voice stores only three phone numbers.

In addition to Voice, DeskSet provides Modem. This is a full telecommunications program with the ability to capture incoming data in a text file for later use.

In this respect, the DeskSet modem program is really designed for a different purpose than the dialer programs in Sidekick and Spotlight.

18.7.   Other Features

There are some other features that are available that are not the same in each program. Sidekick provides a memory-resident ASCII table, which is not offered in DeskSet or Spotlight. Spotlight has a card filing program that is not duplicated in Sidekick or DeskSet. The PopAny program in DeskSet allows you to create a memory area in which you can run a program of your own choosing as a background utility.

18.8.   Conclusion

All three of these programs are worthy of consideration. It might be worthwhile to own two of them. If you already use Sidekick, you might find that some of the individual programs in DeskSet would enhance your work. DOS access and the Alarm program are really quite useful, even with the resident Sidekick features.

Sidekick has the best notepad program, and DeskSet has the best calculator program. Spotlight has the best all-round calendar program. The broadest features are provided by the full DeskSet program.

Sidekick also has the advantage that it is well-integrated with several other outstanding products, such as SuperKey and Turbo Lightning. The combination of those three programs is really quite outstanding.

Any of the three programs has many ways to provide the user with greater productivity from the computer. They all have the ability to justify their cost many times over.

19.

Printing Utilities

This chapter describes some utility programs that perform special functions concerned with printing. The programs are primarily aimed at dot-matrix printers like the IBM Graphics Printer and the Epson family.

Dot-matrix printers have the ability to produce output in a number of different fonts and modes. This ability is not fully supported by most software programs. While many word processing programs do take advantage of some of the special features of these printers, other programs, such as spreadsheets or data bases, make much less use of their abilities.

For example, neither Lotus 1-2-3 or dBASE II or III have any built-in methods for accessing the full printing capacity of the dot printers. dBASE, and to a lesser degree 1-2-3, have places where special codes can be inserted. However, these codes can be a bit complex for most users. Even with these codes, the implementation in 1-2-3 is limited by the number of characters you can enter in a print setup string.

The print utilities in this chapter have the following things in common:

1. They bring to the user methods and styles of printing that many applications do not take advantage of.
2. They present the modes and font options in a menu format. The user is insulated from the character codes that perform the various functions. The user does not have to dig through the printer manual and then try to translate the codes into the correct format for the application.

Printer utilities offer solutions to printing problems that are every bit as novel as the solutions presented by the keyboard and background utilities.

19.1.   C-Printer

C-Printer is a memory-resident utility which allows the user to execute commands that change the font, pitch, or mode of the printer without having to leave the application.

[Some of the functions of this utility can be accomplished by using the DOS Print commands from the DeskSet program, POPDOS. See Chapter 16 for more details.]

C-Printer operates much like the background utilities described in the earlier chapters of Part 4.

[C-Printer can be operated as a normal program from the DOS prompt. However, its main advantage is as a memory-resident background utility.]

To load C-Printer into the memory, enter **cpr /r<Return>**

The program takes up only about three kilobytes of memory. The program is entirely memory resident, so that the disk with the C-Printer program file can be removed from the computer without losing any of C-Printer's functions.

Once C-Printer is loaded, you can proceed to work with other applications as you normally would. When it comes time to print, you can access C-Printer by entering **[Shift PrtSc]**

Instead of performing the normal Print Screen function, the screen will display the C-Printer menu (Fig. 19-1).

[The Print Screen feature of the IBM PC is not disabled by C-Printer. You can still perform a screen print by choosing option 17 from the C-Printer menu.]

19.2.   C-Printer Commands

C-Printer commands fall into five categories:

1. Access Control. These commands activate and deactivate the C-Printer program. The activate command is [Shift PrtSc] and the deactivate command is 0<return>.
2. Basic Commands. These commands cover printer initialization, form feeding, line feeding, continuous line feeding, clearing printer buffer, and sounding the printer buzzer.
3. Format Control. The format commands control the setting of margins, tabs, form length, line spacing, and perforation skip.

```
┌─────────────────────────────────────────────────────────────────────┐
│ Mill Valley Software          C-PRINTER              Version 1.0      │
├───────────────────────────────┬─────────────────────────────────────┤
│ 0 Exit                        │                                     │
│                               │   ENTER SELECTION      ==>          │
│ 1 Initialize Printer          │                                     │
│ 2 Form Feed                   ├─────────────────────────────────────┤
│ 3 Line Feed                   │   Printer Type    ==>   EPSON       │
│ 4 Continuous Line Feed        │                                     │
│ 5 Sound the Buzzer            ├─────────────────────────────────────┤
│ 6 Flush Printer Buffer        │ 17 Invoke Print-Screen              │
│                               │ 18 Printer Test Pattern             │
├───────────────────────────────┼─────────────────────────────────────┤
│ 7 Left Margin      ==>  0     │ 19 Correspondence Mode  ==>  OFF    │
│ 8 Right Margin     ==>  0     │ 20 Enlarged Print       ==>  OFF    │
│ 9 Form Length      ==>  66    │ 21 Condensed Print      ==>  OFF    │
│ 10 Lines per Inch (6|8) ==> 6 │ 22 Emphasized Print     ==>  OFF    │
│ 11 Line Spacing  n/72  ==> OFF│ 23 Double Strike        ==>  OFF    │
│ 12 Line Spacing  n/216 ==> OFF│ 24 Elite Set            ==>  OFF    │
│ 13 Perforation Skip  ==>  0   │ 25 Alternate Set        ==>  OFF    │
│ 14 Paper End Signal  ==>  ON  │ 26 Proportional Spacing ==>  OFF    │
│                               │ 27 International Set     ==>  USA    │
├───────────────────────────────┤                                     │
│ 15 Horizontal Tabs  ==>       │                                     │
│ 16 Vertical Tabs    ==>       │                                     │
└───────────────────────────────┴─────────────────────────────────────┘
```

Fig. 19-1. C-Printer Menu Display.

4. Font Control. These commands allow you to select different styles of printing. They include pica versus elite, enlarged printing, condensed printing,
proportional spacing, double strike mode, emphasized printing, correspondence quality, and use of the international character set or the alternate
character set.

[Many printers support special characters for foreign languages. With this command
you may select the character set which corresponds to the language you are using.

0   U.S. (Default)
1   France
2   Germany
3   England
4   Denmark
5   Sweden
6   Italy
7   Spain
8   Japan]

5. Special Commands. There are two special commands. One invokes a screen
print, the usual function of the [Shift PrtSc] command. The other prints a test
pattern so that you can see how the text will be printed.

C-Printer supports the following printers:

IBM Graphics Printer, or compatible
EPSON LQ-1500
EPSON FX Series
EPSON RX Series
EPSON MX Series
OKIDATA 84
OKIDATA 92
OKIDATA 93
Star Micronics Radix SR10
Star Micronics Radix SR15
Hewlitt Packard Think-Jet

[In most regards the IBM Graphics Printer is the same printer as the Epson MX series printer. Often, what is true for the Epson MX 80 with Graphtrax is true of the IBM Graphics printer.

However, there is one important exception. The built-in character set of the IBM and Epson are the same only for the standard 128-character ASCII code numbered from 0 to 127. The extended codes, i.e., the characters represented by numbers 128 through 255, are not the same in the Epson as they are in the IBM.

The IBM character set corresponds to the graphics characters used on the IBM screen display. The boxes and lines that are often drawn by programs on the screen can be reproduced on the IBM Graphic Printer but not the Epson. The Epson will print italicized letters instead of lines and boxes.

This is due to a difference in built-in character sets. The Printworks program and the Sideways programs have means of making the Epson completely character-compatible with the IBM screen characters.]

19.3. Conclusions: C-Printer

C-Printer is a very handy program for users who want to control printing on their dot-matrix printers without having to use the control codes. The design of many programs makes it difficult if not impossible to control all the functions presented by C-Printer.

Remember that C-Printer's functions are not fully supported by all printers. Before you use the program check the C-Printer documentation to see which features are supported for your printer.

19.4. Printworks

Printworks is a very different program from C-Printer, even though it is designed around the same basic idea, i.e., that most programs do not take advantage of the potential of printers like the Epson or IBM Graphics Printer.

Unlike C-Printer, Printworks is not a background utility. Printworks assumes that you have created an ASCII text file that you want to print. The file can be produced by any of the standard methods.

[See Chapter 1.28 for a description of how some popular programs produce ASCII files.]

Printworks is used to print the ASCII text file with special fonts that enhance the look of the characters in the file. *Font* refers to the style and shape of the printed character. While the ASCII character 65 is invariably the letter "A", font variations change the way the A is printed.

Printworks has four functions:

1. Print a file using standard characteristics of the printer. These are the built-in characteristics, such as changes in pitch, font, and line height.
2. Printing files using special graphics fonts provided by, or designed with, the Printworks program.

ABCDEFGHIJKLMNOPQRSTUVWXYZ
abcdefghijklmnopqrstuvwxyz
1234567890!"#$%&'()*+,-./
:;<=>?@[\]^_`{|}~

ABCDEFGHIJKLMNOPQRSTUVWXYZ
abcdefghijklmnopqrstuvwxyz

ABCDEFGHIJKLMNOPQRSTUVWXYZ
ABCDEFGHIJKLMNOPQRSTUVWXYZ
1234567890!"#$%&'()*+,-./
:;<=>?@[\]^ `{|}~

ABCDEFGHIJKLMNOPQRSTUVWXYZ
abcdefghijklmnopqrstuvwxyz
1234567890!"#$%&'()*+,-./
:;<=>?@[\]^_`{|}~

Fig. 19-2. Sample Fonts.

3. Font Editor. The program allows you to modify the existing font files.
4. Create Fonts. If you are motivated, you can create specification files that define new fonts of your own creation that can be used to print with Printworks.

Printworks supports the following dot-matrix printers:

C.Itoh—Prowriter 1550 EP, 1550 SEP, 1550 SCEP, 7500 EP, 8510 BPI, 8510 SEP, 8510 SCEP
Centronics—Horizon/Quietwriter H80, H136
Epson—FX-80/100, RX-80/100, JX-80, LQ-1500, MX-80/100 III with Graftrax Plus
IBM—Graphics Printer
Inforunner—Riteman Plus, Blue Plus, II, 15
NEC—Pinwriter (P2-3, P3-3)
Okidata—ML 84 Step 2, ML 92 and 93 with or without Plug 'n Play Kit, Pacemark 2350 and 2410
Star Micronics—Gemini 10X/15X, Radix 10/15, Delta 10/15

19.5.   The Main Program

The main Printworks program assumes that you already have created a text file that you wish to print and that the font you want to use already exists. Printworks comes with a variety of fonts, each stored in a file on one of the two disks.

The program is loaded by entering **pw < return >**

The first screen (Fig. 19-3) asks you to select the printer that you will use. One interesting feature of Printworks is that the menu options that appear in the rest of the program differ, depending on which printer you choose. This makes things clearer, since not all printers can perform all of the functions.

After the printer has been selected, you see the main menu (Fig. 19-4). This menu shows you your options.

Most of the options are toggles. The default is to print with the standard font of the printer at ten characters per inch (pica printing).

You can select other options by pressing the letter that corresponds to the command. The commands fall into three areas:

1. *Print Type.* You can select pica or elite, italic, proportional, or a special graphics font. The graphics fonts allow you to choose one of the special font files stored on the disk. For example, Printworks provides an IBM font which prints the full IBM character set on printers that do not normally do so.

SoftStyle| Printer |Printworks
Installation

Select the brand of your printer:

A - C. Itoh
B - Centronics
C - Epson
D - IBM
E - NEC
F - Okidata
G - Riteman
H - Star Micronics

Your choice? ▮

Press the appropriate letter, or
press Ctrl-Brk to quit

Fig. 19-3. Select Printer.

SoftStyle| MX-100 OPTIONS |Printworks
Standard Settings

PRINT MODES:

on S-standard font   on P-pica
   G-graphic font   T-elite
   I-italic   R-proportional

   E-emphasized   U-superscript
   C-condensed   L-subscript
   D-doublestrike
   W-wide

LINE SPACING: PROGRAM OPTIONS:

on 6-6 lines/inch   A-advanced menu
   8-8 lines/inch   X-test pattern
   N-variable space   /-option reset
                       Esc-quit

Use font which is standard with printer
Move cursor and press Enter key, or just

Fig. 19-4. Main Menu.

2. *Print Style.* These options include emphasized print, condensed print, double strike, wide, superscript, or subscript print.

3. *Line Spacing.* You can select six or eight lines per inch or some specific fraction of an inch. For example, the Epson printer will allow you to define the height of a line in movements as small as 1/72 of an inch.

[Line spacing plays a crucial part in reproducing screen images from the IBM PC. Even if you use the IBM character set, vertical lines will appear broken unless you make the line height small.

   If you want a smooth vertical line, you should enter a line height of 24/72 of an inch. Note that this will make the text appear a bit squeezed. A line height of 26/72 of an inch gives a less smooth line but better text appearance.]

19.6. Advanced Options

Pressing "A" displays a second menu of additional options.

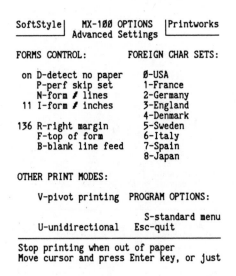

```
SoftStyle|   MX-100 OPTIONS  |Printworks
         |   Advanced Settings

FORMS CONTROL:          FOREIGN CHAR SETS:

   on D-detect no paper  0-USA
      P-perf skip set    1-France
      N-form # lines     2-Germany
   11 I-form # inches    3-England
                         4-Denmark
  136 R-right margin     5-Sweden
      F-top of form      6-Italy
      B-blank line feed  7-Spain
                         8-Japan

OTHER PRINT MODES:

   V-pivot printing  PROGRAM OPTIONS:

                         S-standard menu
   U-unidirectional  Esc-quit

Stop printing when out of paper
Move cursor and press Enter key, or just
```

Fig. 19-5. Advanced Options Menu.

The advanced options are:

1. *Forms Control.* These options control the settings based on the size of the paper you are using. You can specify the length of a page in lines or inches.

You can also specify the width of the form by setting the right margin to the correct number of columns.

2. *Foreign Characters*. You can select the foreign character set that you want to use.

3. *Pivot Printing*. This option prints the text at a 90 degree turn. Instead of printing from top to bottom the program prints from side to side. This type of printing is used mainly by users who have created spreadsheets that are too wide to be printed on normal paper. The pivot print will print a file as wide as you need by turning the direction of the print 90 degrees.

[Printworks can pivot print the text only from an ASCII file. In 1-2-3 you can create a ASCII file by using the Print File command. The command works like the Print Printer command, except that it creates a ASCII file with a PRN extension instead of sending the output to the printer.

dBASE has several methods for creating ASCII files. If you are using the dBASE III report form generator, the command will accept a TO FILE clause which creates an ASCII file. For example:

REPORT FORM sample TO FILE output

The above command will create a file OUTPUT.TXT that is the ASCII text file produced by the REPORT command. You can also use the SET ALTERNATE command to create an ASCII file output from any type of dBASE output. For more information about alternate files, you are referred to my book *Understanding and Using dBASE II and III* (Bowie, MD: Brady Communications Co., 1985).]

19.7.   Font Editor

The font editor allows you to design printer fonts. This can be done by editing an existing font or creating one from scratch. Fonts are created by entering dot patterns in a 8-line by 11-row matrix. Each pattern is assigned an ASCII value that determines which ASCII value in a file will cause that character to print.

This means that ASCII does not have to print an "A" character. You can define the "A" character as some special pattern of dots.

19.8.   Downloading Fonts

Some printers, like the EPSON FX series, contain RAM storage that can be programmed for special fonts. This RAM storage is in addition to the standard fonts provided by the manufacturer.

Printworks contains a number of fonts that can be downloaded into the printer, meaning that the font instructions stay in the printer as long as the printer remains turned on.

What advantage have downloaded fonts?

1. If you have a printer that can accept a font in this manner, you can print directly from an application instead of having to create an ASCII file first and then print the file.
2. Some programs do not contain a facility to create an ASCII output file. Downloading a font allows you to get enhanced outputs from these programs.
3. A downloaded font will print more quickly than the same font used in the normal graphics mode of the printer.

19.9.   Conclusions: Printworks

The Printworks system is an interesting way to create enhanced printing styles on dot-matrix printers. Printworks offers a variety of ready-made fonts, including ones that duplicate the full IBM screen character set.

Printworks prints most of its fonts at a fairly high rate of speed. However, the pivot print mode is considerably slower than the method used by Sideways, (discussed next). If your main purpose is printing spreadsheets sideways, Printworks is not the best choice. If, however, you want to explore some of the characteristics of your dot printer, Printworks is an excellent place to start.

19.10.   Sideways

Sideways is a program designed to print wide data sideways on a dot-matrix printer. Sideways overcomes the width limitation of many printers.

Sideways works in two modes:

1. Indirect—The Sideways program will print an ASCII file turned 90 degrees. In addition, you can change some characteristics of the print, such as type size and line spacing.
2. Direct—Sideways is designed to work directly with Lotus 1-2-3 and Symphony files. In this mode you do not have to produce an ASCII file for output. Sideways will read the 1-2-3 or Symphony files directly.

[Sideways can also function as a Symphony application and can be called using the Symphony application command.]

19.11.   Indirect Processing

The indirect processing mode is used to print ASCII text files sideways. To bring up the program, enter **sideways<return>**

The main menu appears.

```
                    S I D E W A Y S  version 3.00        S/N-2977502-01
                                                        IBM Graphics Printer

Printer port:              LPT1:

Vertical form size (inches):   11.00
Horizontal form size (inches):  8.00

Character font:            Normal        5 x 15 dot matrix
Density:                   Single
Character spacing (dots):       1       12.00 characters per inch
Line spacing (dots):            3        6.66 lines per inch

Left margin (inches):        0.00
Top margin (inches):         0.00
Bottom margin (inches):      0.00           53 lines per page

Starting page:                  1
Glue lines:                     0
Directory:    A:\
Enter name of print file:


F1 for HELP                                          F10 to exit
```

Fig. 19-6. Sideways Main Menu.

The menu allows you to specify:

1. *Form Size*. This means the length and width of the paper you are printing on.
2. *Style*. Sideways allows you to choose the character font as normal, large, extra large, huge, mammoth, minuscule, very tiny, tiny, and small. The density of the type can be single (one pass), double strike, or half (fast draft quality).

   [Sideways will print the full IBM screen character set when it prints an ASCII file.]

3. *Margins*. You can add top, left, and bottom margins.
4. *Options*. These include the starting page and the filename of the ASCII file to print.

19.12.   Direct Spreadsheet Printing

The most exciting feature of Sideways is the direct printing mode. If you are a 1-2-3 user, you will be amazed how quickly and stylishly you can print your spreadsheets.

To begin, enter **sw123 <return>**

The screen displays a spreadsheet that looks a lot like 1-2-3:

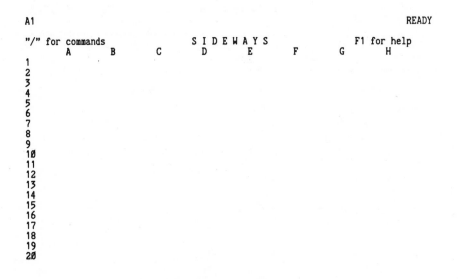

```
A1                                                              READY

"/" for commands              S I D E W A Y S          F1 for help
              A       B       C       D       E       F       G       H
1
2
3
4
5
6
7
8
9
10
11
12
13
14
15
16
17
18
19
20
```

Fig. 19-7. Sideways 1-2-3 Display.

The first step is to load a file. Enter **/**

A Symphony-like menu display appears (Fig. 19-8). Note that it has most of the options offered in the normal Sideways program.

The options presented allow you to choose:

Form Size. This means the length and width of the paper you are printing on.

Style. Sideways allows you to specify the character font as normal, large, extra large, huge, mammoth, minuscule, very tiny, tiny, and small. The density of the type can be single (one pass), double strike, or half (fast draft quality).

Margins. You can add top, left, and bottom margins.

Range. You can specify the range of cells to be included in the printing.

```
                                                                MENU
Range  Go  Options  Clear  File  Interface  Defaults  Quit
Enter print range
 ┌─────────────────────────────────────────────────────────────────┐
 │ Form-size                    Range:          [    Ø pages long ] │
 │    Vertical:     11.ØØ                        [  Ø.ØØ inches wide]│
 │    Horizontal:    8.ØØ                                            │
 │ Character                                                        │
 │    Font:         Normal      [ 5 x 15 dot matrix]                │
 │    Density:      Single                                          │
 │    Char-spacing:      1      [12.ØØ chars/inch]                  │
 │    Line-spacing:      3      [ 6.66 lines/inch]                  │
 │ Margins                                                          │
 │    Top:          Ø.ØØ                                            │
 │    Bottom:       Ø.ØØ         [   53 lines/page]                 │
 │    Left:         Ø.ØØ                                            │
 │    Perf-skip:    Ø.ØØ                                            │
 │ Borders                                                          │
 │    Top:                                                          │
 │    Bottom:                                                       │
 │    Left:                                                         │
 │ Special-effects: No                                             │
 │                                                      Print Settings
 └─────────────────────────────────────────────────────────────────┘
```

Fig. 19-8. Printing Menu.

You can load a file just as you would in 1-2-3. Enter **fr**
Select the file and it appears in the spreadsheet just as it does in 1-2-3.

[You cannot make any changes in the worksheet at this time. You can only print it.]

```
A1                                                              READY


              A            B         C         D         E
 1  * * * * * * * * *  P R O F I T   A N D   L O S S   S T A T E M
 2
 3                       Jan-86    Feb-86    Mar-86    Apr-86
 4
 5   Revenues
 6     Product Sales     325,421   331,929   338,568   345,339
 7     Rentals            81,355    82,982    84,642    86,335
 8     Maintenance Fees   48,813    49,789    50,785    51,8Ø1
 9                       -------   -------   -------   -------
 1Ø                      455,589   464,7Ø1   473,995   483,475
 11
 12  Cost of Sales
 13    Material Costs    177,68Ø   181,234   184,858   188,555
 14    Packaging Costs     7,1Ø7     7,249     7,394     7,542
 15    Shipping Costs     11,194    11,418    11,646    11,879
 16    Sales Commissions  24,146    24,629    25,121    25,624
 17                      -------   -------   -------   -------
 18                      22Ø,127   224,53Ø   229,Ø2Ø   233,6Ø1
 19
 2Ø  Promotional Expense
```

Fig. 19-9. Spreadsheet Displayed.

19.13. Special Effects

One benefit of using the Sideways 1-2-3 program is that it allows you to create printing effects that cannot be accomplished by 1-2-3 or the normal Sideways program alone, such as the entry of printer effects for specific parts of the spreadsheet.

While it is possible to change the style of the entire spreadsheet, e.g., compressed print, you normally cannot choose to print only a part of the spreadsheet underlined. Sideways 1-2-3 makes this possible.

To create special effects enter **/os**

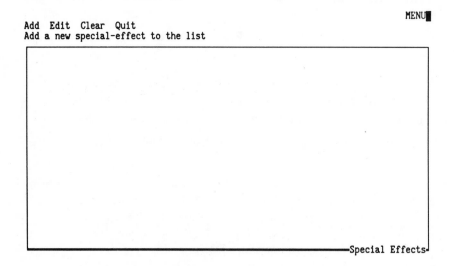

Fig 19-10. Special Effects Screen.

If you want to add a special effect, enter **a**

You can now highlight a range just as you would in 1-2-3. When the range is selected, the screen clears and you now can select the special effects you want for that range. They are:

1. Bold
2. Expanded
3. Underlined

You can choose one or any combination of the three for a given range. The process can be repeated to define several ranges for special printer effects.

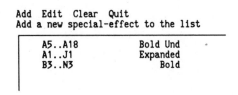

Fig 19-11. Ranges Assigned Printer Effects.

When the final selection has been made, enter **Go** to print the enhanced spreadsheet.

19.14.   Conclusions: Sideways

Sideways is an excellent example of a very narrow utility that fills a badly neglected area. Sideways prints the sideways text quickly enough to make the use of the program quite practical.

If you are a 1-2-3 user, you will find that Sideways is a valuable tool that is quite simple to use. Since Sideways reads the 1-2-3 file directly, you do not have to waste time or disk space to create a ASCII print file. The ability to enhance the spreadsheet with underlines and other special effect in a specified area is an outstanding feature.

Appendix: Product List

Copy II PC, Nokey, Noguard
Central Point Software
9700 S.W. Capitol Hwy, #100
Portland, OR 97219

DeskSet
Bellsoft, Inc.
2820 Northup Way
Bellevue, WA 98004

EASY-DOS-IT
BMS Computers, Inc.
478 N. Wiget Lane
Walnut Creek, CA 94598

GEM
Digital Research, Inc.
P.O. Box 579
Pacific Grove, CA 93950

Microsoft Windows
Microsoft Corporation
10700 Northup Way
Bellevue, WA 98004

Norton Utilities
Peter Norton Computing
2210 Wilshire Blvd.
Santa Monica, CA 90403

Printworks
Softstyle
7192 Kalanianaole Hwy. #205
Honolulu, Hawaii 96825

ProKey
RoseSoft
4710 University Way N.E., #601
Seattle, WA 98105

Recall
YES Software, Inc.
390-10991 Shellbridge Way
Richmond, B.C., Canada V6X 3C6

Sidekick, SuperKey, Turbo Lightning
Borland International
4585 Scotts Valley Drive
Scotts Valley, CA 95066

Sideways
FUNK Software
222 Third Street
Cambridge, MA 02142

SmartKey, SmartPath
Software Research Technologies, Inc.
3757 Wilshire Blvd., #211
Los Angeles, CA 90010

Spotlight
Lotus Development
Corporation
55 Cambridge Pkwy
Cambridge, MA 02142

Xtree
Executive Systems, Inc.
15300 Ventura Blvd., #305
Sherman Oaks, CA 91403

About the Author

Rob Krumm first started using computers in the Philadelphia Public School System. He was one of the first educators to use computers as a teaching aid for students with behavioral problems. In 1982, he left the public school system to go to California, where he founded microCOMPUTER SCHOOLS, Inc. in Walnut Creek. Since his first love is teaching, he continues to teach many of the classes himself.

Rob's credentials include: Business Education Consultant to the State of California; member of the Advisory Board for Business Teachers, San Francisco State University; editorials and how-to articles for *Business Software Magazine*, the San Francisco *Examiner/Chronicle*, and several Bay Area computer journals. In addition, Rob is editor and chief contributor to his own publication, the *mCS Newsletter*.

Index

*
 DOS filenames, 19, 20
/
 in DOS commands, 21
1-2-3 and SuperKey, 312
?
 DOS filenames, 19, 20
A›, 9
Abort, retry, ignore, 11
Alarms
 DeskSet, 448
Alt key
 for typing ASCII characters, 33
ANSI system, 77
 keyboard reassignment, 210
Archive files, 120, 122
ASCII
 files, 25
 IBM extended codes, 32
ASCII codes, 27
ASCII files
 word processing, 29
ASCII table
 Sidekick, 383
ASCII values
 printer codes, 384
Assignment of keys, 210
Autoexec
 batch file, 76
Automatic
 execute batch file, 76

Background programs
 calculators, 491
 calendars, 492
 compared, 489
 DOS access, 493
 notepads, 490
 printing, 496
 telecommunications, 493

Background utilities, 359
 DeskSet, 437
 Sidekick, 363
 Spotlight, 417
 Turbo Lightning, 461
Backup
 archive files, 123
Backup command
 file attributes, 123
Batch commands
 SuperKey, 311
Batch commands
 ProKey, 233
Batch files, 70
 autoexec, 76
 creating, 71
 ECHO command, 74
 EDLIN, 74
Beep
 Norton Utilities, 137
Binary conversion
 Sidekick, 371
Binary files, 25
Binary numbers, 92, 93
Bit
 defined, 26
Boot sector
 discussed, 90
Buffers
 config.sys, 78, 79
Bytes
 binary codes, 26
 defined, 6
 storage codes, 92, 93

C printer, 496
Calculator
 DeskSet, 440
Capturing screen data
 DeskSet, 456

Sidekick, 407
CD
  DOS command, 64
Changing attributes of a file
  Norton Utilities, 97, 98
Changing programs
  Norton Utilities, 134
Character set
  full IBM, 33
Checking disks
  in DOS, 54
CHKDSK, 54
Clearing the screen
  in DOS, 57
CLS
  DOS command, 57
Clusters
  disk storage, 89
  hard disks, 105
Colors
  screen display, 141
Commands
  DOS, 12
  of DOS, 8
Comparison
  background programs, 489
Config.sys, 77
  buffers, 78, 79
  files, 78, 79
  VDISK, 361
Configuration
  of DOS, 77
Conformations
  in DOS, 10
Copy con:
  ASCII files, 29
Copy II PC, 41
Copy protection, 35, 36, 37, 38, 39, 40
  defined, 36, 37, 38, 39, 40
  Spotlight, 417
Copying disks
  protection, 35, 36, 37, 38, 39, 40
Copying files
  DOS, 57
Create
  batch files, 71
Creating macros
  with SuperKey, 256
Customized keyboards, 244

Damaged files
  Norton Utilities, 176
Data
  encryption, 323
dBASE
  ASCII files, 32

dBASE III
  Sidekick phone list, 390
Default
  drive, 9
Defaults
  in DOS, 22
Del
  DOS command, 59
Delays
  ProKey, 223
Delimiters
  DOS, 16
DeskSet
  alarms, 448
  batch commands, 450
  calculator, 440
  calendar, 444
  capturing screen data, 456
  Clipboard, 456
  Date Calendar, 444
  DOS access, 451
  Financial Calculator, 441
  general, 437
  multiple applications, 458
  notepad, 438
  Pop Any, 458
  voice modem, 458
Device drivers, 77
Diablo printers
  changing form length, 384
Directories
  change to, 64
  create in DOS, 62
  in DOS, 23
  listing, 125
  listing of, 67
  paths, 68
  sub-sub, 66
Directory
  Norton Utilities, 94
  of disk, 46, 47
  sorting, 111
Directory command
  Xtree program, 190
Directory display
  Norton Utilities, 95
Directory information
  Norton Utilities, 96
Disk
  directory, 46, 47
Disk data
  viewing, 90
Disk information
  Norton Utilities, 87
Disk map
  Norton Utilities, 99

Disk organization, 22, 90
  Norton Utilities, 88
Disk sectors, 88
Disk storage
  clusters, 89
Disk test
  Norton Utilities, 138
Disks
  names in DOS, 50
Display modes
  Norton Utilities, 95
Displaywrite
  ASCII files, 31
DOS
  batch files, 70
  binary files, 25
  CD command, 64
  checking disks, 54
  CLS, 57
  commands, 8, 12
  configuration, 77
  confirmations, 10
  COPY command, 57
  defaults, 22
  DEL, 59
  delimiters, 16
  directory, 46, 47
  ECHO command, 74
  editing commands, 53
  ERASE, 59
  error messages, 10
  external commands, 13
  file types, 25
  filters, 60
  FIND filter, 61
  grammar, 12
  internal commands, 12
  keyboard codes, 211
  macros, 210
  major tasks, 8
  options, 21
  parameters, 16
  paths, 24
  printing, 59
  PROMPT command, 60
  prompts, 9
  purpose of, 7
  SORT filter, 60
  structure of, 8
  subdirectories, 61
  TREE command, 67
  wildcards, 52
DOS access
  DeskSet, 451
  Spotlight, 432
DOS commands

SmartKey, 341
SuperKey stack, 316
DOS menu, 193, 197
Drive names
  in DOS, 23
Drives
  in DOS, 50

Easy DOS it
  custom menus, 197, 198, 199
  tutor screens, 202
Easy DOS it program, 193
ECHO
  DOS command, 74
Edlin
  ASCII files, 29
  editing batch files, 74
Encryption
  of files with SuperKey, 323
Epson printers
  changing form length, 384
ERASE command
  DOS, 59
Erased data
  locating, 166, 167, 168, 169, 170, 171,
    172, 173
Erased file
  directory, 158
Erased files
  Norton Utilities, 155
  recovering, 155
Error
  abort, retry, ignore, 11
Error messages
  in DOS, 10
Escape codes
  prompt command, 212
Examining
  disk sectors, 94
Extended keyboard codes, 211
External commands
  DOS, 13
  listed, 15
External memory, 5

File attributes
  BACKUP command, 123
  Norton Utilities, 119
File commands
  Xtree program, 191
File encryption
  SmartKey, 349
File management
  Norton Utilities, 109
File size
  Norton Utilities, 114

File status
    Norton Utilities, 161
Filename
    valid characters, 18
Filenames
    * character, 19, 20
    ? character, 19, 20
    reading vs. typing, 19
    wildcards, 19
Files
    attributes, 96
    directory of, 46, 47
    DOS batch, 70
    DOS setting, 78, 79
    encryption, 323
    erased, 155
    hidden attribute, 96
    searching for, 117
    security encryption, 323
    types in DOS, 25
    wiping out, 151
    wiping out data, 148
    Xtree program, 183
Files
    searching for, 51
Filters
    in DOS, 60
Financial calculation
    DeskSet, 441
Find
    DOS filter, 61
Finding erased data, 166, 167, 168, 169,
    170, 171, 172, 173
Finding erased files
    by sector location, 174
Finding files
    Norton Utilities, 117
Flowchart
    Norton Utilities, 107
    unerasing option, 178
Fonts
    Printworks, 498
Form length
    setting for printer, 384
Framework
    ASCII files, 32
Function keys
    in DOS, 53

Grammar
    DOS, 12

Hard disk menus, 193, 197
Hard disk organization
    Xtree, 183
Hard disks, 105

Hex conversion
    Sidekick, 371
Hexadecimal numbers, 92, 93
Hidden files, 96
High order bit
    ASCII codes, 32
How is data stored
    in program files, 28

IBM
    character set, 33
    extended keyboard codes, 211
Information
    storage techniques, 26
Internal commands
    DOS, 12
Internal commands
    listing, 14
Internal memory, 5

Keyboard
    extended codes, 211
    locking, 344
    locking of, 303
    ProKey layout, 244
    ProKey program, 213
    recall program, 331
    SuperKey, 250
Keyboard layout
    SuperKey, 326
Keyboard macros, 208
Keyboard programs
    compared, 351
    defined, 207
Keyboard reassignment, 210
Kilobyte
    defined, 6

Layout
    SuperKey, 326
Line print
    Norton Utilities, 139
Listing directories
    Norton Utilities, 125
Locating
    erased data, 166, 167, 168, 169, 170,
    171, 172, 173
Lotus products
    ASCII files, 31

Macros
    ANSI system, 210
    defined, 207
    keyboard, 208
    keys used, 209
    programs compared, 351

ProKey program, 213
recall program, 331
SmartKey, 340
SuperKey program, 250
window displays, 344
with DOS, 210
Macros
menus, 344
Make directories
DOS command, 62
Maps
disk storage, 99
MD
DOS command, 62
Memory
about, 3
bytes, 6
external, 5
internal, 5
measured, 6
setting buffers, 78, 79
usage discussed, 7
Memory resident programs, 359
Menus
display macros, 308
for hard disks, 193, 197, 198, 199
from macros, 304
MS DOS
defined, 7
Multimate
ASCII files, 30

Norton Utilities, 83
change file attributes, 97, 98
changing programs, 134
damaged files, 176
directory information, 96
disk information, 87
disk map, 99
disk test, 138
erased files, 155
file attributes, 119
file management, 109
file sizes, 114
file status, 161
finding files, 117
flowchart, 107
hex search, 103
list directories, 125
main program, 86
printing, 139
protecting files, 121
searching, 101
security of files, 148
sorting directories, 111
systems information, 144

systems utilities, 137
text search, 125
time mark, 145
unerasing a file, 159
versions, 83
volume labels, 147

Options
in DOS, 21

Parameters
DOS, 16
Passwords
for files, 325
Path problems
with WordStar, 181
Pathnames
i, 24
Paths, 24
in DOS, 68
SmartPath, 179
PC DOS
defined, 7
Phone lists
Sidekick, 386
Printer codes
sending ASCII characters, 384
Printers
form length, 384
Printing
boxes and lines, 35
full IBM character set, 35
Norton Utilities, 139
Printworks, 498
Sideways, 504
Printing programs
Printworks, 498
Sideways, 504
Printing utilities, 495
Printing
in DOS, 59
Program files
how is data stored, 28
Programming
DOS batch files, 70
ProKey, 213
annotating macros, 221
basis use, 215
batch commands, 233
changing commands, 243
clearing macros, 220
conclusion, 248
delays, 223
fixed length fields, 226
guarding macros, 222
interactive mode, 216

layout program, 244
macros suspended, 241
multiple fields, 229
names, 229
notes for macros, 221
other features, 239
pauses in macros, 225
performance, 240
recalling macros, 218
recording macros, 217
restoring macros, 221
saving macros, 218
special features, 215
speed, 240
suspending program, 241
swapping keys, 231
text files, 232, 235
variable length fields, 226
Prompt
change in DOS, 60
systems, 9
Prompt command
ANSI system, 212
Proofing text
Turbo Lightning, 463
Protecting files
Norton Utilities, 121
Protection
from copying, 35, 36, 37, 38, 39, 40

RAM
defined, 5
Ramdisks, 359
Read only files, 120
Recall
debugging mode, 334
fields, 333
macro creation, 331
macro menus, 334
menus, 334
Recall program
general, 331
Recovering
erased files, 155
Recovery of damaged files, 176
ROM
defined, 5
Root directory, 67

Screen attributes
Norton Utilities, 141
Screen colors
Norton Utilities, 141
Searching
directories, 51

for erased text, 166, 167, 168, 169,
170, 171, 172, 173
Searching for data
Norton Utilities, 101
Searching for files, 117
Sectors, 88
erased files, 174
hard disks, 105
Security
Norton Utilities, 148
of files, 349
Selecting files, 188
Xtree program, 188
Sidekick
activating, 367
appointments, 375
ASCII table, 383
basic notepad commands, 398
binary conversion, 371
calculator, 369
calculator memory, 371
calculator modes, 371
calendar, 374
calendar files, 378
capturing screen data, 407
clearing programmed keys, 374
combining files, 405
dBASE III, 390
delete in notepad, 400
dialer, 386
exiting, 373
features, 367
general, 363
help, 368
hex conversion, 371
import and export, 406
indents, 403
insert in notepad, 400
loading files, 404
margins in notepad, 402
notepad, 394
notepad files, 403
other editing command, 401
pasting, 411
pasting numbers, 412
phones lists, 386
printing calendars, 380
programming keys with calculator,
372
reforming paragraph, 401
saving text, 401
selecting files, 405
telecommunications, 386
time stamping, 409
with SuperKey, 317
Sideways, 504

SmartKey
  batch commands, 348
  captured fields, 343
  DOS functions, 343
  editing, 342
  file ecryption, 349
  general, 339
  keyboard layout, 349
  keyboard lock, 344
  list, 342
  macro creation, 340
  menus, 344, 346
  special functions, 343
  sub menus, 348
  windows, 344
SmartPath, 179
Sort
  in DOS, 60
Sorting
  DOS directories, 111
Spelling check
  Turbo Lightning, 463
Spoolers, 359
Spotlight
  appointment calendar, 422
  calculator, 421
  calendar, 422
  copy protection, 417
  data formats, 420
  DOS access, 432
  file format, 420
  filer, 432
  files, 432
  general, 417
  index card file, 434
  menus, 419
  notepad, 418
  phone book, 429
  saving data, 420
  window management, 434
  window positions, 419
Spreadsheets
  with SuperKey, 312
Stop watch
  Norton Utilities, 145
Storage
  maps, 99
Structure
  of DOS, 8
Subdirectories, 61
  change to, 64
  create in DOS, 62
  in DOS, 23
  paths, 68
Sub-subdirectories, 66
SuperKey

advanced editing, 292
advanced functions, 286
alignment in fields, 287
autodisplay, 306
batch commands, 311
batch execution, 314
canceling a macro, 260
clearing a key, 261, 270
command keys, 322
controls on data, 282
creating macros, 256
cut and paste, 294, 300
data entry control, 285
data entry controls, 282
defaults values, 322
delays, 273
display macros, 304, 310
DOS command stack, 316
editing macros, 258, 262, 292
encryption, 323
erasing a macro, 261, 270
field alignment, 287
fields, 278, 282
file passwords, 325
files, 270
fill in characters, 289
fixed fields, 285
fixed length fields, 279
functions in macros, 275
functions, 286, 295
general, 249
interactive mode, 252
keyboard locking, 303
keyboard, 251, 326
layout, 326
listing macros, 263
loading macros, 270
macro menus, 308
macros commands, 272
macros files, 270
macros functions, 275
macros keys, 251
macros menu, 255
memory usage, 250
menus, 253
merging files, 271
multiple fields, 282
nesting macros, 275
numeric formats, 290
options commands, 303
other features, 320
passwords, 325
pauses, 273
playback delays, 302
program, 249
recalling macros, 267

revising macros, 262
saving macros, 267
showing macros, 263
special commands, 272
special symbols, 258
storing macros, 267
submenus, 310
text files, 270
timed delays, 274
variable length fields, 280
with 1-2-3, 312
with Sidekick, 317
Sys files, 77
Systems prompt
i, 9
Systems information
Norton Utilities, 144

Telecommunications
Sidekick, 386
Testing disks
Norton Utilities, 138
Text files
DOS, 25
ProKey, 232, 235
Text search
Norton Utilities, 125
Text searches
Norton Utilities, 101
Thesaurus
Turbo Lightning, 474
Time mark
Norton Utilities, 145
TREE
DOS command, 67
Turbo Lightning
capitalization, 472
command keys, 480
commands, 465
customization, 479
dictionary files, 478
environments, 480
full screen check, 468
general, 461
key commands, 480
main menu, 464
proof reading, 463
sound alike words, 469
thesaurus, 474

with Framework II, 482
with other applications, 480
with word processing, 479
with WordStar 2000, 486
word check, 464
Tutor screens
easy DOS it, 202
TYPE command
DOS, 59

Unerase
Norton Utilities, 158
Unerasing
by text searches, 166, 167, 168, 169,
    170, 171, 172, 173
flowchart, 178
Unerasing a file, 159

VDISK, 361
Volume labels
Norton Utilities, 147
Volumes
in DOS, 23

Wildcards
DOS filenames, 19
in DOS, 52
Wipeout data
from files, 148
Wiping files
Norton Utilities, 151
Wiping out a disk, 149
Word
ASCII files, 30
WordPerfect
ASCII files, 31
Word processing
in Sidekick, 394
WordStar
ASCII files, 30
path problems, 181
WordStar 2000
ASCII files, 30
Writing
batch files, 71

Xtree, 183
directory commands, 190